T0183814

Lecture Notes in Computer Science   9252

Commenced Publication in 1973
Founding and Former Series Editors:
Gerhard Goos, Juris Hartmanis, and Jan van Leeuwen

More information about this series at http://www.springer.com/series/7407

Cristian S. Calude · Michael J. Dinneen (Eds.)

Unconventional Computation and Natural Computation

14th International Conference, UCNC 2015
Auckland, New Zealand, August 30 – September 3, 2015
Proceedings

 Springer

Editors
Cristian S. Calude
University of Auckland
Auckland
New Zealand

Michael J. Dinneen
University of Auckland
Auckland
New Zealand

ISSN 0302-9743   ISSN 1611-3349   (electronic)
Lecture Notes in Computer Science
ISBN 978-3-319-21818-2   ISBN 978-3-319-21819-9   (eBook)
DOI 10.1007/978-3-319-21819-9

Library of Congress Control Number: 2015944175

LNCS Sublibrary: SL1 – Theoretical Computer Science and General Issues

Springer Cham Heidelberg New York Dordrecht London

Printed on acid-free paper

Springer International Publishing AG Switzerland is part of Springer Science+Business Media
(www.springer.com)

Preface

This volume contains the papers presented at The 14th International Conference Unconventional Computation and Natural Computation (UCNC 2015), which was held August 30–September 3, 2015 in Auckland, New Zealand.

The scope of the conference is to create a forum for the presentation of new results in all areas that relate to theoretical and experimental unconventional computation and natural computation and to foster collaboration between researchers working on these topics. Typical, but not exclusive, topics are:

- Molecular (DNA) computing, quantum computing, chaos computing, optical computing, physarum computing, computation in hyperbolic spaces, collision-based computing.
- Cellular automata, neural computation, evolutionary computation, swarm intelligence, nature-inspired algorithms, artificial immune systems, artificial life, membrane computing, amorphous computing.
- Computational systems biology, genetic networks, protein-protein networks, transport networks, synthetic biology, cellular (in vivo) computing.
- Computations beyond the Turing model and philosophical aspects of computing.

For this edition we received 38 submissions. Each submission was reviewed by at least two Programme Committee members. The committee decided to accept 16 papers. The programme also includes six invited talks:

Invited Lectures

1. R. Freivalds: *Ultrametric Algorithms and Automata.*
2. G. Longo: *Models, Simulations and "Reality": A Comparison by Theoretical Symmetries,*
3. M. Sagar: *Behavioural Animation.*
4. Ya. D. Sergeyev: *The Infinity Computer and Numerical Computations with Infinities.*

Invited Tutorials

1. J.P. Lewis: *Textures and Realism: Turing Tests for Visual Computation.*
2. K. Pudenz: *Quantum Computing Meets the Real World.*

The conference has included four satellite workshops:

1. *Biological Cell Information Processing*, organised by M. Cooling
2. *Membrane Computing*, organised by M.J. Dinneen
3. *Physics and Computation*, organised by A. Abbott, V. Kendon, and S. Stepney
4. *Unconventional Computation in Europe*, organised by M. Amos and S. Stepney

The first conference in the series was organised in Auckland New Zealand in January 1998 by the Centre for Discrete Mathematics and Theoretical Computer Science (University of Auckland) and the Santa Fe Institute, USA. The following twelve editions followed: Brussels, Belgium (December 2000), Kobe, Japan (October 2002), Seville, Spain (October 2005), York, UK (September 2006), Kingston, Canada (August 2007), Vienna, Austria (August 2008), Ponta Delgada, Portugal (September 2009), Tokyo, Japan (June 2010), Turku, Finland (June 2011), Orléans, France (September 2012) Milano, Italy (June 2013) and London, Ontario, Canada (July 2014).

The UCNC conference series is overseen by a Steering Committee which includes Thomas Back (Leiden University, The Netherlands), Cristian S. Calude (University of Auckland, New Zealand), as founding chair, Lov K. Grover (Bell Labs, Murray Hill, New Jersey, USA), Nataša Jonoska (University of South Florida, USA), as co-chair, Jarkko Kari (University of Turku, Finland), as co-chair, Lila Kari (University of Western Ontario, Canada), Seth Llloyd (Massachusetts Institute of Technology, USA), Giancarlo Mauri (University of Milano-Bicocca, Italy), Gheorghe Păun (Institute of Mathematics of the Romanian Academy, Romania), Grzegorz Rozenberg (Leiden University, The Netherlands), as emeritus chair, Arto Salomma (University of Turku, Finland), Tommaso Toffoli (Boston University, USA), Carme Torras (Institute of Robotics and Industrial Informatics, Barcelona, Spain), and Jan Van Leeuwen (Utrecht University, The Netherlands).

We thank the Programme Committee, the Organisation Committee, and the additional reviewers for their exemplary work.

Support Groups

- Our sponsors, the CDMTCS, and the Department of Computer Science (University of Auckland) PBRF allocation.
- Springer LNCS team, Alfred Hofmann, Anna Kramer and Christine Reiss for producing another excellent UCNC volume.
- EasyChair for helping with the organisation of UCNC 2015.

June 2015   Cristian S. Calude
                                                                   Michael J. Dinneen

Organisation

Programme Committee

Martyn Amos	Manchester Metropolitan University, UK
Selim G. Akl	Queens University, Canada
Olivier Bournez	École Politechnique, France
Cristian S. Calude	University of Auckland, New Zealand, Co-Chair
Nachum Dershowitz	Tel Aviv University, Israel
Michael J. Dinneen	University of Auckland, New Zealand, Co-Chair
David Doty	Caltech, USA
Marian Gheorghe	Sheffield University, UK
Masami Hagiya	University of Tokyo, Japan
Oscar H. Ibarra	University of California, USA
Kazuo Iwama	Kyoto University, Japan
Natasha Jonoska	University of South Florida, Tampa FL, USA
Jarkko Kari	University of Turku, Finland
Lila Kari	University of Western Ontario, Canada
Viv Kendon	Durham University, UK
Fred Kroon	University of Auckland, New Zealand
Rossella Lupacchini	University of Bologna, Italy
Giancarlo Mauri	Università degli Studi di Milano-Bicocca, Italy
Kenichi Morita	Hiroshima University, Japan
Matthew Patitz	University of Arkansas, USA
Ion Petre	Åbo Akademi University, Finland
Susan Stepney	University of York, UK
Karl Svozil	Vienna University of Technology, Austria
H. Todd Wareham	Memorial University of Newfoundland, Canada
James Whiting	UWE, Bristol, UK
Damien Woods	California Institute of Technology, USA

Additional Reviewers

A. Abbott	V. Rogojin
M. Hirvensalo	A. Rueda-Toicen
T. Isokawa	Z. Sajedinia
A. Keenan	A. Simjour
S. Kopecki	M. Stay
P.-E. Meunier	T. Yokomori

Organisation Committee

Elena Calude   Massey University at Albany, Publicity Chair
Ulrich Speidel   University of Auckland, Chair

Contents

Invited Papers

The Unconventionality of Nature: Biology, from Noise to Functional Randomness

Barbara Bravi[1]([✉]) and Giuseppe Longo[2,3]

[1] Department of Mathematics, King's College London, London, UK
`barbara.bravi@kcl.ac.uk`
[2] Centre Cavaillès, CNRS, École Normale Supérieure, Paris, France
[3] Department of Integrative Physiology and Pathobiology,
Tufts University, Boston, USA
`Giuseppe.Longo@ens.fr`

Abstract. In biology, phenotypes' variability stems from stochastic gene expression as well as from extrinsic fluctuations that are largely based on the contingency of developmental paths and on ecosystemic changes. Both forms of randomness constructively contribute to biological robustness, as resilience, far away from conventional computable dynamics, where elaboration and transmission of information are robust when they resist to noise. We first survey how fluctuations may be inserted in biochemical equations as probabilistic terms, in conjunction to diffusion or path integrals, and treated by statistical approaches to physics. Further work allows to better grasp the role of biological "resonance" (interactions between different levels of organization) and plasticity, in a highly unconventional frame that seems more suitable for biological processes. In contrast to physical conservation properties, thus symmetries, symmetry breaking is particularly relevant in biology; it provides another key component of biological historicity and of randomness as a source of diversity and, thus, of onto-phylogenetic stability and organization as these are also based on variation and adaptativity.

Keywords: Noise biology · Randomness · Resilience · Variability · Diversity

1 Introduction

Conventional computing is the result of a remarkable historical path that originated in the invention of the alphabet: discrete and meaningless signs evocate meaning by composition and by phonemes, that is by sounds, and provide by this a musical notation for the continuum of speech. This revolutionary step is an

B. Bravi—This author's work is supported by the Marie Curie Training Network NETADIS (FP7, grant 290038).

G. Longo—This author's work is part of the project *"Le lois des dieux, des hommes et de la nature"* at IEA–Nantes.

© Springer International Publishing Switzerland 2015
C.S. Calude and M.J. Dinneen (Eds.): UCNC 2015, LNCS 9252, pp. 3–34, 2015.
DOI: 10.1007/978-3-319-21819-9_1

early form of dualism, an invention very far from natural phenomena: ideograms carry or recall meaning in their form, while the signs of an alphabet are perfectly abstract and meaningless. They require phonemes and do not refer per se to the sensible world. We enriched this stepping away from the world by more passages, in history, such as the Cartesian dualism, which further separated a human mental software from physical matter, and, later, by the coding of alphabetic signs by numbers, yet another radical separation of (coded) words from meaning. Gödel and Turing brought to the limelight this later invention for the purpose of . . . showing the internal limits of the (alphabetic) writing of axioms and formal (meaningless) deductions. In order to prove their negative results, the construction of undecidable sentences and functions, they had to formally define computability and decidability. By well-known equivalence results, we know that no finitistic (alpha-numeric) re-writing system computes more functions than the ones invented by the founding fathers and, thus, that it is subject to the same limitations and incompleteness. In these computational frames, which are our fantastic, linguistic invention far away from nature and its material contingency, randomness has no place and all is done to avoid it, as "noise".

However, these limits of formal writing and signs' manipulations may be viewed also as a contribution to understanding the key role of randomness in describing natural phenomena. As a matter of fact, randomness, in all existing physical and computational theories, may be understood as unpredictability w.r.to the intended theory. It is thus a form of (in time) undecidability w.r.to the given (more or less) formal frame (see Calude and Longo 2015; Abbott et al. 2012; Gács et al. 2011 for analyses in relation to algorithmic randomness). In other words, the (joint) analysis of (algorithmic, physical and biological) randomness crucially helps to go beyond formal deductions and computations, as given by conventional theories.

The understanding and the treatment of randomness and unpredictability is at the core of dynamical (non-linear) systems, quantum mechanics, statistical physics. We will discuss common tools for the analysis of unpredictability within some mathematical formalisms, from the Langevin approach to the Fokker-Planck equation for diffusion, from path integrals to limit theorems of probability theory related to the Law of Large Numbers. In biology, though, randomness acquires a peculiar status as it is inherent to the variability, adaptivity and diversity of life, as crucial components of its structural stability. Stochastic gene expression will be introduced as striking example that already provides hints towards a novel, hopefully more proper, definition of biological randomness; the notions of "bio-resonance" and plasticity will be further examples of this. In particular, we will first refer to "noise" in various, very relevant, conventional (physical) representations of randomness, extensively applied to biology. Then, we will stress the essential role of random events in biological processes, whose contribution to life's dynamical stability goes well beyond "noise" and suggests the need for an enriched perspective; that is, for a better, unconventional, conceptualization (and terminology), or possibly mathematization of randomness, encompassing biological variability and diversity. A comparison will be made with the revolutionary change in the laws of causality, randomness and determination proposed by quantum mechanics in the analysis of matter in microphysics.

This poses the question of the suitability of the notion of "law", as inherited from classical and quantum physics, for the investigation of the dynamics of the living state of matter. A key issue for us is that physical laws are given in pre-defined phase spaces.

2   Stochasticity Modelled by Noise

Stochasticity in biological systems is largely denoted as "noise". The use of term noise implicitly assumes a way of thinking about cells shaped by the metaphor that compares genetic and metabolic pathways to signalling "circuits" (Monod 1970; Simpson et al. 2009; Maheshri and O'Shea 2007).

Models, for the sake of simplification and understanding, rely on the choice of relevant objects, properties and some defined degree of detail. In particular, a mathematical (equational) model requires the a priori choice of the pertinent observables and parameters, that is of a "phase space". In this context, invoking analogies with better characterized systems can provide qualitative insights but is not neutral in terms of conceptual implications: discussing the latter is indispensable to assess the suitability of metaphors, including the transfer of mathematical tools between scientific fields. In fact, analogies set the guiding principles for building models (to be considered "representations" first of all), in such a way to shape the mathematical formalism, and how experiments are designed and interpreted. It is thus a matter of vocabulary and, more importantly, of conceptual frameworks that may hinder progress if they prevent from formulating questions in a way pertinent to the intended domain, living beings in our case.

Concepts for studying metabolic and genetic pathways are explicitly drawn from electronic circuit theory (e.g. Bhalla 2003), the richest source of inspiration among various metaphors for signalling. The essential point, in our view, is that the emphasis is placed on particular levels of description, namely functionality and the problem of optimal processing and transmission of information. This is inherent in the very mechanism of a metaphor, which is a *meta-fero*, a transfer of meanings, a mapping to more familiar domains, that does not necessarily imply a complete superposition. Furhermore, the systematic transfer of methodology and concepts from physics to biology should be reframed in terms of dualities as well as (or rather than) similarities, as we will argue below. In the context of this metaphor, "noise" is seen as something that disrupts the system, causes a defective functioning or even the breakdown. Yet, as we will stress, biological "noise" is meant to refer also to *variability*: as a consequence, one attributes the meaning of "disturbance" to something intrinsic to life, as a component of adaptivity and diversity (plasticity is yet another element of these aspects of biology).

Next sections are devoted to a discussion of the mathematical role of this particular notion, *noise*, in the quantitative investigation of stochastic effects in biological systems. Our aim is to focus on its theoretically and practically relevant implications once it acts as a principle to make experimental evidences intelligible, because it then contributes to modelling assumptions and to the construction of the "objectivity" to which scientific analysis is applied, in particular because it affects how we conceive the underlying causal structure.

3   Randomness and Its Mathematical Formulation

The dynamics of a biochemical reaction is believed to be properly treated as a Markov jump process (i.e. changes are seen as discrete events occurring at random times and regardless of the previous chemical history) in a state or phase space specified by the number of molecules (it is a description at the level of "copy numbers"). Typically the abundance of reactants allows a quantification on a continuous scale in terms of concentrations (number/volume). We mention this aspect as, in the following sections, we will discuss the relevance of defining a pertinent phase space when laying the foundations of a theory: in existing physical theories, the laws (of a dynamics, typically) are given in a pre-defined phase space.

In the context of a deterministic macroscopic characterization of biochemical networks, variations of concentrations are assumed to occur by a continuous process and reactions are described in terms of rate equations for the species involved. This temporal evolution can be obtained applying the law of mass action, which states that the rate of a reaction is proportional to the product of the concentrations of the reactants and leads to equations in the form:

Rate of change of concentrations = Total rate of production - Total rate of consumption

Mathematically equivalent to:

$$\frac{dx_i(t)}{dt} = \sum_{j=1}^{R} S_{ij} f_j(\boldsymbol{x}) \tag{3.1}$$

where $i = 1, ..., N$ denotes the chemical species and j runs from 1 to R, the number of chemical reactions. $S_{ij} = s_{ij} - r_{ij}$ contains the stoichiometric coefficients s_{ij} for the reactants and r_{ij} for the products, while $f_j(\boldsymbol{x})$ is the macroscopic rate function for the j-th reaction and accounts for its probability.

As exhaustively explained by Gillespie (1976), in this formulation the cell is considered to be endowed with a well-mixed and spatially homogeneous environment: spatial components and inhomogeneities, compartmentalization of reactions, diffusion phenomena should be then analyzed separately. Moreover, what should be verified is that the occurrence of nonreactive (elastic) collisions or other molecular motions responsible for the maintenance of these conditions of random uniform distribution is more frequent than reactive collisions.

Differential equations for the temporal evolution of concentrations must be interpreted as a deterministic description as, once a set of initial conditions $\boldsymbol{x}_0(t_0)$ is fixed, the future evolution will be univocal. On the other hand, heterogeneous cellular behaviors are thought to be appropriately captured by stochastic models: the lack of accuracy of the deterministic models for essential biological features leads one to introduce stochasticity at the level of the description (Wilkinson 2009). Once the need for a stochastic explanation has been recognized, the first step is to resort to statistical analyses and probability theory. This is presently the only quantitative framework for taking into account any kind of *unpredictability*, either epistemic or intrinsic.

In this spirit, the primary source of stochasticity is identified with fluctuations present in all biochemical systems, as reactions occur at random times and with a random outcome: arguments based on Poisson statistics are then used to affirm that the relative amplitude of fluctuations should scale as the inverse square root of the chemical population. Stochasticity is thus expected to be enhanced by small numbers, for which fluctuations can exceed, in magnitude, the mean molecular level (Elowitz et al. 2002; Simpson et al. 2009; Swain et al. 2002; Raj and Van Oudenaarden 2008).

In light of this expected crucial role, a growing interest towards stochastic behaviors has emerged in the field of biological modelling. Stochastic modelling has been acknowledged as a well-established solution only since late 1990s, once experimental techniques gave precise results showing that including random terms was fundamental in order to fit experimental findings (Arkin et al. 1998).

Molecular fluctuations are usually incorporated by adding a random force term in rate equations according to the so-called *Langevin approach* (see the textbook by Van Kampen 2007 for a discussion), as follows:

$$\frac{dx_i(t)}{dt} = \sum_{j=1}^{R} S_{ij} f_j(\boldsymbol{x}) + \xi_i(t) \tag{3.2}$$

The Langevin approach consists of writing down the deterministic equations of the macroscopic behavior with an additional Langevin force term that exhibits certain properties:

- The average over an ensemble of identical (or similar) systems vanishes, i.e. $\langle \xi_i(t) \rangle = 0$ for any i.
- It stems from the instantaneous collisions between particles, so that, if variations are sufficiently rapid, they are not correlated in successive times. As a consequence, the autocorrelation is supposed to be represented by a delta function, i.e. $\langle \xi_i(t) \xi_j(t') \rangle = \Sigma_{ij}(\boldsymbol{x}) \delta(t - t')$.
  This delta representation is an abstraction, but it is applied for the sake of convenience whenever the time of a collision is negligible w.r.to the relevant timescale of the dynamics.
- $\xi_i(t)$ is Gaussian distributed (i.e. completely characterized by the first two moments).

This term is often referred to as "noise" because of its unpredictable nature; on the other hand, the above properties guarantee a regular behavior in terms of averages. In particular, when the last two properties hold true, one can define a *Gaussian white noise* (*white* refers to the fact that a δ-time correlation is independent on frequency in the Fourier space).

Remarkably, this approach represents a very recurrent strategy in stochastic modelling and it has been adopted to include heuristically every type of fluctuations, also not directly connected to thermal effects in biochemistry: the properties listed above are often given *a priori*, without connections to the physical dynamics of the underlying process[1]. The structure of Langevin equation is taken as conventional justification for affirming that, whenever fluctuations are not relevant, the molecular population evolves *deterministically* according to the set of macroscopic reaction rate equations. Also at the level of mathematical description, it has been often found convenient to invoke analogies from engineering: in fact, Gaussian white noise is a useful model of noise in electronics engineering, for example for instrument errors in filtering theory and for unknown forces in control theory. The analogy in these cases connects the "noise" observed in biochemical networks to what is called "shot noise" of charge carriers in electronic devices, the random timing and discrete nature of molecular processes being the common features (Simpson et al. 2009). Adding a noise term can be conceived as a formal procedure to insert "randomness" in a deterministic equation and the description it conveys is that of an *external* force contribution. The aim is, in parallel, to switch from a deterministic description to a probabilistic one: in this way, in fact, each value is associated with a probability distribution, which is either a peaked or spread function depending on the amplitude of fluctuations, and is characterized in terms of averages.

Adding fluctuations to a dynamics otherwise predictable, enlarging the width of probability distributions reflect the first attempts along an intellectual path going from invariant to structurally stable, from repetition of identical to repetition of similar. In the resulting theoretical account of stochasticity, still a "regularity" in the sense of physics can be found (by means of the average over an hypothetical ensemble) while an always different outcome (that we would call stochastic, unpredictable) can be interpreted as "regular" given an epistemology based on variability as a major invariant, presumably more appropriate in biology (Longo and Montévil 2013).

The Langevin approach is completely equivalent to a *Fokker-Planck equation* (see Risken 1989), a diffusion equation for continuous Markov processes which turns out to be generally more tractable:

$$\frac{\partial}{\partial t}P(\boldsymbol{x},t) = -\sum_{i=1}^{N}\frac{\partial}{\partial x_i}(\boldsymbol{Sf})_i(\boldsymbol{x})P(\boldsymbol{x},t) + \sum_{i,k=1}^{N}\frac{\partial^2}{\partial x_i \partial x_k}\Sigma_{ik}(\boldsymbol{x})P(\boldsymbol{x},t) \qquad (3.3)$$

The *convective* term $(\boldsymbol{Sf})_i(\boldsymbol{x})$ corresponds to the macroscopic deterministic reaction, while the *diffusion* term $\Sigma_{ik}(\boldsymbol{x})$ is meant to mimic how the noise leads the

---

[1] In this regard, Van Kampen critically claims an "indiscriminate application" of the Langevin approach for internal sources of stochasticity, the main reason being that fluctuations cannot be analyzed independently of the global evolution. From the mathematical point of view, in fact, the Eq. (3.2) is rigorously defined only if one specifies which integration rule is chosen (either the Itô or Stratonovich convention, as explained in Van Kampen 2007).

probability distribution to spread around the average value, which coincides with the deterministic one (it is also referred to as "noise-generating" term).

Simplified assumptions are usually needed to solve analytically the Fokker-Planck equation. In this regard, stochastic kinetics methods have been primarily developed for biochemical reactions that exhibit macroscopically stable stationary (or steady) states. We remark that stationarity is a condition that requires steady flows of energy and matter, thus it includes also some out-of-equilibrium, but close to equilibrium, situations. In this perspective, one analyzes small fluctuations w.r.to stationarity, for example by considering suitably large numbers of molecules and by linearizing the dynamics around the stationary states, see the Linear Noise Approximation (LNA) put forward by Van Kampen (2007). According to the solution of the Fokker-Planck equation in this case, deviations follow a Gaussian distribution, thus in average they cancel out. However, in general, intracellular biochemical processes can occur far from the thermodynamic equilibrium and from stationarity, where the noise becomes extremely significant, regardless of the average molecule copy number. Although approximations such as the LNA are very valuable tools for characterizing fluctuations in many scenarios, they still fail to faithfully and accurately describe what we will highlight as "noise-induced" phenomena, i.e. the rich set of dynamical behaviors that stem from the interplay between fluctuations and nonlinearities (Elf and Ehrenberg 2003).

3.1 "Effective" Randomness

It is worth a brief discussion on the meaning of a random term and the corresponding stochastic picture, as it does not necessarily imply the "pure" randomness of the physical underlying mechanism.

As a matter of fact, fluctuation terms can be also representative of a conventional randomness in the description, canalizing the way in which the existence of ignored variables manifests itself (we shall call it "effective" randomness). This point can be exhaustively clarified through the application of *projection methods* (Zwanzig 1961) or other methods for reduced statistical descriptions (Bravi and Sollich 2015). More generally, the projection approach demonstrates that, when a separation of timescales can be identified, the exact equation for "relevant" (slow) variables may be mapped into a stochastic equation with a "random" force stemming from "irrelevant" (fast) degrees of freedom that have been traced out. In the context of this particular description, typically chosen for a matter of convenience and tractability, fast variables act *effectively* as random terms, regardless of the true physical mechanism by which they influence the system (in principle they can act as deterministic forces). Coarse graining procedures, that allow to switch between different levels of detail, rely on the same logic. Random terms indeed arise as a consequence of mapping a finer scale of description into a coarser one where only certain relevant variables are retained. For example, as explained both in conceptual and formal terms by Castiglione et al. (2008) and in the references therein, a microscopically deterministic dynamics, whose unique source of stochasticity is given by uncertain initial conditions, can be translated into a mesoscopic stochastic evolution.

A basic and powerful guiding idea of many models is to trace out degrees of freedom, so that to end up with terms of effective randomness carrying memory effects from the neglected components. This idea has been explicitly elaborated within projection methods but typically underlies several statistical approaches: it must be seen as a way of rearranging in a form suitable for further treatment the complicated contribution of both predictable and intrinsically unpredictable effects, as well as the overall uncertainty on conditions and on factors involved.

To sum up, terms of effective randomness appear as a consequence of the choice to integrate out some levels of detail, in terms both of components and dynamical processes. This randomness "intrinsic" to the formalism from the mathematical point of view adds itself to the one "intrinsic" to the experimental procedure, the unavoidable uncertainty that affects each physical measure and forces one to express it by an interval.

3.2   Path Integrals

The Fokker-Planck equation is deterministic because the value of the solution is fixed once we know the initial conditions, while stochasticity is included in the fact that it *determines* the dynamics for a law of probability, in analogy with the Schrödinger equation of quantum mechanics.

Quantum randomness manifests as unpredictable fluctuations in measurements: if we repeat an experiment under exactly identical conditions, the outcome of any measurement is found to vary with a random behavior that can be assessed only by probabilistic tools. Importantly, this is due not only to our *ignorance* (the epistemic randomness of classical dynamics), but also to Heisenberg principle. The latter states the non-commutativity of measurements (they depend on the order) and it transforms uncertainty into a *principle*, at the very root of the theory, intrinsically. On the other hand, fluctuations are not the only aspect representing randomness, which in quantum theory is accounted for by the complex nature of the wave function: remarkably, this allows a description for the interference phenomena that are observed in microscopic world and whose explanation builds on the superposition principle. This principle is formalized by the *path integral* formulation, which replaces, for calculating quantum amplitudes, the classical notion of a unique trajectory with a sum, or functional integral, over an infinity of possible trajectories.

Path integrals constitute a formalism intended to incorporate naturally interference effects stemming from wave-particle duality and the key intuition behind is to express stochasticity as an intrinsic superposition of possibilities satisfying certain given boundary conditions. This idea can be traced back to the theory of stochastic processes and can be attributed to Wiener (1976), who introduced the integral named after him for the study of Brownian motion and diffusion processes.

The *Wiener integral*, involving Brownian walks, can be regarded as the first historical evaluation of a statistical path integral and, as well, it provides the basis for a rigorous formulation of quantum mechanics in terms of path integrals, to which stochastic processes are related upon transition to imaginary time.

In fact, quantum mechanics relies on real-time (Minkowskian-time) path integrals: by performing a Wick rotation (i.e. an analytical continuation of the integral to an imaginary time variable) one recovers the Wiener integral, that in this way can be immediately interpreted as an Euclidean-time (imaginary time) path integral giving a transition probability for the process. In addition, once integrated over boundary configurations, this path integral turns out to resemble a statistical partition function: this connection between quantum mechanics and statistical mechanics (globally discussed e.g. by Kleinert 2009) is deeply rooted in the theory and not just dependent on the path integrals formulation. It is demonstrated also by the fact (well known to Schrödinger) that the equation bearing his name coincides with a diffusion equation with an imaginary diffusion constant (or, analogously, in imaginary time). The complete path integral formalization for non-relativistic quantum theory was developed by Feynman (1948), who also showed the equivalence of this formulation to the one of Schrödinger differential equation and to the algebraic one of Heisenberg matrices. In quantum mechanics, the probability of an observable (a real quantity) is given by the squared module of a complex number, the probability amplitude. As a consequence of the superposition principle, Feynman's conjecture theorizes that the probability amplitude can be calculated by a sum of all conceivable and alternative ways of evolution in configuration space, in other words, a sum over all *histories* of the system. Each one is weighted by an exponential term whose imaginary phase is given by the classical action for that history divided by the Planck constant $\hbar$. Thus, according to Feynman's interpretation, the classical action is postulated to contribute as a phase acquired by the system during the time evolution: quantum path integrals are in fact denoted as *oscillatory*. This is in opposition to Wiener integrals, where the action in the exponential still represents a particular history but is not multiplied by the imaginary unit: the probability of each path is thus encoded by an exponential decay, the well-known Boltzmann factor of statistical mechanics (Sethna 2006). By this idea of histories with varying phases, the path integral formulation offers a convenient framework for deducing the classical limit of quantum theory. For instance, when the classical action is much larger than the Planck constant, the exponent becomes a very rapidly varying function, positive and negative deviations w.r.to the classical history are suppressed by destructive interference and the path integral can be evaluated by *stationary phase method* (therefore a justification of classical variational principle is also included). The classic limit of quantum path integrals corresponds to the deterministic limit in stochastic path integrals, which is the one that selects the most probable path by minimizing the action.

Both in the quantum and stochastic context, path integrals do no bring conceptual novelties strictly speaking, they are rather a reformulation of the existing theory in a different form[2]. Nevertheless such a different form looks suitable for performing mathematical manipulations and in particular it frames in intuitive

---

[2] Almost ironically, Feynman (1948) notices in this regard: "There are, therefore, no fundamentally new results. However, there is a pleasure in recognizing old things from a new point of view".

terms a common way of thinking about randomness. The interplay between real and complex numbers, objectified by the Wick rotation, is fundamental in transforming a representation of a properly quantum randomness to the one of diffusive processes, but still the same formal framework can summarize both: an inherent co-existence of possibilities is assumed to characterize quantum systems as well as classical systems commonly denoted as *stochastic*.

4   Stochastic Gene Expression

Since the pioneering work by Kupiec (1983) and more recently (see Raj and Van Oudenaarden 2008; Maheshri and O'Shea 2007; Swain et al. 2002), it has been acknowledged that gene expression is best described as a stochastic process, the evidence being that, even in presence of homogeneous and reproducible experimental conditions, single-cell measurements display a significant degree of heterogeneity. This is interpreted as a phenomenon due to stochasticity, or "noise", intended as unpredictability about the outcome and occurrence of chemical reactions: the idea that noise can influence cell fates was thus developed starting from experimental observation of cell-to-cell differences in gene expression levels. In 1940 Delbrück put forward, for the first time, the hypothesis that fluctuations in biological molecule populations, typically consisting of few copies, can have a relevant impact on cellular physiology: later he proposed this might explain, in part, the variability observed in the number of viruses produced per phage-infected cell (Delbrück 1945). The notion of stochastic gene expression has become well established and widely accepted only more recently, since means of a systematic experimental investigation became available (many of early experiments were in fact limited by the difficulties inherent to measuring gene expression in single cells and needed the development of new tools to manipulate organisms genetically). Since then, it has motivated a great research effort and resulted in a long series of publications in the context of "noise biology" (e.g. Rao et al. 2002; Simpson et al. 2009). Among the first experiments aimed at identifying factors influencing gene expression, we recall the studies of Elowitz et al. (2002), who introduced the distinction between extrinsic and intrinsic noise (see next section).

From a quantitative point of view, a measure of the noise affecting a state variable is given by the Coefficient of Variation (CV), a dimensionless quantity defined as standard deviation of the distribution divided by the mean value (we refer to Simpson et al. 2009; Swain et al. 2002 for formulas): this definition implies examining an ensemble of trajectories at a single time or points of a single trajectories over time, given that ergodicity holds true (i.e. time averages and population averages are interchangeable). The "noise" of a stochastic variable thus is identified with fluctuations with respect to the average over the whole statistical ensemble, usually composed by different cells. Already this definition implies that cells can be regarded as independent and identical realizations of the same system, forcing then a symmetry that is far from being verified in biology, as it will be discussed. By means of the Central Limit Theorem and the Law of Large Numbers (LLN), fluctuations are expected to scale as the inverse of the square root of the number of molecules, thus they correspond only to small corrections to the mean value and can be neglected with respect to the latter. In other words, fluctuations average out as the numbers of molecules increases. Once defined the CV as measure of stochasticity, it can be compared with the noise-type term of the Langevin approach, a term, we remark, that reflects and imposes a probabilistic description. Note that, in the context of experimental characterization, noise is found to have a structure that consists of magnitude (i.e. the size of excursions with respect to mean value) and autocorrelation (a characteristic time scale that quantifies the duration of effects due to fluctuations): both are important in determining biological consequences. However, in biological systems, low copy numbers of crucial components, like DNA or of some molecular types in a cell, prevent from the application of the same argument and motivates the interest for fluctuations, as we will acknwoledge below[3].

4.1   Extrinsic-Intrinsic Noise

In the attempt to clarify and interpret results of experiments, two categories have been defined: *extrinsic* noise and *intrinsic* noise. Both types of noise are claimed to be necessary to justify the observed amount of variability and both are suggested to appear in intracellular reactions involving small numbers of reactants (see Elowitz et al. 2002; Wilkinson 2009; Raj and Van Oudenaarden 2008).

First of all, to make progress in terms of understanding and interpretation, it is essential to provide a brief overview of the biological context in relation to which the subdivision intrinsic-extrinsic has been introduced. In this regard, the fundamental work was done by Elowitz et al. (2002), whose aim was to proceed with a quantitative study of gene expression variability in *Escherichia Coli*. They injected 2 copies of the same promoter into a single cell genome, one responsible for the expression of the cyan fluorescent protein (CFP) and the other for the yellow fluorescent protein (YFP). Under different experimental conditions, the two fluorescent species could either fluctuate indipendently (something observable in the very diversified resulting colors of bacteria) or in a correlated way, giving rise to a more homogenoeus population. According to the definition of CV, noise can be quantified looking at the distribution of a state variable (in this case, the relative number of proteins in living cells that can be estimated from fluorescence intensity): uncorrelated fluctuations define the intrinsic noise, the extrinsic component is detected through correlated flucuations. Correlated changes in expression are believed to result from fluctuations of global expression capacity, while uncorrelated variations in protein levels affect copies independently. In this way, if both promoters can be reasonably assumed

---

[3] The intuition beyond can be traced back to E. Schrödinger's words: "Incredibly small groups of atoms, much too small to display exact statistical laws, do play a dominating role in the very orderly and lawful events within a living organism", *What is Life* (1944).

independent and statistically equivalent in the expression, intrinsic noise is taken as proportional to the difference in the number of each protein within a single cell, while cell-to-cell differences in total fluorescent protein expression account for the extrinsic noise. Both the intrinsic and extrinsic component of noise could be thus determined from plots of CFP versus YFP fluorescence intensity in individual cells, where correlated and uncorrelated deviations actually appear as orthogonal contributions to total noise.

The intrinsic noise is classified as the one due to stochasticity of biochemistry inherent in translation and transcription events: it incorporates and expresses the stochastic nature of gene-specific biochemical reactions, which consist of collisions occurring at random times.

On the other hand, cellular variation is known to be predominantly generated by multiple interactions of the system of interest with other stochastic systems, within the cell and in the environment, that become experimentally detectable as extrinsic fluctuations. As a consequence, several studies (see Shahrezaei et al. 2008; Huang et al. 2010) have focused on models that include random terms of both intrinsic and extrinsic type: in particular, the authors claim that extrinsic noise is essential for the sake of a biologically realistic picture. While the treatment for intrinsic stochasticity is relatively well established, the attempts of mathematical formalization of extrinsic stochasticity are still at the beginning. A hypothesis widely accepted on the basis of experimental evidence (Shahrezaei et al. 2008) is to characterize extrinsic noise as nonspecific (it affects equally each component of the system, so that mathematically it modifies the dynamics as multiplicative noise) and colored (the autocorrelation time is not negligible: it exhibits a substantial lifetime, comparable to the cell cycle).

Many factors are believed to be sources of extrinsic noise: cell-to-cell differences in morphology, organelle composition and molecular population structure, microenvironmental changes in temperature, pression, chemicals, radiation, nutrients, influences from upstream regulators that are unknown or neglected at a certain level of description. As a result, in stochastic representations including extrinsic fluctuations, a connotation of "effective" for randomness should be implicitly assumed: effective randomness, in fact, concentrates contributions of unknown initial and boundary conditions. The idea is to focus on a certain subsystem, so that external but connected degrees of freedom can be taken into account as "random" terms in the equations of that particular subsystem, even if in principle they act deterministically (Bravi and Sollich 2015). The importance, in generating extrinsic fluctuations, of variation both in intracellular and extracellular environments lays a great stress on the role of contexts (intracellular crowding, tissue organization) and history (cell divisions cause an accumulation of differences) in cell dynamics. In other words, extrinsic noise expresses the fact that a cell is not an autonomous entity, it is embedded in an organism and maintains connections with it by regulation and integration mechanisms in several directions. In fact, looking at the cells population level, variability is not found to be simply the sum of independent stochastic events occuring at the intracellular level, as it is not averaged out by large numbers: gene expression itself seems to depend also on a collective dynamics of the whole population (see Stolovicki and Braun 2011).

To summarize, firstly we reconsider the importance of stochasticity on the basis of the LLN, which provides an explanation for what in physics is called "intrinsic" noise, as it stems from the very nature of components of the systems and not from external perturbations. In biological data, additional sources of heterogeneity force to introduce a "noise" accounting for the orthogonal contribution in observations: to remark this opposition, it is called "extrinsic". Paradoxically, at a more detailed analysis, the discussion about the different factors contributing to extrinsic noise reveals that, biologically speaking, it can be regarded as more *intrinsic* than the "intrinsic" noise: in fact, it emerges as an operational and mathematical way to take into account the fundamental *specificity* of biological objects. It is thus be considered *intrinsic to the theory* by remote analogy to its treatment in quantum mechanics. In addition, one is somehow forced to resort to the (too) inclusive category of extrinsic noise because of the lack of experimental techniques to isolate all the different factors we listed.

In the overall perspective, extrinsic noise seems a problem still to exhaustively unravel and this, possibly, suggests a change of viewpoint, as we will propose below: reframing the question itself into an alternative epistemology, the one of the living beings, which accounts for the structures of determination inherent to biology and for an autonomous definition of randomness. Sticking to this idea, history and contexts, as well as internal constraints of integration and regulation mechanisms, can be thought to *constrain* possible evolutionary paths that dynamically arise in the interaction with the environment rather than to *determine* the outcome (as determinism requires that the same effects derive from the same causes). The role of constraints, in reference to "enablement", both to be defined below, seems crucial in biology, as we will hint in the sequel.

Our emphasis on the peculiar biological meaning of "noise" may become particularly relevant in connection to the new discipline we mentioned, whose denomination is exactly "noise biology".

5   Noise Biology

Understanding the role of biological "noise" is in some sense an attempt to address the interplay order-disorder, an unresolved problem in biology since Schrödinger (1944): this constitutes the main focus of "noise biology", a rapidly expanding field. As we observed, noise biology relies on engineering approaches to systems biology, in which networks of biochemical processes are conceptualized as circuits. Noise as a disturbance effect is the consequence of the use (and, let us say, abuse) of the electronic circuit metaphor: as we will discuss later, it focuses on functionality features and thus tends to identify the action of factors that do not fall into this category as a disruption. On the other hand, many are the studies that offer alternative points of view with respect to the one of noise as detrimental to organisms, the convincing argument being that, if what is called noise exerted only perturbative effects, there wouldn't be the interesting "noise-induced" phenomena that we observe in metabolism, stress response, growth (Raj and Van Oudenaarden 2008; Eldar and Elowitz 2010). Some examples are epigenetic influences in developmental processes (see Buiatti 2011) and "noise-driven" cell fates (see Arkin et al. 1998; Rao et al. 2002; Bhogale et al. 2014; Munsky et al. 2014). Among the most striking "noise-induced" phenomena, we should then mention self-organizational properties and the spontaneous emergence of patterns in morphogenesis (e.g. see Meyer and Roeder 2014 for a review): random fluctuations, such as inhomogeneities in the spatial distribution of chemical species, can in fact initiate tissue differentiation and patterning mechanisms by breaking the symmetry between cells. Interestingly this research direction is in part reminiscent of what Prigogine (1984) introduced as "order by fluctuations" and, in particular, it continues Turing's studies on pattern formation in reaction-diffusion systems (1952).

Even in this different perspective, the vocabulary often used still derives from the electronic circuit metaphor and thus inherits some notion of "optimality" in the design, a problematic notion itself when referred to organisms (Longo and Montévil 2013). The basic assumption of noise biology is that natural selection has "optimized" the distribution of noise to populations, shaping molecular processes in such a way to "resist" or to functionally "exploit" noise (Vilar et al. 2002; Rao et al. 2002): the aim of noise biology is to understand this distribution, statistical properties of random variables being informative about selective mechanisms that drove such evolution.

The emerging scenario is consistent with the characterization of "canalized" biological randomness previously proposed. In the noise biology literature, heterogeneity is often denoted as "*biased* by environmental and intracellular signals [...] *ordered*" (Rao et al. 2002), "*adjusted* during functional evolution" (Snijder and Pelkmans 2011). In particular, the integration of functional modules and regulatory features are assumed to filter and shape noise, the result being a "*cultivated* noise" or an "environmentally *tuned* heterogeneity in a cell population" (Rao et al. 2002). For instance, stochastic behaviors are inevitably affected by the crowded, diffusion-limiting, highly structured and compartmentalized intracellular media and by molecular mechanisms of regulation and compensation, such as *feedback* and *feedforward* loops (in feed-back loops the output comes back as input, while in feed-forward information is unidirectional). Also at the tissue level, mechanical stresses can either control or amplify cell growth heterogeneity, as suggested by Uyttewaal et al. (2012). In general, noise takes part in the evolutionary and adaptive dynamics thus its "functional role" has been extensively claimed. In this context, the focus is on its interplay with nonlinearities, which leads to phenomena of stochastic amplification, stochastic dumping and focusing of oscillations (see Paulsson et al. 2000). An example worth mentioning is the circadian rhythm, i.e. the biochemical mechanism oscillating in phase with the photoperiod, for which stochastic models are shown (see Guerriero et al. 2012 for plant circadian clock) to better capture experimental observations. Stochasticity ensures a faster, thus more efficient, synchronization to variations in photoperiod and buffers fluctuations in various environmental factors, such as light intensity and temperature. In summary, stochasticity, by facilitating the response to external changes, provides organisms with an increased plasticity and it is directly linked to metabolism and survival through the role played by circadian rhythms in photosynthesis.

Furthermore, fluctuations act in connection with positive feedbacks in cell fate-selection mechanisms, yielding to the so called noise-mediated or stochastic "switches" (Raj and Van Oudenaarden 2008): a positive feedback loop can lead to multiple stationary solutions (multistability) and stochastic fluctuations have the potential to switch between them, causing a variation in the phenotype. Such mechanisms are considered an evidence of functional advantage of noise to respond to environmental changes. The paradigmatic (and firstly studied) system in this regard is the λ-phage lysis-lysogeny decision circuit, where the "noise" canalizes the effect of the environment in such a way to enable the decision between the lytic and lysogenic pathway (Arkin et al. 1998). Other examples can be listed in metabolism and nutrient uptake, such as the lactose-pathway switch in *E.coli* (Bhogale et al. 2014), or in connection to fate selection in viral infection, such as the Pyelonephritis-Associated Pili (PAP) epigenetic switch in *E. Coli* (Munsky et al. 2014). Variability is thus enhanced by networks that can produce multiple, mutually exclusive profiles of gene expression: this fact, in combination with other processes of randomly expressing genes and silencing others, is thought to have a selective advantage, as it allows organisms to display phenotypic variants also in uniform genetic and environmental conditions (Wilkinson 2009). These phenomena can be thought to belong to the class of "variability generators" introduced by Buiatti and Buiatti (2008) and described as exploration tools of the phase space that are essential for the adaptation to changing contexts. This is relevant in the perspective further developped below, that the very phase space is co-constructed by the changing biological structures and their interaction with the ecosystem.

6   Robustness from Noise and Beyond Noise

Dialectically, the problem of "noise" cannot be separated from the one of "robustness": this is often meant as an inherent noise-rejecting property, given implicitly the assumption that a noise-resistant system is likely to exhibit robustness. Many key properties of biological systems, from phenotypes to the capability of performing some task, are recognized to be "robust" in the sense of relatively insensitive to the precise values of biochemical parameters: the degree of robustness can be thus quantitatively and systematically investigated by methods connected to sensitivity analysis (Barkai et al. 1997). Relying on the analogy with an electronic circuit, robustness is described as crucial to ensure a proper functioning of "signal" transduction networks in "noisy" conditions. The explanation of biological robustness in absence of large numbers, not possible by invoking arguments from physics, is attempted rather by focusing on "design" features of biochemical networks (a way of proceeding more akin to engineering). The metaphor biosystem-circuit provides thus the framework to accommodate the interplay between robustness, noise and their respective roles for a reliable operational outcome but, importantly, in such a framework they are conceived as seemingly conflicting notions. "Noise", by enlarging the range of parameters, contributes to variability and, as a consequence, a potential advantage in terms of adaptiveness to changing environments can be argued for (see e.g. Rao et al. 2002): one can indeed analyze robustness in close connection with organisms internal plasticity (Buiatti and Buiatti 2008) and randomness as a key component of structural stability (Longo and Montévil 2013).

Attempts to include a property of robustness into models account for the "individuality" of living objects that strikingly emerges in observations: examples of this evidence are some features of chemotactic response (Barkai et al. 1997), such as adaptation time and steady state tumbling frequency, that vary significantly from one bacterium to another in genetically identical populations, or phyllotaxis (Mirabet et al. 2012), as the arrangement of leaves and flowers is widely diversified both at inter and intra-plant scale. In our perspective, robustness expresses and justifies a notion of organisms as systems endowed with a high degree of historical specificity: it allows changes over time, while preserving varying degrees of individuality, from bacteria to large vertebrates. By virtue of this correspondence, robustness can be regarded as an intrinsic property, as far as variability and individuality within the constraints of structural stability are inherent to life. Thus, stochasticity, far from being just "noise", plays a constructive role towards robustness, by promoting and underlying the adaptive responses of an organism to the environment. Remarkably, this potential positive contribution of randomness is grounded not only in statistical properties but it holds true both by large and by small numbers, in contrast to physics, as we will argue below.

In biology one needs to enrich the notion of robustness with respect to other disciplines (see Lesne 2008 for an extensive review of the notion of robustness in biology): for example one should add forms of "functional", "structural" robustness that stem from regulation mechanisms and are shaped by the evolutionary history (e.g. feedbacks in stochastic "switches" and in morphogenesis act towards a stabilization and a reinforcement of the phenotypic path selected by fluctuations). In particular, the definition of robustness should not be limited simply to "feature persistence" but should include also the meaning of "resilience", to be intended as persistent dynamic reconstruction of a viable coherence structure, viable also because adaptive and diverse, thus changing.

7   Proper Biological Randomness

It should be clear by now that the need to capture heterogeneity, which manifests itself as unpredictability with respect to the deterministic formalism, leads to resort to stochastic models. In particular, a description in probabilistic terms of biochemistry has been the starting point for the physico-mathematical investigation and characterization of biological randomness.

In spite of the major interest of this investigation, we consider it still essentially incomplete (where incompleteness does not mean at all useless). The perspective we want to hint here is based on an attempt to include randomness in the "structure of determination" of biological dynamics, intrinsically. In a sense, we can still refer to mathematical physics, methodologically, for a paradigmatic

change of this kind: Schrödinger equation gives the deterministic dynamics of
...a law (an amplitude) of probability. By this, quantum randomness is integrated in the mathematical determination. We are far from being able to propose
a similar mathematical novelty, in biology, as first a change in the theoretical
frame, including terminology, is required. A preliminary, apparently minor, point
is the idea of avoiding the reference to "noise", when appreciating the role of
random events in biology. As we stressed and as we will further stress below,
in biology, randomness is an integral part of variability, thus of adaptation and
diversity, both in reference to small numbers and to large numbers. Randomness contributes by this to biological structural stability, as a peculiar form of
resilience. It is an evolutionary fact that a population of a few thousand animals
is more stable if diverse; but diversity in large populations as well, or in species,
contributes to stability, far away from the "averaging out" proper to noise in
stochastic dynamics in physics. That is, both within an organism and in the
ecosystem, diversity, variability and number of components play a diverse role,
as we will hint. And randomness, as a component of variability, adaptation and
diversity, becomes functional *as such* to biological dynamics.

7.1 Examples of the Functionality of Diversity in Large Numbers

Within an organism, variability may contribute in different ways to its structural
stability. It is largely claimed that the average functionality of hepathocytes (liver
cells) only matters (Pocock 2006). So, variability seems averaged out in this organ
made of a few hundred million cells, a number considered "large" in biological
applications of statistical physics. Similarly, as for the lungs' function, only the
average functionality of lung's cell seems to matter. Yet, at a closer insight, both
interindividual and intraindividual diversity of the fractal and alveoli's structure
and cells' diversity of lungs in mammals (about five hundred million alveoli,
in an adult human), contributes to the adaptivity of the lungs' functionality
in different contexts: the direct interface with the atmosphere better adapts to
atmospheric changes by its diversity. Even more so, the about 10^9 leukocytes in
the immune system, yet another large number, are effective exactly because of
their variety and diversity: they are produced as a result of variability generators (Buiatti and Buiatti 2004) and subsequently selected when binding antigens.
The immune system is a true evolutionary system within an organism, where
diversity within each leukocytes' population, and between populations, is at the
core of its functionality and is enhanced by selection (Thomas et al. 2008). Thus,
variability, which fluctuates over about 10^{15} potentially different cell receptors,
is the opposite of noise to be averaged out. In conclusion, the biological functionality of randomness is highly unconventional w.r.to physics, by the peculiar role
of adaptivity and diversity, and a reference to two out of these three examples,
say, just in terms of "noise" may be highly misleading.

In biology, a novel and specific notion of randomness has been claimed (see
Buiatti and Longo 2013; Longo and Montévil 2013, 2014). This is also due to the
need to work simultaneously at different levels of organization, that is to grasp, in

a unified way, cellular, tissue, organ, organismal levels, possibly within an evolutionary context. In physics, different scales are enough to force different theories, so far: quantum and relativistic fields are still not unified to describe gravity; classical and quantum randomness are treated differently (they are dealt with different probabilities, in view of the violation of Bell inequalities, see Aspect et al. 1982); hydrodynamics is far from being understood in terms of quantum physics – in spite of water being formed by simple molecules (Chibbaro et al. 2014). This lack of unity, in physics, is relevant for biological theorizing, since both quantum and classical randomness are present at the molecular level (see Buiatti and Longo 2013 for references and a discussion); water, say, has also a relevant role, including by its peculiar "coherence" in the highly compartmentalized structures of eukariota, due to Quantum Electro-Dynamics effects (Del Giudice and Preparata 1998). Moreover, many researchers analyze cell networks in terms of statistical physics, while others work in morphogenesis of organs in terms of non-linear dynamics, since Turing's 1952 paper (Fleury and Gordon 2011).

From an epistemic perspective, these different levels of analysis may be soundly called "different levels of organization" as they require, so far, different mathematical, even conceptual, possibly incompatible, tools. The reduction to the molecular level is a myth that is in contrast to the history of physics, where theoreticians proposed "unifications" (Newton, Boltzmann) not reductions and still search for unification (relativistic vs. quantum fields). Moreover, this myth leads to incomplete theories even at the molecular level, as any relevant molecular cascade, in an organism, be it just a cell, *causally depends on the context*. In particular, macromolecular interactions are largely stochastic, must then be given in probabilities and these probabilities depend on the context. For example, macromolecular syntheses may be "constrained" by enzymes in different ways; a simple pressure on the cell or its nucleus, "constrains" or "canalizes" stochastic gene expression (Farge et al. 2009; Swain et al. 2002; Raj and Van Oudenaarden 2008).

In order to deal with the physical singularity of these phenomena, the notions of "bio-resonance" and "enablement" have been proposed (Buiatti and Longo 2013; Longo et al. 2012a). These notions are proper to organismal biology and evolution and significantly change the biological "structure of determination", in particular in relation to randomness; they enrich by this the contribution by biochemistry, summarized in the previous sections. Bio-resonance has been proposed in analogy to the role of "planetary" resonance in the non-linear analyses of the planetary system: it is the gravitational interaction between planets that "destabilizes" the dynamics by a non-linear amplification of minor fluctuations and perturbations, in particular when planets are aligned with the sun (a sort of noise that destabilizes the perfect clockwork of Creation). This happens though at just one scale, at one level of mathematical description. Bio-resonance instead concerns the interactions, by integration and regulation, between different levels of organization, thus possibly between different mathematical analyses, within an organism. Moreover, on one side, (minor) fluctuations at one level may affect other levels – an endocrine perturbation, say, may change the control of cell reproduction in a tissue, a possible cause of cancer (Soto and Sonnenschein 2010). On the other, bio-resonance enhances regulation and correlates variations, by integration of cells, in a tissue, in an organ, in an organism. By this, it contributes to stabilization of an organism, which continually undergoes Darwin's correlated variations, also in ontogenesis, though in a more constrained way than at the evolutionary space-time scale.

As for enablement (Longo et al. 2012a; Longo and Montévil 2013), its epistemological novelty resides in enriching deterministic causality: phylogenetic and developmental paths are selected according to their "compatibility" in a (phase) space of phylogenetic and morphogenetic trajectories dynamically "co-constituted" with the environment (Longo and Montévil 2014). In short, an ecosystem *enables*, does not causes, in general, the formation of a new phenotype (possibly a species). In light of Darwin's first principle, the default state for biological entities, since they are endowed with a replicative structure, is given by "proliferation with *variation*", as we will stress in the conclusion, following Longo et al. (2015). Then, some variants, some hopeful monsters as suggested by Goldsmith, often produced by sudden bursts of variability (Eldredge and Gould 1972) may be enabled by the (changing) environment. Note that, by modifying the default state, from inertia to Darwin's descent with modification, the causal analysis of an evolutionary and ontogenetic dynamics must be extended to an analysis of "what enables". A doctor who understands the *cause* of a Pneumonia in a bacterium, must also consider the state of the lungs or the general health conditions of the patient that *enabled* the infection to develop – bacteria a priori reproduce with variations and are generally present in an organism: a healthy lung and immune system control their reproduction and do not enable them beyond a viable level.

As for the dynamic nature of the enabling environment and of the organisms that grow in it and compose it, note that, since a quantum event at a molecular level may induce a phenotypic change, a possibility mentioned above, the latter has at least the same nature of unpredictability as the quantum event, though manifested at a very different scale and level of organization. Thus, if one takes as observables the ones proposed since Darwin, namely organisms and phenotypes, in a broad sense, these are a consequence of the dynamics and cannot be pre-given, even not a space of possibilities. This is in sharp contrast with the theoretical attitude in physics, where one of the major duties of theory building is the preliminary invention of the "proper" phase space: the dynamics and its laws will follow, possibly given by equations or evolution functions within those spaces. It should be clear that these may be infinite or even infinite dimensional, such as Hilbert spaces in quantum mechanics, yet they are mathematically pre-defined to the dynamics (by their symmetries, they can be axiomatically defined, by finitely many words). In some cases, in statistical physics, the (finite) dimension may change, yet the new dimensions have the same observable properties as the others and the probabilities of each change of phase space are known (Sethna 2006).

Enablement, compatibility, dynamic and unpredictable co-constitution of the phase space contribute to set up a new conceptual framework to understand and justify variability and diversity as intrinsic properties of life: they are not just "noise", or perturbations within a pre-given frame. Also the analysis of the "living state of the matter" proposed by Buiatti and Buiatti (2004) pays particular attention to variability generators or internal random generators, a set of phenomena and mechanisms that enable organisms to produce new possible paths and variants on which selection processes act or that are enabled. These generators are at the core of plasticity, adaptiveness, evolvability. As we mentioned, within an organism, the immune system is the most typical case of a contribution to biological viability and stability based on variability generators, thus on diversity.

In summary, randomness in biology must be considered as a constitutive component of stability, also or mostly by the peculiar biological role of adaptivity and diversity. It is a massive but "canalized" phenomenon, summarizing the pressure due to internal constraints and to environmental conditions, in such a way that the analysis cannot be performed regardless of the context. Internal mechanisms of integration and regulation, to which upward and downward processes contribute, establish an intertwining of local and global scales in organisms and canalize biological evolutionary and developmental dynamics. They appear as constitutive aspects of the concept of "bio-resonance", proposed in order to include in the description both constraints and amplification of randomness between epistemic organizational levels. Furthermore, living systems are open, they continually interact with the ecosystem, exchanging energy and matter and dynamically modifying their configuration jointly to the ever changing environment. In biology, histories and contexts, "accidents" that are usually neglected in physics, contribute to biological determination (Longo and Montévil 2013): two books and several papers (see Longo's web page) propose a perspective on these aspects of organismal dynamics that need to be taken into consideration, even in investigations at a molecular level.

Note, finally, that the law of large numbers (LLN), in physics, justifies the interest in potential effects of randomness in small populations, as it indirectly stresses the potential role of fluctuations for low numbers and the possibilities of change as opposite to "averaging them out", proper to fluctuations in large numbers of entities. However, LLN does not provide tools for a satisfactory treatment of this phenomenon for low numbers, while it precludes the understanding of functional diversity by randomness in large numbers (see the immune system above). In other words, the LLN implication that fluctuations are negligible is rather a retrieval of the fully deterministic macroscopic model and its "classical" stability. In addition, the statistical theory behind LLN subsumes indipendent copy number fluctuations[4] as sole source of "noise" and this is not sufficient in

---

[4] As a preliminary evidence, recent experiments (see Salman et al. 2012) suggest that the fitted curves for protein abundance resemble limit distributions of strongly correlated stochastic variables: this would reflect the spatial and temporal interdependence of processes regulating gene expression.

biology, as we tried to make clear also by the description of intrinsic and extrinsic components of noise in the previous section and by the examples and notions in this section.

In summary, from our perspective, biological randomness plays an essential explanatory role, in presence of both large and low numbers, by the role of variability, diversity and adaptivity. By focusing on these randomness related components of *biological stability*, we stressed a rather unconvential aspect of life dynamics in comparison both to physical or computational ones. The mathematical form of randomness appropriate to biology reasonably needs a more systematic elaboration and definition, as it should condense the conceptual novelties briefly described here and be conceived as proper to the very dynamics of life.

8   Symmetries

The role of symmetries, in mathematics and physics, is well-known. By symmetry we mean both a regularity in a structure, which may present an invariance with respect to some transformations, and a trasformation that preserves some properties of the intended object. In a sense, in a discipline largely based on invariants and invariance preserving transformations, mathematics, symmetries have this peculiar double status of being both invariants and transformations. By their definition, symmetries are organized as a group, in the intended space. In mathematics and physics, from Euclid to Grothendieck, from Archimedes to Einstein and Weyl or contemporary physics, symmetries are at the core of knowledge construction. Our 3-dimensional continuum possesses a fundamental (rotational and translational) symmetry (groups O(3) and R3) which permeates all physical theories. Lorentz and Poincaré symmetry groups in relativity and gauge groups for elementary particles are at the core of contemporary physics. Symmetries appear in crystals and quasicrystals, in self-similarity for fractals, dynamical systems and statistical mechanics, in monodromies for differential equations . . . . Even more fundamentally, conservation properties, of energy and momentum, are symmetries in the equations (Noether's theorems): these properties allow to write the Hamiltonian, an omnipresent tool in mathematical physics. Similarly, in electromagnetism, inversing charges does not alter the equations (a symmetry), or the aim of the recent experiments on the Higgs boson was to witness a symmetry breaking in fundamental fields in particle physics.

In biology, symmetries allow to understand macromolecular interactions, as well as global structures, such as organisms' bauplans. Yet, *symmetry breaking* as well has a crucial *theoretical* role in biology, as we will hint in the next section. An interesting connection that may help to move from physics to biology, is given by the notion of "critical transition", where both symmetries and their breaking play a key role. This notion has been used, in between physics and biology, since the'80s (see Longo and Montévil 2014 for a survey and details on the following remarks). The main idea is to split first the microscopic and the macroscopic descriptions. The microscopic level may be described by the same equations in different macroscopic states and these equations satisfy certain symmetries (for example, no particular direction in magnetization at high temperature, nor in a fluid). At the transition point, i.e. at a given value of the control parameter (temperature, say), these symmetries are broken and a precise direction dominates in magnetization, in crystal formation .... The space of description changes, at the pertinent scale, as well as its symmetries. Yet, in existing physical theories, this space may be pre-given. Crystals and snow flakes, a typical formation of a coherence structure at a critical transition, yield new, but pre-listable symmetries, in a new, but expected, space of observables, due to forces already present in molecular interaction, but ineffective till the Brownian motion is above a certain threshold. At critical transitions, along the intended parameters, pertinent objects change, yet they may be measured according to pre-given observables.

In the statistical approach to thermodynamics, one can observe a similarly consistent role in the definition of a phase space, at the thermodynamic limit, and this in connection to the "averaging out" of some key features which, in that limit, can be regarded just as microscopic details. Note also that, in this approach, the probability of deviating from the most probable state decreases exponentially, depending on the number of lower-level entities (this result is known as the "fluctuation theorem"). On the grounds of some fundamental assumptions, such as the thermodynamic limit (the assumption of an infinite number of particles leads to a coincidence of averages and macroscopic states) and ergodicity (that is a symmetry assumption between time average and phase space average), the theory allows to go from the properties of a trajectory to the properties of the phase space and vice versa[5].

More generally, the description of a suitable phase space where "trajectories", in a broad sense, may be described, even in presence of critical transitions or asymptotic constructions, is a key issue of the theoretical investigation in physics. As we already observed, since Newton and Kant, we understood physical knowledge as built in "a priori" defined (phase) spaces, where one can describe the intended dynamics by equations and evolution functions, that is once fixed the pertinent parameters and observables. Newton, in space and time, then in suitable, yet different, phase spaces, Hamilton, Poincaré, Gibbs, Boltzman, Einstein, Schrödinger ... gave us the beautiful theories that frame physical theories. Let us see more closely a further key role of symmetries in this very robust methodology.

---

[5] In these contexts, mean values analyses (or central limit theorems) are generally valid. However, in the complex case of second-order phase transitions, in thermodynamics, these analyses fail. For example, the transition between macroscopic order versus disorder in ferro-paramagnetic transitions, does not occur progressively but at a precise (critical) temperature. At that point, fluctuations at every scale dominate and this expresses a tendency to obtain magnetic alignments of every size. Moreover, some physical quantities become infinite, such as susceptibility to an external field. As a consequence of the dominating fluctuations, close or at the transition, mean value analyses fail (Longo et al. 2012b; Toulouse et al. 1977). This may be of interest for biological theoretizing, yet, in this case as well, the phase space is pre-given.

Physical and mathematical objects are *generic*, that is they are invariants in experiments and theories, in a given (abstract) space of observables and objects. As for mathematics, it should be clear that a right triangle or a Banach space are generic: a proof of their properties on one of them, gives them "for all". In physics, a measurement on a falling stone or an electron may be iterated identically, always, in any similar context, within physical approximation, for any stone or electron. This is a theoretical symmetry (a invariance property of objects that may be interchanged, are generic, in the theory – as given by equations, evolution functions . . .), which is also crucial for measurement. As Galileo observed in "Dialoghi sopra i massimi sistemi": errors in measurement are unavoidable, yet small errors are the most probable; errors distribute symmetrically around the mean value; reliability increases with the number of measurements. The symmetries of a Gaussian and the genericity of the physical objects formalize Galileo's early insight.

9 Symmetry Breaking

9.1 Measurement

In order to stress the singularity of biological experiments and subsequent theoretizing, observe first that Galileo's remarks are fundamentally wrong in biology, from cells to plants and animals, and this constitutes a major challenge for experimental work. Indeed, biological objects are *specific*, that is, they are the result of a history, they are individuated and diverse, they are not interchangeable (symmetric). By an extraordinary attention to experimental protocols, biologists care of the history of each organism they work on: its phylogeny, up to a very high number of generations, and its ontogeny are closely considered in order to perform and compare experiments. So mice and cells are internationally numbered, described and used according to these histories. Typically, when increasing the number of experiments, one may be forced to go beyond the (limited) number of organisms with the same phylogenetic history, and this may give very different reactions in a given experiment. Then "errors" and their distance may increase with the number of experiments. The point, of course, is that these are not errors, a priori, but may correspond to increasing interindividual diversity, when a population increases. Similarly, exceptions to mean values are not to be discarded, as they may correspond to an exploration by variability of new onto-phylogenetic paths. As we observed, biologists "symmetrize" (a terminology by M. Montévil in ongoing strongly needed theoretical reflections on biological measurement) as much as they can the objects of experiments, typically by common histories and strictly controlled environments, but the comparative analysis of variability is also a component of the empirical investigation: the fact that Polynesian and Polish patients may react very differently to a molecule is an important information, per se. Specificity of organisms breaks a fundamental symmetry assumption in mathematics and physics, genericity, an invariance under objects' transformations, in experiments and in theories.

9.2 Extended Criticality

A conceptualization of the permanent reconstruction of the coherence structure of an organism, as a state of "extended critical transition" proper to biological onto-phylogenetic trajectories is summarized in Longo and Montévil (2014), following some previous papers (downloadable). Each cell reproduction, in particular in a multicellular organism, yields a critical transition. At the "bifurcation", it produces a new coherence structure of intercellular context, where two similar (almost symmetric, but inherently asymmetric) cells reorganize cell-to-cell connections as well as collagen, tissue's matrix .... The sensitivity to the context of the new symmetries formed at the transition, plus the asymmetric distribution of DNA and proteomes, facilitates cellular differentiation and variation: a minor change in the context (different distance from the source of energy, different pressure ...) may influence the cell fate. Adaptation is a further consequence of this unstable/stable dynamics, as, at criticality, a cell, an organ may better adjust to organismal or ecosystemic changes (see Mora and Bialek 2011, where also some biological functions are described as poised at criticality[6]).

In this perspective, a biological trajectory of an organism is a cascade of symmetry changes of ... a fundamentally symmetric, i.e. locally coherent, structure, yet continually changing its proper coherence (its symmetries). This viewpoint focuses on the contingency of structural stability in biology, but does not exclude stability from the theoretical construction. We just stress the role of time and of changes in an understanding of the resilience, thus of a form of stability, in biological dynamics, on the grounds of a permanent dialogue with physical theories, both by a methodological transfer and by conceptual dualities. Note, typically, that the continual changes of symmetries do not allow to describe biological trajectories as the optimal result of conservation properties (energy, momentum or alike), like in physics. As a consequence of these properties, in physics, the trajectories are geodetics (optimal paths) in a pre-given phase space, thus they are specific[7]. We claim instead that trajectories, in biology, in evolution in particular, are *generic*, that is they are "possible" ones, as a consequence of Darwin's principle of descent with modification and of enablement or selection, in a co-constructed ecosystem as phase space, where pertinent observables and parameters are subject to change[8]. Moreover, a phylogenetic trajectory is the "sum" of ontogenetic trajectories, where each of these trajectories is an extended critical path (ontogeny is an extended critical interval, in the life span, with time as a control parameter, see Longo and Montévil 2014).

---

[6] In reference to a previous footnote, this situation is closer to second order criticality than to the statistical "averaging out".

[7] Geodetics are usually derived by variational or equivalent methods that allow to write a Hamiltonian or extremize a Lagrangian functional that are given in terms of conservation properties.

[8] Note that not only measurable phenotypes, as observables, may change, but pertinent parameters as well: air vibrations at audible frequencies were irrelevant before the formation of hears, in early vertebrates with a double jaw (Allin 1975).

Table 1, below, summarizes the conceptual dualities w.r.to physics that guide the theoretical attempts in biology mentioned here. We already hinted to the dualities in the first three lines that are extensively treated in the references. In the next section, a few ideas will be given on the dualites not yet discussed. This will allow to further stress the functional role of randomness in biology.

Table 1. A possible theoretical differentiation between inert and living state of matter is described through some conceptual dualities, based on the work in Longo and Montévil (2014).

PHYSICS	BIOLOGY
Randomness is non deterministic or deterministic non predictability within a pre-given phase space	Randomness is intrinsic indetermination given also by changing phase spaces (ontogenesis and phylogenesis)
Specific trajectories (geodetics) and generic objects	Generic trajectories (possible/compatible with ecosystem) and specific objects
Point-wise criticality	Extended criticality
Reversible time (or irreversible for degradation-simplified thermodynamics)	Double irreversibility of time (thermodynamics and phenotypic complexity constitution)

10   Symmetry Breaking, Randomness and Time

10.1   Biological Time

Longo and Montévil (2015) observe the co-existence, in existing physical theories, of symmetry breaking, random events and (local) irreversibility of time. In short, measurement as projection of the state vector in quantum mechanics, bifurcations in classical non-linear dynamics, diffusions by random paths . . . , as symmetry breakings, are all associated to random events (or probability values) and are time irreversible. By a direct analogy, in this case, it should be clear that the approach hinted here to biological trajectories in terms of cascades of symmetry changes further stresses the omnipresent and constituive role of randomness in biology. But also the irreversibility of time turns out to be crucial. Of course, there are plenty of thermodynamic effects, in an unicellular organisms as well as in elephants, since energy is used and transformed everywhere. Yet and once more, the physical singularity of life pops out also by the peculiar irreversibility of time that we consider needed for an appropiate theorizing.

First, energy dispersal, as understood in thermodynamics, has a major relevance in biology. The decrease of entalpic oscillations of a macromolecule may have little physical interest, in particular because, by pumping energy, one may restaure the previous situation (like in two mixing gazes, where a centrifugue may separate again the gazes). Yet, in a cell, decreasing oscillations of macromolecules may reduce stochastic interactions and biochemical activities, thus it may irreversibly affect gene expression and metabolic stability (the increasing instability of the latter is often considered at the heart of aging, see Olshansky and Rattan 2005). This stresses the relevance of the thermodynamic irreversibility in biological processes. Second, the very setting up and mantainance of biological organization is a highly irreversible process. Everybody understands that a theory that would allow to conceive a backwards film of embryogenesis should be immediately discarded. Let's examine this point more closely.

As we recalled above, each cell division, on one side, increases order, as having two cells instead of one enriches the order or the organization of the universe; on the other, it produces a slight disorder. The asymmetric division of the proteome, which, for many molecular types that are present in low numbers, does not average out, similarly as for the differences in DNA copies, in the partitioned membrane ... yield irreversible symmetry breakings. This slight production of disorder is also a form of entropy production, while it comes with the production of order "per se", not just by the use of energy. Now, cell division is not proper only to embryogenesis, but it is a critical transition that continually occurs in ontogenesis, by billions of times everyday in a large metazoan. A close analysis of the relevance of this two forms of entropy production for aging is developped by Bailly and Longo (2009). Let's just mention here that this may help to stress a difference between monocellular and multicellular organisms. In a monocellular organism, the entropy produced by the energy transformation processes or at asymmetric reproductions is mostly released in the exterior environment. Some traces of aging are then found in asymmetries in the new membranes – a new vs. an older part – which happens to be the border between interior and exterior, where flows pass through, see (Lindner et al. 2008; Stewart et al. 2005)). In a metazoan, the entropy produced, under all of its forms, is also but inevitably transferred to the environing cells, to the tissue, to the organism. It may contribute to decrease collagen tension and the global tensegrity structures of tissues. It may affect metabolic stability in other cells as well as the oxidative stress (Romano et al. 2010). As this is an additive effect, it increases exponentially: while negligible in embryogenesis and youth, it prevails over the slower reconstruction of organization with aging. Note, here, that we do not want to ascribe aging entirely to this double form of entropy production, as the debate on the nature of aging, a multifactorial process, is extremely open and lively. We just propose a possible further element for the controversial role of many factors, some of which may be unified by this analysis, which differs but is compatible with other recent proposals. In particular, the generation of more connective tissues, a possible biological response to degradation, is another challenging component of aging, (Miquel 2014). Note finally that even the analysis of the entropic component of aging cannot be based on the averaging out of fluctuations or the centrality of means. It is based instead on the key role of reproductive variability as such and the slight creation of disorder associated to it, also during the (re-)construction of order. Moreover, the distinction between thermodynamic irreversibility and the irreversibility of the very setting up and mantainance of organization, encourages to single-out a second observable time, in the same dimension of the physical arrow of time, yet proper to biological investigations: the time of (re-)construction of the organization (in physics, the dimension of energy contains different observable forms of energy). Biological clocks and internal rhythms in organisms provide a natural measurement for this second observable time, at least along metazoans' life span, as they scan it in a relatively independent way from thermodynamic time (Longo and Montévil 2014). Once more, random events are at the core of it and have a constitutive, functional role.

10.2 Plasticity and Variation

So far, variability in biology has been implicitly assumed as the result of random variation at some level of organization, beginning of course, with DNA, from mutations to stochastic gene expression. However, there is an increasing awareness of Lamarckian effects in phylogenesis. Acquired or epigenetic inheritance has been observed in cyliates (Nowacki and Landweber 2009). Proteomic changes due to different environmental levels in lactose are reportedly inherited for several generations (Robert et al. 2010). It is well known that methylation and demethylation, which affect gene expression, may be induced by environmental factors, including emotional situations, from rats to humans. In other words, Darwin's principle of descent with modification is not only based on random effects, but may also be induced by contextual interactions and result in acquired inheritance. In this perspective, *canalization by constraints* may be another suitable concept for the relation between biological dynamics and their contour or internal conditions. Some recent experiences in microgravity (Bizzarri et al. 2014) show that unicellular eukariota develop wild cytoskeleta when they reproduce in geo-stationary satellites. The idea is that gravity constrains development: typically, it canalizes cytoskeletal growth towards relatively flat structures as well as it selects negatively shapes that are unsuitable for subsistance or movement. When this constraint is reduced or disappears, descent with modification yields a larger variety of enabled structures. One may consider then the resulting forms as due to the plasticity of organismal development, as cytoskeleta seem shaped, not just selected, also by gravity. Biological plasticity, of course, reaches its highest point in (large) brains, where the continual dynamics of neurons and their connections undergoes deformations and even critical transitions (Werner 2007) as a consequence of brain's interaction with the ecosystem. In short, from individual eukariota to large organisms, their neural systems at least, both phylogenesis and ontogenesis extensively present random variations as well as forms of induced or canalized changes by plasticity, where selection or enablement apply.

11 Conclusion and Opening: Some Principles of Biological Organization

Cell proliferation has been called "ground state' in the context of embryonic stem cells, because it is inherent to the system, and does not require stimulation (Wray et al. 2010). Morevoer, all cells move. In pioneering work on cancer

(Soto and Sonnenschein 1999) proposed to consider proliferation and motility as default state of all cells, also within organisms, where this default state is highly constrained. Even neurons or heart's cells, which are known not to reproduce or to reproduce very rarely, when extracted from their organismal context proliferate at high pace. As we already mentioned, in Darwin's theory, reproduction is always *with modification* and will happen as long as there are sufficient available nutrients – up to potentially covering Earth, says Darwin. The addition of "modification" is thus fundamental; variation begins at the cell division that generates two overall similar, but not identical cells. Adding modification at reproduction is at the core of this paper not just in view of random molecular events (Kupiec 1983; Raj and Van Oudenaarden 2008), but also by the plasticity mentioned above. In Longo et al. (2015), this has been synthesized as a default state of all organisms:

Proliferation with variation and motility

and as a Framing Principle:

Life phenomena are never identical iterations of a morphogenetic process

Generating diversity from a single cell, be it LUCA (Last Common Universal Ancestor) or a zygote, is an essential component of phylogenesis and ontogenesis. The Framing Principle is a way to express a principle of iterated organization at all scales and levels, not just cells and organisms. For example, branching morphogenesis in organs is an ubiquitous iterative process that generates a repetitive, yet always changing pattern, e.g. branching angles vary (in vascular systems, in ducts of all sorts). This is due to the combined action of the default state of the cells producing the corresponding tissues and the varying pressures, frictions . . . in the context.

An analysis of "organization with variation" has been recently proposed by Montévil and Mossio (2015), where an explicit distinction betweeen causal relations and constraints provides a major conceptual clarification. By the introduction of characteristic times for processes within an organism and by the role given to variation and scales, their novel diagrammatic approach to ontogenesis may open the way to new mathematical ideas, which may add relevant theoretical understanding to the transfer of tools from physics. We recall that the work at the right scale of observation has been the key step originating all theories in physics, from falling bodies and celestial mechanics to thermodynamics and quantum mechanics or hydrodynamics, originally all based on very different or incompatible principles (and many are still now). Then, new and suitable principles and mathematical tools where invented, both for the analysis at the intended scale or, later, for theoretical unifications, whenever possible, as there has been no "reduction" in physics, but remarkable unifications – even the (partial) understanding of some chemical laws in terms of quantum mechanics should be viewed in this way (Chibbaro et al. 2014). Thus, we shouldn't just use conventional tools from mathematical physics in the analysis of the living state of matter, but also develop intrinsic insights and possibly new mathematics, following the methodology of physics along history, including the choice of a suitable scale – with the cell as least component, in this perspective. Unification will then be possible, as a long term project, like within physics, but if one does not have two or more theories, there is nothing to unify. The analysis of the conceptual dualities summarized above (see also Table 1) and the peculiar yet comparable role of randomness in different contexts may be a way to this.

Acknowledgements. We thank Angelo Vulpiani for stimulating remarks on a preliminary draft and Peter Sollich for a careful reading of part of the manuscript.

References

Abbott, A.A., Calude, C.S., Conder, J., Svozil, K.: Strong Kochen-Specker theorem and incomputability of quantum randomness. Phys. Rev. A **86**, 062109 (2012)

Allin, E.F.: Evolution of the mammalian middle ear. J. Morphol. **147**(4), 403–437 (1975)

Arkin, A., Ross, J., McAdams, H.H.: Stochastic kinetic analysis of developmental pathway bifurcation in phage λ-infected escherichia coli cells. Genetics **149**, 1633–1648 (1998)

Aspect, A., Grangier, P., Roger, G.: Experimental tests of Bell's inequalities using time-varying analyzers. Phys. Rev. Lett. **49**, 1804–1807 (1982)

Bailly, F., Longo, G.: Biological organization and anti-entropy. J. Biol. Syst. **17**(1), 63–96 (2009)

Barkai, N., Leibler, S.: Robustness in simple biochemical networks. Nature **387**, 913–917 (1997)

Bhalla, U.S.: Understanding complex signaling networks through models and metaphors. Prog. Biophys. Mol. Biol. **81**, 45–65 (2003)

Bhogale, P.M., Sorg, R.A., Veening, J.W., Berg, J.: What makes the *lac*-pathway switch: identifying the fluctuations that trigger phenotype switching in gene regulatory systems. Nucleic Acid Res. **42**(18), 11321–11328 (2014)

Bizzarri, M., Cucina, A., Palombo, A., Masiello, M.G.: Gravity sensing cells: mechanisms and theoretical grounds. Rend. Fis. Acc. Lincei **25**, S29–S38 (2014)

Bravi, B., Sollich, P.: Gaussian Variational Approximation (2015, in preparation)

Buiatti, M., Buiatti, M.: Towards a statistical characterisation of the living state of matter. Chaos Soliton. Fract. **20**, 55–61 (2004)

Buiatti, M.: Plants: individuals or epigenetic cell populations? In: Jablonka, E., Gissis, S.B. (eds.) Transformations of Lamarckism. MIT Press, Cambridge (2011)

Buiatti, M., Buiatti, M.: Chance vs. necessity in living systems: a false antinomy. Biol. Forum **101**, 29–66 (2008)

Buiatti, M., Longo, G.: Randomness and multi-level interactions in biology. Theory Biosci. **132**(3), 139–158 (2013)

Calude, C.S., Longo, G.: Classical, quantum and biological randomness as relative incomputability. Nat. Comput. (Spec. Issue) (2015, in press)

Castiglione, P., Falcioni, M., Lesne, A., Vulpiani, A.: Chaos and Coarse Graining in Statistical Mechanics. Cambridge University Press, Cambridge (2008)

Chibbaro, S., Rondoni, L., Vulpiani, A.: Reductionism, Emergence and Levels of Reality. Springer, Berlin (2014)

Del Giudice, E., Preparata, G.: A new QED picture of water: understanding a few fascinating phenomena. In: Sassaroli, E., et al. (eds.) Macroscopic Quantum Coherence. World Scientific, London (1998)

Delbrück, M.: The burst size distribution in the growth of bacterial viruses. J. Bacteriol. **50**(2), 131–135 (1945)

Elf, J., Ehrenberg, M.: Fast evaluation of fluctuations in biochemical networks with the linear noise approximation. Genome Res. **13**(11), 2475–2484 (2003)

Eldar, A., Elowitz, M.B.: Functional roles for noise in genetic circuits. Nature **467**(7312), 167–173 (2010)

Eldredge, N., Gould, S.J.: Punctuated equilibria: an alternative to phyletic gradualism. In: Schopf, T.J.M. (ed.) Models in Paleo-Biology, vol. 72, pp. 82–115. Freeman, San Francisco (1972)

Elowitz, M.B., Levine, A.J., Siggia, E.D., Swain, P.S.: Stochastic gene expression in a single cell. Science **297**, 1183–1186 (2002)

Farge, E.: L'embryon sous l'emprise des gènes et de la pression. Pour la Sci. **379**, 42–49 (2009)

Feynman, R.: Space-time approach to non-relativistic quantum mechanics. Rev. Mod. Phys. **20**(2), 367–387 (1948)

Fleury, V., Gordon, R.: Coupling of growth differentiation and morphogenesis, and integrated approach to design in embryogenesis. In: Swan, L., Gordon, R., Seckbach, J. (eds.) Origin of Design in Nature, vol. 23, pp. 385–428. Springer, Heidelberg (2011)

Gács, P., Hoyrup, M., Rojas, C.: Randomness on computable probability spaces - a dynamical point of view. Theor. Comput. Syst. **48**, 465–485 (2011)

Gillespie, D.T.: A general method for numerically simulating the stochastic time evolution of coupled chemical reactions. J. Comput. Phys. **22**, 403–434 (1976)

Guerriero, M.L., Pokhilko, A., Fernández, A.P., Halliday, K.J., et al.: Stochastic properties of the plant circadian clock. J. R. Soc. Interface **9**, 69 (2012)

Huang, M.C., Wu, J., Luo, Y., Petrosyan, K.G.: Fluctuations in gene regulatory networks as gaussian colored noise. J. Chem. Phys. **132**, 155101 (2010)

Kleinert, H.: Path Integrals in Quantum Mechanics, Statistics, and Polymer Physics, and Financial Markets. World Scientific, Singapore (2009)

Kupiec, J.J.: A probabilistic theory for cell differentiation, embryonic mortality and DNA C-value paradox. Specul. Sci. Technol. **6**, 471–478 (1983)

Lesne, A.: Robustness: confronting lessons from physics and biology. Biol. Rev. Camb. Philos. Soc. **83**(4), 509–532 (2008)

Lindner, A.B., Madden, R., Demarez, A., Stewart, E.J., Taddei, F.: Asymmetric segregation of protein aggregates is associated with cellular aging and rejuvenation. PNAS **8**(105), 3076–3081 (2008)

Longo, G., Montévil, M.: Extended criticality, phase spaces and enablement in biology. Chaos Soliton. Fract. **55**, 64–79 (2013)

Longo, G., Montévil, M.: Perspectives on Organisms: Biological Time, Symmetries and Singularities. Springer, Berlin (2014)

Longo, G., Montévil, M.: Models vs. simulations: a comparison by their theoretical symmetries. In: Springer Handbook of Model-Based Science (2015, to appear)

Longo, G., Montévil, M., Kauffman, S.: No entailing laws, but enablement in the evolution of the biosphere. In: ACM Proceedings of GECCO (2012)

Longo, G., Montévil, M., Pocheville, A.: From bottom-up approaches to levels of organization and extended critical transitions. Front. Physiol. **3**, 232 (2012)

Longo, G., Montévil, M., Sonnenschein, C., Soto, A.M. In Search of Principles for a Theory of Organisms (2015, submitted)

Maheshri, N., O'Shea, E.K.: Living with noisy genes: how cells function reliably with inherent variability in gene expression. Annu. Rev. Biophys. Biomol. Struct. **36**, 413–434 (2007)

Meyer, H.M., Roeder, A.H.K.: Stochasticity in plant cellular growth and patterning. Front. Plant Sci. **5**, 420 (2014)

Miquel, P.A.: Aging as alteration. In: Robert, L., Fulop, T. (eds.) Aging: Facts and Theories. Krager, Basel, vol. 39, pp. 187–197 (2014)

Mirabet, V., Besnard, F., Vernoux, T., Boudaoud, A.: Noise and robustness in phyllotaxis. Plos Comput. Bio. **8**, 2 (2012)

Monod, J.: Le Hasard et la Nécessité. PUF, Paris (1970)

Montévil, M., Mossio, M.: Biological organisation as closure of constraints. J. Theor. Biol. **372**, 179–191 (2015)

Mora, T., Bialek, W.: Are biological systems poised at criticality? J. Stat. Phys. **144**, 268–302 (2011)

Munsky, B., Hernday, A., Low, D., Kammash, M.: Stochastic modeling of the Pap Pili epigenetic switch. In: Proceedings of FOSBE Conference, pp. 145–148 (2014)

Nowacki, M., Landweber, L.F.: Epigenetic inheritance in ciliates. Curr. Opin. Microbiol. **12**(6), 638–643 (2009)

Olshansky, S.J., Rattan, S.I.S.: At the heart of aging: is it metabolic rate or stability? Biogerontology **6**, 291–295 (2005)

Paulsson, J., Berg, O.G., Ehrenberg, M.: Stochastic focusing: fluctuation-enhanced sensitivity of intracellular regulation. PNAS **97**(13), 7148–7153 (2000)

Pocock, G.: Human Physiology, 3rd edn. Oxford University Press, Oxford (2006)

Prigogine, I., Stengers, I.: Order out of Chaos: Man's new Dialogue with Nature. Bantam Books, New York (1984)

Raj, A., Van Oudenaarden, A.: Nature, nurture, or chance: stochastic gene expression and its consequences. Cell **135**, 216–226 (2008)

Rao, C.V., Wolf, D.M., Arkin, A.P.: Control, exploitation and tolerance of intracellular noise. Nature **420**, 231–237 (2002)

Risken, H.: The Fokker Planck Equation: Methods of Solution and Applications. Springer, Heidelberg (1989)

Robert, L., Paul, G., Chen, Y., Taddei, F., Baigl, D., Lindner, A.B.: Pre-dispositions and epigenetic inheritance in the Escherichia coli lactose operon bistable switch. Mol. Syst. Biol. **6**, 357 (2010)

Romano, A.D., Serviddio, G., De Matthaeis, A., Bellanti, F., Vendemiale, G.: Oxidative stress and aging. J. Nephrol. **23**(15), S29–S36 (2010)

Salman, H., Brenner, N., Tung, C., Elyahu, N., Stolovicki, E., Moore, L., Libchaber, A., Braun, E.: Universal protein fluctuations in populations of microorganisms. PRL **108**(23), 238105 (2012)

Schrödinger, E.: What is Life. Cambridge University Press, Cambridge (1944)

Sethna, J.P.: Statistical Mechanics: Entropy, Order Parameters, and Complexity. Oxford University Press, New York (2006)

Shahrezaei, V., Olivier, J.F., Swain, P.S.: Colored extrinsic fluctuations and stochastic gene expression. Mol. Syst. Biol. **4**, 196 (2008)

Simpson, M.L., Cox, C.D., Allen, M.S., McCollum, J.M., Dar, R.D., Karig, D.K., Cooke, J.F.: Noise in biological circuits. WIREs Nanomed. Nanotechnol. **1**, 214–225 (2009)

Snijder, B., Pelkmans, L.: Origins of regulated cell-to-cell variability. Nature **12**, 119–125 (2011)

Sonnenschein, C., Soto, A.M.: The Society of Cells: Cancer and Control of Cell Proliferation. Springer, New York (1999)

Soto, A.M., Sonnenschein, C.: Environmental causes of cancer: endocrine disruptors as carcinogens. Nat. Rev. Endocrinol. **6**(7), 363–370 (2010)

Stewart, E.J., Madden, R., Paul, G., Taddei, F.: Aging and death in an organism that reproduces by morphologically symmetric division. PLoS Biol. **3**(2), e45 (2005)

Stolovicki, E., Braun, E.: Collective dynamics of gene expression in cell populations. PLoS One **6**(6), e20530 (2011)

Swain, P.S., Elowitz, M.B., Siggia, E.D.: Intrinsic and extrinsic contributions to stochasticity in gene expression. PNAS **99**(20), 12795–12800 (2002)

Thomas-Vaslin, V., Altes, H.K., De Boer, R.J., Klatzmann, D.: Comprehensive assessment and mathematical modeling of T cell population dynamics and homeostasis. J. Immunol. **180**(4), 2240–2250 (2008)

Toulouse, G., Pfeuty, P., Barton, G.: Introduction to the Renormalization Group and to Critical Phenomena. Wiley, New York (1977)

Turing, A.M.: The chemical basis of morphogenesis. Phil. Trans. R. Soc. Lond. B **237**, 37–72 (1952)

Uyttewaal, M., Burian, A., Alim, K., Landrein, B., et al.: Mechanical stress acts via katanin to amplify differences in growth rate between adjacent cells in Arabidopsis. Cell **149**, 439–451 (2012)

Van Kampen, N.G.: Stochastic Processes in Physics and Chemistry, 3rd edn. Elsevier, Amsterdam (2007)

Vilar, J.M.G., Kueh, H.Y., Barkai, N., Leibler, S.: Mechanisms of noise-resistance in genetic oscillators. PNAS **99**(9), 5988–5992 (2002)

Werner, G.: Metastability, criticality and phase transitions in brain and its models. Biosystems **90**(2), 496–508 (2007)

Wiener, N., Masani, P.: Collected Works: with Commentaries. MIT Press, Cambridge (1976)

Wilkinson, D.J.: Stochastic modelling for quantitative description of heterogeneous biological systems. Nature **10**, 122–133 (2009)

Wray, J., Kalkan, T., Smith, A.G.: The ground state of pluripotency. Biochem. Soc. Trans. **38**, 1027–1032 (2010)

Zwanzig, R.: Memory effects in irreversible thermodynamics. Phys. Rev. **124**, 4 (1961)

Ultrametric Algorithms and Automata

Rūsiņš Freivalds$^{(\boxtimes)}$

Institute of Mathematics and Computer Science,
University of Latvia, Raiņa bulvāris 29, Riga 1459, Latvia
Rusins.Freivalds@lu.lv

Abstract. We introduce a notion of ultrametric automata and Turing machines using p-adic numbers to describe random branching of the process of computation. These automata have properties similar to the properties of probabilistic automata but complexity of probabilistic automata and complexity of ultrametric automata can differ very much.

1 Introduction

Irrational numbers can be represented by decimal digits

$$2.718281828\ldots$$

In this representation infinitely many digits are allowed on the right-hand side but only a finite number of them on the left-hand side. Informally, non-terminating decimals are easily understood, because it is clear that a real number can be approximated to any required degree of precision by a terminating decimal. If two decimal expansions differ only after the 10th decimal place, they are quite close to one another; and if they differ only after the 20th decimal place, they are even closer.

10-adic numbers use a similar non-terminating expansion, but with a different concept of "closeness". Whereas two decimal expansions are close to one another if their difference is a large negative power of 10, two 10-adic expansions are close if their difference is a large positive power of 10.

Thus 3333 and 4333, which differ by 10^3, are close in the 10-adic world, and 33333333 and 43333333 are even closer, differing by 10^7.

More precisely, a rational number r can be expressed as $10^a \cdot \frac{p}{q}$, where p and q are positive integers and q is relatively prime to p and to 10. For each $r \neq 0$ there exists the maximal a such that this representation is possible. Let the 10-adic norm of r to be

$$\mid r \mid_{10} = \frac{1}{10^a},$$

$$\mid 0 \mid_{10} = 0.$$

The research was supported by Grant No. 271/2012 from the Latvian Council of Science and by the project ERAF Nr.2DP/2.1.1.1/13/APIA/VIAA/027. Partially supported by Latvian State Research programme NexIT project No.1 "Technologies of ontologies, semantic web and security".

C.S. Calude and M.J. Dinneen (Eds.): UCNC 2015, LNCS 9252, pp. 35–52, 2015.
DOI: 10.1007/978-3-319-21819-9_2

Closeness in any number system is defined by a metric. Using the 10-adic metric the distance between numbers x and y is given by $\mid x - y \mid_{10}$.

The "closeness" in the 10-adic metric may seem strange. This reminds me an occasion in the seminar "Algebra and Logics" lead by Professor Anatoly Maltsev in Novosibirsk University nearly 50 years ago. A young student was presenting a paper on modifications of the Tarski-Kuratowski algorithm. I do not remember whether the paper was by the student himself or whether he presented some foreign paper. At some moment the presenter proudly announced that the best earlier known version of the algorithm had time complexity $\exp\exp\ldots\exp n$ (9 times exponent) but the version in the paper was much better, namely, $\exp\exp\ldots\exp n$ (7 times exponent). Professor Maltsev immediately commented that he did not see much difference there. Boris Trakhtenbrot came to the presenter's help and noticed that the improvement is not just exponential but exponent-of-exponential. After short but emotional discussion the participants agreed that the improvement is essential but the difference is negligible.

On that day I learned that humans do not distinguish between huge and very huge numbers. Similarly, they not distinguish between small and very small numbers. The Archimedean metric is good in mathematics but not in the everyday life.

An interesting consequence of the 10-adic metric (or of a p-adic metric) is that there is no longer a need for the negative sign. As an example, by examining the following sequence we can see how unsigned 10-adics can get progressively closer and closer to the number 1:

$$
\begin{array}{ll}
9 = -1 + 10 & \mid 9 - 1 \mid_{10} = \frac{1}{10} \\
99 = -1 + 100 & \mid 99 - 1 \mid_{10} = \frac{1}{100} \\
999 = -1 + 1000 & \mid 999 - 1 \mid_{10} = \frac{1}{1000} \\
9999 = -1 + 10000 & \mid 9999 - 1 \mid_{10} = \frac{1}{10000} \\
99999 = -1 + 100000 & \mid 99999 - 1 \mid_{10} = \frac{1}{100000}
\end{array}
$$

$$\ldots 99999999999999999999999999999999999999 = -1$$

10-adic numbers have a major drawback. It is possible to find pairs of non-zero 10-adic numbers (having an infinite number of digits, and thus not rational) whose product is 0.

The reason for this property turns out to be that 10 is a composite number which is not a power of a prime. This problem is simply avoided by using a prime number p as the base of the number system instead of 10 and indeed for this reason p in p-adic is usually taken to be prime.

Let p be an arbitrary prime number. We will call *p-adic digit* a natural number between 0 and $p - 1$ (inclusive). A *p-adic integer* is by definition a sequence $(a_i)_{i \in N}$ of p-adic digits. We write this conventionally as

$$\cdots a_i \cdots a_2 a_1 a_0$$

(that is, the a_i are written from left to right).

If n is a natural number, and

$$n = \overline{a_{k-1}a_{k-2}\cdots a_1 a_0}$$

is its p-adic representation (in other words $n = \sum_{i=0}^{k-1} a_i p^i$ with each a_i a p-adic digit) then we identify n with the p-adic integer (a_i) with $a_i = 0$ if $i \geq k$. This means that natural numbers are exactly the same thing as p-adic integer only a finite number of whose digits are not 0. The number 0 is the p-adic integer all of whose digits are 0, and that 1 is the p-adic integer all of whose digits are 0 except the right-most one (digit 0) which is 1.

If $\alpha = (a_i)$ and $\beta = (b_i)$ are two p-adic integers, we will now define their sum. To that effect, we define by induction a sequence (c_i) of p-adic digits and a sequence (ϵ_i) of elements of $\{0,1\}$ (the "carries") as follows:

- ϵ_0 is 0.
- c_i is $a_i + b_i + \epsilon_i$ or $a_i + b_i + \epsilon_i - p$ according as which of these two is a p-adic digit (in other words, is between 0 and p - 1). In the former case,$\epsilon_i + 1 = 0$ and in the latter, $\epsilon_i + 1 = 1$.

Under those circumstances, we let $\alpha + \beta = (c_i)$ and we call $\alpha + \beta$ the sum of α and β. Note that the rules described above are exactly the rules used for adding natural numbers in p-adic representation. In particular, if α and β turn out to be natural numbers, then their sum as a p-adic integer is no different from their sum as a natural number. So $2 + 2 = 4$ remains valid (whatever p is but if $p = 2$ it would be written $\cdots 010 + \cdots 010 = \cdots 100$). Here is an example of a 7-adic addition:

$$
\begin{array}{r}
\cdots 2\,5\,1\,4\,1\,3 \\
\cdots 1\,2\,1\,1\,0\,2 \\
\hline
\cdots 4\,0\,2\,5\,1\,5
\end{array}
$$

This addition of p-adic integers is associative, commutative, and verifies $\alpha + 0 = \alpha$ for all α (recall that 0 is the p-adic integer all of whose digits are 0). Subtraction of p-adic integers is also performed in exactly the same way as that of natural numbers in p-adic form. Note that this subtraction scheme gives us the negative integers readily: for example, subtract 1 from 0 (in the 7-adics) :

$$
\begin{array}{r}
\cdots 0\,0\,0\,0\,0\,0 \\
\cdots 0\,0\,0\,0\,0\,1 \\
\hline
\cdots 6\,6\,6\,6\,6\,6
\end{array}
$$

(each column borrows a 1 from the next one on the left). So $-1 = \cdots 666$ as 7-adics. More generally, -1 is the p-adic all of whose digits are $p - 1$, -2 has all of its digits equal to $p - 1$ except the right-most which is $p - 2$, and so on. In fact, (strictly) negative integers correspond exactly to those p-adics all of whose digits except a finite number are equal to $p - 1$.

It can then be verified that p-adic integers, under addition, form an abelian group.

We now proceed to describe multiplication. First note that if n is a natural number and α is a p-adic integer, then we have a naturally defined $n \cdot \alpha = \alpha + \alpha + \ldots + \alpha$ (n times, with $0 \cdot \alpha = 0$, of course). This limited multiplication satisfies some obvious equalities, such as $(m + n)\alpha = m\alpha + n\alpha, n(\alpha + \beta) = n\alpha + n\beta, m(n\alpha) = (mn)\alpha$, and so on. Note also that multiplying by $p = \cdots 0010$ is the same as adding a 0 on the right. Multiplying two p-adic integers on the other hand requires some more work. To do that, we note that if $\alpha_0, \alpha_1, \alpha_2, \cdots$ are p-adic integers, with α_1 ending in (at least) one zero, α_2 ending in (at least) two zeros, and so on, then we can define the sum of all the α_i, even though they are not finite in number. Indeed, the last digit of the sum is just the last digit of α_0 (since $\alpha_1, \alpha_2, \cdots$ all end in zero), the second-last is the second-last digit of $\alpha_0 + \alpha_1$ (because $\alpha_2, \alpha_3, \cdots$ all end in 00), and so on: every digit of the (infinite) sum can be calculated with just a finite sum. Now we suppose that we want to multiply α and $\beta = (b_i)$ two p-adic integers. We then let $\alpha_0 = b_0\alpha$ (we know how to define this since b_0 is just a natural number), $\alpha_1 = pb_1\alpha$, and so on: $\alpha_i = p^ib_i\alpha$. Since α_i is a p-adic integer multiplied by p_i, it ends in i zeros, and therefore the sum of all the α_i can be defined. This procedure may sound complicated, but, it is the usual algorithm to multiply two natural numbers. Here is an example of a 7-adic multiplication:

$$
\begin{array}{r}
\cdots 2\,5\,1\,4\,1\,3 \\
\cdots 1\,2\,1\,1\,0\,2 \\
\hline
\cdots 5\,3\,3\,1\,2\,6 \\
\cdots 0\,0\,0\,0\,0 \\
\cdots 1\,4\,1\,3 \\
\cdots 4\,1\,3 \\
\cdots 2\,6 \\
\cdots 3 \\
\hline
\cdots 3\,1\,0\,4\,2\,6
\end{array}
$$

To have p-adic representations of all rational numbers, $\frac{1}{p}$ is represented as $\cdots 00.1$, the number $\frac{1}{p^2}$ as $\cdots 00.01$, and so on. For any p-adic number it is allowed to have infinitely many (!) digits to the left of the "decimal" point but only a finite number of digits to the right of it.

However, p-adic numbers is not merely one of generalizations of rational numbers. They are related to the notion of *absolute value* of numbers.

If X is a nonempty set, a distance, or metric, on X is a function d from pairs of elements (x, y) of X to the nonnegative real numbers such that

1. $d(x, y) = 0$ if and only if $x = y$,
2. $d(x, y) = d(y, x)$,
3. $d(x, y) \leq d(x, z) + d(z, y)$ for all $z \in X$.

A set X together with a metric d is called a *metric space*. The same set X can give rise to many different metric spaces.

The *norm* of an element $x \in X$ is the distance from 0:

1. $\| x \| = 0$ if and only if $x = y$,
2. $\| x.y \| = \| x \| . \| xy \|$,
3. $\| x + y \| \leq \| x \| + \| y \|$.

We know one metric on Q induced by the ordinary absolute value. However, there are other norms as well.

A norm is called *ultrametric* if the third requirement can be replaced by the stronger statement: $\| x + y \| \leq \max\{\| x \|, \| y \|\}$. Otherwise, the norm is called *Archimedean*.

Definition 1. *Let $p \in \{2, 3, 5, 7, 11, 13, \cdots\}$ be any prime number. For any nonzero integer a, let the p-adic ordinal (or valuation) of a, denoted $\mathrm{ord}_p a$, be the highest power of p which divides a, i.e., the greatest m such that $a \equiv 0 (\mathrm{mod} p^m)$. For any rational number $x = a/b$, denote $\mathrm{ord}_p x$ to be $\mathrm{ord}_p a - \mathrm{ord}_p b$. Additionally, $\mathrm{ord}_p x = \infty$ if and only if $x = 0$.*

Definition 2. *Let $p \in \{2, 3, 5, 7, 11, 13, \cdots\}$ be any prime number. For arbitrary rational number x, its p-norm is:*

$$||x||_p = \begin{cases} \frac{1}{p^{\mathrm{ord}_p x}}, \text{if} & x \neq 0, \\ \neg p_i, \text{if} & x = 0 ; \end{cases}$$

Rational numbers are p-adic integers for all prime numbers p. The nature of irrational numbers is more complicated. For instance, $\sqrt{2}$ just does not exist as a p-adic number for some prime numbers p. More precisely, $\sqrt{a}$ can be represented as a p-adic number if and only if a is a quadratic residue modulo p, i.e. if the congruence $x^2 = a(\mathrm{mod} p)$ has a solution. On the other hand, there is a continuum of p-adic numbers not being real numbers. Moreover, there is a continuum of 3-adic numbers not being 5-adic numbers, and vice versa.

p-adic numbers are described in much more detail in [7,11,14].

ascal and Fermat believed that every event of indeterminism can be described by a real number between 0 and 1 called *probability*. Quantum physics introduced a description in terms of complex numbers called *amplitude of probabilities* and later in terms of probabilistic combinations of amplitudes most conveniently described by *density matrices*.

String theory [18], chemistry [12] and molecular biology [2,10] have introduced p-adic numbers to describe measures of indeterminism.

Popularity of usage of p-adic numbers can be explained easily. There is a well-known difficulty to overcome the distinction between *continuous* and *discrete* processes. For instance, according to Rutherford's model of atoms, the electrons can be situated only on specific orbits. When energy of an electron increases, there is a quantum leap. Niels Bohr proposed, in 1913, what is now called the Bohr model of the atom. He suggested that electrons could only have certain classical motions:

1. Electrons in atoms orbit the nucleus.
2. The electrons can only orbit stably, without radiating, in certain orbits (called by Bohr the "stationary orbits"): at a certain discrete set of distances from the nucleus. These orbits are associated with definite energy levels. In these orbits, the electron's acceleration does not result in radiation and energy loss as required by classical electromagnetics.
3. Electrons can only gain and lose energy by jumping from one allowed orbit to another, absorbing or emitting electromagnetic radiation with a frequency determined by the energy difference of the levels according to the Planck relation.

One of the methods to model such quantum leaps is to consider p-adic numbers and there norms. The p-adic numbers can have continuum distinct values but their norms can have only denumerable values. If a variable gradually changes taking p-adic values, its norm performs quantum leaps. Hence usage of p-adic numbers as measures of indeterminism provides a mechanism which is similar to probabilistic model but mathematically different from it.

There were no difficulties to implement probabilistic automata and algorithms practically. Quantum computation [9] has made a considerable theoretical progress but practical implementation has met considerable difficulties. However, prototypes of quantum computers exist, some quantum algorithms are implemented on these prototypes, quantum cryptography is already practically used. Some people are skeptical concerning practicality of the initial spectacular promises of quantum computation but nobody can deny the existence of quantum computation.

We consider a new type of indeterministic algorithms called *ultrametric* algorithms. They are very similar to probabilistic algorithms but while probabilistic algorithms use real numbers r with $0 \leq r \leq 1$ as parameters, ultrametric algorithms use *p-adic* numbers as the parameters. Slightly simplifying the description of the definitions one can say that ultrametric algorithms are the same probabilistic algorithms, only the interpretation of the probabilities is different.

Our choice of p-adic numbers instead of real numbers is not quite arbitrary. In 1916 Alexander Ostrowski [16] proved that any non-trivial absolute value on the rational numbers Q is equivalent to either the usual real absolute value or a p-adic absolute value. This result shows that using p-adic numbers is not merely one of many possibilities to generalize the definition of deterministic algorithms but rather the only remaining possibility not yet explored.

Moreover, Helmut Hasse's local-global principle states that certain types of equations have a rational solution if and only if they have a solution in the real numbers and in the p-adic numbers for each prime p.

There are many distinct p-adic absolute values corresponding to the many prime numbers p. These absolute values are traditionally called *ultrametric*. Absolute values are needed to consider *distances* among objects. We have used to rational and irrational numbers as measures for distances, and there is a psychological difficulty to imagine that something else can be used instead of irrational numbers. However, there is an important feature that distinguishes p-adic numbers from real numbers. Real numbers (both rational and irrational) are linearly ordered. p-adic numbers cannot be linearly ordered. This is why *valuations* and *norms* of p-adic numbers are considered.

The situation is similar in Quantum Computation. Quantum amplitudes are complex numbers which also cannot be linearly ordered. The counterpart of valuation for quantum algorithms is *measurement* translating a complex number $a + bi$ into a real number $a^2 + b^2$. Norms of p-adic numbers are rational numbers.

Ultrametric finite automata and ultrametric Turing machines are reasonably similar to probabilistic finite automata and Turing machines.

2   First Examples

The notion of p-adic numbers widely used in mathematics but not so much in Computer Science. It seems that the first author having proposed to use p-adic numbers to analyze finite automata has been A.G.Lunts [13]. The first papers containing definition of ultrametric finite automata in the sense used in this survey were [5,6].

The aim of our next sections is to show that the notion of ultrametric automata and ultrametric Turing machines is natural.

In mathematics, a stochastic matrix is a matrix used to describe the transitions of a Markov chain. A *right stochastic matrix* is a square matrix each of whose rows consists of nonnegative real numbers, with each row summing to 1. A *stochastic vector* is a vector whose elements consist of nonnegative real numbers which sum to 1. The *finite probabilistic automaton* is defined [3,4] as an extension of a non-deterministic finite automaton $(Q, \Sigma, \delta, q_0, F)$, with the initial state q_0 replaced by a stochastic vector giving the probability of the automaton being in a given initial state, and with stochastic matrices corresponding to each symbol in the input alphabet describing the state transition probabilities. It is important to note that if A is the stochastic matrix corresponding to the input symbol a and B is the stochastic matrix corresponding to the input symbol b, then the product AB describes the state transition probabilities when the automaton reads the input word ab. Additionally, the probabilistic automaton has a threshold λ being a real number between 0 and 1. If the probabilistic automaton has only one *accepting state* then the input word x is said to be accepted if after reading x the probability of the accepting state has a probability exceeding λ. If there are several accepting states, the word x is said to be accepted the total of probabilities of the accepting states exceeds λ.

Ultrametric automata are defined exactly in the same way as probabilistic automata, only the parameters called *probabilities of transition from one state to another one* are real numbers between 0 and 1 in probabilistic automata, and they are p-adic numbers called *amplitudes* in the ultrametric automata. Formulas to calculate the amplitudes after one, two, three, $\cdots$ steps of computation are exactly the same as the formulas to calculate the probabilities in the probabilistic automata. Following the example of finite quantum automata, we demand that the input word x is followed by a special end-marker. At the beginning of the work, the states of the automaton get *initial amplitudes* being p-adic numbers. When reading the current symbol of the input word, the automaton changes the amplitudes of all the states according to the transition matrix corresponding to this input symbol. When the automaton reads the end-marker, the *measurement* is performed, and the amplitudes of all the states are transformed into the p-norms of these amplitudes. The norms are rational numbers and it is possible to compare whether or not the norm exceeds the threshold λ. If total of the norms for all the accepting states of the automaton exceeds λ, we say that the automaton accepts the input word.

Ultrametric algorithms are described by finite directed acyclic graphs (DAG), where exactly one node is marked as root. As usual, the root does not have any incoming edge. Furthermore, every node having outdegree zero is said to be a *leaf*. The leaves are the output nodes of the DAG.

Let v be a node in such a graph. Then each outgoing edge is labeled by a p-adic number which we call *amplitude*. We require that the sum of all amplitudes that correspond to v is 1. In order to determine the *total amplitude* along a computation path, we need the following definition.

Definition 3. *The total amplitude of the root is defined to be 1. Furthermore, let v be a node at depth d in the DAG, let α be its total amplitude, and let $\beta_1, \beta_2, \cdots, \beta_k$ be the amplitudes corresponding to the outgoing edges $e_1, \ldots, e_k$ of v. Let $v_1, \ldots, v_k$ be the nodes where the edges $e_1, \ldots, e_k$ point to. Then the total amplitude of v_ℓ, $\ell \in \{1, \ldots, k\}$, is defined as follows.*

(1) *If the indegree of v_ℓ is one, then its total amplitude is $\alpha\beta_\ell$.*
(2) *If the indegree of v_ℓ is bigger than one, i.e., if two or more computation paths are joined, say m paths, then let $\alpha, \gamma_2, \ldots, \gamma_m$ be the corresponding total amplitudes of the predecessors of v_ℓ and let $\beta_\ell, \delta_2, \ldots, \delta_m$ be the amplitudes of the incoming edges The total amplitude of the node v_ℓ is then defined to be $\alpha\beta_\ell + \gamma_2\delta_2 + \cdots + \delta_m\gamma_m$.*

Note that the total amplitude is a p-adic integer.

It remains to define what is meant by saying that a p-ultrametric algorithm produces a result with a certain probability. This is specified by performing a so-called *measurement* at the leaves of the corresponding DAG. Here by measurement we mean that we transform the total amplitude β of each leaf to β_p. We refer to β_p as the *p-probability* of the corresponding computation path.

Definition 4. *We say that a p-ultrametric algorithm produces a result m with a probability q if the sum of the p-probabilities of all leaves which correctly produce the result m is no less than q.*

Comment. Just as in Quantum Computation, there is something counterintuitive in ultrametric algorithms. The notion of probability which is the result of measurement not always correspond to our expectations. It was not easy to accept that L. Grover's query algorithm [8] does not read all the input on any computation path. There is a similar situation in ultrametric algorithms. It is more easy to accept the definition of ultrametric algorithms in the case when there is only one accepting state in the algorithm. The 2-ultrametric algorithm in Theorem 10 has only one accepting state.

Paavo Turakainen considered various generalizations of finite probabilistic automata in 1969 and proved that there is no need to demand in cases of probabilistic branchings that total of probabilities for all possible continuations equal 1. He defined generalized probabilistic finite automata where the "probabilities" can be arbitrary real numbers, and that languages recognizable by these generalized probabilistic finite automata are the same as for ordinary probabilistic finite automata. Hence we also allow usage of all possible p-adic numbers in p-ultrametric machines. Remembering the theorem by P.Turakainen [17] we start with the most general possible definition hoping to restrict it if we below find examples of not so natural behavior of ultrametric automata. (Moreover, we do not specify all the details of the definitions in Theorems 1–4, and make the definition precise only afterwards. The reader may consider such a presentation strange but we need some natural examples of ultrametric automata before we concentrate on one standard definition.)

However, it is needed to note that if there is only one accepting state then the possible probabilities of acceptance are discrete values $0, p^1, p^{-1}, p^2, p^{-2}, p^3, \cdots$. Hence there is no natural counterpart of *isolated cut-point* or *bounded error* for ultrametric machines. On the other hand, a counterpart of Turakainen's theorem for probabilistic automata with isolated cut-point still does not exist. We also did not succeed to prove such a theorem for ultrametric automata. Most probably, there are certain objective difficulties.

Theorem 1. *There is a continuum of languages recognizable by finite ultrametric automata.*

Proof. Let $\beta = \cdots 2a_3 2a_2 2a_1 2a_0 2$ be an arbitrary p-adic number (not p-adic integer) where $p \geq 3$ and all $a_i \in \{0, 1\}$. Denote by B the set of all possible such β. Consider an automaton A_β with 3 states, the initial amplitudes of the states being $(\beta, -1, -1)$. The automaton is constructed to have the following property. If the input word is $2a_0 2a_1 2a_2 2a_3 2 \cdots 2a_n 2$ then the amplitude of the first state becomes $\cdots 2a_{n+4} 2a_{n+3} 2a_{n+2} 2a_{n+1} 2$. To achieve this, the automaton adds -2, multiplies to p, adds $-a_n$ and again multiplies to p.

Now let β_1 and β_2 be two different p-adic numbers. Assume that they have the same first symbols $a_m \cdots 2a_3 2a_2 2a_1 2a_0 2$ but different symbols a_{m+1} and b_{m+1}. Then the automaton accepts one of the words $a_{m+1} 2a_m \cdots 2a_3 2a_2 2a_1 2a_0 2$ and rejects the other one $b_{m+1} 2a_m \cdots 2a_3 2a_2 2a_1 2a_0 2$. Hence the languages are distinct.   □

Definition 5. *Finite p-ultrametric automaton is called* **integral** *if all the parameters of it are p-adic integers.*

Automata recognizing nonrecursive languages cannot be considered natural. Hence we are to restrict our definition.

Theorem 2. *There exists a finite integral p-ultrametric automaton recognizing the language $\{0^n 1^n\}$.*

Proof. When the automaton reads 0 it multiplies the amplitude to 2, and when it reads 1 it multiplies it to $\frac{1}{2}$. The norm of the amplitude equals p^0 iff the number of zeros is equal to the number of ones.   □

We consider the following language.

$$L = \{w|w \in \{0,1\}^* \text{ and } w = w^{rev}\}$$

Theorem 3. *For every prime number $p \geq 5$, there is an integral p-ultrametric automaton recognizing L.*

Proof. The automaton has two special states. If the input word is

$$a(1)a(2)\cdots a(n)a(n+1)a(n+2)\cdots a(2n+1)$$

then one of these states has amplitude

$$a(1)p^n+\cdots+a(n)p^{+1}+a(n+1)p^0+a(n+2)p^{-1}+\cdots+a(2n)p^{-n+1}+a(2n+1)p^{-n}$$

and the other one has amplitude

$$-a(1)p^{-n}-\cdots-a(n)p^{-1}-a(n+1)p^0-a(n+2)p^{+1}-\cdots-a(2n)p^{+n-1}+a(2n+1)p^{+n}$$

If the sum of these two amplitudes equals 0 then the input word is a palindrome. Otherwise, the sum of amplitudes has a norm removed from p^0.   □

Definition 6. *A square matrix with elements being p-adic numbers is called **balanced** if for arbitrary row of the matrix the product of p-norms of the elements equals 1.*

Definition 7. *A finite ultrametric automaton is called **balanced** if all the matrices in its definition are balanced.*

Theorem 4. *If a language M can be recognized by a finite ultrametric automaton then M can be recognized also by a balanced finite ultrametric automaton.*

Proof. For every state of the automaton we add its duplicate. If the given state has an amplitude γ then its duplicate has the amplitude $\frac{1}{\gamma}$. Product of balanced matrices is balanced.   □

Definition 8. *A balanced finite ultrametric automaton is called **regulated** if there exist constants λ and c such that $0 < c < 1$ and for arbitrary input word x and for arbitrary state of the automaton the norm $c\lambda <\| \gamma \|_p< \frac{\lambda}{c}$. We say that the word x is accepted if $\| \gamma \|_p> \lambda$ and it is rejected if $\| \gamma \|_p\leq \lambda$.*

Theorem 5. *[6] (1) If a language M is recognized by a regulated finite ultrametric automaton then M is regular.*
(2) For arbitrary prime number p there is a constant c_p such that if a language M is recognized by a regulated finite p-ultrametric automaton with k states then there is a deterministic finite automaton with $(c_p)^{k.logk}$ states recognizing the language M.

3   Non-regulated Finite Automata

Since the numbers 1 and 0 are also p-adic numbers, every deterministic finite automaton can be described in terms of matrices for transformation of amplitudes. Hence every regular language is recognizable by a regulated p-ultrametric automaton. There is a natural problem : are there languages for which regulated p-ultrametric automata can have smaller complexity, i.e. smaller number of states.

The following 3 theorems seem to present such an example but there is a catch: these automata are not regulated because the norm of the amplitude to be measured can be arbitrary small (for lengthy input words).

Theorem 6. *For arbitrary prime number $p \geq 3$ the language*

$$L_{p-1} = \{1^n \mid n \equiv p - 1(\ mod \ p)\}$$

is recognizable by a p-ultrametric finite automaton with 2 states.

Proof. A primitive root modulo n is any number g with the property that any number coprime to n is congruent to a power of g modulo n. In other words, g is a generator of the multiplicative group of integers modulo n. Existence of primitive roots modulo prime numbers was proved by Gauss. The initial amplitude 1 of a special state in our automaton is multiplied to an arbitrary primitive root modulo p. When the end-marker is read the amplitude -1 of the other state is added to this amplitude. The result has p-norm p^0 iff $n \equiv p - 1$.   □

Theorem 7. *For arbitrary prime number $p \geq 3$ the language*

$$L_p = \{1^n \mid n \equiv p(\ mod \ p)\}$$

is recognizable by a p-ultrametric finite automaton with 2 states.

Proof. The value 1 of the amplitude of the second state is added to the amplitude of the accepting state at every step of reading the input word. The result has p-norm p^0 iff $n \equiv p$.   □

Theorem 8. *For arbitrary natural number m there are infinitely many prime numbers p such that the language*

$$L_m = \{1^n \mid n \equiv 0(\ mod \ m)\}$$

is recognizable by a p-ultrametric finite automaton with 2 states.

Proof. Dirichlet prime number theorem, states that for any two positive coprime integers m and d, there are infinitely many primes of the form $m + nd$, where $n \geq 0$. In other words, there are infinitely many primes which are congruent to m modulo d. The numbers of the form $mn + d$ form an arithmetic progression

$$d, \ m + d, \ 2m + d, \ 3m + d, \ \ldots,$$

and Dirichlet's theorem states that this sequence contains infinitely many prime numbers.

Let p be such a prime and g be a primitive root modulo p. Then the sequence of remainders $g, g^2, g^3, \cdots$ modulo p has period m and $n \equiv 0(\bmod\ m)$ is equivalent to $g^n \equiv d(\bmod\ p)$. Hence the automaton multiplies the amplitude of the special state to g and and adds $-d$ when reading the end-marker. $\square$

4   Regulated Finite Automata

We wish to complement Theorem 5 by a proof showing that the gap between the complexity of regulated finite ultrametric automata and the complexity of deterministic finite automata is not overestimated. It turns out that this comparison is related to well-known open problems.

First, we consider a sequence of languages where the advantages of ultrametric automata over deterministic ones are super-exponential but the advantages are achieved only for specific values of the prime number p.

It is known that every p-permutation can be generated as a product of sequence of two individual p-permutations:

$$a = \begin{pmatrix} 1\ 2\ 3\ \cdots\ p-1\ p \\ 2\ 3\ 4\ \cdots\quad p\quad 1 \end{pmatrix}$$

$$b = \begin{pmatrix} 1\ 2\ 3\ \cdots\ p-1\ p \\ 2\ 1\ 3\ \cdots\ p-1\ p \end{pmatrix}$$

A string $x \in \{a, b\}^*$ is in the language M_p if the product of these p-permutations equals the trivial permutation.

Theorem 9. *(1) For arbitrary prime p, the language M_p is recognized by a p-ultrametric finite automaton with $p + 2$ states.*
(2) If a deterministic finite automaton has less than $p! = c^{p \cdot \log p}$ states then it does not recognize M_p.

Idea of the proof. The ultrametric automaton gives initial amplitudes $0, 1, 2, \cdots, p-1$ to p states of the automaton and after reading any input letter only permutes these amplitudes. After reading the endmarker from the input the automaton subtracts the values $0, 1, 2, \cdots, p-1$ from these amplitudes. $\square$

5   Ambainis' Function

A. Ambainis exhibited a function f that provides the first superlinear separation between polynomial degree and quantum query complexity [1].

Ambainis' function f of 4 Boolean variables is defined as follows:

$$f(x_1, x_2, x_3, x_4) = x_1 + x_2 + x_3 x_4 - x_1 x_4 - x_2 x_3 - x_1 x_2.$$

It is easy to check that for arbitrary 4-tuple (x_1, x_2, x_3, x_4), if $(x_1, x_2, x_3, x_4) \in \{0,1\}^4$ then $f(x_1, x_2, x_3, x_4) \in \{0,1\}$. To explore properties of the Ambainis' function we introduce 6 auxiliary sets of variables.

$$
\begin{aligned}
S_1 &= \{x_1, x_2\} & T_1 &= \{x_1\} \\
S_2 &= \{x_2, x_3\} & T_2 &= \{x_2\} \\
S_3 &= \{x_1, x_4\} & T_3 &= \{x_3, x_4\}
\end{aligned}
$$

By S we denote the class (S_1, S_2, S_3) and by T we denote the class (T_1, T_2, T_3). By $\alpha(x_1, x_2, x_3, x_4)$ we denote the cardinality of those $S_i = (x_j, x_k)$ such that $x_j = x_k = 1$. By $\beta(x_1, x_2, x_3, x_4)$ we denote the cardinality of those T_i such that it contains at least one element x_j which equals 0.

Lemma 1. *For arbitrary 4-tuple $(x_1, x_2, x_3, x_4) \in \{0,1\}^4$, $f(x_1, x_2, x_3, x_4) = 0$ iff $\alpha(x_1, x_2, x_3, x_4) + \beta(x_1, x_2, x_3, x_4)$ is congruent to 1 modulo 2.*

Proof. Immediately from Table 1. $\square$

Theorem 10. *There exists a 2-ultrametric automaton with two one-way input tapes recognizing the language L.*

Proof. The desired algorithm branches its computation path into 6 branches at the root. We assign to each starting edge of the computation path the amplitude $\frac{1}{7}$.

Table 1. Values of the functions

x_1	x_2	x_3	x_4	$\alpha(x_1, x_2, x_3, x_4)$	$\beta(x_1, x_2, x_3, x_4)$	$f(x_1, x_2, x_3, x_4)$
0	0	0	0	0	3	0
0	0	0	1	0	3	0
0	0	1	0	0	3	0
0	0	1	1	0	2	1
0	1	0	0	0	2	1
0	1	0	1	0	2	1
0	1	1	0	1	2	0
0	1	1	1	1	1	1
1	0	0	0	0	2	1
1	0	0	1	1	2	0
1	0	1	0	0	2	1
1	0	1	1	1	1	1
1	1	0	0	1	1	1
1	1	0	1	2	1	0
1	1	1	0	2	1	0
1	1	1	1	3	0	0

The first 3 branches (labeled with numbers $1, 2, 3$) correspond to exactly one set S_i.

Let S_i consist of elements x_j, x_k. If the two computed values equal 1 then the algorithm goes to the state q_3. If at least one of the computed values equals 0 then the algorithm goes to the state q_4.

The next 3 branches (labeled with numbers $4, 5, 6$) correspond to exactly one set T_i. Let T_i consist of elements x_j, x_k. If at least one of the results equals 0 then the algorithm goes to the state q_3. If all the results equal 1 then the algorithm goes to the state q_4.

1 branch (labeled with number 7) asks no query and the algorithm goes to the state q_3.

In result of this computation the amplitude A_3 of the states q_3 has become

$$A_3 = \frac{1}{7}(1 + \alpha(x_1, x_2, x_3, x_4) + \alpha(x_1, x_2, x_3, x_4)),$$

The 2-ultrametric query algorithm performs measurement of the state q_3. The amplitude A_3 is transformed into a rational number A_3. 2-adic notation for the number 7 is $\ldots 000111$ and 2-adic notation for the number $\frac{1}{7}$ is $\ldots 110110110111$. Hence, for every 2-adic integer γ, $\gamma = \frac{1}{7}\gamma$.

By Lemma 1, $1 + \alpha(x_1, x_2, x_3, x_4) + \alpha(x_1, x_2, x_3, x_4)_2$ equals 1, if $f(x_1, x_2, x_3, x_4) = 0$ and it equals $\frac{1}{2}$, if $f(x_1, x_2, x_3, x_4) = 0$ □

6   Kushilevitz's Function

E. Kushilevitz exhibited a function f that provides the largest gap in the exponent of a polynomial in $deg(f)$ that gives an upper bound on $bs(f)$. Never published by Kushilevitz, the function appears in footnote 1 of the Nisan-Wigderson paper [15].

Kushilevitz's function h of 6 Boolean variables is defined as follows:
$h(z_1, \ldots, z_6) = \Sigma_i z_i - \Sigma_{i \neq j} z_i z_j + z_1 z_3 z_4 + z_1 z_2 z_5 + z_1 z_4 z_5 + z_2 z_3 z_4 + z_2 z_3 z_5 + z_1 z_2 z_6 + z_1 z_3 z_6 + z_2 z_4 z_6 + z_3 z_5 z_6 + z_4 z_5 z_6.$

To explore properties of the Kushilevitz's function we introduce 10 auxiliary sets of variables.

$$
\begin{array}{l|l}
S_1 = \{z_1, z_3, z_4\} & T_1 = \{z_2, z_5, z_6\} \\
S_2 = \{z_1, z_2, z_5\} & T_2 = \{z_3, z_4, z_6\} \\
S_3 = \{z_1, z_4, z_5\} & T_3 = \{z_2, z_3, z_6\} \\
S_4 = \{z_2, z_3, z_4\} & T_4 = \{z_1, z_5, z_6\} \\
S_5 = \{z_2, z_3, z_5\} & T_5 = \{z_1, z_4, z_6\} \\
S_6 = \{z_1, z_2, z_6\} & T_6 = \{z_3, z_4, z_5\} \\
S_7 = \{z_1, z_3, z_6\} & T_7 = \{z_2, z_4, z_5\} \\
S_8 = \{z_2, z_4, z_6\} & T_8 = \{z_1, z_3, z_5\} \\
S_9 = \{z_3, z_5, z_6\} & T_9 = \{z_1, z_2, z_4\} \\
S_{10} = \{z_4, z_5, z_6\} & T_{10} = \{z_1, z_2, z_3\}
\end{array}
$$

By S we denote the class $(S_1, \ldots, S_{10})$ and by T we denote the class $(T_1, \ldots, T_{10})$.

Lemma 2. *For every $i \in \{1, \ldots, 6\}$, the union $S_i \cup T_i$ equals $\{1, \ldots, 6\}$.*

Lemma 3. *For every $i \in \{1, \ldots, 6\}$, the variable z_i is a member of exactly 5 sets in S and a member of exactly 5 sets in T.*

Lemma 4. *For every $i \in \{1, \ldots, 6\}$, the variable z_i has an empty intersection with exactly 5 sets in S and with exactly 5 sets in T.*

Lemma 5. *For every pair (i, j) such that $i \neq j$ and $i \in \{1, \ldots, 6\}, j \in \{1, \ldots, 6\}$, the pair of variables (z_i, z_j) is a member of exactly 2 sets in S and a member of exactly 2 sets in T.*

Lemma 6. *For every pair (i, j) such that $i \neq j$ and $i \in \{1, \ldots, 6\}, j \in \{1, \ldots, 6\}$, the pair of variables (z_i, z_j) has an empty intersection with exactly 2 sets in S and with exactly 2 sets in T.*

Lemma 7. *For every triple (i, j, k) of pairwise distinct elements of $\{1, \ldots, 6\}$, the triple of variables (z_i, z_j, z_k) coincides either with some set $S_i \in S$ or with some set T_j.*

Lemma 8. *No triple (i, j, k) of pairwise distinct elements of $\{1, \ldots, 6\}$ is such that the triple of variables (z_i, z_j, z_k) is a member of both S and T.*

Lemma 9. *For every quadruple (i, j, k, l) of pairwise distinct elements of $\{1, \ldots, 6\}$, the quadruple of variables (z_i, z_j, z_k, z_l) contains exactly 2 sets $S_i \in S$ and exactly 2 sets $T_i \in T$.*

Proof. Immediately from Lemma 5.   □

Lemma 10. *For every quintuple (i, j, k, l, m) of pairwise distinct elements of $\{1, \ldots, 6\}$, the quintuple of variables $(z_i, z_j, z_k, z_l, z_m)$ contains exactly 5 sets $S_i \in S$ and exactly 5 sets $T_i \in T$.*

Proof. Immediately from Lemma 3.   □

Lemma 11. *(1) If $\Sigma_i z_i = 0$ then $h(z_1, \ldots, z_6) = 0$.*
(2) If $\Sigma_i z_i = 1$ then $h(z_1, \ldots, z_6) = 1$,
(3) If $\Sigma_i z_i = 2$ then $h(z_1, \ldots, z_6) = 1$,
(4) If $\Sigma_i z_i = 4$ then $h(z_1, \ldots, z_6) = 0$,
(5) If $\Sigma_i z_i = 5$ then $h(z_1, \ldots, z_6) = 0$,
(6) If $\Sigma_i z_i = 6$ then $h(z_1, \ldots, z_6) = 1$,
(7) If $\Sigma_i z_i = 3$ and there exist 3 pairwise distinct (j, k, l) such that $(z_j = z_k = z_l = 1)$ and $(z_j, z_k, z_l) \in S$ then $h(z_1, \ldots, z_6) = 1$,
(8) If $\Sigma_i z_i = 3$ and there exist 3 pairwise distinct (j, k, l) such that $(z_j = z_k = z_l = 1)$ and $(z_j, z_k, z_l) \in T$ then $h(z_1, \ldots, z_6) = 0$.

Proof. If $\Sigma_i z_i = 0$ then all monomials in the definition of $h(z_1, \ldots, z_6)$ equal zero. If $\Sigma_i z_i = 1$ then $\Sigma_i z_i = 1$ but all the other monomials in the definition of $h(z_1, \ldots, z_6)$ equal zero. If $\Sigma_i z_i = 2$ then $h(z_1, \ldots, z_6) = \Sigma_i z_i - \Sigma_{i \neq j} z_i z_j = 2 - 1$. If $\Sigma_i z_i = 3$ and $(z_j, z_k, z_l) \in S$ then $h(z_1, \ldots, z_6) = \Sigma_i z_i - \Sigma_{i \neq j} z_i z_j = 3 - 3 + 1$. If $\Sigma_i z_i = 3$ and $(z_j, z_k, z_l) \in T$ then $h(z_1, \ldots, z_6) = \Sigma_i z_i - \Sigma_{i \neq j} z_i z_j = 3 - 3 + 0$. If $\Sigma_i z_i = 4$ then, by Lemma 9, $h(z_1, \ldots, z_6) = \Sigma_i z_i - \Sigma_{i \neq j} z_i z_j = 4 - 6 + 2$. If $\Sigma_i z_i = 5$ then, by Lemma 10, $h(z_1, \ldots, z_6) = \Sigma_i z_i - \Sigma_{i \neq j} z_i z_j = 5 - 10 + 5$. If $\Sigma_i z_i = 6$ then $h(z_1, \ldots, z_6) = \Sigma_i z_i - \Sigma_{i \neq j} z_i z_j = 6 - 15 + 10$. $\square$

By $\alpha(z_1, \ldots, z_6)$ we denote the cardinality of those $S_i = (z_j, z_k, z_l)$ such that $z_j = z_k = z_l = 1$. By $\beta(z_1, \ldots, z_6)$ we denote the cardinality of those $S_i = (z_j, z_k, z_l)$ such that $z_j = z_k = z_l = 0$.

Lemma 12. *(1) For arbitrary 6-tuple $(z_1, \ldots, z_6) \in \{0,1\}^6$, $h(z_1, \ldots, z_6) = 1$ iff $\alpha(z_1, \ldots, z_6) - \beta(z_1, \ldots, z_6)$ is congruent to 1 modulo 3.*
(2) For arbitrary 6-tuple $(z_1, \ldots, z_6) \in \{0,1\}^6$, $h(z_1, \ldots, z_6) = 0$ iff $\alpha(z_1, \ldots, z_6) - \beta(z_1, \ldots, z_6)$ is congruent to 2 modulo 3.

Proof. If $\Sigma_i z_i = 0$ then $\alpha(z_1, \ldots, z_6) - \beta(z_1, \ldots, z_6) = 0 - 10 \equiv 2 \pmod 3$. If $\Sigma_i z_i = 1$ then, by Lemma 4, $\alpha(z_1, \ldots, z_6) - \beta(z_1, \ldots, z_6) = 0 - 5 \equiv 1 \pmod 3$. If $\Sigma_i z_i = 2$ then, by Lemma 6, $\alpha(z_1, \ldots, z_6) - \beta(z_1, \ldots, z_6) = 0 - 2 \equiv 1 \pmod 3$. If $\Sigma_i z_i = 3$ and there exist 3 pairwise distinct (j, k, l) such that $(z_j = z_k = z_l = 1)$ and $(z_j, z_k, z_l) \in S$ then, by Lemmas 7 and 8, $\alpha(z_1, \ldots, z_6) - \beta(z_1, \ldots, z_6) = 1 - 0 \equiv 1 \pmod 3$. If $\Sigma_i z_i = 3$ and there exist 3 pairwise distinct (j, k, l) such that $(z_j = z_k = z_l = 1)$ and $(z_j, z_k, z_l) \in T$ then, by Lemmas 7 and 8, $\alpha(z_1, \ldots, z_6) - \beta(z_1, \ldots, z_6) = 0 - 1 \equiv 2 \pmod 3$. If $\Sigma_i z_i = 4$ then, by Lemma 9, $\alpha(z_1, \ldots, z_6) - \beta(z_1, \ldots, z_6) = 2 - 0 \equiv 2 \pmod 3$. If $\Sigma_i z_i = 5$ then, by Lemma 10, $\alpha(z_1, \ldots, z_6) - \beta(z_1, \ldots, z_6) = 5 - 0 \equiv 2 \pmod 3$. If $\Sigma_i z_i = 5$ then $\alpha(z_1, \ldots, z_6) - \beta(z_1, \ldots, z_6) = 10 - 0 \equiv 1 \pmod 3$. These results correspond to Lemma 11. $\square$

Theorem 11. *There exists a 3-ultrametric query algorithm computing the Kushilevitz's function using 3 queries.*

Proof. The desired algorithm branches its computation path into 31 branches at the root. We assign to each starting edge of the computation path the amplitude $\frac{1}{61}$.

The first 10 branches (labeled with numbers $1, \ldots, 10$) correspond to exactly one set S_i.

Let S_i consist of elements z_j, z_k, z_l. Then the algorithm queries z_j, z_k, z_l. If all the queried values equal 1 then the algorithm goes to the state q_3. If all the queried values equal 0 then the algorithm goes to the state q_3 but multiplies the amplitude to (-1). (For the proof it is important that for every 3-adic number a the norm $-a = a$.) If the queried values are not all equal then the algorithm goes to the state q_4.

The next 10 branches (labeled with numbers $11, \ldots, 20$) also correspond to exactly one set S_i. Let S_i consist of elements z_j, z_k, z_l. Then the algorithm queries z_j, z_k, z_l. If all the queried values equal 1 then the algorithm goes to the state q_5.

If all the queried values equal 0 then the algorithm goes to the state q_3. If the queried values are not all equal then the algorithm goes to the state q_4 but multiplies the amplitude to (-1).

11 branches (labeled with numbers $21, \ldots, 31$) ask no query and the algorithm goes to the state q_3.

In result of this computation the amplitude A_3 of the states q_3 has become

$$A_3 = \frac{1}{31}(11 + \alpha(z_1, \ldots, z_6) - \beta(z_1, \ldots, z_6)),$$

The 3-ultrametric query algorithm performs measurement of the state q_3. The amplitude A_3 is transformed into a rational number A_3. As it was noted in Sect. 1, 3-adic notation for the number 31 is $\ldots 000112$ and 3-adic notation for the number $\frac{1}{31}$ is $\ldots 0212111221021$. Hence, for every 3-adic integer γ, $\gamma = \frac{1}{31}\gamma$.

By Lemma 12, $11 + \alpha(z_1, \ldots, z_6) - \beta(z_1, \ldots, z_6) = 1$ if $h(z_1, \ldots, z_6) = 1$ and $11 + \alpha(z_1, \ldots, z_6) - \beta(z_1, \ldots, z_6) = \frac{1}{3}$ if $h(z_1, \ldots, z_6) = 0$. $\square$

7   Iterated Kushilevitz's Function

The iterated Kushilevitz's function is defined as follows. Let $f_1(x_1, \ldots, x_6)$ be the Kushilevitz's function.

$$f_{d+1} = f(f_d(x_1, \ldots, x_{6^d}), f_d(x_{6^d+1}, \ldots, x_{2 \cdot 6^d}), \ldots, f_d(x_{5 \cdot 6^d+1}, \ldots, x_{6 \cdot 6^d})$$

Theorem 12. *There exists a 3-ultrametric query algorithm computing the function g_d using $\cdot 3^d$ queries.*

References

1. Ambainis, A.: Polynomial degree vs. quantum query complexity. J. Comput. Syst. Sci. **72**(2), 220–238 (2006)
2. Radu, V.: Application. In: Radu, V. (ed.) Stochastic Modeling of Thermal Fatigue Crack Growth. ACM, vol. 1, pp. 63–70. Springer, Heidelberg (2015)
3. Freivalds, R.: Complexity of probabilistic versus deterministic automata. In: Bārzdiņš, J., Bjørner, D. (eds.) Baltic Computer Science. LNCS, vol. 502, pp. 565–613. Springer, Heidelberg (1991)
4. Freivalds, R.: Non-constructive methods for finite probabilistic automata. Int. J. Found. Comput. Sci. **19**(3), 565–580 (2008)
5. Freivalds, R.: Ultrametric automata and Turing machines. In: Voronkov, A. (ed.) Turing-100. EPiC Series, vol. 10, pp. 98–112. EasyChair (2012)
6. Freivalds, R.: Ultrametric finite automata and turing machines. In: Béal, M.-P., Carton, O. (eds.) DLT 2013. LNCS, vol. 7907, pp. 1–11. Springer, Heidelberg (2013)
7. Gouvea, F.Q.: p-adic Numbers: An Introduction. Universitext, 2nd edn. Springer, Heidelberg (1983)
8. Grover, L.K.: A fast quantum mechanical algorithm for database search. In: Proceedings of the 28th ACM Symposium on Theory of Computing, pp. 212–219 (1996)

9. Hirvensalo, M.: Quantum Computing. Springer, Heidelberg (2001)
10. Khrennikov, A.Yu.: Non-Archimedean Analysis: Quantum Paradoxes, Dynamical Systems and Biological Models. Kluwer Academic Publishers, Dordrecht (1997)
11. Koblitz, N.: p-adic Numbers, p-adic Analysis, and Zeta-Functions. Graduate Texts in Mathematics, vol. 58, 2nd edn. Springer, Heidelberg (1984)
12. Kozyrev, S.V.: Ultrametric analysis and interbasin kinetics. In: Proceedings of the 2nd International Conference on p-Adic Mathematical Physics, American Institute Conference Proceedings, vol. 826, pp. 121–128 (2006)
13. Lunts, A.G.: A method of analysis of finite automata. Sov. Phys. Dokl. **10**, 102–105 (1965)
14. Madore, D.A.: A first introduction to p-adic numbers. http://www.madore.org/david/math/padics.pdf
15. Nisan, N., Wigderson, A.: On rank vs. communication complexity. Combinatorica **15**(4), 557–565 (1995)
16. Ostrowski, A.: Über einige Lösungen der funktionalgleichung $\varphi(x)\varphi(y) = \varphi(xy)$. Acta Math. **41**(1), 271–284 (1916)
17. Turakainen, P.: Generalized automata and stochastic languages. Proc. Am. Math. Soc. **21**(2), 303–309 (1969)
18. Vladimirov, V.S., Volovich, I.V., Zelenov, E.I.: p-Adic Analysis and Mathematical Physics. World Scientific, Singapore (1995)

Realism and Texture: Benchmark Problems for Natural Computation

John P. Lewis[✉]

Victoria University, Wellington, New Zealand
noisebrain@gmail.com

Abstract. We consider the problems of the realistic image synthesis, and texture synthesis, from the point of view of natural computation. These problems provide an interesting and relatively simple setting for considering issues such as the depth of simulation and the role of perception. We conclude with a discussion of recent results on the fundamental limits of image synthesis programs. Interpreting these results more generally suggests that "natural" signals may be exactly those that are compressible. This characterization provides a further link between the fields of natural computation and algorithmic information theory.

1 Realism

The best current computer graphics images are sufficiently realistic that human observers are sometimes unsure if they are photographs or synthetic scenes [2]. In other cases, the images are impressive, but observers can guess that they are synthetic. Curiously, people are often not able to report exactly what is wrong–different people may give different and vague answers, such as "something is wrong with the lighting".

Creating very realistic synthetic images requires simulating a small part of a virtual universe. The transport of light is simulated with geometric optics (although there have been alternative proposals [21]): a virtual book on a shelf is illuminated by light from a window, but it is also illuminated by light that first strikes the floor and then scatters, then hits the book, scattering again, and finally arriving at the virtual camera or eye, and also by light that first hits the ceiling, then the floor, then the book, and so on. These indirect bounces continue indefinitely, though with rapidly diminishing strength.

With the simplifying assumption that light scatters from surfaces equally in all directions (Lambert assumption), the steady-state lighting at a small surface element can be described as

$$b_i = e_i + \rho_i \sum_{j=1}^{N} F_{ij} b_j$$

where b_i is the radiosity (i.e. brightness) of the particular surface element, e_i is the light emitted from the surface (non-zero only if surface element i is part

© Springer International Publishing Switzerland 2015
C.S. Calude and M.J. Dinneen (Eds.): UCNC 2015, LNCS 9252, pp. 53–65, 2015.
DOI: 10.1007/978-3-319-21819-9_3

of a light source), F_{ij} describes how much surface element i is illuminated by surface element j, and ρ_i is the fraction of incident light that is reflected from this surface patch. Rewriting this in vector-matrix form, and merging ρ and F into a single light transfer operator $\mathbf{R}$ we have

$$\mathbf{b} = \mathbf{e} + \mathbf{R}\mathbf{b} \tag{1}$$

where $\mathbf{b}$ is the vector of brightness of each surface element, and $\mathbf{e}$ is the self-illumination of each surface. This equation describes the complete light interchange between every surface in the scene. The multiple-bounce light scattering can be identified by expanding this as

$$\mathbf{b} = \mathbf{e} + \mathbf{R}\mathbf{e} + \mathbf{R}^2\mathbf{e} + \mathbf{R}^3\mathbf{e} + \cdots$$

Here $\mathbf{e}$ is the emission, $\mathbf{R}\mathbf{e}$ is direct illumination, $\mathbf{R}^2\mathbf{e}$ is the first bounce lighting, and so on. Recognizing this as a Neumann series (or working directly from Eq. 1) the scene lighting can be solved as

$$\mathbf{b} = (\mathbf{I} - \mathbf{R})^{-1}\mathbf{e} \tag{2}$$

The Lambert assumption is very approximately accurate for some materials, but is not true for glossy or shiny materials. A mirror is an extreme case, in which an incoming ray of light reflects in a single direction. Other materials are more complex. Skin is an interesting example: some portion of the incident light directly scatters from the skin surface. Some of the remaining light penetrates the skin, is scattered inside the body, and then may reemerge from the skin a small distance away. Accurately simulating this "subsurface scattering" effect is crucial for creating believable human and animal characters – without it, the characters look as if they are made of wood or plastic [5,10,14].

Further aspects of the virtual scene must also be simulated. For example, it is generally accepted that the motion of clothing and hair is too complicated to manually specify, and so it must be created using a physically based computer simulation. The motion of water is particularly complex and is often accomplished with physical simulation. Visual effects movies often portray buildings and other objects that are destroyed [28]; physical simulations are used in these cases as well.

There is an underlying issue of representation. We expect that an elegant model of the virtual scene is one with a short description, and perhaps one that allows the image to be generated with a short computation. Computer graphics the rendering software (such as [4]) encodes some of the regularities of making an image, such as the laws describing light scattering from common materials. The input to the rendering software is a file that describes the particular scene. The situation might be compared to the concept of a two-part code in algorithmic information theory. However, unlike the two-part code, in practice the scene description typically still has considerable regularity.

In fact, scene descriptions are larger than one would expect and require more lengthy computations then might be initially imagined. The description of the scene generally contains descriptions of the geometry, for example as a mesh of polygons. The size of this description (measured in bits) is often considerably larger than the size of the final image. In part this is because the scene description is sufficiently accurate to generate images from many viewpoints and distances. The scene description becomes economical if a sufficiently long movie of the scene is produced. The compute time involved in making a movie image is also remarkable. It varies considerably depending on the particular image, but visual effects companies generally require large compute clusters. Thinking of scene descriptions as providing a compressed representation does not capture the situation. Laplace's demon [24] provides an alternate analogy: the scene description and computation allow multiple images at near future times to be computed from a more fundamental description of the initial state of the virtual world.

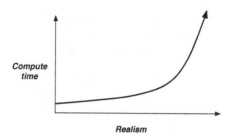

Fig. 1. Hypothetical relation between image realism and compute time.

Comparison of synthetic images in movies and games might initially suggest that the required compute time rises dramatically with rendering quality (Fig. 1). A single image in a videogame can usually be computed in 1/60 of a second, whereas a movie image requires minutes or even hours of computation. A movie image that takes one hour of computation requires about 200,000 times more computation than a game image. The image from the movie is certainly of higher quality than a game image, but few would say that it is 200,000 times better. One might object that this comparison is not strictly valid, since the game images contain precomputed approximations of the light transport, and the precomputation requires substantial time. However, this merely shifts the focus onto the difference between the approximate precomputed transport and the more exact calculations used in movies.

Analysis of rendering algorithms indicates that the relation suggested in Fig. 1 is not correct. For example, the matrix inverse in Eq. 2 indicates an $\mathcal{O}(N^3)$ compute time as a function of the geometric scene complexity N (e.g. triangle count). In classic ray tracing algorithms a dominant cost is the ray-triangle intersection, leading to an expected $N \log N$ dependence on scene complexity due to the role of sorting in finding the closest triangle. In general, we expect that compute time does not rise dramatically with scene complexity.

This issue might be resolved if Fig. 1 describes the relationship between *perceived* realism and compute time, whereas increasing *objective* realism requires more reasonable and modest investment in computation. We propose that this difference between the objective and perceived character of computational processes may be a suitable subject of enquiry for the field of natural computation. In the next section we consider how this question arises with the particular subject of texture.

2 Texture

Texture generally refers to the appearance and feel of the surface. The fields of computer graphics, computer vision, and image processing use the word in a more general sense, as an image of an object that would satisfy the traditional definition. In this usage the requirement for textures to have a tactile component is omitted.

At present there does not appear to be a definition of texture suitable for formal discussion, nor even a clear idea as to why the concept is necessary. For example, [9] surveyed existing definitions and concluded

> "Texture is an apparently paradoxical notion. On the one hand, it is commonly used in early processing of visual information, especially for practical classification purposes. On the other hand, no one has succeeded in producing a commonly accepted definition of texture."

One common example of a working definition is that a texture consists of a *primitive* and a *placement rule* [1,25]. An image of a brick wall satisfies this definition: an individual brick is the primitive, with the placement rule describing how the bricks are stacked to create the wall. Similarly, an image of a field of grass satisfies the definition, with the primitive being an individual blade of grass, and the placement rule being an appropriate random process. This definition is overly inclusive however. We might choose "sock" as the primitive, and "in the drawer" as the placement rule, but few people would say that a drawer of socks is a texture.

Despite the lack of a formal definition, we believe that the concept of texture involves perception. Early investigation of perception of textures resulted in the Julesz conjecture [15], which asserted that humans cannot "preattentively" (i.e. without close scrutiny) distinguish textures that differ only in their higher-order statistics.

For an image $I(\mathbf{p})$ indexed by pixel location $\mathbf{p}$, and assuming stationary (translation-invariant) statistics, the nth-order statistics are

$$P(I(\mathbf{p} + \mathbf{0}) = g_1, I(\mathbf{p} + \mathbf{\Delta}_2) = g_2, I(\mathbf{p} + \mathbf{\Delta}_3) = g_3, \cdots)$$

over n-tuples of pixels $\{I(\mathbf{p} + \mathbf{0}), I(\mathbf{p} + \mathbf{\Delta}_2), I(\mathbf{p} + \mathbf{\Delta}_3), \cdots\}$ and grey values g_k, where $\mathbf{\Delta}_k = (x_k, y_k)$ are offsets within the image. (The first-order statistics comprise the probability density of the image pixels).

The nth-order statistics require considerable information to specify. For example, for a grayscale image that is quantized to 256 code values, representing

Fig. 2. Landscape images created with a texture-synthesis process using second-order moments [18].

the 2nd order statistics over a neighborhood of N pixels requires $(N-1) \cdot 256^2$ probabilities. The 2nd or 3rd order statistics may easily be more voluminous than the image itself.

Because of this, the statistics are usually summarized for the purpose of computation. Gray level co-occurrence matrices (GLCM) [13] represent the second-order statistics, but typically over small neighborhoods or with heavily quantized luminance values (e.g. two bits per pixel). For the purpose of texture classification the full GCLM are often further summarized with a set of computed statistics [3]. An alternate approach is to use the nth-order moments (or expectations) rather than the full nth-order density. The 2nd order moments (with the mean removed) are the autocovariance (also called autocorrelation). An example of texture synthesis using second-order moments is shown in Fig. 2. By the Wiener-Khinchin theorem the autocovariance is the Fourier transform of the power spectrum. This relation indicates that texture modeling with the second-order moments is somewhat limited – it can capture only "random phase" textures.

Julesz and collaborators found that the original statement of the conjecture is not strictly correct – while there are texture pairs with identical second-order statistics that cannot be distinguished [17], certain texture pairs with identical third-order statistics *can* be distinguished [16]. Nevertheless the approximate conclusion that humans have limited ability to recognize increasingly high order statistics is plausible and supported by evidence.

In general, however, both the nth-order statistics and their moments may be the wrong representation of the problem. To this author, they seem analogous to trying to represent a square wave using a Taylor series. The failure of the Julesz conjecture reveals that these statistics do not correspond in a simple way to perception.

Another approach to texture synthesis involves sampling from an example of the desired texture [11,12,27]. Specifically, a neighborhood of pixels at the edge of a partially synthesized texture is compared to all neighborhoods in the reference texture image. The k neighborhoods that are most similar are noted.

The partially synthesized texture is then expanded by including pixels bordering one of these k neighborhoods, chosen at random. The basic algorithm can be regarded as sampling from the probability of the new pixels conditioned on the neighborhood, where the conditional probability is estimated from the histogram of border regions of the k neighbors.

This general approach is often successful, and has inspired a number of specific methods that accelerate the high-dimensional nearest neighbor lookup required by the neighborhood search. However, these methods are also sometimes "brittle", in that seemingly small changes in the choice of reference image can cause the synthesis to fail. Also, these methods do not provide a model of texture – they can be applied to any image (texture or not).

As discussed above, directly modeling pixel statistics is currently intractable except over small neighborhoods. The most promising approaches instead model the statistics of features that characterize a texture. The features then implicitly provide a larger neighborhood and the possibility of long-range interactions. Reference [29] defined a Markov random field (MRF) via the Gibbs energy on the histograms of predefined (e.g. Gabor) filter responses. Reference [26] builds higher-order MRFs over a hierarchy of texture-specific features, thus allowing the unique structure of each texture to be economically modeled.

2.1 Texture from an AIT Point of View

Most of the existing texture modeling approaches do not give an explicit definition of texture, nor do they motivate why this concept is needed. We would like to consider texture from an alternate point of view, that of algorithmic information theory (AIT) [6], in hopes of making progress towards a definition. Informally, AIT defines the algorithmic complexity (AC) of the digital object as (approximately) the length of the shortest computer program that generates that object.[1] The complexity does not depend on the choice of programming language, other than through an additive constant: any language can emulate any other language by way of an interpreter, and among the possible languages there is a language that can express an optimal compression of a particular object. The length of the interpreter is a constant that becomes in unimportant in the limit of increasingly large objects. The AC is not computable, but it can be bounded from above. In fact, even the use of crude approximate upper bounds has occasionally resulted in useful algorithms [8].

Figure 3 considers possible functional relationships between AC and the perceived complexity (PC) of images. Figure 3(a) and (b) depict polynomial or other functional relationships. Figure 3(c) depicts the situation where there is *no* relationship between AC and PC. Figure 3(d) depicts a situation where there is a relationship below some threshold in AC, but no relationship above that threshold.

---

[1] Important technical considerations such as the means by which programs are delimited are omitted in this brief description.

Fig. 3. Hypothetical relationships between objective complexity (horizontal axis) and perceived visual complexity (vertical axis).

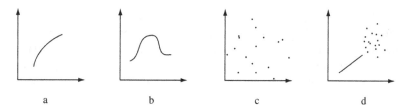

Fig. 4. Abstract patterns differing in their distribution of edges.

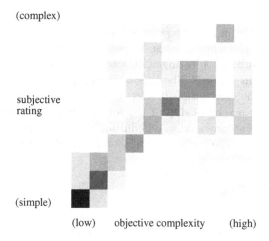

Fig. 5. Plot of subjective rating versus objective complexity for the patterns in Fig. 4. Darker values indicate more people selected the particular rating.

Establishing such a relationship initially seems not easy, since PC is subjective, while AC is not computable! Nevertheless, we obtain suggestive results using the following approach: First, patterns are generated using an approximate complexity measure. The subjective complexity of the patterns is then estimated using a psychological survey, i.e. by averaging the ratings of a number of observers. Figures 4 and 5 show patterns and results from a small exploratory study.

The patterns vary according to their distribution of edges. Specifically, we sample from a probability density with specified entropy, and gather the results into a histogram. The entries in histogram are interpreted as as edge strengths, and edge polarity is assigned at random. Lastly, the edges are wrapped around a circle to create a shape. The entropy of the distribution of edges provides the approximate objective complexity measure.

To obtain the subjective complexity, viewers were given the following instructions that provide an operational definition of PC: *You will see pairs of shapes that resemble evil spaceships. Imagine that you have to pick one of each pair and describe it to a police artist. For each pair, quickly pick the shape that would be easier to describe.*

Table 1. Subjective/objective chi-square significance and association strength

	All patterns	Low complexity	High complexity
χ^2 probability	.0000	.0061	0.14

Viewers were shown randomly generated patterns from each of 10 complexity levels, resulting in 45 pair comparisons. 23 people completed the study. The χ^2 association between subjective ratings (PC) and objective complexity (approximate AC) is shown in Table 1. There is a significant association overall, and at low complexity. The association breaks down for high complexity patterns, tentatively suggesting a relationship of the form in Fig. 3(d). We speculatively propose that this finding may lead to a definition of texture, as a signal that has too much complexity for the human visual system to fully process.

3   Image Synthesis

In the final section of the paper we step back and take a deeper and more philosophical look at the problem of computer graphics: is it possible to simply create a program that can generate all possible images? Can such a program even exist?

Before considering the answer to that question, we will mention examples of existing algorithms that invent images. A wide variety of pattern synthesis algorithms have been devised. These include L-systems [22], fractals [20], shape grammars [23], and others.

Figure 6 shows examples of randomly synthesized images created using a "meta" shape grammar [19]. As can be seen in the figure, the approach can be adapted to generate a variety of image classes. This approach is elegantly express using the closure concept in functional languages such as Lisp. Consider the example:

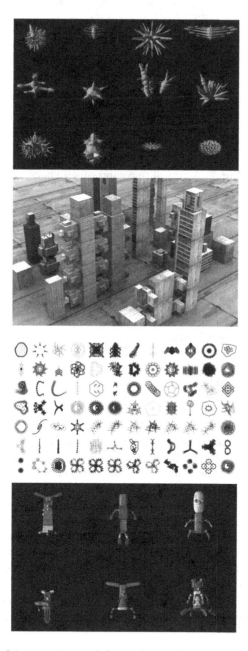

Fig. 6. A variety of images invented by a "meta shape grammar" approach [19]: Radiolaria-like shapes, futuristic buildings, doodles, toy robots. Please enlarge to see details.

Fig. 7. A typical (incompressible) image.

```
(define gen-radial
   (lambda (recursion-level)
   (let ((child (generate-child
                    (+ 1 recursion-level)))
          (vc-scale (rndin 0.15 0.7))
          (n (rndin-lowbias 3 12))))
      (lambda ()
         (dotimes (i n)
                  (save-transform
                   (rotate (/ (* i 2PI) n))
                   (scale vc-scale)
                   (child)))))))
```

Here, gen-radial is a function that defines and returns another anonymous
(lambda) function. The constructed inner function executes a loop with n iterations, at each iteration performing a rotation, scale, and calling some child
function that is randomly generated. Notice that while the iteration count n is
randomly chosen, it is chosen in the closure (lexical environment) of the inner
function. Thus, the same value of n is used each time the anonymous function is called. This construct provides a clean separation between choices that
are intended to be random (which can be effected through a pseudo-random
generator called inside the inner function), and "structural" inventions, that
are pseudo-randomly chosen in the outer scope. In simple situations the inner
function(s) can be seen as rewrite rules in a shape grammar, while the outer
function(s) serves to invent that grammar.

This is an example of an image synthesis approach that can produce a fairly
wide range of images (Fig. 6). Can this (or some other program) produce all
possible images?

3.1   A Universal Image Synthesizer?

Reference [7] considered the question of whether there is a single program than
can generate all possible "natural" images. There are certainly programs that

generate all possible images, for example, by enumerating all combinations of pixel values, or by choosing pixels randomly or pseudo-randomly. However, from AIT arguments we know that almost all images look like Fig. 7. While a program that enumerates all possible images will eventually produce images that document all aspects of your life, one would have to wait a very long time before seeing anything that resembles a real-world image. Thus, the restriction in [7] that we would like a program that produces all and only "natural" images.

The issue is that almost all images are incompressible, and (equivalently) lack structure. Is there a program that produces all images *except* those that lack structure? [7] proposes that:

"Natural" images are exactly those that can be compressed.

With this definition, the natural images are computably enumerable (c.e.), but not computable.[2]

Reference [7] considered a further requirement on admissible "natural" images. This requirement starts from the reasonable assumption that large images should contain more information than small ones. Simple programs such as fractal generators can produce an image of arbitrary size. The AC of such images is $C(x) \approx \log |x| + \text{constant}$ where $|x|$ denotes the size of the image x and the constant reflects the encoding of the program. Running a fractal generator to produce a large image does in some sense produce more detail, but one might argue that this detail is merely an effect of the increased number of pixels, rather than truly additional information. As a comparison, plotting a step function

$$H(x) = \begin{cases} 0 & x < \pi \\ 1 & x \geq \pi \end{cases}$$

on a series of images of increasing size provides increasing resolution on the exact location of the discontinuity at π, but a large image of the step function might not be considered as more complex than a smaller image. Indeed, the change in AC in each case reflects only the cost of encoding the size of the image.

The second requirement in [7] is thus that large images have more complexity than small images (i.e. beyond that generated by the encoding of the image size itself), expressed as $C(x) > \log |x| + \text{constant}$. With this requirement, and a precise definition of what a compressible image is, "natural" images are not even computably enumerable. Specifically, they are an infinite subset of an immune set, i.e. a set containing no infinite c.e. subset [7]. The natural images are in a sense much less computable than the halting set!

4   Conclusions

Considering computer graphics from the point of view of natural computation highlights several fundamental issues, including the role of perception, and the

---

[2] That is, they are not computable in the same sense that the set of programs that halt is not computable.

depth of simulation of physical and natural processes. While exploring the ultimate limits of computer graphics programs, we arrived at a definition of natural images as those that are compressible. We propose that this definition may hold for other types of signals, suggesting a further link between natural computation and the field of algorithmic information theory.

Acknowledgements. Thanks to Cris Calude for discussion of several topics.

References

1. Dictionary entry for texture in the Free On-line Dictionary of Computing. University of London Imperial College of Science, Technology, and Medicine, Department of Computing, foldoc.org (2002)
2. Fake or foto (2015). http://area.autodesk.com/fakeorfoto
3. Albregtsen, F.: Statistical texture measures computed from gray level coocurrence matrices. Image Processing Laboratory, Department of Informatics, University of Oslo, pp. 1–14 (2008)
4. Apodaca, A.A., Gritz, L.: Advanced RenderMan: Creating CGI for Motion Picture, 1st edn. Morgan Kaufmann Publishers Inc., San Francisco (1999)
5. Borshukov, G., Lewis, J.: Realistic human face rendering for the matrix reloaded. In: Proceedings of the SIGGRAPH 2003 Conference Sketches and Applications, pp. 1. ACM Press (2003)
6. Calude, C.S.: Information and Randomness: An Algorithmic Perspective, 2nd edn. Springer-Verlag New York Inc, Secaucus (2002)
7. Calude, C.S., Lewis, J.P.: Is there a universal image generator? Appl. Math. Comput. **218**(16), 8151–8159 (2012)
8. Cilibrasi, R., Vitanyi, P.: Clustering by compression. IEEE Trans. Inf. Theory **51**(4), 1523–1545 (2005)
9. Coggins, J.M.: A framework for texture analysis based on spatial filtering. Michigan State University Ph.D. thesis (1982)
10. D'Eon, E., Irving, G.: A quantized-diffusion model for rendering translucent materials. In: ACM SIGGRAPH 2011 Papers, pp. 56:1–56:14. ACM, New York (2011). http://doi.acm.org/10.1145/1964921.1964951
11. Efros, A.A., Leung, T.K.: Texture synthesis by non-parametric sampling. In: Proceedings of the International Conference on Computer Vision ICCV 1999, vol. 2, pp. 1033. IEEE Computer Society, Washington (1999)
12. Garber, D.: Computational Models for Texture Analysis and Textures Synthesis. University of Southern California, Los Angeles (1981)
13. Haralick, R.M., Shanmugam, K., Dinstein, I.: Textural features for image classification. IEEE Trans. SMC Syst. Man Cybern. **36**(6), 610–621 (1973). http://dx.doi.org/10.1109/tsmc.1973.4309314
14. Jensen, H.W., Marschner, S.R., Levoy, M., Hanrahan, P.: A practical model for subsurface light transport. In: SIGGRAPH 2001 Proceedings of the 28th Annual Conference on Computer Graphics and Interactive Techniques, pp. 511–518. ACM, New York (2001)
15. Julesz, B.: Visual pattern discrimination. IEEE Trans. Info. Theory **8**, 84–92 (1962)
16. Julesz, B., Gilbert, E., Victor, J.: Visual discrimination of textures with identical third-order statistics. Biol. Cybern. **31**(3), 137–140 (1978)

17. Julesz, B.: A theory of preattentive texture discrimination based on first-order statistics of textons. Biol. Cybern. **41**(2), 131–138 (1981). http://dx.doi.org/10.1007/BF00335367
18. Lewis, J.P.: Generalized stochastic subdivision. ACM Trans. Graph. **6**(3), 167–190 (1987)
19. Lewis, J.P., Rosenholtz, R., Fong, N., Neumann, U.: Visualids: automatic distinctive icons for desktop interfaces. ACM Trans. Graph. **23**(3), 416–423 (2004)
20. Mandelbrot, B.: The Fractal Geometry of Nature. Freeman, San Francisco (1983)
21. Moravec, H.P.: 3D graphics and the wave theory. SIGGRAPH Comput. Graph. **15**(3), 289–296 (1981). http://doi.acm.org/10.1145/965161.806817
22. Prusinkiewicz, P., Hanan, J.: Lindenmayer Systems, Fractals, and Plants. Springer Verlag, New York (1989)
23. Stiny, G.: Shape: Talking about Seeing and Doing. MIT Press, Cambridge (2006)
24. Svozil, K.: Randomness & Undecidability in Physics. World Scientific, Singapore (1993)
25. Tuceryan, M., Jain, A.: Texture analysis. In: Handbook of Pattern Recognition and Computer Vision. 2 edn, pp. 207–248. World Scientific (1998)
26. Versteegen, R., Gimel'farb, G., Riddle, P.: Learning high-order generative texture models. In: IVCNZ 2014 Proceedings of the 29th International Conference on Image and Vision Computing New Zealand, pp. 90–95. ACM, New York (2014). http://doi.acm.org/10.1145/2683405.2683420
27. Wei, L.Y., Levoy, M.: Fast texture synthesis using tree-structuredvector quantization. In: SIGGRAPH 2000 Proceedings of the 27th Annual Conference on ComputerGraphics and Interactive Techniques, pp. 479–488. ACMPress/Addison-Wesley Publishing Co., New York (2000). http://dx.doi.org/10.1145/344779.345009
28. Zafar, N., Stephens, D., Larsson, M., Sakaguchi, R., Clive, M., Sampath, R., Museth, K., Blakey, D., Gazdik, B., Thomas, R.: Destroying LA for 2012. In: ACM SIGGRAPH Talk (2010)
29. Zhu, S.C., Wu, Y.N., Mumford, D.: Filters, random fields and maximum entropy (FRAME): towards a unified theory for texture modeling. Int. J. Comput. Vis. **27**(2), 107–126 (1998)

Quantum Computing Meets the Real World

Kristen L. Pudenz[✉]

Advanced Development Programs,
Lockheed Martin Aeronautics Company,
Fort Worth, TX, USA
kristen.l.pudenz@lmco.com

1 Practical Quantum Information Processing

Quantum information processing as a scalable experimental pursuit has experienced significant progress in recent years. Multiple laboratories at large research organizations have constructed working systems with multiple interacting qubits, focused on the implementation of small-scale computational problems or the demonstration of quantum error correction techniques. This stage of development is particularly interesting because the engineering issues related to controlling multiple quantum systems in a noisy environment are being clarified as the various systems progress, illuminating where the best hopes for quantum computation may lie. These practical pathways are not always the same as what has been predicted in the closed-system theoretical context, so creative algorithmic thinking is needed to unlock the potential of the real devices.

2 Models and Implementations

2.1 Circuit Model

The circuit model is the first scheme proposed for a quantum computer, and the closest to the architecture and operation of classical computing system. In a circuit model computation, the qubits are initialized into some quantum state, then operated on by a series of discrete gates, which may introduce quantum effects such as entanglement into the system. Many of the canonical quantum algorithms were developed for the circuit model of quantum computation.

Several circuit model quantum information processing systems are currently under development. IBM recently announced a four-qubit system based on superconducting technology; the interactions between their four qubits were designed for the purpose of state preservation on two of the qubits, while measurement of the other two allows the detection of an arbitrary quantum error [1]. The National Institute for Standards and Technology (NIST) has been working on quantum computation using trapped ions for many years, and has been able to generate entangled states of at least six atoms in the laboratory [2].

© Springer International Publishing Switzerland 2015
C.S. Calude and M.J. Dinneen (Eds.): UCNC 2015, LNCS 9252, pp. 66–70, 2015.
DOI: 10.1007/978-3-319-21819-9_4

2.2 Adiabatic

Most of the recent efforts to construct a scalable quantum processor, however, have focused on the adiabatic model of quantum computation (AQC). AQC involves initializing a set of qubits to a known state, then slowly and continuously changing the parameters of the experimental Hamiltonian. If the noise is low enough and the changes are sufficiently slow, the state of the qubits at the end of the computation will represent the low-energy state of an entirely different energy function than that which initialized the computation [3]. Both the circuit model and the adiabatic model are universal for quantum computation, and a translation with polynomial overhead exists for mapping circuit-model quantum algorithms to adiabatic target energy functions [4].

The best-known implementation of the adiabatic model is the D-Wave Systems quantum optimization processor. Their commercially available quantum chips have grown in size from 128 to over 1000 superconducting qubits, which interact via a fixed local connectivity structure [5]. Google is also developing a superconducting quantum information processing system based on the adiabatic model. Their most recent chip has nine qubits fabricated in a row, allowing users to study dynamics of chained quantum systems or do limited error correction [6]. Other groups working on experimental AQC systems include the University of Maryland (trapped ions) [7] and Sandia National Laboratories (superconducting) [8].

2.3 Limitations

None of the currently available experimental systems is a universal quantum computer; each has its own limitations. Coupling between qubits is difficult for superconducting systems because of space and routing limitations on the chip. All of the superconducting implementations have a specific connectivity structure that is much more sparse than a complete graph connecting all qubits; most are limited to nearest-neighbor interactions. Of the superconducting circuits, the IBM chip is the only one to incorporate all of the coupler types necessary for universal quantum computation, but currently is still limited to state preservation rather than computation. The ion trap implementations have more flexibility in the interactions available to them because all of the ions reside in the same trap and can be coupled with laser pulses. However, these systems face a serious scalability hurdle because the number of ions that a trap can hold is limited, so a way to move ions between traps while preserving their state must be developed and integrated.

3 Applications

3.1 Factoring

Shor's algorithm for factoring numbers is the most famous example of an application for quantum computers [9]. The algorithm is attractive because it offers an exponential quantum speed advantage over the best known classical algorithm and it solves a cryptographic problem that is widely used. It may not be the first application to be realized on a large scale, however, because it demands much of a quantum information processor. A device to solve the factoring problem must be able to implement universal interactions between qubits, and be extremely low-noise in order to preserve small variations in quantum states. Other, more flexible applications will be needed to take advantage of the initial generations of quantum information processors.

3.2   Quantum Simulation

The application that inspired the concept of a quantum computer was the simulation of quantum systems, once it became clear that solving the Schrodinger equation using classical computers becomes intractable very quickly as the system size increases [10]. The idea is to build a quantum system that is controllable and measurable in the laboratory, yet will naturally undergo the same processes as the system we wish to study. Of course a universal quantum computer can simulate an arbitrary quantum system, but perhaps of more immediate interest is the idea of a special-purpose quantum simulator, constructed to emulate a particular system or class of systems. This idea is particularly appealing because the constraints that hamper the construction of a universal quantum computer also apply to natural systems (particularly locality of interactions and restrictions on the number of particles that may interact significantly at once). If such a quantum simulator is built for the right quantum system, it may become the first great success for quantum computing.

3.3   Optimization

The largest and most functional quantum processor currently in existence, the D-Wave chip, is an optimizer by design. It uses the adiabatic model to solve an Ising spin glass (or, equivalently, a quadratic binary optimization) problem, finding the configuration of spins that minimizes the energy of the system. Because the adiabatic model is probabilistic and the process occurs in a system with noise, approximate solutions may be generated in addition to or, under certain conditions, in lieu of the global optimum [11]. This will also be true for the other adiabatic systems under development that were discussed in Sect. 2.2. Though many efforts have been made to develop applications for [12–14] and characterize the performance of the D-Wave family of processors, whether and for what type of problem these systems can offer a genuine quantum speed-up is still an open question [15, 16].

3.4   Error Correction

Efforts are also beginning to implement error correction for quantum information systems, which will be an essential component of any quantum computer operating at large scale in a real environment, and therefore must be a concern for any group seeking to implement quantum computation. The circuit model system at IBM and the adiabatic system at Google are addressing the problem directly in their small-scale devices, designing from the ground up to implement a robust quantum error correction scheme known as the surface code [1,6]. D-Wave has not incorporated error correction in the design of their systems, but there are user-side constructions that provide some amount of error suppression and correction [17,18], which would also be applicable to future adiabatic implementations.

4   A Path Forward

The new generation of quantum computing systems is producing novel open questions for the field at a rapid pace and creating opportunities for work which will have a real impact on computation. Of particular importance among these open problems is the creation of new algorithms for practical devices which are useful at small scales, robust to noise, and capable of taking advantage of the special features of implemented systems (e.g. the distribution of approximate solutions returned by adiabatic devices). Such development should keep in mind the capabilities of classical computing, and use the quantum processor as a complement and enhancement to the resources we already have available to us. In this way, classical and quantum algorithms will advance together, each providing feedback to the other, to the overall enhancement of useful computation.

References

1. Corcoles, A. D., et al.: Demonstration of a quantum error detection code using a square lattice of four superconducting qubits. Nature Commun. 6, 6979 (2015)
2. Leibfried, D., et al.: Creation of a 'six-atom Schrodinger' cat state. Nature **438**, 639–642 (2005)
3. Farhi, E., et al.: Quantum computation by adiabatic evolution (2000). arXiv preprint quant-ph/0001106
4. Aharonov, D., et al.: Adiabatic quantum computation is equivalent to standard quantum computation. SIAM Rev. **50**(4), 755–787 (2008)
5. Johnson, M.W., et al.: Quantum annealing with manufactured spins. Nature **473**(7346), 194–198 (2011)
6. Kelly, J., et al.: State preservation by repetitive error detection in a superconducting quantum circuit. Nature **519**, 66–69 (2015)
7. Kielpinski, D., Monroe, C., Wineland, D.J.: Architecture for a large-scale ion-trap quantum computer. Nature **417**, 709–711 (2002)
8. Blume-Kohout, R.: Robust, self-consistent, closed-form tomography of quantum logic gates on a trapped ion qubit (2013). arXiv preprint quant-ph/1310.4492
9. Shor, P.W.: Algorithms for quantum computation: discrete logarithms and factoring. In: 1994 Proceedings of 35th Annual Symposium on Foundations of Computer Science, pp. 124–134. IEEE (1994)
10. Feynman, R.P.: Simulating physics with computers. Int. J. Theor. Phys. **21**(6), 467–488 (1982)

11. Amin, M.H.S., Love, P.J., Truncik, C.J.S.: Thermally assisted adiabatic quantum computation. Phys. Rev. Lett. **100**(6), 060503 (2008)
12. Denchev, V., Ding, N., Neven, H.: Robust classification with adiabatic quantum optimization. In: Proceedings of the 29th International Conference on Machine Learning, pp. 863–870 (2012)
13. Rieffel, E.G., et al.: A case study in programming a quantum annealer for hard operational planning problems. Quantum Inf. Process. **14**(1), 1–36 (2015)
14. Santra, S., et al.: MAX 2-SAT with up to 108 qubits. New J. Phys. **16**(4), 045006 (2014)
15. Troels, R.F., et al.: Defining and detecting quantum speedup. Science **345**(6195), 420–424 (2014)
16. Hen, I., et al.: Probing for quantum speedup in spin glass problems with planted solutions (2015). arXiv preprint arXiv:1502.01663
17. Pudenz, K.L., Albash, T., Lidar, D.A.: Error-corrected quantum annealing with hundreds of qubits. Nature Commun. **5**, 3243 (2014)
18. Pudenz, K.L., Albash, T., Lidar, D.A.: Quantum annealing correction for random Ising problems. Phys. Rev. A **91**, 042302 (2015)

BL: A Visual Computing Framework for Interactive Neural System Models of Embodied Cognition and Face to Face Social Learning

Mark Sagar[✉], Paul Robertson, David Bullivant, Oleg Efimov,
Khurram Jawed, Ratheesh Kalarot, and Tim Wu

University of Auckland, Auckland, New Zealand
m.sagar@auckland.ac.nz
http://www.abi.auckland.ac.nz/en/about/our-research/
animate-technologies.html

Keywords: Visualisation · Simulation · Animation · Computational
neuroscience · Cognitive modelling · Behavioural modelling

1 Introduction

Our behaviour emerges as the result of many systems interacting at different scales, from low level biology to high level social interaction. Is it possible to create naturalistic explanatory models which can integrate these factors? This paper describes the general approach and design of a framework to create autonomous expressive embodied models of behaviour based on affective and cognitive neuroscience theories. The goal of our research is to integrate many different current theories and models to create a large functioning sketch of several fundamental aspects of human behaviour including face to face interaction, to explore how it may emerge from interaction of low level and high level systems in a top-down bottom up approach. A key feature of the approach is (given the constraints of the medium), to create as naturalistic models as possible in order to elicit and respond to the appropriate behaviours from the user, involving both sensing and synthesis of visual and auditory stimuli. The models are intended to be as autonomous as possible, so interactions are unscripted and co-created. In order to develop an overall generative model of behaviour that, where possible, remains grounded in biologically plausible models and thus has more explanatory power than statistical approaches, we are developing BL, a modular Lego-like neural network modelling language, sensing and visual simulation framework, to facilitate integration of a range of emerging and established models from diverse sources such as cognitive science, developmental psychology, computational neuroscience and physiology with high quality interactive computer graphics. While some models are still highly theoretical it is still beneficial to explore how these can be integrated with more established models to see the contribution each sub-process has to the overall system. As a result of combining many diverse

C.S. Calude and M.J. Dinneen (Eds.): UCNC 2015, LNCS 9252, pp. 71–88, 2015.
DOI: 10.1007/978-3-319-21819-9_5

models, the neurobehavioural architectures created in BL often form large, complex networks and simulations form complex dynamic systems justifying a visual computing approach in which systems and subsystems can be explored visually as the simulation proceeds. As the users behaviour as an interactive partner is a key factor in social learning, it is important to capture and visualize the effect of internal and external events on the network.In this overview we describe BL and its user interface, before detailing some simple test cases utilizing the various features of the interface, and then illustrate a more complex application in a psychobiological simulation of an infant Baby X currently under development, which aims to combine models of the facial motor system and models of basic neural systems involved in early interactive behaviour and learning.

2 Background and Related Work

Our research integrates a wide range of fields, so due to space requirements a brief summary is given here of key areas.

2.1 Embodied Cognition and Social Learning

Embodied Cognition and Grounded Cognition theories suggest our cognitive activity is grounded in sensorimotor processes situated in specific contexts and situations [8]. The embodied cognition hypothesis suggests. The brain is not the sole cognitive resource we have available to us to solve problems. Our bodies and their perceptually guided motions through the world do much of the work required to achieve our goals, replacing the need for complex internal mental representations [56]. Social learning is the primary process through which knowledge and behaviour central to successful functioning in human groups is transmitted [6,13,14,19,25,26,28,56,59].

2.2 Developmental and Social Robotics

The importance of embodied and grounded cognition and social learning is being explored in the fields of developmental and social robotics [10]. Interactive robots or intelligent virtual agents share many of the same components, such as computer vision based object tracking, speech recognition, memory and cognition, reactive behavior, reasoning, planning, action scheduling, and articulation enabling them to participate autonomously in real-time in dynamic environments [5].

2.3 Affective Computing and Social Signal Processing

The study of emotion is a vast field [52] still under considerable debate. Recent higher level approaches to synthesis of social emotion are surveyed in [58]. Affective computing [44] aims to enable machines to interpret the emotional state of humans and adapt their behaviour to give an appropriate response, and facilitate social learning [43]. Incorporating developmental learning processes is thought to be fundamental in achieving intelligent embodied agents [3,4]. A relatively recent survey of the detection and synthesis of social signals using virtual humans, and the challenges faced can be found in [58]. Simulating conversational interaction and social reasoning [11,42] requiring higher levels of abstraction is not our focus here (we are concerned with the lower level building blocks of basic behaviour) but our system has been designed to be efficiently integrated with higher level cognitive architectures and conversational systems.

2.4 Affective Neuroscience

Affective neuroscience is the study of the neural mechanisms of emotion. Panksepp [39] has described the core emotional systems in mammals based on their neuro-chemistries, many of which likely have human analogies. Emotional circuits discovered to date are complex and also have many redundant features [21]. Effectively simulating complexity of emotions is likely to require a dynamic architecture [51], and dynamic systems modelling of emotion using neurobiological models have been proposed [34,47].

2.5 Neural Networks and Cognitive System Simulators

Computational Neuroscience [16,57] encompasses biologically based neural models of information processing, cognition and behaviour with numerical models. Although much work involves specific modelling of isolated components, a range of more general biological neural network simulators have been developed (with various specializations) to study systems. Publically available neural network simulators are summarized in [9,35]. A range of biologically inspired cognitive architectures [50] have been developed for both explanatory purposes and also for the potential flexibility they can offer. A good example is the "Leabra" framework [38] which covers many aspects of cognition using biologically based models including goal driven learning and behaviour.

2.6 Autonomous Behaviour

Autonomy is viewed in the context of our work as an emergent property of low level biological processes based on homeostasis, incentive salience, novelty, action discovery and self organization modulated by higher level goal directed process [7,15,22,29,30,37]. Rich behaviour can emerge from physical (or virtual) constraints and fundamental low level mechanisms. For example, intrinsic goal free motor activity which underlies babbling may lay an essential foundation for play and cognitive development [33]. Intrinsically motivated behaviour has arguably been demonstrated in biologically based models of action discovery [22].

2.7 Visual Simulation Frameworks

Various visual simulation environments for biological models have been developed, from problem solving environments such to simulation architectures.

An example of an established problem solving environment is SCIRun [41] which is described as a "computational workbench" in which a user selects software modules that can be connected in a visual programing environment to create a high level workflow for experimentation. Each module exposes all the available parameters necessary for scientists to adjust the outcome of their simulation or visualization. An example simulation architecture is SOFA (Simulation Open Framework Architecture) [1], which is an Open Source framework primarily targeted at real-time physical simulation, with an emphasis on medical simulation.

2.8 Face to Face Interaction

A vital component of effective social interaction is dynamic facial expression. To capture the user's affect, interactive virtual humans and robots commonly use computer vision (and audio analysis) as key components of the system. For agents interacting with humans, detailed tracking of the face is still challenging and is still an active area of research. A wide range of techniques have been developed for video face tracking. A survey of affect recognition methods is given in [61,62].

The other critical side of the interaction involves the generation of facial expression which is difficult to achieve realistically in both robotics and computer graphics. Facial animation is a complex task which must account for both extremely subtle and also dramatic changes in appearance, form and movement. In virtual human models animatable faces are typically represented through deforming geometry using weighted joints, blendshape methods or hybrids [40]. Joint based methods suffer from loss of detail, whereas blendshape based models suffer from combinatorial explosion in representing the complex manifold of facial expression. The highest quality models used in the visual effects industry currently incorporate a large number of blendshapes to form piecewise linear approximations to non-linear deformations. Creating these models is labour intensive, especially accurately representing material point motion. A small number of researchers have approached this problem using physically based simulation [48,53,55,60].

The neural control of facial movements is complex and uses multiple parallel systems (including voluntary and emotive systems), which are anatomically and functionally distinct up to the facial nucleus [12]. To our knowledge no previous work has been done to generate facial animation through modelling neural control over the face.

3   BL: Brain Language Overview

While a range of range of a neural simulation software packages and architectures exist [9,35,38,50] few if any of these have an intimate link with realistic computer graphics and animation as an output. In order to allow models from diverse sources to communicate with one another and drive realistic real time computer graphics animation and visualization we have developed a specialized framework called Brain Language (BL). BL is focused on creating psychobiologically-driven animation models, combining neural systems modelling with advanced interactive computer graphics. In creating BL we have adopted a modular approach which facilitates model modification and comparison, as well as allowing models from diverse sources to communicate with one another and drive the required graphical elements. BL allows users to create and control real-time interactive visualizations and realistic animations driven by neural network models.

Given the highly visual environment of BL, there is a natural link between simulation visualization and model development. BL supports both abstract and anatomically-based data visualization and gives real-time feedback in many forms. This is valuable for model development as it enables "soft exploration" of model parameter spaces.

Models in BL are created by linking modular computation units together. Each computation unit, or module, functions as a self-contained black-box and may implement virtually any model at any scale (e.g. from a single neuron to a network). The inputs and outputs of the model are exposed as a module's "variables" which can then be connected to the variables of other modules or used to drive animation parameters. BL supports algorithmic model generation and modification. Within a module, the behaviour of the encapsulated model may change in response to external stimuli and internal feedback. As a simple example, consider a module encapsulating a neural network model. Within the module, the synaptic strengths between neurons are subject to plasticity and may change according to a specified (e.g. Hebbian) learning algorithm. These synaptic strengths may be influenced by feedback as well as external modulatory signals such as phasic dopamine activity.

BL also enables more direct model modification. A user interface system allows users to directly change the values of model parameters using a set of widgets which link to different variables in the system. Variables may directly control the behaviour of an underlying model. As an example, consider the omnipause neurons of the oculomotor system [36]. By changing the time constant of the neuron model, the firing frequency can be adjusted, which in turn affects the nature of saccadic motion. This also may serve as an example of the previously mentioned "soft exploration" of parameter space; the firing rate of the omnipause neuron can be adjusted with reference to the observed behaviour until realistic saccadic motion is observed that is consistent with measurement. The user may do this without having to previously know the exact numerical value of the firing rate or the time constant.

BL is written purely in C for speed and compatibility. It is designed to communicate with other programs via custom interface modules. It can also communicate over sockets and has been successfully used to control remote devices and software systems.

3.1 Modules

The fundamental computational unit of BL is the module. Modules in BL are treated as "black boxes" implementing a time-stepped model. A range of different modules have been implemented in BL embodying relatively simple models such as Leaky-Integrate-and-Fire or Izhikevich-type [27] point neurons to more complex recurrent networks and larger scale models such as a Deep Learning module based on LeCun et al. [31]. There is no theoretical limit on the complexity of a the model contained within a module; BL only requires that the model may be time-stepped. BL provides a range of modules but is intended to be user-extensible; e.g. specific module types can be developed on an as-needed basis.

3.2 Variables

Variables provide access points to modules in BL. Any model input or output may be be accessed as a variable, be it a single value or a multi-dimensional array. In the case of module inputs, the associated variable can be written to and read, while module outputs may only be read (as they are written by the module's internal model).

3.3 Connectors

Connectors link variables together to enable both intra- and inter-module communication. Aside from direct connections, one connector can link several variables and may also perform intermediate calculations on variables. An example of this is the linear transformation connector, which reads one or more variables and combines them in a linear combination before writing the result of this calculation to its destination variable.

3.4 Model Definition

Models in BL are defined by a set of text-based configuration files in a directory structure. This directory structure becomes a hierarchical model structure based on a scene graph; a single root module contains all the modules and connectors as children, grandchildren, great-grandchildren etc. Module files contain parameter and initial values for a module's model, while connector files contain "equations" of variable paths.

3.5 Geometry Definition

Geometry, textures and shaders are also specified in text/image files and are attached to specific modules (and sometimes connectors). Shader uniforms and geometry transformations are accessible to the model as variables of the associated module allowing a tight link between the neurobehavioural model and its visualisation.

4   BL: Interface

The 3D visualisation linked to a BL model can be thought of as the primary end-user interface. Users can see and react to a high quality 3D character (or other visualisation). BL contains modules to receive audio and video input as well as standard keyboard/mouse input, so the model can in turn react to external stimuli.

BL's 3D graphics models are constructed externally, in standard computer graphics formats, and are incorporated into model design. When developing BL models, a user might wish to change the structure of the model, trace/visualise a range of variables or tweak various model parameters and observe the effect on the 3D visualisation. There is hence a definite need for an interface which can visualise and modify any valid BL scene without the need for extensive prior planning.

The user interface developed for BL addresses these needs by providing:

- a general visualisation of any scene's underlying model as a node-graph network
- a general visualisation of any module/connector type and a listing of its associated variables
- tools to view and edit variables
- tools to add new modules and connectors to a scene

The central view of the user interface is a node-graph network visualisation of the scene. Both hierarchical and connector-based relationships are visualised between modules (orange and blue lines respectively). Various graph layout algorithms are used to produce different network layouts. The combination of a hierarchical tree and a directed graph (the hierarchy and "connectome" of a scene) presents challenges in choosing a layout algorithm, as does the potential size and connection density of typical scenes. Presently the hierarchy is taken into account when computing a layout; layouts computed using a force-directed algorithm based on the Fruchterman-Rheingold algorithm [18] have also been experimented with but further work is needed to determine which algorithms may be best suited to BL, and we aim to provide a variety of choices. We also give the user control over direct graphical placement of modules to mimic textbook diagrams of neural circuits.

Larger networks are best visualised using a simple "dots and lines" view, however each module and connector may also be viewed in a more expanded form where each variable is a node on a larger icon. The module icon in particular also contains a visualisation feature allowing any of a module's variables to be viewed, either as a time trace (for a single value) or as a dynamic 2D texture (for arrays). By viewing different variables across several modules the effects of a stimulus can be viewed and traced through a network in real time.

Each module's variables are visible in a collapsible tree view separate from the main network view. By navigating to the appropriate entry in this view, a user may edit single values directly by entering the desired value in a text box or by adjusting a slider. We have found the slider feature to be particularly useful when attempting "soft exploration" of a parameter space, that is, moving a slider within a desired range until the appropriate behaviour is observed, either in a 3D visualisation or in variable time traces.

Modules and connectors may be added to a scene via a wizard interface. In the case of a module, a user specifies where in the hierarchy the module is to be inserted, provides and name and a type, and specifies any necessary parameter values. For a connector, the user must provide a name and a type, and then specify the connections by either searching in the hierarchy for the relevant variables or by manually entering an expression. The interface determines the correct location in the hierarchy for a connector based on the variables used.

The user interface is built using the Qt library. The choice of Qt was motivated by several factors including a need for cross-platform compatibility and extensive and well-developed feature set. Qt also offered extensive documentation and ongoing development as well as an established track record including use in large-scale commercial applications (e.g. Autodesk Maya). Using Qt has also enabled us to add access points to BL for use with a separate interface based on the QML engine. QML user interfaces are interpreted from a set of text files at runtime which allows them to be developed independently of BL's source code making them ideal for end-user-developed interfaces.

5   BL: Examples

This section presents examples in BL of increasing complexity intended to illustrate some of the features previously discussed.

5.1   Simple Oscillator

This model (Fig. 1) implements a simple oscillator circuit using leaky integrator neurons in an excitatory-inhibitory loop. Neuron 1 also has a tonic excitatory input. The neurons are connected using a simple connector type which does not perform any extra mathematical operations on its input variables. In this example there is no 3D geometry supplied so no 3D visualisation appears.

Fig. 1. Simple two neuron circuit (left). Editing the membrane constant of the neurons using a slider. The time trace shows the gradual change in oscillation amplitude as the membrane constant is increased (Centre). Creating a new connection linking the membrane constants of both neurons (Right).

5.2 Knee Jerk

This model (Fig. 2) is an implementation of the patellar reflex as found in [45]. As in the simple oscillator example, the neurons are all modeled as leaky integrators. As the circuit is only described qualitatively in [45], exact parameter values had to be chosen to give reasonable behaviour. There is a 3D visualisation whose movement is controlled linking simulated neuronal voltages to activation weights controlling animation parameters. The relative activation of the two muscles is further visualised by linking a shader uniform controlling brightness to the activation voltages. This connection is achieved using the same syntax (and in fact the same connector) as is used to link the neurons' voltages and inputs.

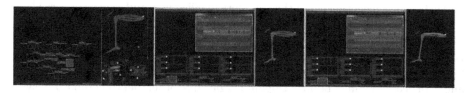

Fig. 2. A network visualisation of the patellar reflex circuit in which the modules have been placed by hand. Custom network layouts in BL can be saved and loaded at a later time. This layout is intended to approximate the layout in the original schematic found in [45] (left) Before and during stimulation of the reflex. Note the time traces showing the stimulus on the muscle spindle (left), the membrane voltages of the extensor (middle) and flexor (right) muscles as well as the 3D visualisation on the left, with the extensor and flexor muscles changing brightness in relation to activation (right).

Fig. 3. The full model hierarchy (orange) and connectome (cyan) of a virtual 3D avatar viewed as a hierarchical tree with two different layout configurations (centre and right). Note the high degree of 'between layers' and long range connections. A small subcircuit is highlighted (left) (Color figure online).

5.3 Virtual Infant Model Baby X

This section gives an overview the demonstrates how the simulation framework applies to a more complex interactive system, an experimental computer generated psychobiological simulation of an infant (BabyX) currently under development, which aims to combine models of the facial motor system and models of basic neural systems involved in early interactive behaviour and learning.The neural models implemented so far in the virtual infant model span the neuroaxis and create muscle activation based animation as motor output from continuously integrated neural models (Fig. 3).

Neural Models. The neural models implemented so far in the virtual infant model span the neuroaxis and create muscle activation based animation as motor output from continuously integrated neural models.

Sensory input is taken live from camera, microphone and other devices. Details of the various computational models from the literature incorporated to date are outside the scope of this overview, but the models have been selected for their wider acceptance and their numerical efficiency, and currently cover key elements of motor control, behaviour selection, reflex, visual attention, learning, salience, emotion and motivation. Neural systems being modelled include the Basal Ganglia, Hippocampus, Hypothalamus, Amygdala, Oculomotor system, Superior Colliculus, Facial Nucleus, and other brainstem nuclei, Cortico-Basal and Cortico-Thalamic Loops, Dopaminergic and other neuromodulatory systems, and higher level models of episodic and working memory.

An example of the interconnected systems in the virtual infant model in action: The camera maps to the simulated retina which detects luminance change and maps to activity on the superior colliculus which resolves competing inputs and directs the oculomotor system (comprised of multiple nuclei) to generate saccadic eye motion which is sent to the animation system. Unexpected stimuli causes dopamine release via the tectonigral pathway. The eyes foveate on the stimuli and if novel or rewarding dopamine is released which affects the Basal Ganglia modifying current motor activity and future response through hebbian plasticity. The amygdala associates the current emotional state with the stimuli, and may trigger hormone release in the hypothalamus and activation of brainstem motor circuits driving facial muscles which produce animation by activating precomputed biomechanically simulated deformations. The response and plasticity of the subsystems are affected by the levels of different neuromodulators and hormones, which also influence the affective state. Because the behaviour of the model is affected by its history as well as external events, the virtual infants's animation results from complex nonlinear system dynamics, self regulated through parametric physiological constraints.

The virtual infant incorporates multiple learning models including unsupervised learning, reinforcement learning, temporal learning, conditioning and action discovery. The microdynamics of early social learning [46] are key in developing realistic interaction, and in related collaborations with the School of Psychology and the Early Learning Laboratory (ELLA) at the University of Auckland we are analyzing and modelling the nuances of more complex behaviours of parent-child interaction which will inform the quality of simulation over time.

Facial Animation. The facial animation of the virtual infant is driven through a neuroanatomical model based on the known architecture of the facial motor system (See [12] for an overview). The model includes both voluntary and emotional facial motor systems. Facial Motor signals are generated by multiple different areas of the brain which project directly or indirectly to the facial nucleus, including the motor cortex, amygdala, hypothalamus, and various brainstem nuclei. The effects of the various drivers can be seen through 'synthetic lesions', for example disabling cortical control of the face. Brainstem pattern generators are modeled using biologically plausible recurrent neural network models and produce activity which is resolved in the facial nucleus before being output as animation weights. For more details of the facial simulation model see [49].

Sensing. A core part of the BL framework is its ability to support sensory input. BL provides connections to a variety of sensors for input to neural network and computer vision models of perception. The virtual infant model uses both video and audio input, and can analyze affect using real time facial tracking, pitch analysis and pattern recognition. For efficiency and accuracy the facial landmarks tracked with computer vision are passed to a specialized solver for facial expression activation weights. In general, most facial expressions can be parameterized using the Facial Action Coding System (FACS) where each AU corresponds to skin motion caused by the contraction of individual or group of muscles [17]. For more details see [49]. For more general object recognition we are using deep convolutional neural networks which exhibit good performance.

Visualization. BL has been designed to visualize simulated neural circuits through multiple modalities including 3D neuroanatomical models. This allows the viewer to see the neural circuits giving rise to behaviour in action in neuroanatomical context at any given time, or in more schematic displays. A key feature of the virtual infant is to graphically look below the skin, to see the activity of the neural circuit models contributing to the activation the facial muscles in action in real-time.

A range of visualisation modalities are available in BL, each being suited to examining different aspects of a simulation. These include time traces and spike raster plots, which may be integrated into the 3D scene or viewed separately, and detailed 3D geometry of anatomical and neuroanatomical features (Fig. 4).

The range of viewing modalities available in BL allows users to viewer various parts of a model in a neuroanatomical context at will as well as offering more traditional "numerically focused" displays which may be better suited for more abstract models and for live model parameter modification.

Realistic facial simulation (Fig. 5) is one of the core objectives of BL's visualization system. BL's rendering engine is based on OpenGL and supports multipass rendering for advanced state of the art shading effects. Custom shaders can be used for the anatomy to add richness to users' visual feedback for example neuroanatomical circuits and regions light up according to their activation.

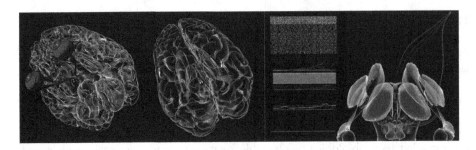

Fig. 4. Different angles of interactive Brain model (left). BL visualization screenshot showing Spike Raster (Centre Top Left) and Neuromodulator Levels (Centre Top Left). Basal Ganglia Model showing a Thalamo-Cortical-BG Feedback Loop (Far Right).

Learning. Various biologically based learning models can be implemented in BL. BL gives the flexibility to view these in different user-definable ways allowing the user a direct insight into the activity and progress of learning circuits, and their inputs and outputs. For example the user can see how various synaptic weights are changing as a result of events during a simulation essentially getting live feedback from the low-level components of a neural network while simultaneously interacting with the high level model.

Example: Facial Mimicry. An example of a fundamental learning mechanism we are exploring is facial mimicry. Facial mimicry is a key example used in the debate over the mirror neuron system [24]. The emergence of Facial mimicry behaviour in the virtual infant is modeled using motor babbling, sensorimotor association and reinforcement learning (Fig. 5, Top).

Intrinsic motor babbling activity is thought to be a fundamental way by which an animal can bootstrap exploration of its motor space (e.g. a specialized circuit for vocal babbling has been discovered in the Songbird [2]) and it is argued that babbling is a fundamental to cognitive development in autonomous intelligent agents [33]. In the model, motor babbling is produced by a specialized recurrent neural network which forms part of the basal ganglia thalamic circuit [20]. The babbling is modulated by the degree of novelty and activity and other physiological parameters. Babbling input contributes to the activation of motor pattern generators which produce a facial animation via the facial nucleus. If the caregiver responds to the virtual infant's expression by mimicking it, intrinsic sensory novelty of the sensed facial activity in the caregiver's response causes phasic DA release in the model modulating the plasticity of the sensorimotor association of the virtual infant's active expression with the caregiver's. Changes in striatal plasticity in the BG model increase the likelihood of the mimicked expression. All of the elements can be visualized simultaneously in BL during a learning session, from dopamine levels to individual synaptic weights to camera input. Without substantial use of visualization constructing and testing an interactive learning model of this nature would be difficult to achieve.

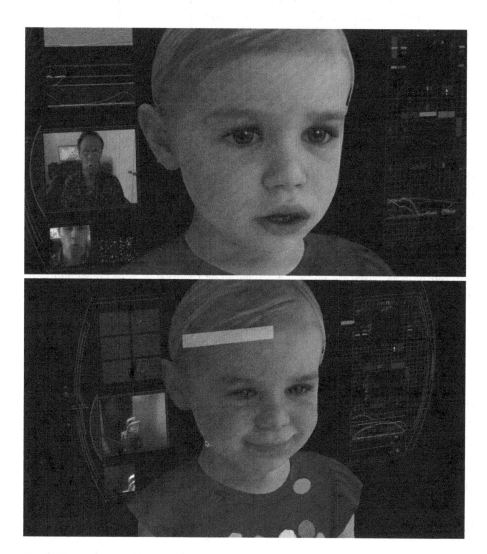

Fig. 5. Sensorimotor learning session screenshot in which multiple inputs and outputs of the model can be viewed simultaneously including: scrolling displays, spike rasters, plasticity, activity of specific neurons, camera input, animated output. This gives the user insight into the performance of the potentially complex system and low level neural circuits during an interaction (Top). Learning to play the classic video game Pong through action discovery. The Bat and Ball are superimposed onto the camera input so no modification to the visual architecture is made, and Motor channels are connected to the bat, so the avatar discovers through motor babbling the control of the bat. The reward from hitting the ball gives the model intrinsic enjoyment (Bottom).

Example: Learning a Video Game Through Intrinsic Motivation. As a simplistic but fun example to demonstrate action discovery and learning through intrinsic motivation we set up the virtual infant to learn to play the classic video game 'Pong' (Fig. 5). The initial setup involved connecting Motor CPGs in the virtual infant to the bat controls, and the mapping the visual input of the pong game to the virtual infant's retina. Motor babbling causes the virtual infant to inadvertently move the bat, much like a baby may flail its arms and hit a rattle. Moving the bat causes a novel change in the visual field and causes phasic dopamine activity, which modulates the plasticity of the striatum and sensorimotor associative neural networks. If the bat hits the ball further environmental response is caused by action, leading to further dopamine release reinforcing the producing behaviour selection associated with the sensory context (Fig. 5, Bottom).

Emotion. Our approach to emotion synthesis is a relatively low level biologically based one, and involves modeling where possible fundamental physiological systems which influence and trigger behaviour. Where available biologically inspired models based on current knowledge or theories of core emotional systems and circuits are being implemented in BL to constitute an initial dynamic systems model of emotion which regulates fundamental behaviour. For example our model of the amygdala has both synaptic connections to the facial nuclei [32,54], but also to the hypothalamus which modulates the release of Corticotrophin releasing hormone (CRH) which triggers a feedback system involving three endocrine glands, the hypothalamic-pituitary-adrenal (HPA) axis [23]. These determine the production of adrenocorticotrophic hormone (ACTH) and then cortisol, which form a physiological correlation of stress in the model, and modulate various behaviours. The use of such low level models means that the user can change the levels (or the receptor weights) of various physiological parameters (such as CRH or tonic Dopamine) to adjust behavioural dynamics and sensitivities (even temperament). The BL architecture allows for low level emotional responses to be driven by higher level cognitive models.

6   Conclusion

We have started to tackle the complexity of interactive expressive facial behaviours involved in autonomous behaviour, social interaction and learning using a bottom up top down approach, through the use of generative low level neurobiological models which are be modulated by higher level neural system models.

We have been able to construct complex (yet relatively simple) interactive neurobehavioural models which are able to be investigated visually in real time using a novel framework, Brain Language (BL). Because of the modular nature of BL we are able to easily modify and update existing subsystems and add new models representing new functionality and anatomy.

An application of the framework has been described in the construction of a virtual infant model, which is an example of a complex system incorporating and embodying a wide range of biologically-based models. This is an example of a bottom up top down approach to represent a complex system, in order to lay the foundations for emergent highly expressive autonomous facial animation involved in social learning and behaviour. We are continuously updating both the graphics and behavioural models.

The BL language and its visual interface are under active development, including the ability for users to dynamically create systems models from scratch as well as modify existing models using intuitive tools. Design goals include the ability to support a wide range of neural models, and to connect with higher level cognitive architectures. The BL architecture may also be suitable for use in other biological system modeling. Developers can add their own custom modules to interface with existing software or devices, and we are interested in collaborations with researchers who wish to implement their models in the BL framework or form live connections with BL based models.

The enormous complexity of modeling human behaviour and dyadic interaction cannot be underestimated, but through developing naturalistic autonomous virtual humans who can embody and process theoretical models of our behaviour and reflect them back at us may give us new insight into fundamental aspects of our nature and interaction with other people.

Acknowledgement. We would like to acknowledge the support of the University of Auckland Strategic Development Fund, CFRIF, and SRIF, Auckland UniServices, Peter Hunter, Andrew Wong, Kieran Brennan, Auckland Bioengineering Institute (ABI): Paul Corballis, Ben Thompson, Centre for Brain Research (CBR), Annette Henderson, Early Learning Lab (ELLA), John Reynolds (Basal Ganglia Research Group and Alistair Knott, (University of Otago).

References

1. Allard, J., Cotin, S., Faure, F., Bensoussan, P.J., Poyer, F., Duriez, C., Delingette, H., Grisoni, L.: Sofa-an open source framework for medical simulation. In: MMVR 15-Medicine Meets Virtual Reality, vol. 125, pp. 13–18. IOP Press (2007)
2. Aronov, D., Andalman, A.S., Fee, M.S.: A specialized forebrain circuit for vocal babbling in the juvenile songbird. Science **320**(5876), 630–634 (2008)
3. Asada, M., Hosoda, K., Kuniyoshi, Y., Ishiguro, H., Inui, T., Yoshikawa, Y., Ogino, M., Yoshida, C.: Cognitive developmental robotics: a survey. IEEE Trans. Auton. Ment. Dev. **1**(1), 12–34 (2009)
4. Asada, M., MacDorman, K.F., Ishiguro, H., Kuniyoshi, Y.: Cognitive developmental robotics as a new paradigm for the design of humanoid robots. Rob. Auton. Syst. **37**(2), 185–193 (2001)
5. Aylett, R., Krenn, B., Pelachaud, C., Shimodaira, H. (eds.): IVA 2013. LNCS, vol. 8108. Springer, Heidelberg (2013)
6. Bandura, A.: Social Foundations of Thought and Action: A Social-cognitive View. Prentice-Hall, New York (1986)
7. Berridge, K.C., Kringelbach, M.L.: Neuroscience of affect: brain mechanisms of pleasure and displeasure. Curr. Opin. Neurobiol. **23**(3), 294–303 (2013)

8. Borghi, A.M., Pecher, D.: Introduction to the special topic embodied and grounded cognition. Front. Psychol. **2**, 187 (2011)
9. Brette, R., Rudolph, M., Carnevale, T., Hines, M., Beeman, D., Bower, J.M., Diesmann, M., Morrison, A., Goodman, P.H., Harris Jr, F.C., et al.: Simulation of networks of spiking neurons: a review of tools and strategies. J. Comput. Neurosci. **23**(3), 349–398 (2007)
10. Cangelosi, A., Schlesinger, M., Smith, L.B.: Developmental Robotics: From Babies to Robots. The MIT Press, Cambridge (2015)
11. Cassell, J.: Embodied Conversational Agents. MIT press, Cambridge (2000)
12. Cattaneo, L., Pavesi, G.: The facial motor system. Neurosci. Biobehav. Rev. **38**, 135–159 (2014)
13. Csibra, G., Gergely, G.: Social learning and social cognition: the case for pedagogy. In: Processes of Change in Brain and Cognitive Development. Attention and Performance XXI, vol. 21, pp. 249–274 (2006)
14. Cultural, E.C.: Culture-gene coevolutionary theory and childrens selective social learning. In: Banaji, M.R., Gelman, S.A.(eds.) Navigating the Social World: What Infants, Children, and Other Species Can Teach us, p. 181 (2013)
15. Damasio, A.: Self Comes to Mind: Constructing the Conscious Brain. Knopf Doubleday Publishing Group, Pantheon (2010)
16. Dayan, P., Abbott, L.F.: Theoretical Neuroscience. MIT Press, Cambridge, MA (2001)
17. Ekman, P., Friesen, W.V., Hager, J.C.: Facial Action Coding System: The Manual. Consulting Psychologists Press, Salt Lake City (2002)
18. Fruchterman, T.M., Reingold, E.M.: Graph drawing by force-directed placement. Softw. Pract. Experience **21**(11), 1129–1164 (1991)
19. Galef Jr, B.G.: Imitation in animals: history, definition, and interpretation of data from the psychological laboratory. In: Zentall, T.R. (ed.) Social learning: Psychological and biological perspectives, pp. 3–28. Lawrence Erlbaum Associates, New Jersey (1988)
20. Goldberg, J.H., Fee, M.S.: Vocal babbling in songbirds requires the basal ganglia-recipient motor thalamus but not the basal ganglia. J. Neurophysiol. **105**(6), 2729–2739 (2011)
21. Gothard, K., Hoffman, K.: Circuits of emotion in the primate brain. In: Platt, M.L., Ghazanfar, A.A. (eds.) Primate Neuroethology, pp. 292–315. Oxford University Press, New York (2010)
22. Gurney, K., Lepora, N., Shah, A., Koene, A., Redgrave, P.: Action discovery and intrinsic motivation: a biologically constrained formalisation. In: Baldassarre, G., Mirolli, M. (eds.) Intrinsically Motivated Learning in Natural and Artificial Systems, pp. 151–181. Springer, Heidelberg (2013)
23. Herman, J.P., Cullinan, W.E.: Neurocircuitry of stress: central control of the hypothalamo-pituitary-adrenocortical axis. Trends Neurosci. **20**(2), 78–84 (1997)
24. Heyes, C.: Where do mirror neurons come from? Neurosci. Biobehav. Rev. **34**(4), 575–583 (2010)
25. Heyes, C.M.: Social learning in animals: categories and mechanisms. Biol. Rev. **69**(2), 207–231 (1994)
26. Heyes, C.M., Galef Jr, B.G.: Social Learning In Animals: The Roots of Culture. Elsevier, Burlington (1996)
27. Izhikevich, E.M., et al.: Simple model of spiking neurons. IEEE Trans. Neural Networks **14**(6), 1569–1572 (2003)
28. Jones, S.S.: Imitation in infancy the development of mimicry. Psychol. Sci. **18**(7), 593–599 (2007)

29. Kohonen, T.: Self-Organization and Associative Memory, 100 figs. XV, p. 312. Springer-Verlag, Berlin Heidelberg New York. Also Springer Series in Information Sciences, vol. 8(1) (1988)

30. Krichmar, J.L., Edelman, G.M.: Machine psychology: autonomous behavior, perceptual categorization and conditioning in a brain-based device. Cereb. Cortex **12**(8), 818–830 (2002)

31. LeCun, Y., Bottou, L., Bengio, Y., Haffner, P.: Gradient-based learning applied to document recognition. Proc. IEEE **86**(11), 2278–2324 (1998)

32. Ledoux, J.: The Emotional Brain: The Mysterious Underpinnings of Emotional Life. Simon & Schuster, New York (1996)

33. Lee, M.H.: Intrinsic activity: from motor babbling to play. In: Proceedings of the First Joint International Conference on Development and Learning (ICDL) and on Epigenetic Robotics (EpiRob) (2011)

34. Lewis, M.D.: Bridging emotion theory and neurobiology through dynamic systems modeling. Behav. Brain Sci. **28**(02), 169–194 (2005)

35. Mingus, B.: Comparison of neural network simulators. http://grey.colorado.edu/emergent/index.phptitle=Comparison_of_Neural_Network_Simulators& oldid=10307. Accessed 27 April 2015

36. Moschovakis, A., Scudder, C., Highstein, S.: The microscopic anatomy and physiology of the mammalian saccadic system. Prog. Neurobiol. **50**(2), 133–254 (1996)

37. O'Reilly, R.C., Hazy, T.E., Mollick, J., Mackie, P., Herd, S.: Goal-driven cognition in the brain: a computational framework (2014). arXiv preprint arXiv:1404.7591

38. O'Reilly, R.C., Hazy, T.E., Herd, S.A.: The leabra cognitive architecture: how to play 20 principles with nature and win! (2012)

39. Panksepp, J.: Affective Neuroscience: The Foundations of Human and Animal Emotions. Oxford University Press, New York (1998)

40. Parke, F.I., Waters, K.: Computer Facial Animation, vol. 289. AK Peters Ltd., Wellesley (1996)

41. Parker, S.G., Johnson, C.R.: Scirun: a scientific programming environment for computational steering. In: Proceedings of the 1995 ACM/IEEE Conference on Supercomputing, p. 52. ACM (1995)

42. Pelachaud, C.: Modelling multimodal expression of emotion in a virtual agent. Philos. Trans. R. Soc. B: Biol. Sci. **364**(1535), 3539–3548 (2009)

43. Picard, R.W., Papert, S., Bender, W., Blumberg, B., Breazeal, C., Cavallo, D., Machover, T., Resnick, M., Roy, D., Strohecker, C.: Affective learning-a manifesto. BT Technol. J. **22**(4), 253–269 (2004)

44. Picard, R.W.: Affective computing. Technical report, M.I.T. Media Laboratory (1995)

45. Purves, D., Augustine, G.J., Fitzpatrick, D., Hall, W.C., LaMantia, A.S., McNamara, J.O., Williams, S.M. (eds.): Neuroscience. Sinauer Associates, Inc., Sunderland (2004)

46. Rohlfing, K., Deak, G.: Microdynamics of interaction: capturing and modeling infants' social learning. IEEE Trans. Auton. Ment. Dev. **5**(3), 189–191 (2013)

47. Rolls, E.T.: Emotion and Decision-making Explained. Oxford University Press, New York (2013)

48. Sagar, M.: Creating models for simulating the face. In: Whittle, J., Clark, T., Kühne, T. (eds.) MODELS 2011. LNCS, vol. 6981, pp. 394–394. Springer, Heidelberg (2011)

49. Sagar, M., Bullivant, D., Robertson, P., Efimov, O., Jawed, K., Kalarot, R., Wu, T.: A neurobehavioural framework for autonomous animation of virtual human faces. In: SIGGRAPH Asia 2014 Autonomous Virtual Humans and Social Robot for Telepresence, p. 2. ACM (2014)

50. Samsonovich, A.V.: Toward a unified catalog of implemented cognitive architectures. In: BICA, vol. 221, pp. 195–244 (2010)

51. Scherer, K.R.: Emotions are emergent processes: they require a dynamic computational architecture. Philos. Trans. R. Soc. B: Biol. Sci. 364(1535), 3459–3474 (2009)

52. Scherer, K.R., Ekman, P., et al. (eds.): Approaches to Emotion. Psychology Press, New York (2014)

53. Sifakis, E., Neverov, I., Fedkiw, R.: Automatic determination of facial muscle activations from sparse motion capture marker data. ACM Trans. Graph. (TOG) 24(3), 417–425 (2005)

54. Snell, R.: Clinical Neuroanatomy. Wolters Kluwer Health/Lippincott Williams & Wilkins, Philadelphia (2010)

55. Terzopoulos, D., Waters, K.: Physically-based facial modelling, analysis, and animation. J. Visual. Comput. Animation 1(2), 73–80 (1990)

56. Tomasello, M., Kruger, A.C., Ratner, H.H.: Cultural learning. Behav. Brain Sci. 16(03), 495–511 (1993)

57. Trappenberg, T.: Fundamentals of Computational Neuroscience. Oxford University Press, New York (2010)

58. Vinciarelli, A., Pantic, M., Heylen, D., Pelachaud, C., Poggi, I., D'Errico, F., Schröder, M.: Bridging the gap between social animal and unsocial machine: a survey of social signal processing. IEEE Trans. Affect. Comput. 3(1), 69–87 (2012)

59. Whiten, A.: Primate culture and social learning. Cogn. Sci. 24(3), 477–508 (2000)

60. Wu, T., Mithraratne, K., Sagar, M., Hunter, P.J.: Characterizing facial tissue sliding using ultrasonography. In: Lim, C.T., Goh, J.C.H. (eds.) WCB 2010, vol. 31, pp. 1566–1569. Springer, Heidelberg (2010)

61. Zeng, Z., Pantic, M., Roisman, G.I., Huang, T.S.: A survey of affect recognition methods: Audio, visual, and spontaneous expressions. IEEE Trans. Pattern Anal. Mach. Intell. 31(1), 39–58 (2009)

62. Zhang, T., Gomes, H.M.: Technology survey on video face tracking. In: IS&T/SPIE Electronic Imaging, pp. 90270F–90270F. International Society for Optics and Photonics (2014)

Computations with Grossone-Based Infinities

Yaroslav D. Sergeyev[1,2,3](✉)

[1] University of Calabria, Rende, Italy
[2] Lobatchevsky State University, Nizhni Novgorod, Russia
[3] Institute of High Performance Computing and Networking, C.N.R., Naples, Italy
yaro@si.dimes.unical.it,
http://wwwinfo.dimes.unical.it/~yaro

Abstract. In this paper, a recent computational methodology is described. It has been introduced with the intention to allow one to work with infinities and infinitesimals numerically in a unique computational framework. It is based on the principle 'The part is less than the whole' applied to all quantities (finite, infinite, and infinitesimal) and to all sets and processes (finite and infinite). The methodology uses as a computational device the Infinity Computer (patented in USA and EU) working numerically with infinite and infinitesimal numbers that can be written in a positional system with an infinite radix. On a number of examples dealing mainly with infinite sets and Turing machines with different infinite tapes it is shown that it becomes possible to execute a fine analysis of these mathematical objects. The accuracy of the obtained results is continuously compared with results obtained by traditional tools used to work with mathematical objects involving infinity.

Keywords: Numbers and numerals · Numerical infinities and infinitesimals · Infinite sets · Turing machines · Infinite sequences

1 Introduction

There exists an important distinction between *numbers* and *numerals*. A *numeral* is a symbol (or a group of symbols) that represents a *number*. A *number* is a concept that a *numeral* expresses. The same number can be represented by different numerals. For example, the symbols '10', 'ten', 'IIIIIIIIII','X', '$\doteq$', and 'Ĩ' are different numerals, but they all represent the same number[1]. Rules used to write

---

Y.D. Sergeyev—This research was partially supported by the Russian Foundation for Basic Research, grant no. 15-01-06612.

[1] The last two numerals, $\doteq$ and Ĩ, are probably less known. The former belongs to the Maya numeral system where one horizontal line indicates five and two lines one above the other indicate ten. Dots are added above the lines to represent additional units. For instance, $\doteq$ means eleven in this numeral system. The latter symbol, Ĩ, belongs to the Cyrillic numeral system derived from the Cyrillic script. This numeral system was developed in the late X^{th} century and was used by South and East Slavic peoples. The system was used in Russia as late as the early XVIIIth century when

C.S. Calude and M.J. Dinneen (Eds.): UCNC 2015, LNCS 9252, pp. 89–106, 2015.
DOI: 10.1007/978-3-319-21819-9_6

down numerals together with algorithms for executing arithmetical operations form a *numeral system*.

In our everyday activities with finite numbers the *same* finite numerals are used for *different* purposes (e.g., the same numeral 10 can be used to express the number of elements of a set, to indicate the position of an element in a sequence, and to execute practical computations). In contrast, when we face the necessity to work with infinities or infinitesimals, the situation changes drastically. In fact, in this case *different* numerals are used to work with infinities and infinitesimals in *different* situations. To illustrate this fact it is sufficient to mention that we use the symbol ∞ in standard analysis, ω for working with ordinals, $\aleph_0, \aleph_1, \ldots$ for dealing with cardinalities.

Many theories dealing with infinite and infinitesimal quantities have a symbolic (not numerical) character. For instance, many versions of non-standard analysis (see [23]) are symbolic, since they have no numeral systems to express their numbers by a finite number of symbols (the finiteness of the number of symbols is necessary for organizing numerical computations). Namely, if we consider a finite n than it can be taken $n = 134$, or $n = 65$ or any other numeral used to express finite quantities and consisting of a finite number of symbols. In contrast, if we consider a non-standard infinite m then it is not clear which numerals can be used to assign a concrete value to m.

Analogously, in non-standard analysis, if we consider an infinitesimal h then it is not clear which numerals consisting of a finite number of symbols can be used to assign a value to h and to write $h = \ldots$ In fact, very often in non-standard analysis texts, a *generic* infinitesimal h is used and it is considered as a symbol, i.e., only symbolic computations can be done with it. Approaches of this kind leave unclear such issues, e.g., whether the infinite $1/h$ is integer or not or whether $1/h$ is the number of elements of an infinite set. If one wishes to consider two infinitesimals h_1 and h_2 then it is not clear how to compare them because numeral systems that can express infinitesimals are not provided by non-standard analysis techniques. In fact, when we work with finite quantities, then we can compare x and y if they assume numerical values, e.g., $x = 25$ and $y = 78$ then, by using rules of the numeral system the symbols 25 and 78 belong to, we can compute that $y > x$.

Even though there exist codes allowing one to work symbolically with ∞ and other symbols related to the concepts of infinity and infinitesimals, traditional computers work numerically only with finite numbers and situations where the usage of infinite or infinitesimal quantities is required are studied mainly theoretically (see [2,3,8,10,11,15,16,23,45] and references given therein). The fact that numerical computations with infinities and infinitesimals have not been implemented so far on computers can be explained by several difficulties. Obviously, among them we can mention the fact that arithmetics developed for this purpose are quite different with respect to the way of computing we use when

---

it was replaced with Arabic numerals. To distinguish numbers from text, a titlo, ̃, is drawn over the symbols showing so that this is a numeral and, therefore, it represents a number and not just a character of text.

we deal with finite quantities. For instance, there exist undetermined operations ($\infty - \infty$, $\frac{\infty}{\infty}$, etc.) that are absent when we work with finite numbers. There exist also practical difficulties that preclude an implementation of numerical computations with infinity and infinitesimals. For example, it is not clear how to store an infinite quantity in a finite computer memory.

A computational methodology introduced recently in [26,32,36,40] allows one to look at infinities and infinitesimals in a new way and to execute *numerical* computations with infinities and infinitesimals on the Infinity Computer patented in USA (see [30]) and other countries. Moreover, this approach proposes a numeral system that uses *the same numerals* for several different purposes for dealing with infinities and infinitesimals: for measuring infinite sets; for indicating positions of elements in ordered infinite sequences; for working with functions and their derivatives that can assume different infinite, finite, and infinitesimal values and can be defined over infinite and infinitesimal domains; for describing Turing machines, etc.

An international scientific community developing a number of interesting theoretical and practical applications in several research areas by using the new methodology grows rapidly. Among these studies it is worthy to mention papers connecting the new approach to the historical panorama of ideas dealing with infinities and infinitesimals (see [17–19,41]). In particular, relations of the new approach to bijections are studied in [19] and metamathematical investigations on the new theory and its non-contradictory can be found in [18]. Then, the new methodology has been applied for studying Euclidean and hyperbolic geometry (see [20,21]), percolation (see [12,13,44]), fractals (see [25,27,35,44]), numerical differentiation and optimization (see [4,28,33,47]), infinite series and the Riemann zeta function (see [29,34,46]), the first Hilbert problem, Turing machines, and lexicographic ordering (see [31,39,41–43]), cellular automata (see [5–7]), ordinary differential equations (see [37,38]), etc. The interested reader is invited to have a look also at surveys [26,32,36] and the book [24] written in a popular way.

In this paper, we briefly describe the new methodology and the numeral system showing how they can be used in a number of situations where infinities and infinitesimals are useful. Infinite sets, bijections, and Turing machines are mainly discussed.

2   Numeral Systems, their Accuracy, and Numbers they can Express

It is necessary to remind that different numeral systems can express different sets of numbers and they can be more or less suitable for executing arithmetical operations. Even the powerful positional system is not able to express, e.g., the number $\sqrt{2}$ by a finite number of symbols (the finiteness is essential for executing numerical computations) and this special numeral, $\sqrt{2}$, is deliberately introduced to express the desired quantity. There exist many numeral systems that are weaker than the positional one. For instance, Roman numeral system is not able to express zero and negative numbers and such expressions as III – VIII or X-X are indeterminate forms in this numeral system. As a result, before appearing the positional numeral system and inventing zero mathematicians were not able to create theorems involving zero and negative numbers and to execute computations with them. Thus, numeral systems seriously bound the possibilities of human beings to compute and developing new, more powerful than existing ones, numeral systems can help a lot both in theory and practice of computations.

Even though Roman numeral system is weaker than the positional one it is not the weakest numeral system. There exist really feeble numeral systems allowing their users to express very few numbers and one of them is illuminating for our study. This numeral system is used by a tribe, Pirahã, living in Amazonia nowadays. A study published in *Science* in 2004 (see [9]) describes that these people use an extremely simple numeral system for counting: one, two, many. For Pirahã, all quantities larger than two are just 'many' and such operations as 2+2 and 2+1 give the same result, i.e., 'many'. Using their weak numeral system Pirahã are not able to see, for instance, numbers 3, 4, and 5, to execute arithmetical operations with them, and, in general, to say anything about these numbers because in their language there are neither words nor concepts for that.

It is worthy to mention that the result 'many' is not wrong. It is just *inaccurate*. Analogously, when we observe a garden with 343 trees, then both phrases: 'There are 343 trees in the garden' and 'There are many trees in the garden' are correct. However, the accuracy of the former phrase is higher than the accuracy of the latter one. Thus, the introduction of a numeral system having numerals for expressing numbers 3 and 4 leads to a higher accuracy of computations and allows one to distinguish results of operations 2+1 and 2+2.

The poverty of the numeral system of Pirahã leads also to the following results

$$\text{'many'} + 1 = \text{'many'}, \quad \text{'many'} + 2 = \text{'many'},$$

$$\text{'many'} - 1 = \text{'many'}, \quad \text{'many'} - 2 = \text{'many'},$$

$$\text{'many'} + \text{'many'} = \text{'many'}$$

that are crucial for changing our outlook on infinity. In fact, by changing in these relations 'many' with ∞ we get relations used to work with infinity in the traditional calculus and Cantor's cardinals

$$\infty + 1 = \infty, \quad \infty + 2 = \infty, \quad \infty - 1 = \infty, \quad \infty - 2 = \infty, \quad \infty + \infty = \infty,$$

$$\aleph_0 + 1 = \aleph_0, \quad \aleph_0 + 2 = \aleph_0, \quad \aleph_0 - 1 = \aleph_0, \quad \aleph_0 - 2 = \aleph_0, \quad \aleph_0 + \aleph_0 = \aleph_0.$$

It should be mentioned that the astonishing numeral system of Pirahã is not an isolated example of this way of counting. In fact, the same counting system, one, two, many, is used by the Warlpiri people, aborigines living in the Northern Territory of Australia (see [1]). The Pitjantjatjara people living in the Central Australian desert use numerals one, two, three, big mob (see [14]) where 'big mob' works as 'many'. It makes sense to remind also another Amazonian tribe – Mundurukú (see [22]) who fail in exact arithmetic with numbers larger than 5 but are able to compare and add large approximate numbers that are far beyond their naming range. Particularly, they use the words 'some, not many' and 'many, really many' to distinguish two types of large numbers. Their arithmetic with 'some, not many' and 'many, really many' reminds strongly the rules Cantor uses to work with $\aleph_0$ and $\aleph_1$, respectively. For instance, compare

'some, not many'+ 'many, really many' = 'many, really many'

with

$$\aleph_0 + \aleph_1 = \aleph_1.$$

This comparison suggests that our difficulty in working with infinity is not connected to the *nature* of infinity but is a result of inadequate numeral systems used to express infinite numbers. Traditional numeral systems have been developed to express finite quantities and they simply have no sufficiently high number of numerals to express different infinities (and infinitesimals). In other words, the difficulty we face is not connected to the object of our study – infinity – but is the result of weak instruments – numeral systems – used for our study.

The way of reasoning where the object of the study is separated from the tool used by the investigator is very common in natural sciences where researchers use tools to describe the object of their study and the used instrument influences the results of the observations and determine their accuracy. When a physicist uses a weak lens A and sees two black dots in his/her microscope he/she does not say: The object of the observation *is* two black dots. The physicist is obliged to say: the lens used in the microscope allows us to see two black dots and it is not possible to say anything more about the nature of the object of the observation until we change the instrument - the lens or the microscope itself - by a more precise one. Suppose that he/she changes the lens and uses a stronger lens B and is able to observe that the object of the observation is viewed as eleven (smaller) black dots. Thus, we have two different answers: (i) the object is viewed as two dots if the lens A is used; (ii) the object is viewed as eleven dots by applying the lens B. Both answers are correct but with the *different accuracies* that depend on the lens used for the observation.

The same happens in Mathematics studying natural phenomena, numbers, objects that can be constructed by using numbers, sets, etc. Numeral systems used to express numbers are among the instruments of observations used by mathematicians. As we have illustrated above, the usage of powerful numeral systems gives the possibility to obtain more precise results in Mathematics in the same way as usage of a good microscope gives the possibility of obtaining more precise results in Physics.

3   Grossone-Based Numerals

In order to increase the accuracy of computations with infinities and infinitesimals, the computational methodology developed in [24, 26, 32] proposes a numeral system that allows one to observe infinities and infinitesimals with a higher accuracy. This numeral system avoids situations similar to 'many' $+1 =$ 'many' and $\infty - 1 = \infty$ providing results ensuring that if a is a numeral written in this numeral system then for any a (i.e., a can be finite, infinite, or infinitesimal) it follows $a + 1 > a$ and $a - 1 < a$.

The numeral system is based on a new infinite unit of measure expressed by the numeral ① called *grossone* that is introduced as the number of elements of the set of natural[2] numbers

$$\mathbb{N} = \{1, 2, 3, \dots \}. \tag{1}$$

Concurrently with the introduction of ① in the mathematical language all other symbols (like ∞, Cantor's ω, $\aleph_0, \aleph_1, \dots$, etc.) traditionally used to deal with infinities and infinitesimals are excluded from the language because ① and other numbers constructed with its help not only can be used instead of all of them but can be used with a higher accuracy. Analogously, when zero and the positional numeral system had been introduced in Europe, Roman numerals I, V, X, etc. had not been involved and new symbols 0, 1, 2, etc. had been used to express numbers. The new element – zero expressed by the numeral 0 – had been introduced by describing its properties in the form of axioms. Analogously, ① is introduced by describing its properties postulated by the Infinite Unit Axiom added to axioms for real numbers (see [26, 32] for a detailed discussion). Let us comment upon some of properties of ①.

If we consider a finite integer k, then the number of elements of the set $\{1, 2, 3, \dots k - 1, k\}$ is its largest element, i.e., k. For instance, the number 4 in the set

$$A = \{1, 2, 3, 4\} \tag{2}$$

is the largest element in the set A and the number of elements of A. Grossone has been introduced as the number of elements of the set of natural numbers and, therefore, we have the same situation as in (2), i.e., ① $\in \mathbb{N}$. As a consequence, the introduction of ① allows us to write down the set of natural numbers as follows

$$\mathbb{N} = \{1, 2, \ \dots \ \frac{①}{2} - 2, \frac{①}{2} - 1, \frac{①}{2}, \frac{①}{2} + 1, \frac{①}{2} + 2, \ \dots \ ① - 2, \ ① - 1, \ ①\}. \tag{3}$$

Infinite natural numbers

$$\dots \ \frac{①}{2} - 2, \frac{①}{2} - 1, \frac{①}{2}, \frac{①}{2} + 1, \frac{①}{2} + 2, \ \dots \ ① - 2, ① - 1, ① \tag{4}$$

that are invisible if traditional numeral systems are used to observe the set of natural numbers can be viewed now thanks to the introduction of ①. The two records, (1) and (3), refer to the same set – the set of natural numbers – and

---

[2] Notice that nowadays not only positive integers but also zero is frequently included in $\mathbb{N}$. However, since zero has been invented significantly later than positive integers used for counting objects, zero is not include in $\mathbb{N}$ in this text.

infinite numbers (4) also take part[3] of $\mathbb{N}$. Both records, (1) and (3), are correct and do not contradict each other. They just use two different numeral systems to express $\mathbb{N}$. Traditional numeral systems do not allow us to see infinite natural numbers that we can observe now thanks to grossone. Thus, we have the same object of observation – the set $\mathbb{N}$ – that can be observed by different instruments – numeral systems – with different accuracies.

Similarly, Pirahã are not able to see finite natural numbers 3, 4, and 5. In spite of the fact that Pirahã do not see them, these numbers 3, 4, and 5, belong to $\mathbb{N}$ and are visible if one uses a more powerful numeral system. Even the numeral system of Mundurukú is sufficient to observe 3, 4, and 5. Notice also that the weakness of their numeral system does not allow Pirahã to define the set (2) while Mundurukú would be able to do this.

In general, in the new methodology it is necessary always to indicate a numeral system used for computations and theoretical investigations. For instance, the words 'the set of all finite numbers' do not define a set completely in this methodology. It is always necessary to specify which instruments (numeral systems) are used to describe (and to observe) the required set and, as a consequence, to speak about 'the set of all finite numbers expressible in a fixed numeral system'. For instance, for Pirahã and Warlpiri 'the set of all finite numbers' is the set $\{1, 2\}$, for the Pitjantjatjara people 'the set of all finite numbers' is the set $\{1, 2, 3\}$ and for Mundurukú 'the set of all finite numbers' is the set $\{1, 2, 3, 4, 5\}$. We stress again that in Mathematics, as it happens in Physics, the instrument used for an observation bounds the possibility of the observation and defines the accuracy of this observation. It is not possible to say how we shall see the object of our observation if we have not clarified which instruments will be used to execute the observation.

Let us see now how one can write down different numerals expressing different infinities and infinitesimals and to execute computations with all of them. Instead of the usual symbol ∞ different infinite and/or infinitesimal numerals can be used thanks to ①. Indeterminate forms are not present and, for example, the following relations hold for infinite numbers ①, ①^2 and ①$^{-1}$, ①$^{-2}$ (that are infinitesimals), as for any other (finite, infinite, or infinitesimal) number expressible in the new numeral system

$$0 \cdot ① = ① \cdot 0 = 0, \quad ① - ① = 0, \quad \frac{①}{①} = 1, \quad ①^0 = 1, \quad 1^① = 1, \quad 0^① = 0,$$

$$0 \cdot ①^{-1} = ①^{-1} \cdot 0 = 0, \quad ①^{-1} > 0, \quad ①^{-2} > 0, \quad ①^{-1} - ①^{-1} = 0,$$

$$\frac{①^{-1}}{①^{-1}} = 1, \quad (①^{-1})^0 = 1, \quad ① \cdot ①^{-1} = 1, \quad ① \cdot ①^{-2} = ①^{-1},$$

$$\frac{①^{-2}}{①^{-2}} = 1, \quad \frac{①^2}{①} = ①, \quad \frac{①^{-1}}{①^{-2}} = ①, \quad ①^2 \cdot ①^{-1} = ①, \quad ①^2 \cdot ①^{-2} = 1.$$

---

[3] This is a difference with respect to non-standard analysis where infinities it works with do not belong to $\mathbb{N}$.

The introduction of the numeral ① allows us to represent infinite and infinitesimal numbers in a unique framework. For this purpose a numeral system similar to traditional positional numeral systems was introduced in [24, 26]. To construct a number C in the numeral positional system with the radix grossone, we subdivide C into groups corresponding to powers of ①:

$$C = c_{p_m} ①^{p_m} + \ldots + c_{p_1} ①^{p_1} + c_{p_0} ①^{p_0} + c_{p_{-1}} ①^{p_{-1}} + \ldots + c_{p_{-k}} ①^{p_{-k}}. \quad (5)$$

Then, the record

$$C = c_{p_m} ①^{p_m} \ldots c_{p_1} ①^{p_1} c_{p_0} ①^{p_0} c_{p_{-1}} ①^{p_{-1}} \ldots c_{p_{-k}} ①^{p_{-k}} \quad (6)$$

represents the number C, where all numerals $c_i \neq 0$, they belong to a traditional numeral system and are called *grossdigits*. They express finite positive or negative numbers and show how many corresponding units $①^{p_i}$ should be added or subtracted in order to form the number C. Note that in order to have a possibility to store C in the computer memory, values k and m should be finite.

Numbers p_i in (6) are sorted in the decreasing order with $p_0 = 0$

$$p_m > p_{m-1} > \ldots > p_1 > p_0 > p_{-1} > \ldots p_{-(k-1)} > p_{-k}.$$

They are called *grosspowers* and they themselves can be written in the form (6). In the record (6), we write $①^{p_i}$ explicitly because in the new numeral positional system the number i in general is not equal to the grosspower p_i. This gives the possibility to write down numerals without indicating grossdigits equal to zero.

The term having $p_0 = 0$ represents the finite part of C since $c_0 ①^0 = c_0$. Terms having finite positive grosspowers represent the simplest infinite parts of C. Analogously, terms having negative finite grosspowers represent the simplest infinitesimal parts of C. For instance, the number $①^{-1} = \frac{1}{①}$ mentioned above is infinitesimal. Note that all infinitesimals are not equal to zero. In particular, $\frac{1}{①} > 0$ since it is a result of division of two positive numbers.

A number represented by a numeral in the form (6) is called *purely finite* if it has neither infinite nor infinitesimals parts. For instance, 14 is purely finite and $14 + 5.3①^{-1.5}$ is not. All grossdigits c_i are supposed to be purely finite. Purely finite numbers are used on traditional computers and for obvious reasons have a special importance for applications. All of the numbers introduced above can be grosspowers, as well, giving thus a possibility to have various combinations of quantities and to construct terms having a more complex structure. *

We conclude this section by emphasizing that different numeral systems, if they have different accuracies, cannot be used together. For instance, the usage of '*many*' from the language of Pirahã in the record $5 + $'*many*' has no any sense because for Pirahã it is not clear what 5 is and for people knowing what 5 is the accuracy of the answer 'many' is too low. Analogously, the records of the type $①+\omega$, $①-\aleph_0$, $①/\infty$, etc. have no sense because they include numerals developed under different methodological assumptions, in different mathematical contests, for different purposes, and, finally, numeral systems these numerals belong to have different accuracies.

4 Measuring Infinite Sets and Relations to Bijections

By using the ①-based numeral system it becomes possible to measure certain infinite sets. As we have seen above, relations of the type 'many' $+ 1 =$ 'many' and $\aleph_0 - 1 = \aleph_0$ are consequences of the weakness of numeral systems applied to express numbers (finite or infinite). Thus, one of the principles of the new computational methodology consists of adopting the principle 'The part is less than the whole' to all numbers (finite, infinite, and infinitesimal) and to all sets and processes (finite and infinite). Notice that this principle is a reformulation of Euclid's Common Notion 5 saying 'The whole is greater than the part'.

Let us show how, in comparison to the traditional mathematical tools used to work with infinity, the new numeral system allows one to obtain more precise answers in certain cases. For instance, Table 1 compares results obtained by the traditional Cantor's cardinals and the new numeral system with respect to the measure of a dozen of infinite sets (for a detailed discussion regarding the results presented in Table 1 and for more examples dealing with infinite sets see [18, 19, 31, 32, 41]). Notice, that in $\mathbb{Q}$ and $\mathbb{Q}'$ we calculate different numerals and not numbers. For instance, numerals $\frac{4}{1}$ and $\frac{8}{2}$ have been counted two times even though they represent the same number 4. Then, four sets of numerals having the cardinality of continuum are shown in Table 1 (these results are discussed more in detail in the next section). Among them we denote by A_2 the set of numbers $x \in [0, 1)$ expressed in the binary positional numeral system, by A'_2 the set being the same as A_2 but with x belonging to the closed interval $[0, 1]$, by A_{10} the set of numbers $x \in [0, 1)$ expressed in the decimal positional numeral system, and finally we have the set $C_{10} = A_{10} \cup B_{10}$, where B_{10} is the set of numbers

Table 1. Measuring infinite sets using ①-based numerals allows one in certain cases to obtain more precise answers in comparison with the traditional cardinalities, $\aleph_0$ and $\mathcal{C}$, of Cantor.

Description of sets	Cardinality	Number of elements
the set of natural numbers $\mathbb{N}$	countable, $\aleph_0$	①
$\mathbb{N} \cup \{0\}$	countable, $\aleph_0$	① $+ 1$
$\mathbb{N} \setminus \{3, 5, 10, 23, 114\}$	countable, $\aleph_0$	① $- 5$
the set of even numbers $\mathbb{E}$	countable, $\aleph_0$	$\frac{①}{2}$
the set of odd numbers $\mathbb{O}$	countable, $\aleph_0$	$\frac{①}{2}$
the set of integers $\mathbb{Z}$	countable, $\aleph_0$	$2① + 1$
$\mathbb{Z} \setminus \{0\}$	countable, $\aleph_0$	$2①$
the set of square natural numbers $\mathbb{G} = \{x : x = n^2, x \in \mathbb{N}, n \in \mathbb{N}\}$	countable, $\aleph_0$	$\lfloor \sqrt{①} \rfloor$
the set of pairs of natural numbers $\mathbb{P} = \{(p, q) : p \in \mathbb{N}, q \in \mathbb{N}\}$	countable, $\aleph_0$	$①^2$
the set of numerals $\mathbb{Q}' = \{-\frac{p}{q}, \frac{p}{q} : p \in \mathbb{N}, q \in \mathbb{N}\}$	countable, $\aleph_0$	$2①^2$
the set of numerals $\mathbb{Q} = \{0, -\frac{p}{q}, \frac{p}{q} : p \in \mathbb{N}, q \in \mathbb{N}\}$	countable, $\aleph_0$	$2①^2 + 1$
the set of numerals A_2	continuum, $\mathcal{C}$	$2^①$
the set of numerals A'_2	continuum, $\mathcal{C}$	$2^① + 1$
the set of numerals A_{10}	continuum, $\mathcal{C}$	$10^①$
the set of numerals C_{10}	continuum, $\mathcal{C}$	$2 \cdot 10^①$

$x \in [1, 2)$ expressed in the decimal positional numeral system. It is worthwhile to notice also that grossone-based numbers from Table 1 can be ordered as follows

$$\lfloor\sqrt{①}\rfloor < \frac{①}{2} < ① - 5 < ① < 2① < 2① + 1 <$$

$$①^2 < 2①^2 + 1 < 2^① < 2^① + 1 < 10^① < 2 \cdot 10^①.$$

It can be seen from Table 1 that Cantor's cardinalities say only whether a set is countable or uncountable while the ①-based numerals allow us to express the exact number of elements of the infinite sets. However, both numeral systems – the new one and the numeral system of infinite cardinals – do not contradict one another. Both Cantor's numeral system and the new one give correct answers, but their answers have *different accuracies*. By using an analogy from physics we can say that the lens of our new 'telescope' used to observe infinities and infinitesimals is stronger and where Cantor's 'telescope' allows one to distinguish just two dots (countable sets and the continuum) we are able to see many different dots (infinite sets having different number of elements).

The ①-base numeral system, as all numeral systems, cannot express all numbers and give answers to all questions. Let us consider, for instance, the set of *extended natural numbers* indicated as $\widehat{\mathbb{N}}$ and including $\mathbb{N}$ as a proper subset

$$\widehat{\mathbb{N}} = \{\underbrace{1, 2, \ldots, ① - 1, ①}_{\text{Natural numbers}}, ① + 1, ① + 2, \ldots, 2① - 1, 2①, 2① + 1, \ldots$$

$$①^2 - 1, ①^2, ①^2 + 1, \ldots 3①^① - 1, 3①^①, 3①^① + 1, \ldots\}. \tag{7}$$

What can we say with respect to the number of elements of the set $\widehat{\mathbb{N}}$? The introduced numeral system based on grossone is too weak to give an answer to this question. It is necessary to introduce in a way a more powerful numeral system by defining new numerals (for instance, ②, ③, etc.).

In order to see how the principle 'The part is less than the whole' agrees with traditional views on infinite sets, let us consider two illustrative examples. The first of them is related to the one-to-one correspondence that can be established between the sets of natural and odd numerus. Namely, odd numbers can be put in a one-to-one correspondence with all natural numbers in spite of the fact that $①$ is a proper subset of $\mathbb{N}$

$$\begin{array}{lll} \text{odd numbers:} & 1, 3, 5, 7, 9, 11, \ldots \\ & \updownarrow \updownarrow \updownarrow \updownarrow \updownarrow \updownarrow & \tag{8} \\ \text{natural numbers:} & 1, 2, 3, 4\ 5, 6, \ldots \end{array}$$

The usual conclusion is that both sets are countable and they have the same cardinality $\aleph_0$.

Let us see now what we can say from the new methodological positions. We know now that when one executes the operation of counting, the accuracy of the result depends on the numeral system used for counting. Proposing to Pirahã to measure sets consisting of four apples and five apples would give us the answer that both sets of apples have many elements. This answer is correct but its precision is low due to the weakness of the numeral system used to measure the sets.

Thus, the introduction of the notion of accuracy for measuring sets is very important and should be applied for infinite sets also. Since for cardinal numbers it follows

$$\aleph_0 + 1 = \aleph_0, \quad \aleph_0 + 2 = \aleph_0, \quad \aleph_0 + \aleph_0 = \aleph_0,$$

these relations suggest that the accuracy of the cardinal numeral system of Alephs an is not sufficiently high to see the difference with respect to the number of elements of the two sets from (8).

In order to look at the record (8) using the new numeral system we need the following fact from [24]: the sets of even and odd numbers have $①/2$ elements each and, therefore, $①$ grossone is even. It is also necessary to remind that numbers that are larger than $①$ are not natural, they are extended natural numbers. For instance, $① + 1$ is odd but not natural, it is extended natural, see (7). Thus, the last odd natural number is $① - 1$. Since the number of elements of the set of odd numbers is equal to $\frac{①}{2}$, we can write down not only initial (as it is usually done traditionally) but also the final part of (8)

$$
\begin{array}{cccccccccc}
1, & 3, & 5, & 7, & 9, & 11, & \ldots & ① - 5, & ① - 3, & ① - 1 \\
\updownarrow & \updownarrow & \updownarrow & \updownarrow & \updownarrow & \updownarrow & & \updownarrow & \updownarrow & \updownarrow \\
1, & 2, & 3, & 4 \ 5, & 6, & \ldots & & \frac{①}{2} - 2, & \frac{①}{2} - 1, & \frac{①}{2}
\end{array}
\tag{9}
$$

concluding so (8) in a complete accordance with the principle 'The part is less than the whole'. Both records, (8) and (9), are correct but (9) is more accurate, since it allows us to observe the final part of the correspondence that is invisible if (8) is used.

The accuracy of the $①$-based numeral system allows us to measure also, for instance, such sets as $\mathbb{O}' = \mathbb{O}\backslash\{3\}$ and $\mathbb{O}'' = \mathbb{O}\backslash\{1, ① - 1\}$. The set $\mathbb{O}'$ is constructed by excluding one element from $\mathbb{O}$ and the set $\mathbb{O}''$ by excluding from $\mathbb{O}$ two elements. Thus, $\mathbb{O}'$ and $\mathbb{O}''$ have $\frac{①}{2} - 1$ and $\frac{①}{2} - 2$ elements, respectively. In case one wishes to establish the corresponding bijections, starting with natural numbers $1, 2, 3, \ldots$ we obtain for these two sets

$$
\begin{array}{cccccccccc}
1, & 5, & 7, & 9, & 11, & 13, & \ldots & ①-5, & ①-3, & ①-1 \\
\updownarrow & \updownarrow & \updownarrow & \updownarrow & \updownarrow & \updownarrow & & \updownarrow & \updownarrow & \updownarrow \\
1, & 2, & 3, & 4 \ 5, & 6, & \ldots & & \frac{①}{2} - 3, & \frac{①}{2} - 2, & \frac{①}{2} - 1
\end{array}
\tag{10}
$$

$$
\begin{array}{cccccccccc}
3, & 5, & 7, & 9, & 11, & 13, & \ldots & ① - 7, & ① - 5, & ① - 3 \\
\updownarrow & \updownarrow & \updownarrow & \updownarrow & \updownarrow & \updownarrow & & \updownarrow & \updownarrow & \updownarrow \\
1, & 2, & 3, & 4 \ 5, & 6, & \ldots & & \frac{①}{2} - 4, & \frac{①}{2} - 3, & \frac{①}{2} - 2
\end{array}
\tag{11}
$$

In order to become more familiar with natural and extended natural numbers let us consider one more example where we multiply each element of the set of natural numbers, $\mathbb{N}$, by 2. We would like to study the resulting set, that is called $\mathbb{E}^2$ hereinafter, to calculate the number of its elements, and to specify which among its elements are natural and which ones are extended natural numbers and how many they are.

The introduction of the new numeral system allows us to write down the set, $\mathbb{N}$, of natural numbers in the form (7). By definition, the number of elements of $\mathbb{N}$ is equal to ①. Thus, after multiplication of each of the elements of $\mathbb{N}$ by 2, the resulting set, $\mathbb{E}^2$, will also have grossone elements. In particular, the number $\frac{①}{2}$ multiplied by 2 gives us ① and $\frac{①}{2}+1$ multiplied by 2 gives us $①+2$ that is even extended natural number, see (7). Analogously, the last element of $\mathbb{N}$, i.e., ①, multiplied by 2 gives us 2①. Thus, the set of even numbers $\mathbb{E}^2$ can be written as follows

$$\mathbb{E}^2 = \{2, 4, 6, \ \ldots \ ① - 4, ① - 2, ①, ① + 2, ① + 4, \ \ldots \ 2① - 4, 2① - 2, 2①\},$$

where numbers $\{2, 4, 6, \ \ldots \ ① - 4, ① - 2, ①\}$ are even and natural (they are $\frac{①}{2}$) and numbers $\{① + 2, ① + 4, \ \ldots \ 2① - 4, 2① - 2, 2①\}$ are even and extended natural, they also are $\frac{①}{2}$.

5 Turing Machines and Infinite Sequences

In this section we present some results related to Turing machines with infinite tapes (the presentation has been simplified, see [41,42] for a comprehensive discussion). Traditionally, an *infinite sequence* $\{a_n\}, a_n \in A, n \in \mathbb{N}$, is defined as a function having the set of natural numbers, $\mathbb{N}$, as the domain and a set A as the codomain. A *subsequence* $\{b_n\}$ is defined as a sequence $\{a_n\}$ from which some of its elements have been removed. In spite of the fact that the removal of the elements from $\{a_n\}$ can be directly observed, the traditional point of view on sequences does not allow one to register, in the case where the obtained subsequence $\{b_n\}$ is infinite, the fact that $\{b_n\}$ has less elements than the original infinite sequence $\{a_n\}$.

Let us study what happens when the new approach is used. The definition of infinite sequences should be done more precise in a complete analogy to finite sequences. In the finite case, to define a sequence $a_1, a_2, \ldots, a_n$ the number, n, of its elements should be explicitly declared. Thanks to the introduction of ①-based numerals we are able to express infinite numbers, as well and, as a consequence, we extend this definition directly to the infinite case, i.e., to define an infinite sequence $a_1, a_2, \ldots, a_n$ its infinite number of elements, n, should be provided.

Since the new numeral system allows us to express the number of elements of the set $\mathbb{N}$ as ① grossone and due to the sequence definition given above, any sequence having $\mathbb{N}$ as the domain has grossone elements. Such sequences are called *complete*. Notice that, among other things, this definition states that there cannot exist infinite sequences having more than ① elements. However, since we can express infinite integers less than ①, infinite sequences having less than ① elements can exist and can be described using ①-based numerals. In fact, the notion of subsequence is introduced as a sequence from which some of its elements have been removed. This means that the resulting subsequence will have less elements than the original sequence and the infinite number of elements of infinite subsequences can be expressed.

For instance, let us consider two infinite sequences: $\{a_n\}$ and $\{b_n\}$. The first sequence $\{a_n\}$, $1 \leq n \leq ①$, with $a_n = n - 1$. This sequence has $①$ elements and it is, therefore, complete. Its first element is $a_1 = 0$ and its last element is $a_① = ① - 1$. The second infinite sequence, $\{b_n\}$, that is a subsequence of the first one is defined as follows: $\{b_n\}$, $1 \leq n \leq 0.5①$, with $b_n = n - 1$. Thus, both sequences, $\{a_n\}$ and $\{b_n\}$, have the same general element, $a_n = b_n = n - 1$, the same first element, $a_1 = b_1 = 0$, and both are infinite but the first sequence is complete and the second one is not since it has $0.5① < ①$ elements and its last element is $b_{0.5①} = 0.5① - 1$.

Suppose now that we have a Turing machine with an infinite tape that contains an output written using symbols $\{0, 1, \ldots b - 2, b - 1\}$ with a finite b. The traditional point of view allows us to distinguish neither tapes having different infinite lengths nor machines using different alphabets, i.e., $\{0, 1, \ldots B - 2, B - 1\}$ with $B \neq b$. The question of the possibility to have different infinite tapes is not discussed and it is supposed that machines with all output alphabets have the same computational power if their tapes are infinite. This happens because the traditional numeral systems used to describe Turing machines do not allow us to see these differences. The new numeral system offers such a possibility giving a chance to describe Turing machines in a more precise way and to distinguish them at infinity.

In the new framework, it is not sufficient to say that the tape is infinite. It is necessary to define the infinite length of the tape explicitly. As an example, let us consider a Turing machine having the tape $①$ positions long. Output sequences are written on the tape using symbols from an output alphabet, let it be again $\{0, 1, \ldots b - 2, b - 1\}$ with a finite b. The importance of the discussion on the infinite sequences provided above for Turing machines becomes clear now: the output sequences of symbols, as all sequences, though infinite cannot have more than $①$ elements.

Moreover, we can make a more accurate analysis and count the precise number of infinite output sequences of symbols that the machine can produce. It is obvious that its outputs can be viewed as numerals in the positional numeral system with the finite radix b

$$(a_1 a_2 \ldots a_{①-1} a_①)_b, \quad a_i \in \{0, 1, \ldots b - 2, b - 1\}, \quad 1 \leq i \leq ①. \tag{12}$$

This means that we have $①$ positions that can be filled in with b symbols each, i.e., this machine called hereinafter T_1 can produce $b^①$ different outputs. Then, if we consider another machine, T_2, having the tape with $① - 1$ positions and outputs written using the same base, b, the number of its outputs is $b^{①-1} < b^①$ and each of them is one position shorter than outputs of T_1. Moreover, if we consider the third machine, T_3, having the tape with $①$ positions and outputs written using a base $B > b$, the number of its outputs is $B^① > b^①$. In other words, the machine T_3 is more powerful then the machine T_1 that, in its turn, is more powerful than the machine T_2.

Let us give a couple of illustrations. We start by considering a Turing machine T_4 working with the alphabet $\{0, 1, 2\}$, the tape with ①/2 positions, and computing the following output

$$\underbrace{0, 1, 2, 0, 1, 2, 0, 1, 2, \ \ldots \ 0, 1, 2, 0, 1, 2}_{①/2 \text{ positions}}. \tag{13}$$

Then a Turing machine T_5 working with the output alphabet $\{0, 1\}$ and the tape with ①/2 positions cannot produce a sequence of symbols computing (13). In fact, since the numeral 2 does not belong to the alphabet $\{0, 1\}$ it should be coded by more than one symbol. One of codifications using the minimal number of symbols in the alphabet $\{0, 1\}$ necessary to code numbers $0, 1, 2$ is $\{00, 01, 10\}$. Then the output corresponding to (13) and computed in this codification should be

$$00, 01, 10, 00, 01, 10, 00, 01, 10, \ \ldots \ 00, 01, 10, 00, 01, 10. \tag{14}$$

Since the output (13) contains ①/2 positions, the output (14) should contain ① positions. However, by the definition of T_5 it can produce outputs that have only ①/2 positions.

Let us consider now a Turing machine T_6 working with the alphabet $\{0, 1, 2\}$ as T_4 but the infinite tape of T_6 is one position longer than the tape of T_4, i.e., it has ①/2+1 positions, and T_6 computes the following output

$$\underbrace{0, 1, 2, 0, 1, 2, 0, 1, 2, \ \ldots \ 0, 1, 2, 0, 1, 2, 0}_{①/2+1 \text{ positions}}. \tag{15}$$

Then there is no a Turing machine working with the output alphabet $\{0, 1\}$ and coding the numbers $0, 1, 2$ as $\{00, 01, 10\}$ such that it is able to compute the output corresponding to (15) in this codification. The proof is very easy and is based on the fact that infinite sequences cannot have more than ① elements. Since the output (15) contains ①/2 + 1 positions, the output

$$00, 01, 10, 00, 01, 10, 00, 01, 10, \ \ldots \ 00, 01, 10, 00, 01, 10, 00.$$

should contain ① + 2 positions. However, infinite sequences cannot have more than ① elements. Notice that significantly more sophisticated results for deterministic and non-deterministic Turing machines can be found in [41–43].

6   Concluding Remarks

In this paper infinite sets and Turing machines with different infinite tapes have been studied using a recently introduced positional numeral system with the infinite radix ①. It has been shown that in certain cases the new numerals allow one to obtain more precise results in dealing with infinite quantities in comparison to numeral systems traditionally used for this purpose.

In particular, the following observation (see [31] for a detailed discussion) can be made for the set C_b^k of numerals expressible in the positional numeral system with the finite radix b and k digits $\{0, 1, \ldots b - 2, b - 1\}$ where k is infinite

$$(a_1 a_2 \ldots a_{k-1} a_k)_b, \qquad a_i \in \{0, 1, \ldots b - 2, b - 1\}, \ \ 1 \le i \le k. \tag{16}$$

Clearly, this is a simple generalization of the record (12) where we have $k = ①$. Analogously to the analysis made above it follows that the number of numerals expressible in the system (16) is b^k and for infinite values of k the set C_b^k should have the cardinality of continuum in the traditional language. Let us consider now $k_1 = \lfloor \log_b ① \rfloor$ where $\lfloor x \rfloor$ is the integer part of x. Note that k_1 is infinite since $①$ is infinite. It follows then that

$$b^{\lfloor \log_b ① \rfloor} < b^{\log_b ①} = ①,$$

i.e., with respect to the traditional language the set $C_b^{\log_b ①}$ would be countable. Analogously, many different instances of infinite sets that are constructed starting from the continuum framework and resulting at the end to be countable can be exhibited. For example, for infinite $k = 3\lfloor \log_b ① \rfloor$ and $k = 0.5\lfloor \log_b ① \rfloor$ it follows that

$$b^{3\lfloor \log_b ① \rfloor} < b^{3\log_b ①} = ①^3 < b^①, \qquad b^{0.5\lfloor \log_b ① \rfloor} < b^{0.5\log_b ①} = \sqrt{①} < b^①,$$

i.e., the sets $C_b^{3\log_b ①}$ and $C_b^{0.5\log_b ①}$ would be also countable from the traditional point of view.

Thus, the $①$-based numeral system allows us to distinguish new infinite sets that were invisible using traditional instruments both within continuum and numerable sets. Thanks to the $①$-based numerals it becomes possible to calculate the exact number of elements of old (see Table 1) and new sets and to exhibit sets that were constructed as continuum but are indeed countable bridging so the gap between the two groups of sets (see [31] for a detailed discussion). This fact, among other things, allows us to see that the computational power of Turing machines with different infinite tapes is different. Reminding our example with the microscope we are able now to see instead of two dots (countable and continuum) many different dots.

In this paper only two applications where $①$-based numerals are useful have been discussed: infinite sets and Turing machines. More examples showing how these numerals can be successfully used can be found in the following publications: Euclidean and hyperbolic geometry (see [20,21]), percolation (see [12,13,44]), fractals (see [25,27,35,44]), infinite series and the Riemann zeta function (see [29,34,46]), the first Hilbert problem and lexicographic ordering (see [31,39,41–43]), cellular automata (see [5–7]).

In particular, numerical computations with infinities and infinitesimals expressed by $①$-based numerals are discussed in the following papers: numerical differentiation, solutions of systems of linear equations, and optimization (see [4,28,33,47]), ordinary differential equations (see [37,38]).

References

1. Butterworth, B., Reeve, R., Reynolds, F., Lloyd, D.: Numerical thought with and without words: Evidence from indigenous Australian children. Proc. National Acad. Sci. United States Am. **105**(35), 13179–13184 (2008)
2. Cantor, G.: Contributions to the Founding of the Theory of Transfinite Numbers. Dover Publications, New York (1955)
3. Conway, J.H., Guy, R.K.: The Book of Numbers. Springer-Verlag, New York (1996)
4. De Cosmis, S., De Leone, R.: The use of grossone in mathematical programming and operations research. Appl. Math. Comput. **218**(16), 8029–8038 (2012)
5. D'Alotto, L.: Cellular automata using infinite computations. Appl. Math. Comput. **218**(16), 8077–8082 (2012)
6. D'Alotto, L.: A classification of two-dimensional cellular automata using infinite computations. Indian J. Math. **55**, 143–158 (2013)
7. D'Alotto, L.: A classification of one-dimensional cellular automata using infinite computations. Appl. Math. Comput. **255**, 15–24 (2015)
8. Gödel, K.: The Consistency of the Continuum-Hypothesis. Princeton University Press, Princeton (1940)
9. Gordon, P.: Numerical cognition without words: evidence from Amazonia. Science **306**, 496–499 (2004)
10. Hardy, G.H.: Orders of Infinity. Cambridge University Press, Cambridge (1910)
11. Hilbert, D.: Mathematical problems: lecture delivered before the international congress of mathematicians at paris in 1900. Bull. Am. Math. Soci. **8**, 437–479 (1902)
12. Iudin, D.I., Sergeyev, Y.D., Hayakawa, M.: Interpretation of percolation in terms of infinity computations. Appl. Math. Comput. **218**(16), 8099–8111 (2012)
13. Iudin, D.I., Sergeyev, Y.D., Hayakawa, M.: Infinity computations in cellular automaton forest-fire model. Commun. Nonlinear Sci. Numer. Simul. **20**(3), 861–870 (2015)
14. Leder, G.C.: Mathematics for all? The case for and against national testing. In: Cho, S.J. (ed.) The Proceedings of the 12th International Congress on Mathematical Education: Intellectual and Attitudinal Chalenges, pp. 189–207. Springer, New York (2015)
15. Leibniz, G.W., Child, J.M.: The Early Mathematical Manuscripts of Leibniz. Dover Publications, New York (2005)
16. Levi-Civita, T.: Sui numeri transfiniti. Rend. Acc. Lincei, Series 5a **113**, 7–91 (1898)
17. Lolli, G.: Infinitesimals and infinites in the history of mathematics: a brief survey. Appl. Math. Comput. **218**(16), 7979–7988 (2012)
18. Lolli, G.: Metamathematical investigations on the theory of grossone. Appl. Math. Comput. **255**, 3–14 (2015)
19. Margenstern, M.: Using grossone to count the number of elements of infinite sets and the connection with bijections. p-Adic Numbers, Ultrametric Anal. Appl. **3**(3), 196–204 (2011)
20. Margenstern, M.: An application of grossone to the study of a family of tilings of the hyperbolic plane. Appl. Math. Comput. **218**(16), 8005–8018 (2012)
21. Margenstern, M.: Fibonacci words, hyperbolic tilings and grossone. Commun. Nonlinear Sci. Numer. Simul. **21**(1–1), 3–11 (2015)
22. Pica, P., Lemer, C., Izard, V., Dehaene, S.: Exact and approximate arithmetic in an amazonian indigene group. Science **306**, 499–503 (2004)

23. Robinson, A.: Non-standard Analysis. Princeton Univ. Press, Princeton (1996)
24. Sergeyev, Y.D.: Arithmetic of infinity. Edizioni Orizzonti Meridionali, CS, 2003, 2d electronic ed. 2013
25. Sergeyev, Y.D.: Blinking fractals and their quantitative analysis using infinite and infinitesimal numbers. Chaos, Solitons, Fractals **33**, 50–75 (2007)
26. Sergeyev, Y.D.: A new applied approach for executing computations with infinite and infinitesimal quantities. Informatica **19**(4), 567–596 (2008)
27. Sergeyev, Y.D.: Evaluating the exact infinitesimal values of area of Sierpinski's carpet and volume of Menger's sponge. Chaos, Solitons, Fractals **42**(5), 3042–34046 (2009)
28. Sergeyev, Y.D.: Numerical computations and mathematical modelling with infinite and infinitesimal numbers. J. Appl. Math. Comput. **29**, 177–195 (2009)
29. Sergeyev, Y.D.: Numerical point of view on Calculus for functions assuming finite, infinite, and infinitesimal values over finite, infinite, and infinitesimal domains. Nonlinear Anal. Seri. A: Theor. Methods Appl. **71**(12), e1688–e1707 (2009)
30. Sergeyev, Y.D.: Computer system for storing infinite, infinitesimal, and finite quantities and executing arithmetical operations with them. USA Patent **7**, 860–914 (2010)
31. Sergeyev, Y.D.: Counting systems and the First Hilbert problem. Nonlinear Anal. Ser. A: Theor. Methods Appl. **72**(3–4), 1701–1708 (2010)
32. Sergeyev, Y.D.: Lagrange Lecture: methodology of numerical computations with infinities and infinitesimals. Rend. del Seminario Matematico dell'Università e del Politecnico di Torino **68**(2), 95–113 (2010)
33. Sergeyev, Y.D.: Higher order numerical differentiation on the infinity computer. Optim. Lett. **5**(4), 575–585 (2011)
34. Sergeyev, Y.D.: On accuracy of mathematical languages used to deal with the Riemann zeta function and the Dirichlet eta function. p-Adic Numbers, Ultrametric Anal. Appl. **3**(2), 129–148 (2011)
35. Sergeyev, Y.D.: Using blinking fractals for mathematical modelling of processes of growth in biological systems. Informatica **22**(4), 559–576 (2011)
36. Sergeyev, Y.D.: Numerical computations with infinite and infinitesimal numbers: theory and applications. In: Sorokin, A., Pardalos, P.M. (eds.) Dynamics of Information Systems: Algorithmic Approaches. SPMS, vol. 51. Springer, New York (2013)
37. Sergeyev, Y.D.: Solving ordinary differential equations by working with infinitesimals numerically on the infinity computer. Appl. Math. Comput. **219**(22), 10668–10681 (2013)
38. Sergeyev, Y.D.: Infinity computer and calculus. In: Simos, T.E., Tsitouras, C. (ed.), AIP Proceedings of the International Conference on Numerical Analysis and Applied Mathematics 2014 (ICNAAM-2014), vol. 1648, pp. 150018. Melville, New York (2015)
39. Sergeyev, Y.D.: The olympic medals ranks, lexicographic ordering, and numerical infinities. The Mathematical Intelligencer, **37**(2), 4–8 (2015)
40. Sergeyev, Y.D.: Un semplice modo per trattare le grandezze infinite ed infinitesime. Matematica nella Società e nella Cultura: Rivista della Unione Matematica Italiana Series I **8**, 111–147 (2015)
41. Sergeyev, Y.D., Garro, A.: Observability of Turing machines: a refinement of the theory of computation. Informatica **21**(3), 425–454 (2010)
42. Sergeyev, Y.D., Garro, A.: Single-tape and multi-tape Turing machines through the lens of the Grossone methodology. J. Supercomput. **65**(2), 645–663 (2013)

43. Ivoghlian, A., Wang, K.I.-K., Salcic, Z., Catapang, S.A.: An ultra-low power miniaturised wireless mote for ubiquitous data acquisition. In: Mason, A., Mukhopadhyay, S.C., Jayasundera, K.P. (eds.) Sensing Technology: Current Status and Future Trends IV. SSMI, vol. 12, pp. 139–169. Springer, Heidelberg (2015)

44. Vita, M.C., De Bartolo, S., Fallico, C., Veltri, M.: Usage of infinitesimals in the Menger's Sponge model of porosity. Appl. Math. Comput. **218**(16), 8187–8196 (2012)

45. Wallis, J.: Arithmetica infinitorum. 1656

46. Zhigljavsky, A.A.: Computing sums of conditionally convergent and divergent series using the concept of grossone. Appl. Math. Comput. **218**(16), 8064–8076 (2012)

47. Žilinskas, A.: On strong homogeneity of two global optimization algorithms based on statistical models of multimodal objective functions. Appl. Math. Comput. **218**(16), 8131–8136 (2012)

Regular Papers

Exploring the Effect of Cell Heterogeneity in Wound Healing Using a 3D Multicellular Tissue Growth Model

Belgacem Ben Youssef[(✉)]

Department of Computer Engineering,
College of Computer and Information Sciences,
King Saud University, Riyadh, Saudi Arabia
BBenyoussef@ksu.edu.sa

Abstract. We explore some aspects of cell population dynamics in a wound-healing environment using a three-dimensional simulation model for multicellular tissue growth. The computational model uses a discrete approach based on cellular automata to simulate wound-healing times and tissue growth rates of multiple populations of proliferating and migrating cells. Each population of cells has its own division, motion, collision, and aggregation characteristics resulting in a number of useful system parameters that allow us to investigate their emergent effects. These random dynamic processes can be modeled by appropriately choosing the governing rules of the state transitions of each computational site. Discrete systems of this kind constitute an important approach for studying the temporal dynamics of complex biological systems.

Keywords: 3D model · Multicellular · Tissue growth · Wound healing · Cellular automata

1 Introduction

Natural tissues are multicellular and have a specific three-dimensional architecture [1]. This structure is supported by an extracellular matrix (ECM). The ECM often has the form of a three-dimensional network of cross-linked protein strands (see Fig. 1, for an example). In addition to determining the mechanical properties of a tissue, the ECM plays many important roles in tissue development. Biochemical and biophysical signals from the ECM modulate fundamental cellular activities, including adhesion, migration, proliferation, differentiation, and programmed cell death [2]. Scaffold properties, cell activities like adhesion or migration, and external stimuli that modulate cellular functions are among the many factors that affect the growth rate of tissues [3]. For these reasons, the development of bio-artificial tissue substitutes involves extensive and time-consuming experimentation. The availability of computational models with predictive abilities may greatly speed up progress in this area.

© Springer International Publishing Switzerland 2015
C.S. Calude and M.J. Dinneen (Eds.): UCNC 2015, LNCS 9252, pp. 109–120, 2015.
DOI: 10.1007/978-3-319-21819-9_7

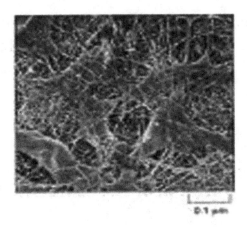

Fig. 1. A scanning electron micrograph displaying the three-dimensional structure of an extracellular matrix. A scale of 0.1 μm is shown

This research describes a three-dimensional cellular automata (CA) model to simulate the growth of three-dimensional tissues consisting of more than one cell type in a wound-healing environment. The corresponding discrete model is an extension of a previously developed base model that accounted for only a single type of cells [4]. The model incorporates all the elementary features of cell division and locomotion including the complicated dynamic phenomena occurring when cells collide and aggregate. Each computational element is represented by a site within a cubic lattice. While the assumption of cubic living cells does not reflect the true morphology of migrating or confluent mammalian cells, it allows us to use data structures that minimize memory and computational time requirements. Here, each computational site interacts with its neighbors that are to its north, east, west, south, and immediately above it or below it. This is known as the von Neumann neighborhood in three dimensions [5].

We analyze the effects of key system parameters on the tissue growth rate and wound-healing time, the latter being approximated by the time to reach full volume coverage, in the context of two wound-seeding topologies employing two types of cell populations. In particular, we explore the following two questions:

1. What are the effects of cell heterogeneity on the wound-healing time and tissue growth rate?
2. Under what circumstances, a given type of wound-seeding mode may be the better choice of cell seeding distribution for faster wound healing?

We begin the paper by defining cellular automata in the next section. This is followed by a short review of related work and a concise description of the development of the model. We then present the corresponding sequential algorithm. Before concluding, we give an overview of the important parameters and inputs of the model and discuss our simulation results.

2   Cellular Automata Concepts

Cellular automata were originally introduced by John von Neumann and Stanislaw Ulam as a possible idealization of biological systems with a particular purpose of modeling biological self-reproduction [6]. This approach has been used since then to study a wide variety of physical, chemical, biological, and other complex natural systems [6].

We consider d-dimensional cellular automata consisting of an array D of lattice cells covering a finite domain. Any cell c is uniquely identified by d integer coordinates $(i_1, i_2, \ldots, i_d)$, where $1 \leq i_1 \leq N_1$, $1 \leq i_2 \leq N_2$, ..., and $1 \leq i_d \leq N_d$. Let Ω be the set of all computational sites in the cellular space and N be the total number of such sites such that $N = N_1 \times N_2 \times \ldots \times N_d$. A cellular automaton satisfies the following properties:

1. Each cell c interacts only with its neighbor cells defined by a neighborhood relation that associates with the cell c a finite list of neighbor cells $c + \nu_1, c + \nu_2, \ldots, c + \nu_k$. In general, the neighborhood vector (or neighborhood index), $V = [\nu_1, \nu_2, \ldots, \nu_k]$, may vary from one cell to another.
2. Each cell can exist in one of a finite number of states. This finite list of states will be listed by Q. In the simplest case of two-state automata, $Q = \{0, 1\}$.
3. Each function $X : \Omega \longrightarrow Q$ defining an assignment of states to all cells in the cellular space Ω is called a configuration. Then, x_c is called the state of the cell c under configuration X.
4. For any cell c in the cellular space, there exists a local transition function (or rule) f_c, from Q^k to Q, specifying the state of the cell at time level $t + 1$ as a function of the states of its neighbors at time level t. That is, $x_c^{t+1} = q^{t+1}(c) = f_c(x_{c+\nu_1}^t, x_{c+\nu_2}^t, \ldots, x_{c+\nu_k}^t)$.
5. The simultaneous application of the local transition functions f_c to all the cells in a cellular space defines a global transition function F which acts on the entire array transforming any configuration X^t to a new configuration X^{t+1} according to $X^{t+1} = F(X^t)$.

These properties imply that each cellular automaton is a discrete dynamical system. Starting from an initial configuration X^0, the cellular array follows a trajectory of configurations defined by the global transition function F. All possible configurations of the cellular automaton define a set Φ, whose cardinality can be quite large. For instance, using $N_1 = N_2 = N_3 = 5$ and $Q = \{0, 1\}$, the number of configurations in Φ would be equal to $2^{5 \times 5 \times 5} \approx 4.254 \times 10^{37}$ configurations.

We can now define parallel discrete iterations for a cellular automaton as follows:

$$\begin{cases} X^0 & \text{is given in } \Phi \\ X^{t+1} = F(X^t), \end{cases} \tag{1}$$

for $t = 0, 1, 2, \ldots$ or equivalently:

$$\begin{cases} X^0 = (x_1^0, x_2^0, \ldots . x_N^0) \text{ is given in } \Phi \\ X_f^{t+1} = f_i(x_1^t, x_2^t, \ldots, x_N^t), \end{cases} \tag{2}$$

for $t = 0, 1, 2, \ldots$ and $i = 1, 2, 3, \ldots, N$. The preceding two equations, or rules, imply that the parallel discrete iterations update the states of all cells at the same time. It should be noted here that the transition functions of cellular automata need not be algebraic in form and may be rule-based. A potentially important feature of cellular automata is the capability for *self-reproduction* through which the evolution of a configuration yields several separated, yet identical copies of the configuration. Moreover, cellular automata rules may map several initial configurations into the same final configuration, thus leading to microscopically *irreversible* time evolution in which trajectories of different states may merge [7].

3   Related Work

Various modeling approaches have been used to simulate the population dynamics of proliferating cells. These models can be classified as: deterministic, stochastic, or based on cellular automata and agents. We briefly review a few of the agent-based lattice-free models to simulate tissue growth [8]. These models apply the dynamics of cell proliferation and death to describe tissue pattern formation and growth. Other related models are suitable for describing the locomotion of a fixed number of cells where cells move relatively slowly with respect to other processes like the diffusion of soluble substances [9]. Additional models employ feedback mechanisms between cells and the substrate to model cells entering and leaving the tissue and to establish homeostasis in such systems [10]. Some of the agent-based models use regular triangulation to generate the neighborhood topology for the cells, thus allowing for a continuous representation of cell sizes and locations in contrast to grid-based models [11]. Others utilize multiscale approaches to model collective phenomena in multicellular assemblies, including inflammation and wound healing [12].

4   The Computational Model

The growth of tissues is a complex biological process. In this model, the migration and proliferation of mammalian cells are considered to be mainly characterized by the following four subprocesses: cell division, cell motion, cell collision, and cell aggregation. For a detailed account of the modeling steps of each of these subprocesses, we refer the reader to related reference [4].

4.1   States of the Cellular Automaton

The model is a discrete system operating in a cellular space containing $N = N_x \times N_y \times N_z$ computational sites. Cells in the cellular space interact with their neighbors at equally spaced time intervals $t_1, t_2, \ldots, t_r, t_{r+1}, \ldots$ where $t_{r+1} = t_r + \Delta t$ for all r. An occupied computational site must describe the current state of a given cell using a set of values. These values must describe the asynchronous proliferation and persistent random walks of multiple cell types. In building an adequate state definition, sufficient information must be provided about the history so that given the current state, the past is statistically irrelevant for predicting all future behavior pertinent to the application at hand [13]. Based on these specifications, the state x_i of an automaton containing a living cell must specify the following set of parameters:

1. The cell type.
2. The direction of cell motion.
3. The cell speed.
4. The time remaining until the next direction change.
5. The time remaining until the next cell division.

The average speed of migrating cells is controlled by varying the value of the time interval, . This is due to the fact that migrating cells cover a fixed distance in each step. Another means of regulating the speed of locomotion is the ability to adjust the transition probability for the stationary state. Therefore, a migrating cell of type j in automaton i must only specify the direction of locomotion and the times which remain until the next direction change and the next cell division in its state x_i. The state of an arbitrary automaton i, thus, takes values from the following set of eight-digit integer numbers $\Psi = \{klmnpqrs/k, l, m, n, p, q, r, \text{and } s \in \mathbb{N}\}$, where k is the cell type. The direction of motion is identified by the direction index l. When l is equal to 0, the cell is in the collision stationary state. When the value of l is in the range of 1 to 6, it represents one of six directions the cell is currently moving in. When the value of l is 7, it enters an aggregation stationary state where it "sticks" to another cell of the same type potentially forming cellular aggregates. The digits mn denote the persistence counter. This counter represents the time remaining until the next change in the direction of cell movement. The cell phase counter is given by the remaining four digits $pqrs$ and holds the time remaining before the cell divides.

5   Sequential Algorithm

5.1   Initial Conditions

The initial parameters for the simulation are first read from the input data file. Then, the computational sites to be occupied by the cells at the start of this simulation run are selected based on the seeding mode of the initial cell distribution. For each occupied site, we assign a cell state based on the population characteristics of that cell type. The direction index is randomly selected, the persistence counter is assigned a properly chosen value, and the cell phase counter is set based on experimentally determined cell division data.

5.2 Iterative Operations

At each time step $t_{r+1} = t_r + \Delta t$, for $r = 0, 1, 2, \ldots$

1. Randomly select a computational site.
2. If this site is occupied by a cell c and the phase counter is zero then it is time for this cell to divide and the division routine is called.
3. If this site is occupied by a cell c and the persistence counter is zero, then it is time for this cell to change directions and the direction change routine is called.
4. If this site is occupied by a cell c and both the phase and persistence counters are not zero, attempt to move this cell to a neighboring site in the direction indicated by the direction index of its current state.
   (a) If this neighboring site is free, then mark it for cell c and decrement the phase and persistence counters by one.
   (b) If this neighboring site is occupied by a cell from a different type, then cell c remains in the current site and both cells enter the stationary state due to collision. Their persistence counters are set accordingly while their respective phase counters are decremented by one.
   (c) If this neighboring site is occupied by a cell from the same type, then cell c remains in the current site and both cells enter the aggregation stationary state. The persistence counters for both cells are set to the appropriate waiting time and their phase counters are decremented by one.
5. Select another site (randomly) and repeat Steps 2–4 until all sites have been processed.
6. Update the states of all sites so that the new locations of all cells are computed.
7. If confluence has not been reached, proceed to the next time step.

In regards to the details of the division and direction change routines, we refer the reader to [4].

6 Simulation Parameters for Wound Healing

6.1 Cell Seeding Distributions

In this study, we consider a wound-seeding topology where a wound in the shape of an empty cylinder is centered in the cellular grid with all surrounding sites occupied by two types of cells. This topology simulates the cell migration and proliferation phase of wound healing. This model does not attempt to describe all the steps of the complicated wound-healing process [14]. We associate two types of cell distributions with this seeding topology:

– Segmented Distribution: Each cell type is seeded in a separate area of the cellular space around the denuded area of the wound environment. During the simulation, cells can migrate freely in the wound area, and can enter spaces that were initially seeded with a different cell type.
– Mixed Distribution: All cell types are seeded together in all areas surrounding the wound using a uniformly random placement of cells. Figure 2 illustrates an example of each distribution.

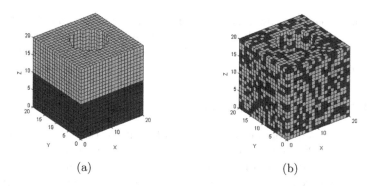

Fig. 2. Two examples of a wound-seeding topology, displaying two cell types in a segmented distribution (a) and a mixed one (b), are depicted. In both, a wound of cylindrical shape, with a diameter of 10 and a height of 20, inside a $20 \times 20 \times 20$ cellular grid is exhibited

6.2   Cell Population Dynamics

Starting with a total number of seed cells equal to N_0, the cellular automata rules transform the cellular array to simulate the dynamic process of tissue growth inside the wound environment. At some time t after the start of the simulation, $N_c(t)$ sites of the cellular automaton are occupied by cells. We define a measure to indicate the volume coverage at time t inside the wound area as the cell volume fraction $k(t)$, as follows:

$$k(t) = \frac{N_c(t) - N_0}{N - N_0} = \frac{\sum_{i=1}^{n}(N_{c_i}(t) - N_{c_i}(0))}{N - \sum_{i=1}^{n} N_{c_i}(0)},$$

with $N_0 = N_c(0) = \sum_{i=1}^{n} N_{c_i}(0)$ and where $N(= N_x \times N_y \times N_z)$ is the size of the cellular space, $N_{c_i}(t)$ is the number of occupied computational sites by cell type i at time t, $N_{c_i}(0)$ is the number of seed cells of type i surrounding the wound, and n is the number of cell types ($n \geq 1$). For the wound seeding, the cell volume fraction indicates the fraction of cells occupying the wound area at a given time. The overall tissue growth rate represents the increase in volume coverage, within the wound area, with respect to time. To this end, the tissue growth rate measure is given by the following formula:

$$\frac{dk(t)}{dt} = \frac{\sum_{i=1}^{n}(N_{c_i}(t) - N_{c_i}(t - \Delta t))}{\Delta t \times (N - N_0)} = \frac{\sum_{i=1}^{n}(N_{c_i}(t) - N_{c_i}(t - \Delta t))}{\Delta t \times (N - \sum_{i=1}^{n} N_{c_i}(0))}.$$

Here, $k(t)$ is the cell volume fraction at time t as given above and Δt is the time step in hours or days, depending on the resolution of the time scale utilized in the model. The simulation continues until all sites are occupied by cells, that is until $k(t)$ equals one.

6.3   Additional Simulation Inputs

The simulation results of the proliferation of multiple cell types are obtained for a $200 \times 200 \times 200$ cellular array where two cell populations are used with a wound diameter of 100 and a height of 200. Cells of population 1 are considered to be the faster moving cells with an assigned "swimming" speed of $10\,\mu$m per hour while cells of population 2 are the slower moving ones with a speed set to $1\mu m$ per hour. We define the cell heterogeneity measure as the ratio of the initially seeded number of cells from population 1 to that from population 2. This is given by:

$$H = \frac{\text{initial number of (faster) cells from population 1}}{\text{initial number of (slower) cells from population 2}}.$$

That is, when $H = 9$ there are 9 cells from population 1 for every cell from population 2. Throughout these simulations, a confluence parameter of $100\,\%$ and an average waiting time of 2 hours for the six directions of motion and 1 hour for the two stationary states are utilized. For the purposes of this study, the time to reach confluence is estimated to be nearly equal to the time necessary for the wound to heal. Each cell is modeled as a cubic computational element whose sides are assumed to be equal to $10\,\mu$m in length. We also employ different division time distributions for these two cell populations. Their division times are given in Table 1.

Table 1. Division time distributions for the two cell populations

	Cell Populations	
Division Times	Cell Population 1	Cell Population 2
12 - 18 hrs	64 %	4 %
18 - 24 hrs	32 %	32 %
24 - 30 hrs	4 %	64 %

7   Simulation Results and Discussion

We discuss our results that simulate the effect of varying the cell heterogeneity ratio on the wound-healing time and the tissue growth rate, and then compare the results of the two seeding modes.

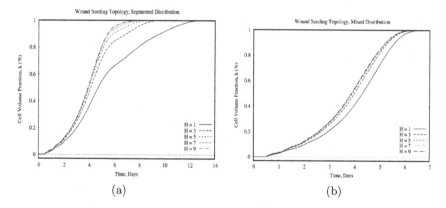

Fig. 3. Effect of varying the cell heterogeneity ratio, H, on the cell volume fraction for the segmented (a) and mixed (b) cell distribution modes of wound seeding

7.1 Effect of Cell Heterogeneity on Wound-Healing Time and Tissue Growth Rate

Figure 3 shows the temporal evolution of volume coverage as the heterogeneity measure, H, is varied for both the segmented and mixed wound-seeding modes. In these simulation runs, the value of H is varied according to the set $\{1, 3, 5, 7, 9\}$. We observe that volume coverage inside the wound increases with time until it reaches confluence for all values of H and that as H is increased, wound healing is achieved sooner. This is because an increase in the value of this ratio results in a larger number of fast cells initially seeded in the part of the cellular space surrounding the wound; thus, allowing these cells to dominate the proliferation process as they go through their mitotic cycle. Faster moving cells are the first to enter the denuded wound areas seeking empty sites, which delays the formation of cell colonies and leads to faster proliferation by mitigating the impact of contact inhibition. This also results in an increase in the overall tissue growth rate as depicted in Fig. 4. Such an impact is more pronounced in the segmented distribution for values of $1 \leq H \leq 5$. This indicates that fast moving cells tend to seek the nearby empty sites initially neighboring the cellular space segment containing the slower cells in order to divide. In all cases, the tissue growth rate increases initially, reaches a maximum and then decreases as a result of contact inhibition brought about by the formation of cell colonies and their associated merging events.

7.2 Comparison of the Two Wound-Seeding Modes

Figure 5 shows comparisons between the cell volume fraction and tissue growth rates obtained by using the segmented and mixed modes of wound seeding. Here, two different values of the ratio H were used, $H = 1$ and $H = 9$, respectively. We also observe that when $H = 1$, the mixed seeding mode takes less time to reach full volume coverage and thus, heals the wound faster (7 days vs. 13 days for the

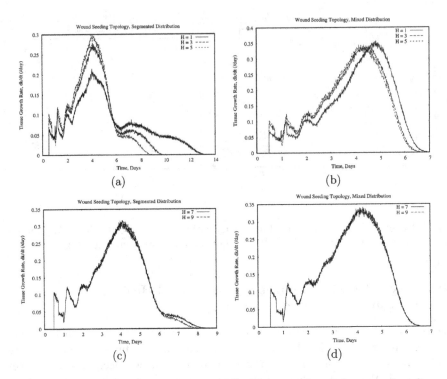

Fig. 4. The temporal evolution of the overall tissue growth rate for wound seeding as the cell heterogeneity ratio, H, is varied from 1–5 (top), then 7–9 (bottom) for the segmented seeding mode ((a) and (c)) and the mixed mode ((b) and (d)).

segmented mode). It also yields a higher tissue growth rate reaching a maximum value of 0.35 versus 0.21 for the segmented mode. This may be attributed to the fact that contact inhibition has less of an effect in the mixed seeding mode where faster cells can access nearby empty spaces faster to move and divide into which in turn frees up sites for the slower-moving cells as well. Increasing the value of H to 9 shows a stronger positive impact on the time to heal the wound and the tissue growth rate for the segmented wound-seeding mode than the mixed one. In the former, the increased number of faster moving cells affords them the opportunity to rapidly move into the empty sites of the wound area and eventually dominate the proliferation process. This results in a nearly similar overall tissue growth behavior for both seeding modes when $H = 9$. As parts (c) and (d) of Fig. 5 clearly illustrate, the distinction between the two wound-seeding modes of cell distribution becomes less apparent when the faster moving cells constitute at least 90 % of the total seeded cells around the wound site. Hence, we observe that when using equal proportions of seed cell types, the mixed mode may be chosen over the segmented one. In the event that larger cell heterogeneity ratios are employed, the segmented mode could be beneficial in yielding a high tissue growth rate and a reasonably reduced wound-healing time.

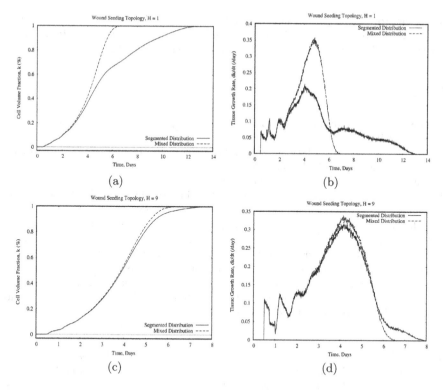

Fig. 5. Comparison of the cell volume fraction ((a) and (c)) and the overall tissue growth rate ((b) and (d)) between the segmented and mixed wound-seeding modes for two cell heterogeneity ratios: $H = 1$ (top) and $H = 9$ (bottom)

8   Conclusion

We presented in this paper the description of a three-dimensional computational model for the growth of multicellular tissues based on the concept of cellular automata to simulate wound healing. The model incorporates many aspects of cell behavior involving cell migration, division, collision, and aggregation while including multiple cell types. The flexibility of the model permits the exploration of the influence of several system parameters on the wound healing time and tissue growth rate. We presented simulation results from the serial implementation of the model using two wound-seeding distribution modes. Our results indicate that the use of a mixed wound-seeding mode may be more advantageous when using equal proportions of fast and slow moving cell types seeded around the wound area. This advantage diminishes, however, when a much larger proportion of fast cells are employed. In that case, the segmented seeding mode could be used as a reasonable alternative.

Acknowledgments. The author would like to acknowledge the support for this research work from the Research Centre in the College of Computer and Information Sciences as well as the Deanship of Scientific Research at King Saud University.

References

1. Palsson, B.O., Bhatia, S.N.: Tissue Engineering. Pearson Prentice Hall, Upper Saddle River (2004)
2. Soll, D., Wessels, D.: Motion Analysis of Living Cells: Techniques in Modern Biomedical Microscopy. Wiley-Liss, New York (1998)
3. Langer, R., Vacanti, J.P.: Tissue engineering. Sci. **260**, 920–926 (1993)
4. Ben Youssef, B.: A visualization tool of 3-D time-varying data for the simulation of tissue growth. Multimed. Tools Appl. **73**(3), 1795–1817 (2014)
5. Tchuente, M.: Computation on automata networks. In: Soulie, F.G., Robert, Y., Tchuente, M. (eds.) Automata Networks in Computer Science: Theory and Applications, pp. 101–129. Princeton University Press, Princeton (1987)
6. Deutsch, A., Dormann, S.: Cellular Automaton Modeling of Biological Pattern Formation: Characterization, Applications, and Analysis. Birkhauser, Boston (2005)
7. Chopard, B., Droz, M.: Cellular Automata Modeling of Physical Systems. Cambridge University Press, Cambridge (1998)
8. Schaller, G., Meyer-Hermann, M.: Multicellular tumor spheroid in an off-lattice voronoi-delaunay cell model. Phys. Rev. E **71**(5 Pt 1), 051910 (2005)
9. Beyer, T., Meyer-Hermann, M.: Delauny object dynamics for tissues involving highly motile cells. In: Chauviere, A., Preziosi, L., Verdier, C. (eds.) Cell Mechanics: From Single Scale-Based Models to Multiscale Modeling, pp. 417–442. CRC Press, London (2010)
10. Fu, Y.X., Chaplin, D.D.: Development and maturation of secondary lymphoid tissues. Annu. Rev. Immunol. **17**, 399–433 (1999)
11. Beyer, T., Schaller, G., Deutsch, A., Meyer-Hermann, M.: Parallel dynamic and kinetic regular triangulation in three dimensions. Comput. Phys. Commun. **172**(2), 86–108 (2005)
12. Cordelia, Z., Mi, Q., An, G., Vodovotz, Y.: Computational modeling of inflammation and wound healing. Adv. Wound Care **2**(9), 527–537 (2013)
13. Bratley, P., Fox, B.L., Schrage, L.E.: A Guide to Simulation, 2nd edn. Springer-Verlag, New York (1987)
14. Majno, G., Joris, I.: Cells, Tissues, and Disease: Principles of General Pathology. Oxford University Press, New York (2004)

Regularized Linear and Nonlinear Autoregressive Models for Dengue Confirmed-Cases Prediction

Larissa Braz Sousa[1]([✉]), Claudio J. Von Zuben[1], and Fernando J. Von Zuben[2]

[1] Zoology Department on Bioscience Institute,
Sao Paulo State University, Rio Claro, SP, Brazil
{larissabs,vonzuben}@rc.unesp.br
[2] Department of Computer Engineering and Industrial Automation,
University of Campinas, Campinas, SP, Brazil
vonzuben@dca.fee.unicamp.br

Abstract. Based solely on the dengue confirmed-cases of six densely populated urban areas in Brazil, distributed along the country, we propose in this paper regularized linear and nonlinear autoregressive models for one-week ahead prediction of the future behaviour of each time series. Though exhibiting distinct temporal behaviour, all the time series were properly predicted, with a consistently better performance of the nonlinear predictors, based on MLP neural networks. Additional local information associated with environmental conditions will possibly improve the performance of the predictors. However, without including such local environmental variables, such as temperature and rainfall, the performance was proven to be acceptable and the applicability of the methodology can then be directly extended to endemic areas around the world characterized by a poor monitoring of environmental conditions. For tropical countries, predicting the short-term evolution of dengue confirmed-cases may represent a decisive feedback to guide the definition of effective sanitary policies.

Keywords: Regularized linear predictor · Regularized nonlinear predictor · MLP neural network · Dengue time series

1 Introduction

Learning from data [8] is a powerful machine learning technique whose main purpose is to automatically obtain mathematical models capable of synthesizing the intrinsic relationships exhibit by data collected from processes under investigation. When the process evolves with time and there is a fixed sample period, the obtained data is denoted a time series [26]. Box and Jenkins [5] properly formalized mathematical models to describe time series and since then the study of time series gained much more attention. The analysis of time series can be divided into two main branches [6]: (1) A more qualitative approach, devoted

© Springer International Publishing Switzerland 2015
C.S. Calude and M.J. Dinneen (Eds.): UCNC 2015, LNCS 9252, pp. 121–131, 2015.
DOI: 10.1007/978-3-319-21819-9_8

to extracting statistical properties and temporal attributes of the time series, such as predictability and stationarity [1]; (2) A more quantitative viewpoint, mainly concentrated in obtaining a regression model capable of predicting one-step ahead, given the historical evolution of the time series [26]. This paper is devoted to the more quantitative perspective, looking for high-performance prediction of one-week ahead dengue confirmed-cases time series of densely populated urban areas in Brazil.

Linear and nonlinear prediction models have been proposed in the literature. The advantage of linear models is the simplicity associated with the parameter setting, and the disadvantage is the absence of flexibility to represent more complex behaviours [5]. On the other hand, the flexibility of nonlinear models characterizes their main advantage, at the price of a more challenging computational procedure to determine the parameters of the predictor. Besides, having enough flexibility is not a guarantee of high performance, because the obtained model should exhibit a suitable degree of flexibility, according to the demands of the application. Even linear models with many parameters may overfit the data. That is why we are going to develop linear and nonlinear predictors endowed with regularization procedures [11,24], in an attempt to improve the performance of the predictor for data not used to synthesize the predictor. In machine learning terms, the purpose is to maximize the generalization capability of the predictor [20].

The paper is organized as follows: Sect. 2 is devoted to the motivation of the research and data collection, and Sect. 3 presents a brief review of linear and nonlinear models for time series prediction. Section 4 discusses the experimental setup. The experimental results are outlined in Sect. 5. Concluding remarks are given in Sect. 6.

2   Motivation for Predicting Dengue Confirmed-Cases Time Series and Procedure for Data Collection

Dengue is a major public health problem in many tropical regions, being reported to the World Health Organization about a million confirmed cases per year, all around the world, but with estimates of over 50 million cases annually, without notification [9]. Between 2001 and 2009 there were more than six million cases, in more than 30 countries in the regions of the Americas, and over 2,000 deaths by DHF (Dengue Haemorrhagic Fever) reported in the same period. Especially, in Brazil, 591,080 cases were registered only in 2014 [4]. Totally eradicated in Brazil in the 50 s, period when the Brazilian government has developed numerous campaigns for control cases of yellow fever (present in urban areas by the same vector of dengue), dengue again expressed cases of disease in the 80's, and since then the increase in the number of cases has been significant [19,23].

Dengue is an acute fever disease caused by virus representatives of the genus *Flavivirus*. Currently, there are four known different dengue serotypes, DEN-1, DEN-2, DEN-3 and DEN-4, wherein the clinical presentation may vary from asymptomatic to serious cases of dengue hemorrhagic fever, which can be fatal [10]. In 2013, it was described a fifth serotype disease, discovered in Malaysia, the DEN-5. In Brazil, this arbovirus infection is transmitted to humans by the bite of *Aedes (Stegomyia) aegypti*. The disease has caused great concern for international health authorities in the last 60 years; the increase in cases is strongly associated with human habit changes, such as population and urbanization increase and the society's living standards, that have benefited environments conducive to the development of favourable conditions for the mosquito vector. Furthermore, increased air travel has allowed the transport of different serotypes of dengue to other localities [18].

The dynamics of dengue transmission involves a complex relationship between climate, human and environment. Its main vector, *Ae. aegypti*, develops mainly in urban environments, using artificial water reservoirs as breeding [13]. According to the World Health Organization (WHO) (2010), dengue is in the list of neglected tropical diseases. Because it is a present disease mostly in poor countries, it offers little incentive for industries to develop new products for control and treatment. Thus, methods of prevention mainly involve monitoring techniques and combating the vector.

The reported cases of dengue data for the period 2000–2014 were obtained through the Brazilian Unified Health System database (SUS), from previous registration in the portal Electronics Information to citizen service. The data were organized according to the 52 weeks of the year (epidemiological weeks), over 15 years in the comprehensive study. Six densely populated Brazilian cities were selected for the study: São Paulo, Porto Alegre, Manaus, Goiânia, Salvador and Fortaleza. All selected municipalities are capitals of their respective states and have a high number of inhabitants, besides having great airports and thus promoting a high flow of people. Moreover, apart from Porto Alegre, they are cities that have shown a high number of cases of the disease in recent years [4].

Table 1. Reorganization of the time series to produce the input-output dataset.

s_{k-p}	s_{k-p+1}	$\cdots$	s_{k-1}	x_k
s_1	s_2	$\cdots$	s_p	s_{p+1}
s_2	s_3	$\cdots$	s_{p+1}	s_{p+2}
$\vdots$	$\vdots$	$\vdots$	$\vdots$	$\vdots$
s_{N-p}	s_{N-p+1}	$\cdots$	s_{N-1}	s_N
$\Downarrow$	$\Downarrow$		$\Downarrow$	$\Downarrow$
$\overrightarrow{a_p}$	$\overrightarrow{a}_{p-1}$		$\overrightarrow{a_1}$	$\overrightarrow{y}$

3   Linear and Nonlinear Models for Time Series Prediction

In this section, we are going to properly formalize the mathematical models that will characterize the time series predictors. The main notation is:

- s_k: Real value of the time series at the k-th sample instant;
- x_k: Predicted value of the time series at the k-th sample instant;
- N: Number of samples that compose the available time series.

3.1   Linear Models

Linear models will be directly based on the Box and Jenkins proposals [5]. Basically, they assert that the next value of the time series is a linear combination of p precedent values and q previous random impacts, plus the current random impact. The p precedent values compose the autoregressive (AR) components and the q previous impacts compose the moving average (MA) components. We then have the well-known ARMA models. The modelling procedure is thus characterized by setting p and q, followed by the estimation of the coefficients of the linear combination. Here, we will simplify the approach and work with AR models as follows:

$$x_k = b_1 s_{k-1} + b_2 s_{k-2} + ... + b_p s_{k-p} + b_{p+1}. \tag{1}$$

To estimate the vector of coefficients $b = \begin{bmatrix} b_1 & b_2 & \cdots & b_p & b_{p+1} \end{bmatrix}^T$, it is necessary to reorganize the time series to produce the configuration of Table 1. Matrix A can thus be built as follows:

$$A = \begin{bmatrix} a_1 & \cdots & a_p & 1 \end{bmatrix} \tag{2}$$

where 1 is a column vector of ones. It is now possible to interpret vector b^* as the optimal solution of the following linear optimization problem:

$$b^* = \arg \min_{b \in \Re^{p+1}} \|Ab - y\|_2^2 \tag{3}$$

that has a single global optimal solution given by:

$$b^* = (A^T A)^{-1} A^T y. \tag{4}$$

3.2   Definition of the Parameter p for Linear Models

The number p of precedent values is generally defined by the degree of correlation between each column vector a_i and the column vector y. The correlation [22] belongs to the interval $[-1; +1]$, and it is possible to specify a threshold so that the columns to be considered exhibit correlations above (in absolute value) the threshold. In this way, it is possible to define a subset of columns among the p candidates, given that the behaviour of the correlation may be non monotonic and some columns with index below p may violate the threshold and be excluded.

3.3   Regularization of the Linear Model

Depending on the value of p, the linear model may be too flexible so that there is a high risk of overfitting. To obtain a proper regularization of the linear model, a penalization term may be added to the linear optimization problem, with the purpose of enforcing the reduction of the norm of vector $\boldsymbol{b}$:

$$\boldsymbol{b}^* = \arg \min_{\boldsymbol{b} \in \Re^{p+1}} \|A\boldsymbol{b} - \boldsymbol{y}\|_2^2 + c \times \|\boldsymbol{b}\|_2^2, \tag{5}$$

where $c \geq 0$ is a parameter to be further defined. A vector with a reduced norm tends to regularize better [24]. The solution of this regularized version of the linear optimization problem is given by:

$$\boldsymbol{b}^* = (A^T A + cI)^{-1} A^T \boldsymbol{y}. \tag{6}$$

There is no systematic way to define parameter c, and it is usual to evaluate the performance of the predictor considering the following set of candidate values for c:$\{0,\ 2^{-24}, 2^{-23}, ..., 2^{+24}, 2^{+25}\}$ as suggested by Huang $et\ al.$ [15]. To do that, the $N - p$ samples of Table 1 should be divided into training and validation set. Subsequently, problem (5) is then solved by considering the training set and the performance of the obtained vector $\boldsymbol{b}$ is evaluated considering the validation set. Given that $c = 0$ is taken as a candidate solution, this means that the regularized version includes the non-regularized solution as a special case.

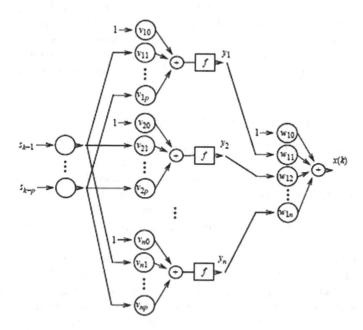

Fig. 1. Illustration of a one-hidden-layer MLP architecture.

3.4 Nonlinear Models

Nonlinear models may be conceived by a multitude of alternative mathematical structures. However, neural networks are generally adopted in the context of time series prediction, motivated by two main aspects of the design: (1) There are powerful techniques to train neural networks given a training dataset [2,16]; (2) Neural networks are universal approximators [14], so that the necessary nonlinear input-output mapping that will characterize the predictor can assume any configuration. The practical consequence is the popularization of neural network as nonlinear prediction models [7,12,26]. The multilayer perceptron (MLP) is the usual neural network model [3] and Fig. 1 presents the main aspects of the MLP architecture. The synaptic weights $v_{ij}(i = 1,...,n; j = 0,...,p)$ and w_{qi} $(i = 0,...,n; q = 1)$ are the parameters to be adjusted during the learning phase. The activation function of the hidden neurons, $f(\cdot)$, is generally taken as the hyperbolic tangent function. The constant input received by each neuron is denoted the bias input. The number of neurons at the output layer may vary depending on the application. In the case of time series prediction, a single output is sufficient to provide the one-step ahead estimation. The output neuron has the identity function as the activation function, so that there is no restriction to the interval of values at the output.

3.5 Definition of the Parameter p for Nonlinear Models

For nonlinear models, mutual information is generally considered in replacement to linear correlation indices [27]. However, given that we are going to perform a comparative analysis involving linear and nonlinear models, it seems reasonable to adopt the same regression vector (input vector) for all the contenders. That is why we are going to consider linear correlation in the definition of p for both types of models.

3.6 Regularization of the Nonlinear Model

By regularizing the neural network we mean the definition of a proper number n of hidden neurons and a proper stopping criterion for the training phase. Given the training and the validation dataset, both extracted from the input-output dataset presented in Table 1, e.g. following the proportions of 70 % for training and 30 % for validation, the definition of the number of hidden neurons may be achieved by an exhaustive search, testing candidate values for n in the interval 1,2,...,20. Of course, the maximum number 20 was arbitrarily defined and may vary depending on the demands of the application. For each candidate value of n (the number of hidden neurons), 30 neural networks with randomly initialized weights are trained using the training dataset and the average validation error is taken as the figure of merit. The stopping condition for the training phase is the minimization of the validation error [21]. The value of n that resulted in the best figure of merit will be selected. Due to computational restrictions, particularly the necessity of training 30 neural networks for each value of n, in the experiments we are going to consider $n \in \{5,10\}$ and not $n \in \{1,2,...,20\}$.

4   Experimental Setup

The experimental setup was defined as follows:

- Six time series were selected. They represent weekly confirmed-cases of dengue, from the year 2000 to the year 2014 of six densely populated urban areas in Brazil, distributed along the five official regions that compose the Brazilian Federation. The Northeast Region contributed two time series, given that the geographical conditions of both areas are divergent.
- The time series were scaled to fit the interval $[0,+1]$ (see Fig. 2).
- After the definition of parameter p, using the Pearson correlation [22], the dataset was split into training and validation, following the proportions of 70–30 %, respectively. This partition was kept the same for all the models. Notice that, from Table 1, there is no necessity of performing a contiguous partition. Any row at Table 1 may belong to the training or to the validation dataset.
- Performance was measured using RMSE (root mean square error), and it is given by the average value produced by 30 independent executions for each time series. For each one of those 30 execution, the 70–30 % partition is distinct. Notice that the 30 distinct partitions for the linear predictors are the same 30 distinct partitions for the nonlinear predictors.
- All the algorithms were implemented by the authors using Matlab® and executed in an CPU Intel® CORE i7-3520M of 2.90 GHz with 6 Gb of RAM. The MLPs were trained with the conjugate gradient algorithm [2,17,25].

Figure 2 presents the six rescaled time series, indicating that they exhibit distinct temporal behaviours, particularly in the location of the most prominent picks.

5   Experimental Results

The first analytical procedure is to determine parameter p, more specifically, the number of precedent values of the time series that hold a significant correlation with the one-week ahead value to be predicted (see Fig. 3). Though exhibiting a slightly distinct behaviour for each of the six time series, it is reasonable to take $p = 5$ for all time series, including all the lags, from $k - 1$ to $k - 5$, being k the current instant of time. Hence, the regression vector will be composed of the most recent five lags, for all the time series. The autocorrelation with index 0 and unitary value is the correlation of the vector to be predicted with itself, just to serve as a reference for the other points of the curve.

Given that we have 30 distinct partitions for the training and validation datasets, we have to synthesize:

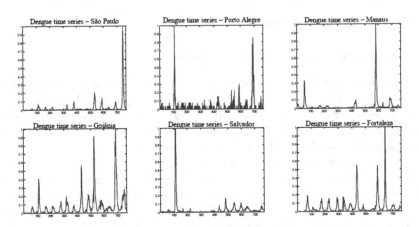

Fig. 2. Time series being investigated in the experiment.

- 30 × 51 linear predictors for each time series, because we have 51 possible values for the parameter c (see Eq. (6) and the text that follows it).
- 30 × 2 nonlinear predictors for each time series, because we are going to consider 2 distinct values for the number of hidden nodes in the MLP neural network: 5 and 10.

Table 2 indicates the number of times that some regularized linear predictor ($c > 0$ in Eq. (6)), among the tested ones, performed better than the non-regularized linear predictor ($c = 0$ in Eq. (6)), for each time series and considering 30 execution with distinct partitions for training and validation datasets. Notice that, in the literature, generally the non-regularized predictor is adopted and this initiative should be revised.

Table 2. Number of times, in 30 possibilities, that the regularization shows to be effective in producing linear predictors of better performance.

	Sao Paulo	Porto Alegre	Manaus	Goiania	Salvador	Fortaleza
No. of times	24	26	27	15	24	20

Table 3 indicates the number of times that the 5- and 10-hidden-nodes MLP neural networks produced a better performance, for each time series and considering 30 execution with distinct partitions for training and validation datasets (the same partitions adopted in the linear case). There is an equilibrium, indicating that the initialization of the weights is probably determining the regularization capability of both neural network architectures. Those results are indicating that both choices for the number of hidden nodes are suitable for the intended application

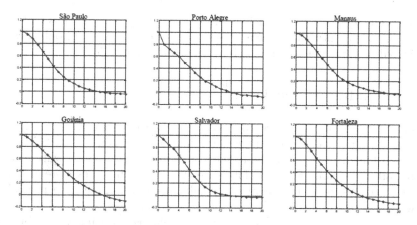

Fig. 3. Sample autocorrelation for the time series being investigated.

Table 3. Number of times, in 30 possibilities, that the 5- and 10-hidden-nodes MLP neural networks were chosen to be the predictors with the best performance for that specifc partition of the dataset.

	Sao Paulo	Porto Alegre	Manaus	Goiania	Salvador	Fortaleza
5-hidden nodes	19	18	15	18	15	19
10-hidden nodes	11	12	15	12	15	11

Table 4. Root mean square error (RMSE) for the average result of linear and nonlinear best predictors, considering the best results of 30 independent executions.

	Sao Paulo	Porto Alegre	Manaus	Goiania	Salvador	Fortaleza
Linear pred.	0.016938	0.055457	0.018188	0.036097	0.029619	0.025131
Nonlinear pred.	0.013244	0.052979	0.015378	0.034378	0.023746	0.018791

Finally, Table 4 presents the average performance of the best linear predictors against the best nonlinear predictors, for each time series, and considering the root mean square error (RMSE).

The nonlinear predictors produced a result in average 19 % better than the linear predictors. Given that the variance of the RMSE along the executions is low, there is a statistical significance in the observed difference in performance for all the time series, using the Wilcoxon test.

Taking into account that the time series are restricted to the interval $[0, +1]$, the RMSE shows that the error is between 1,5 % and 3,5 %, except for the Porto Alegre time series, for which the RMSE achieved 5,5 %. It is not possible to see in Fig. 2 (due to rescaling) that the number of dengue confirmed-cases in Porto

Alegre is much lower than what happens in the other localities, thus making it more difficult to capture tendencies. Notice that Porto Alegre is the only location considered in the experiments that is outside the Tropical Zone.

6   Concluding Remarks

This paper contributes in three directions. Firstly, the obtained results, though restricted to a particular endemic scenario, indicate that non-regularized predictors, even linear ones, should be avoided. In other words, regularization tends to promote significant gain in performance. The design becomes more elaborate and generally requires more computational resources, but we have formalized the whole procedure, both for the linear and the nonlinear cases, and the actual computational power of personal computers is enough to support the burden. The authors believe that the technical procedures adopted along the experimental phase of the research have been presented in a manner so that the reader is capable of reproducing all the fundamental steps. Notice that the non-regularized predictor is considered a candidate solution in our regularized strategy, so that our results will never be inferior to the ones produced by purely non-regularized approaches. Secondly, following other similar remarks in the literature [7,26], we have demonstrated that there are relevant applications in time series prediction in which nonlinear models are capable of guiding to consistently better results when compared to linear models. The average gain in performance of 19 % is a reasonable quantitative indicator of the merit of adopting nonlinear models for time series prediction. However, it is necessary to control the high flexibility of those nonlinear models toward good regularization of the proposed model. Finally, the obtained results suggest that it is possible to achieve good predictors for dengue confirmed-cases based solely on the time series itself, without enriching the model with additional environmental conditions. The applicability of our methodology is thus much higher and the computational approach is general enough to admit an immediate application to other areas of the world where dengue and/or other diseases are endemic.

Acknowledgements. The authors would like to thank FAPESP (São Paulo Research Foundation), process [2014/05101-2], and CNPq for the financial support.

References

1. Anderson, T.W.: Estimating linear statistical relationships. Ann. Stat. **12**(1), 1–45 (1984)
2. Battiti, R.: First and Second-order methods for learning: between steepest descent and Newton's method. Neural Comput. **4**, 141–166 (1992)
3. Bishop, C.M.: Neural Networks for Pattern Recognition. Clarendon Press, New York (1995)
4. Ministério da Saúde.: Monitoramento dos casos de dengue e febre de chikungunya até a Semana Epidemiológica (SE) 53 de 2014. Bol. Epidemiológico **46**, 3 (2015)

5. Box, G.E.P., Jenkins, G.M.: Time Series Analysis, Forecasting and Control. Holden Day, San Francisco (1976)
6. Bradley, E.: Time-series analysis. In: Berthold, M., Hand, D. (eds.) Intelligent Data Analysis: An Introduction, 2nd edn. Springer, Heidelberg (2003)
7. Chakraborty, K., Mehrotra, K., Mohan, C.K., Ranka, S.: Forecasting the behavior of multivariate time series using neural networks. Neural Netw. **5**, 961–970 (1992)
8. Cherkassky, V., Mulier, F.: Learning from Data: Concepts, Theory, and Methods, 2nd edn. Wiley IEEE Press, New York (2007)
9. Crompton, D.W.T., Peters, P. (eds.): World Health Organization. Working to overcome the Global Impact of Neglected Tropical Diseases, First WHO Report on Neglected Tropical Diseases, Switzerland, 172 p. (2010)
10. Forattini, O.P.: Culicidologia Médica, vol. 1, 864 p. EDUSP, São Paulo (2002)
11. Girosi, F., Jones, M., Poggio, T.: Regularization theory and neural network architectures. Neural Comput. **7**(2), 219–269 (1995)
12. Haykin, S.: Neural Networks and Learning Machines, 3rd edn. Prentice-Hall, Upper Saddle River (2008)
13. Hopp, M.J., Foley, J.A.: Global-scale relationships between climate and the dengue fever vector Aedes aegypti. Clim. Change **48**, 441–463 (2001)
14. Hornik, K., Stinchcombe, M., White, H.: Multilayer feedforward networks are universal approximators. Neural Netw. **2**(5), 359–366 (1989)
15. Huang, G.B., Wang, D.H., Lan, Y.: Extreme learning machines: a survey. Int. J. Mach. Learn. Cybernet. **2**, 107–122 (2011)
16. Kulaif, A.C.P., Von Zuben, F.J.: Improved regularization in extreme learning machines. In: 11th Brazilian Congress on Computational Intelligence, pp 1–6 (2013)
17. Luenberger, D.G.: Introduction to Linear and Nonlinear Programming. Addison-Wesley, Reading (1973)
18. Mairuhu, A.T.A., Wangenaar, J., Brandjes, D.M.P., Gorp, E.C.M.: Dengue: an arthropod-borne disease of global importance. Eur. J. Clin. Microbiol. Infect. Dis. **23**, 425–433 (2004)
19. Ministério da Saúde 1996. Plano Diretor de Erradicação do Aedes aegypti no Brasil, Brasília, pp. 78–79 (1996)
20. Moody, J.E.: The effective number of parameters:an analysis of generalization and regularization in nonlinear learning systems. In: Moody, J.E., Hanson, S.J., Lippmann, R.P. (eds.) Advances in Neural Information Processing Systems, vol. 4, pp. 847–854. Morgan Kaufmann, San Mateo (1992)
21. Prechelt, L.: Automatic early stopping using cross validation: quantifying the criteria. Neural Netw. **11**(4), 761–767 (1998)
22. Rodgers, J.L., Nicewander, W.A.: Thirteen ways to look at the correlation coefficient. Am. Stat. **42**(1), 59–66 (1988)
23. Teixeira, M.G.: Epidemiologia e medidas de prevenção do dengue. Informe Epidemiológico do SUS-IESUS **8**, 5–8 (1999)
24. Tibshirani, R.: Regression shrinkage and selection via the lasso. J. R. Stat. Soc. B **58**(1), 267–288 (1996)
25. van der Smagt, P.: Minimization methods for training feedforward neural networks. Neural Netw. **7**(1), 1–11 (1994)
26. Weigend, A.S., Gershenfeld, N.A.: Time Series Prediction: Forecasting the Future and Understanding the Past. Perseus Press, New York (1993)
27. Wentian, L.: Mutual information functions versus correlation functions. J. Stat. Phys. **60**(5–6), 823–837 (1990)

Asynchronous Spiking Neural P Systems with Structural Plasticity

Francis George C. Cabarle[1]([✉]), Henry N. Adorna[1],
and Mario J. Pérez-Jiménez[2]

[1] Algorithms and Complexity Lab, Department of Computer Science,
University of the Philippines Diliman, Diliman, 1101 Quezon City, Philippines
fccabarle@up.edu.ph, hnadorna@dcs.upd.edu.ph
[2] Department of Computer Science and AI, University of Sevilla,
Avda. Reina Mercedes s/n, 41012 Sevilla, Spain
marper@us.es

Abstract. Spiking neural P (in short, SNP) systems are computing devices inspired by biological spiking neurons. In this work we consider SNP systems with structural plasticity (in short, SNPSP systems) working in the asynchronous (in short, *asyn* mode). SNPSP systems represent a class of SNP systems that have dynamic synapses, i.e. neurons can use plasticity rules to create or remove synapses. We prove that for *asyn* mode, bounded SNPSP systems (where any neuron produces at most one spike each step) are not universal, while unbounded SNPSP systems with weighted synapses (a weight associated with each synapse allows a neuron to produce more than one spike each step) are universal. The latter systems are similar to SNP systems with extended rules in *asyn* mode (known to be universal) while the former are similar to SNP systems with standard rules only in *asyn* mode (conjectured not to be universal). Our results thus provide support to the conjecture of the still open problem.

Keywords: Membrane computing · Spiking neural P systems · Structural plasticity · Asynchronous systems · Turing universality

1 Introduction

Spiking neural P systems (in short, SNP systems) are parallel, distributed, and nondeterministic devices introduced into the area of membrane computing in [7]. Neurons are often drawn as ovals, and they process only one type of object, the *spike* signal represented by a. Synapses between neurons are the arcs between ovals: neurons are then placed on the vertices of a directed graph. Since their introduction, several lines of investigations have been produced, e.g. (non)deterministic computing power in [7,13]; language generation in [4]; function computing devices in [11]; solving computationally hard problems in [9]. Many neuroscience inspirations have also been included for computing use, producing several variants (to which the previous investigation lines are also applied), e.g. use of weighted synapses [15], neuron division and budding [9], the

© Springer International Publishing Switzerland 2015
C.S. Calude and M.J. Dinneen (Eds.): UCNC 2015, LNCS 9252, pp. 132–143, 2015.
DOI: 10.1007/978-3-319-21819-9_9

use of astrocytes [10]. Furthermore, many restrictions have been applied to SNP systems (and variants), e.g. asynchronous SNP systems as in [3,6] and [14], and sequential SNP systems as in [6].

In this work the variant we consider are SNP systems with structural plasticity, in short, SNPSP systems. SNPSP systems were first introduced in [1], then extended and improved in [2]. The biological motivation for SNPSP systems is structural plasticity, one form of neural plasticity, and distinct from the more common functional (Hebbian) plasticity. SNPSP systems represent a class of SNP systems using plasticity rules: synapses can be created or deleted so the synapse graph is dynamic. The restriction we apply to SNPSP systems is asynchronous operation: imposing synchronization on biological functions is sometimes "too much", i.e. not alway realistic. Hence, the asynchronous mode of operation is interesting to consider. Such restriction is also interesting mathematically, and we refer the readers again to [3,6] and [14] for further details.

In this work we prove that (i) asynchronous bounded (i.e. there exists a bound on the number of stored spikes in any neuron) SNPSP systems are not universal, (ii) asynchronous weighted (i.e. a positive integer weight is associated with each synapse) SNPSP systems, even under a normal form (provided below), are universal. The open problem in [3] whether asynchronous bounded SNP systems with standard rules are universal is conjectured to be false. Also, asynchronous SNP systems with extended rules are known to be universal [5]. Our results provide some support to the conjecture, since neurons in SNPSP systems produce at most one spike each step (similar to standard rules) while synapses with weights function similar to extended rules (more than one spike can be produced each step). This work is organized as follows: Section 2 provides preliminaries for our results; syntax and semantics of SNPSP systems are given in Sect. 3; our (non)universality results are given in Sect. 4. Lastly, we provide final remarks and further directions in Sect. 5.

2   Preliminaries

It is assumed that the readers are familiar with the basics of membrane computing (a good introduction is [12] with recent results and information in the P systems webpage (http://ppage.psystems.eu/) and a recent handbook [13]) and formal language theory (available in many monographs). We only briefly mention notions and notations which will be useful throughout the paper.

We denote the set of positive integers as $\mathbb{N} = \{1, 2, \ldots\}$. Let V be an alphabet, V^* is the set of all finite strings over V with respect to concatenation and the identity element λ (the empty string). The set of all non-empty strings over V is denoted as V^+ so $V^+ = V^* - \{\lambda\}$. If $V = \{a\}$, we simply write a^* and a^+ instead of $\{a\}^*$ and $\{a\}^+$. If a is a symbol in V, we write $a^0 = \lambda$ and we write the language generated by a regular expression E over V as $L(E)$.

In proving computational universality, we use the notion of register machines. A register machine is a construct $M = (m, I, l_0, l_h, R)$, where m is the number of registers, I is the set of instruction labels, l_0 is the start label, l_h is the halt label, and R is the set of instructions. Every label $l_i \in I$ uniquely labels only one instruction in R. Register machine instructions have the following forms:

- $l_i : (\text{ADD}(r), l_j, l_k)$, increase n by 1, then nondeterministically go to l_j or l_k;
- $l_i : (\text{SUB}(r), l_j, l_k)$, if $n \geq 1$, then subtract 1 from n and go to l_j, otherwise perform no operation on r and go to l_k;
- $l_h : \text{HALT}$, the halt instruction.

Given a register machine M, we say M computes or generates a number n as follows: M starts with all its registers empty. The register machine then applies its instructions starting with the instruction labeled l_0. Without loss of generality, we assume that l_0 labels an ADD instruction, and that the content of the output register is never decremented, only added to during computation, i.e. no SUB instruction is applied to it. If M reaches the halt instruction l_h, then the number n stored during this time in the first (also the output) register is said to be computed by M. We denote the set of all numbers computed by M as $N(M)$. It was proven that register machines compute all sets of numbers computed by a Turing machine, therefore characterizing NRE [8]. A strongly monotonic register machine is one restricted variant: it has only one register which is also the output register. The register initially stores zero, and can only be incremented by 1 at each step. Once the machine halts, the value stored in the register is said to be computed. It is known that strongly monotonic register machines characterize $SLIN$, the family of length sets of regular languages.

3   Spiking Neural P Systems with Structural Plasticity

In this section we define SNP systems with structural plasticity. Initial motivations and results for SNP systems are included in the seminal paper in [7]. A *spiking neural P system with structural plasticity* (SNPSP system) of degree $m \geq 1$ is a construct of the form $\Pi = (O, \sigma_1, \ldots, \sigma_m, syn, out)$, where:

- $O = \{a\}$ is the singleton alphabet (a is called spike);
- $\sigma_1, \ldots, \sigma_m$ are neurons of the form $(n_i, R_i), 1 \leq i \leq m$; $n_i \geq 0$ indicates the initial number of spikes in σ_i; R_i is a finite rule set of σ_i with two forms:
    1. Spiking rule: $E/a^c \rightarrow a$, where E is a regular expression over O, $c \geq 1$;
    2. Plasticity rule: $E/a^c \rightarrow \alpha k(i, N)$, where E is a regular expression over O, $c \geq 1$, $\alpha \in \{+, -, \pm, \mp\}$, $k \geq 1$, and $N \subseteq \{1, \ldots, m\} - \{i\}$;
- $syn \subseteq \{1, \ldots, m\} \times \{1, \ldots, m\}$, with $(i, i) \notin syn$ for $1 \leq i \leq m$ (synapses between neurons);
- $out \in \{1, \ldots, m\}$ indicate the output neuron.

Given neuron σ_i (we also say neuron i or simply σ_i) we define the set of presynaptic (postsynaptic, resp.) neurons $pres(i) = \{j | (i, j) \in syn\}$ (as $pos(i) = \{j | (j, i) \in syn\}$, resp.). Spiking rule semantics in SNPSP systems are similar with SNP systems in [7]. In this work we do not use forgetting rules (rules of the form $a^s \rightarrow \lambda$) or rules with delays of the form $E/a^c \rightarrow a; d$ for some $d \geq 1$.

Spiking rules (also known as *standard rules*) are applied as follows: If neuron σ_i contains b spikes and $a^b \in L(E)$, with $b \geq c$, then a rule $E/a^c \rightarrow a \in R_i$ can be applied. Applying such a rule means consuming c spikes from σ_i, thus only $b - c$ spikes remain in σ_i. Neuron i sends one spike to every neuron with label in $pres(i)$ at the same step as rule application. A nonzero delay d means that if σ_i spikes at step t, then neurons receive the spike at $t + d$. Spikes sent to σ_i from t to $t + d - 1$ are lost (i.e. σ_i is closed), and σ_i can receive spikes (i.e. σ_i is open) and apply a rule again at $t + d$ and $t + d + 1$, respectively. If a rule $E/a^c \rightarrow a$ has $L(E) = \{a^c\}$, we simply write this as $a^c \rightarrow a$. *Extended rules* are of the form $E/a^c \rightarrow a^p, p \geq 1$, where more than one spike can be produced.

Plasticity rules are applied as follows. If at step t we have that σ_i has $b \geq c$ spikes and $a^b \in L(E)$, a rule $E/a^c \rightarrow \alpha k(i, N) \in R_i$ can be applied. The set N is a collection of neurons to which σ_i can connect to or disconnect from using the applied plasticity rule. The rule application consumes c spikes and performs one of the following, depending on α:

- If $\alpha := +$ and $N - pres(i) = \emptyset$, or if $\alpha := -$ and $pres(i) = \emptyset$, then there is nothing more to do, i.e. c spikes are consumed but no synapses are created or removed. Notice that with these semantics, a plasticity rule functions similar to a forgetting rule, i.e. the former can be used to consume spikes without producing any spike.
- for $\alpha := +$, if $|N - pres(i)| \leq k$, deterministically create a synapse to every $\sigma_l, l \in N_j - pres(i)$. If however $|N - pres(i)| > k$, nondeterministically select k neurons in $N - pres(i)$, and create one synapse to each selected neuron.
- for $\alpha := -$, if $|pres(i)| \leq k$, deterministically delete all synapses in $pres(i)$. If however $|pres(i)| > k$, nondeterministically select k neurons in $pres(i)$, and delete each synapse to the selected neurons.

If $\alpha \in \{\pm, \mp\}$: create (respectively, delete) synapses at step t and then delete (respectively, create) synapses at step $t + 1$. Only the priority of application of synapse creation or deletion is changed, but the application is similar to $\alpha \in \{+, -\}$. Neuron i is always open from t until $t + 1$, but σ_i can only apply another rule at time $t + 2$.

An important note is that for σ_i applying a rule with $\alpha \in \{+, \pm, \mp\}$, creating a synapse always involves an *embedded* sending of one spike when σ_i connects to a neuron. This single spike is sent at the time the synapse creation is applied, i.e. whenever σ_i *attaches* to σ_j using a synapse during synapse creation, we have σ_i immediately transferring one spike to σ_j.

Let t be a step during a computation: we say a σ_i is *activated* at step t if there is at least one $r \in R_i$ that can be applied; σ_i is *simple* if $|R_i| = 1$, with a nice biological and computing interpretation, i.e. some neurons do not need to be complex, but merely act as spike repositories or relays. We have the following nondeterminism levels: *rule-level*, if at least one neuron has at least two rules with regular expressions E_1 and E_2 such that $E_1 \neq E_2$ and $L(E_1) \cap L(E_2) \neq \emptyset$; *synapse-level*, if initially Π has at least one σ_i with a plasticity rule where $k < |N - pres(i)|$; *neuron-level*, if at least one activated neuron with rule r can choose to apply its rule r or not (i.e. asynchronous).

By default SNP and SNPSP systems are locally sequential (at most one rule is applied per neuron) but globally parallel (all activated neurons must apply a rule). The application of rules in neurons is usually synchronous, i.e. a global clock is assumed. However, in the asynchronous (*asyn*, in short) mode we release this synchronization so that neuron-level nondeterminism is implied. A configuration of an SNPSP system is based on (a) distribution of spikes in neurons, and (b) neuron connections based on *syn*. For some step t, we can represent: (a) as $\langle s_1, \ldots, s_m \rangle$ where $s_i, 1 \le i \le m$, is the number of spikes contained in σ_i; for (b) we can derive $pres(i)$ and $pos(i)$ from *syn*, for a given σ_i. The initial configuration therefore is represented as $\langle n_1, \ldots, n_m \rangle$, with the possibility of a disconnected graph, or $syn = \emptyset$. A computation is defined as a sequence of configuration transitions, from an initial configuration, and following rule application semantics. A computation halts if the system reaches a halting configuration, i.e. no rules can be applied and all neurons are open.

A result of a computation can be defined in several ways in SNP systems literature. For SNP systems in *asyn* mode however, and as in [3,5,14], the output is obtained by counting the total number of spikes sent out by σ_{out} to the environment (in short, Env) upon reaching a halting configuration. We refer to Π as generator, if Π computes in this asynchronous manner. Π can also work as an acceptor but this is not given in this work.

For our universality results, the following simplifying features are used in our systems as the normal form: (*i*) plasticity rules can only be found in purely plastic neurons (i.e. neurons with plasticity rules only), (*ii*) neurons with standard rules are simple, and (*iii*) we do not use forgetting rules or rules with delays. We denote the family of sets computed by asynchronous SNPSP systems (under the mentioned normal form) as generators as $N_{tot}SNPSP^{asyn}$: subscript *tot* indicates the total number of spikes sent to Env as the result; Other parameters are as follows: $+syn_k$ ($-syn_j$, respectively) where at most k (j, resp.) synapses are created (deleted, resp.) each step; $nd_\beta, \beta \in \{syn, rule, neur\}$ indicate additional levels of nondeterminism source; $rule_m$ indicates at most m rules (either standard or plasticity) per neuron; Since our results for k and j for $+syn_k$ and $-syn_j$ are equal, we write them instead in the compressed form $\pm syn_k$, where $\pm$ in this sense is not the same as when $\alpha := \pm$. A bound p on the number of spikes stored in any neuron of the system is denoted as $bound_p$. We omit nd_{neur} from writing since it is implied in *asyn* mode.

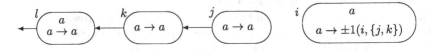

Fig. 1. An SNPSP system Π_{ej}.

To illustrate the notions and semantics in SNPSP systems, we take as an example the SNPSP system Π_{ej} of degree 4 in Fig. 1, and describe its computations. The initial configuration is as follows: spike distribution is $\langle 1, 0, 0, 1 \rangle$ for the neuron order σ_i, σ_j, σ_k, σ_l, respectively; $syn = \{(j, k), (k, l)\}$; output neuron is σ_l, indicated by the outgoing synapse to Env.

Given the initial configuration, σ_i and σ_l can become activated. Due to $asyn$ mode however, they can decide to apply their rules at a later step. If σ_l applies its rule before it receives a spike from σ_i, then it will spike to Env twice so that $N_{tot}(\Pi_{ej}) = \{2\}$. Since $k = 1 < |\{j, k\}|$ and $pres(i) = \emptyset$, σ_i nondeterministically selects whether to create synapse (i, j) or (i, k); if (i, j) $((i, k)$, resp.) is created; a spike is sent from σ_i to σ_j (σ_k, resp.) due to the embedded sending of a spike during synapse creation. Let this be step t. If (i, j) is created then $syn' := syn \cup \{(i, j)\}$, otherwise $syn'' := syn \cup \{(i, k)\}$. At $t + 1$, σ_i deletes the created synapse at t (since $\alpha := \pm$), and we have syn again. Note that if σ_l does not apply its rule and collects two spikes (one spike from σ_i), the computation is aborted or blocked, i.e. no output is produced since $a^2 \notin L(a)$.

4   Main Results

In this section we use at most two nondeterminism sources: nd_{neur} (in $asyn$ mode), and nd_{syn}. Recall that in $asyn$ mode, if σ_i is activated at step t so that an $r \in R_i$ can be applied, σ_i can choose to apply r or not. If σ_i did not choose to apply r, σ_i can continue to receive spikes so that for some $t' > t$, it is possible that: r can never be applied again, or some $r' \in R_i, r' \neq r$, is applied.

For the next result, each neuron can store only a bounded number of spikes (see for example [3, 6, 7] and references therein). In [6], it is known that bounded SNP systems with extended rules in $asyn$ mode characterize $SLIN$, but it is open whether such result holds for systems with standard rules only. In [3], a negative answer was conjectured for the following open problem: are asynchronous SNP systems with standard rules universal? First, we prove that bounded SNPSP systems in $asyn$ mode characterize $SLIN$, hence they are not universal.

Lemma 1. $N_{tot}SNPSP^{asyn}(bound_p, nd_{syn}) \subseteq SLIN, p \geq 1.$

Proof. Taking any asynchronous SNPSP system Π with a given bound p on the number of spikes stored in any neuron, we observe that the number of possible configurations is finite: Π has a constant number of neurons, and that the number of spikes stored in each neuron are bounded. We then construct a right-linear grammar G, such that Π generates the length set of the regular language $L(G)$. Let us denote by $\mathcal{C}$ the set of all possible configurations of Π, with C_0 being the initial configuration. The right-linear grammar $G = (\mathcal{C}, \{a\}, C_0, P)$, where the production rules in P are as follows:

(1) $C \rightarrow C'$, for $C, C' \in \mathcal{C}$ if Π has a transition $C \Rightarrow C'$ in which the output neuron does not spike;

(2) $C \rightarrow aC'$, for $C, C' \in \mathcal{C}$ if Π has a transition $C \Rightarrow C'$ in which the output neuron spikes;

(3) $C \rightarrow \lambda$, for any $C \in \mathcal{C}$ in which Π halts.

Due to the construction of G, Π generates the length set of $L(G)$, hence the set is semilinear. □

Lemma 2. $SLIN \subseteq N_{tot}SNPSP^{asyn}(bound_p, nd_{syn}), p \geq 1.$

The proof is based on the following observation: A set Q is semilinear if and only if Q is generated by a strongly monotonic register machine M. It suffices to construct an SNPSP system Π with restrictions given in the theorem statement, such that Π simulates M. Recall that M has precisely register 1 only (it is also the output register) and addition instructions of the form $l_i : (\text{ADD}(1), l_j, l_k)$. The ADD module for Π is given in Fig. 2. Next, we describe the computations in Π.

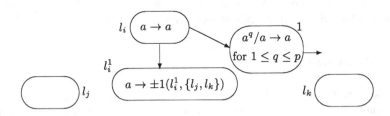

Fig. 2. Module ADD simulating $l_i : (\text{ADD}(1) : l_j, l_k)$ in the proof of Lemma 2

Once ADD instruction l_i of M is applied, σ_{l_i} is activated and it sends one spike each to σ_1 and $\sigma_{l_i^1}$. At this point we have two possible cases due to *asyn* mode, i.e. either σ_1 spikes to Env before $\sigma_{l_i^1}$ spikes, or after. If σ_1 spikes before $\sigma_{l_i^1}$, then the number of spikes in Env is immediately incremented by 1. After some time, the computation will proceed if $\sigma_{l_i^1}$ applies its only (plasticity) rule. Once $\sigma_{l_i^1}$ applies its rule, either σ_{l_j} or σ_{l_k} becomes nondeterministically activated.

However, if σ_1 spikes after $\sigma_{l_i^1}$ spikes, then the number of spikes in Env is not immediately incremented by 1 since σ_1 does not consume a spike and fire to Env. The next instruction, either l_j or l_k, is then simulated by Π. Furthermore, due to *asyn* mode, the following "worst case" computation is possible: σ_{l_h} becomes activated (corresponding to l_h in M being applied, thus halting M) before σ_1 spikes. In this computation, M has halted and has applied an m number of ADD instructions since the application of l_i. Without loss of generality we can have the arbitrary bound $p > m$, for some positive integer p. We then have the output neuron σ_1 storing m spikes. Since the rules in σ_1 are of the form $a^q/a \rightarrow a, 1 \leq q \leq p$, σ_1 consumes one spike at each step it decides to apply a rule, starting with rule $a^m/a \rightarrow a$, until rule $a \rightarrow a$. Thus, Π will only halt once σ_1 has emptied all spikes it stores, sending m spikes to Env in the process.

The FIN module is not necessary, and we add σ_{l_h} without any rule (or maintain $pres(l_h) = \emptyset$). Once M halts by reaching instruction l_h, a spike in Π is sent to neuron l_h. Π is clearly bounded: every neuron in Π can only store at most p spikes, at any step. We then have Π correctly simulating the strongly monotonic register machine M. This completes the proof. □

From Lemmas 1 and 2, we can have the next result.

Theorem 1. $SLIN = N_{tot}SNPSP^{asyn}(bound_p, nd_{syn}), p \geq 1$.

Next, in order to achieve universality, we add an additional ingredient to asynchronous SNPSP systems: weighted synapses. The ingredient of weighted synapses has already been introduced in SNP systems literature, and we refer the reader to [15] (and references therein) for computing and biological motivations. In particular, if σ_i applies a rule $E/a^c \rightarrow a^p$, and the weighted synapse (i, j, r) exists (i.e. the weight of synapse (i, j) is r) then σ_j receives $p \times r$ spikes.

It seems natural to consider weighted synapses for asynchronous SNPSP systems: since asynchronous SNPSP systems are not universal, we look for other ways to improve their power. SNPSP systems with weighted synapses (in short, WSNPSP systems) are defined in a similar way as SNPSP systems, except for the plasticity rules and the synapse set. Plasticity rules in σ_i are now of the form

$$E/a^c \rightarrow \alpha k(i, N, r),$$

where $r \geq 1$, and E, c, α, k, N are as previously defined. Every synapse created by σ_i using a plasticity rule with weight r receives the weight r. Instead of one spike sent from σ_i to a σ_j during synapse creation, $j \in N$, r spikes are sent to σ_j. The synapse set is now of the form

$$syn \subseteq \{1, 2, \ldots, m\} \times \{1, 2, \ldots, m\} \times \mathbb{N}.$$

We note that SNPSP systems are special cases of SNPSP systems with weighted synapses where $r = 1$, and when $r = 1$ we omit it from writing. In weighted SNP systems with standard rules, the weights can allow neurons to produce more than one spike each step, similar to having extended rules. In this way, our next result parallels the result that asynchronous SNP systems with extended rules are universal in [5]. However, our next result uses nd_{syn} with $asyn$ mode, while in [5] their systems use nd_{rule} with $asyn$ mode. We also add the additional parameter l in our universality result, where the synapse weight in the system is at most l. Our universality result also makes use of the normal form given in Sect. 3.

Theorem 2. $N_{tot}WSNPSP^{asyn}(rule_m, \pm syn_k, weight_l, nd_{syn}) = NRE, m \geq 9, k \geq 1, l \geq 3$.

Proof. We construct an asynchronous SNPSP system with weighted synapses Π, with restrictions given in the theorem statement, to simulate a register machine M. The general description of the simulation is as follows: each register r of M corresponds to σ_r in Π. If register r stores the value n, σ_r stores $2n$ spikes. Simulating instruction $l_i : (\text{OP}(r) : l_j, l_k)$ of M in Π corresponds to σ_{l_i} becoming activated. After σ_{l_i} is activated, the operation OP is performed on σ_r, and σ_{l_j} or σ_{l_k} becomes activated. We make use of modules in Π to perform addition, subtraction, and halting of the computation.

Module ADD: The module is shown in Fig. 3. At some step t, σ_{l_i} sends a spike to $\sigma_{l_i^1}$. At some $t' > t$, $\sigma_{l_i^1}$ sends a spike: the spike sent to σ_r is multiplied by two, while 1 spike is received by $\sigma_{l_i^2}$. For now we omit further details for σ_r, since it is never activated with an even number of spikes.

At some $t'' > t'$, $\sigma_{l_i^2}$ nondeterministically creates (then deletes) either (l_i^2, l_j) or (l_i^2, l_k). The chosen synapse then allows either σ_{l_j} or σ_{l_k} to become activated. The ADD module thus increments the contents of σ_r by 2, simulating the increment by 1 of register r. Next, only one among σ_{l_j} or σ_{l_k} becomes nondeterministically activated. The addition operation is correctly simulated.

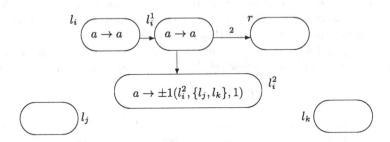

Fig. 3. Module ADD simulating $l_i : (\text{ADD}(r) : l_j, l_k)$ in the proof of Theorem 2.

Module SUB: The module is shown in Fig. 4. Let $|S_r|$ be the number of instructions with form $l_i : (\text{SUB}(r), l_j, l_k)$, and $1 \leq s \leq |S_r|$. $|S_r|$ is the number of SUB instructions operating on register r, and we explain in a moment why we use a size of a set for this number. Clearly, when no SUB operation is performed on r, then $|S_r| = 0$, as in the case of register 1. At some step t, σ_{l_i} spikes, sending 1 spike to σ_r, and $4|S_r| - s$ spikes to $\sigma_{l_i^1}$ (the weight of synapse (l_i, l_i^1)).

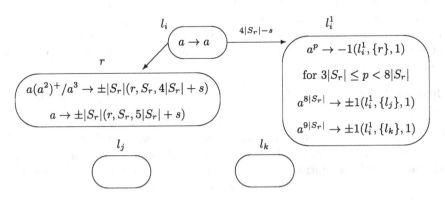

Fig. 4. Module SUB simulating $l_i : (\text{SUB}(r) : l_j, l_k)$ in the proof of Theorem 2.

$\sigma_{l_i^1}$ has rules of the form $a^p \to -1(l_i^1, \{r\}, 1)$, for $3|S_r| \leq p < 8|S_r|$. When one of these rules is applied, it performs similar to a forgetting rule: p spikes are consumed and deletes a nonexisting synapse (l_i^1, r). Since $\sigma_{l_i^1}$ received $4|S_r| - s$

spikes from σ_{l_i}, and $3|S_r| \leq 4|S_r| - s < 8|S_r|$, then one of these rules can be applied. If $\sigma_{l_i^1}$ applies one of these rules at $t' > t$, no spike remains. Otherwise, the $4|S_r| - s$ spikes can combine with the spikes from σ_r at a later step.

In the case where register r stores $n = 0$ (respectively, $n \geq 1$), then instruction l_k (respectively, l_j) is applied next. This case corresponds to σ_r applying the rule with $E = a$ (respectively, $E = a(a^2)^+$), which at some later step allows σ_{l_k} (respectively, σ_{l_j}) to be activated.

For the moment let us simply define $S_r = \{l_i^1\}$. For case $n = 0$ (respectively, $n \geq 1$), σ_r stores 0 spikes (respectively, at least 2 spikes), so that at some $t'' > t$ the synapse $(r, l_i^1, 5|S_r| + s)$ (respectively, $(r, l_i^1, 4|S_r| + s)$) is created and then deleted. $\sigma_{l_i^1}$ then receives $5|S_r| + s$ spikes (respectively, $4|S_r| + s$ spikes) from σ_r. Note that we can have $t'' \geq t'$ or $t'' \leq t'$, due to $asyn$ mode, where t' is again the step that $\sigma_{l_i^1}$ applies a rule. If $\sigma_{l_i^1}$ previously removed all of its spikes using its rules with $E = a^p$, then it again removes all spikes from σ_r because $3|S_r| \leq x < 8|S_r|$, where $x \in \{4|S_r| + s, 5|S_r| + s\}$. At this point, no further rules can be applied, and the computation aborts, i.e. no output is produced. If however $\sigma_{l_i^1}$ did not remove its spikes previously, then it collects a total of either $8|S_r|$ or $9|S_r|$ spikes. Either σ_{l_j} or σ_{l_k} is then activated by $\sigma_{l_i^1}$ at a step after t''.

To remove the possibility of "wrong" simulations when at least two SUB instructions operate on register r, we give the general definition of S_r: $S_r = \{l_v^1 | l_v$ is a SUB instruction on register $r\}$. In the SUB module, a rule application in σ_r creates (and then deletes) an $|S_r|$ number of synapses: one synapse from σ_r to all neurons with label $l_v^1 \in S_r$. Again, each neuron with label l_v^1 can receive either $4|S_r| + s$, or $5|S_r| + s$ spikes from σ_r, and $4|S_r| - s$ spikes from σ_{l_v}.

Let l_i be the SUB instruction that is currently being simulated in Π. In order for the correct computation to continue, only $\sigma_{l_i^1}$ must not apply a rule with $E = a^p$, i.e. it must not remove any spikes from σ_r or σ_{l_i}. The remaining $|S_r| - 1$ neurons of the form l_v^1 must apply their rules with $E = a^p$ and remove the spikes from σ_r. Due to $asyn$ mode, the $|S_r| - 1$ neurons can choose not to remove the spikes from σ_r: these neurons can then receive further spikes from σ_r in future steps, in particular they receive either $4|S_r| + s'$ or $5|S_r| + s'$ spikes, for $1 \leq s' \leq S_r$; these neurons then accumulate a number of spikes greater than $8|S_r|$ (hence, no rule with $E = a^p$ can be applied), but not equal to $8|S_r|$ or $9|S_r|$ (hence, no plasticity rule can be applied). Similarly, if these spikes are not removed, and spikes from $\sigma_{l_{v'}}$ are received, $v \neq v'$ and $l_{v'} \in S_r$, no rule can again be applied: if $l_{v'}$ is the s'th SUB instruction operating on register r, then $s \neq s'$ and $\sigma_{l_{v'}}$ accumulates a number of spikes greater than $8|S_r|$ (the synapse weight of $(l_{v'}, l_{v'}^1)$ is $4|S_r| - s'$), but not equal to $8|S_r|$ or $9|S_r|$. No computation can continue if the $|S_r| - 1$ neurons do not remove their spikes from σ_r, so computation aborts and no output is produced. This means that only the computations in Π that are allowed to continue are the computations that correctly simulate a SUB instruction in M.

The SUB module correctly simulates a SUB instruction: instruction l_j is simulated only if r stores a positive value (after decrementing by 1 the value of r), otherwise instruction l_k is simulated (the value of r is not decremented).

Module FIN: The module FIN for halting the computation of Π is shown in Fig. 5. The operation of the module is clear: once M reaches instruction l_h and halts, σ_{l_h} becomes activated. Neuron l_h sends a spike to σ_1, the neuron corresponding to register 1 of M. Once the number of spikes in σ_1 become odd (of the form $2n + 1$, where n is the value stored in register 1), σ_1 keeps applying its only rule: at every step, 2 spikes are consumed, and 1 spike is sent to Env. In this way, the number n is computed since σ_1 will send precisely n spikes to Env.

The ADD module has nd_{syn}: initially it has $pres(l_i^2) = \emptyset$, and its $k = 1 < |N|$. We also observe the parameter values: m is at least 9 by setting $|S_r| = 1$, then adding the two additional rules in $\sigma_{l_i^1}$; k is clearly at least 1; lastly, the synapse weight l is at least 3 by again setting $|S_r| = 1$. This completes the proof. $\square$

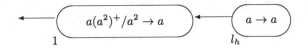

Fig. 5. Module FIN in the proof of Theorem 2.

5   Conclusions and Final Remarks

In [5] it is known that asynchronous SNP systems with extended rules are universal, while the conjecture is that asynchronous SNP systems with standard rules are not [3]. In Theorem 1, we showed that asynchronous bounded SNPSP systems are not universal where, similar to standard rules, each neuron can only produce at most one spike each step. In Theorem 2, asynchronous WSNPSP systems are shown to be universal. In WSNPSP systems, the synapse weights perform a function similar to extended rules in the sense that a neuron can produce more than one spike each step. Our results thus provide support to the conjecture about the nonuniversality of asynchronous SNP systems with standard rules. It is also interesting to realize the computing power of asynchronous unbounded (in spikes) SNPSP systems.

It can be argued that when $\alpha \in \{\pm, \mp\}$, the synapse creation (resp., deletion) immediately followed by a synapse deletion (resp., creation) is another form of synchronization. Can asynchronous WSNPSP systems maintain their computing power, if we further restrict them by removing such semantic? Another interesting question is as follows: in the ADD module in Theorem 2, we have nd_{syn}. Can we still maintain universality if we remove this level, so that nd_{neur} in *asyn* mode is the only source of nondeterminism? In [5] for example, the modules used *asyn* mode and nd_{rule}, while in [14], only *asyn* mode was used (but with the use of a new ingredient called local synchronization).

In Theorem 2, the construction is based on the value $|S_r|$. Can we have a uniform construction while maintaining universality? i.e. can we construct a Π such that $N(\Pi) = NRE$, but is independent on the number of SUB instructions of M? Then perhaps parameters m and l in Theorem 2 can be reduced.

Acknowledgments. Cabarle is supported by a scholarship from the DOST-ERDT of the Philippines. Adorna is funded by a DOST-ERDT grant and the Semirara Mining Corp. Professorial Chair of the College of Engineering, UP Diliman. M.J. Pérez-Jiménez acknowledges the support of the Project TIN2012-37434 of the "Ministerio de Economía y Competitividad" of Spain, co-financed by FEDER funds. Anonymous referees are also acknowledged in helping improve this work.

References

1. Cabarle, F.G.C., Adorna, H., Ibo, N.: Spiking neural P systems with structural plasticity. In: Pre-proceedings of 2nd Asian Conference on Membrane Computing, pp. 13–26, Chengdu, 4–7 November 2013
2. Cabarle, F.G.C., Adorna, H.N., Pérez-Jiménez, M.J., Song, T.: Spiking neural P systems with structural plasticity. Neural Comput. Appl. **26**(131), 1129–1136 (2015). doi:10.1007/s00521-015-1857-4
3. Cavaliere, M., Egecioglu, O., Ibarra, O.H., Ionescu, M., Păun, G., Woodworth, S.: Asynchronous spiking neural P systems: decidability and undecidability. In: Garzon, M.H., Yan, H. (eds.) DNA 2007. LNCS, vol. 4848, pp. 246–255. Springer, Heidelberg (2008)
4. Chen, H., Ionescu, M., Ishdorj, T.-I., Păun, A., Păun, G., Pérez-Jiménez, M.J.: Spiking neural P systems with extended rules: universality and languages. Natural Comput. **7**, 147–166 (2008)
5. Cavaliere, M., Ibarra, O., Păun, G., Egecioglu, O., Ionescu, M., Woodworth, S.: Asynchronous spiking neural P systems. Theor. Com. Sci. **410**, 2352–2364 (2009)
6. Ibarra, O.H., Woodworth, S.: Spiking neural P systems: some characterizations. In: Csuhaj-Varjú, E., Ésik, Z. (eds.) FCT 2007. LNCS, vol. 4639, pp. 23–37. Springer, Heidelberg (2007)
7. Ionescu, M., Păun, G., Yokomori, T.: Spiking neural P systems. Fundam. Inform. **71**(2–3), 279–308 (2006)
8. Minsky, M.: Computation: Finite and infinite machines. Prentice Hall, Englewood Cliffs (1967)
9. Pan, L., Păun, G., Pérez-Jiménez, M.J.: Spiking neural P systems with neuron division and budding. Sci. China Inf. Sci. **54**(8), 1596–1607 (2011)
10. Pan, L., Wang, J., Hoogeboom, J.H.: Spiking neural P systems with astrocytes. Neural Comput. **24**, 805–825 (2012)
11. Păun, A., Păun, G.: Small universal spiking neural P systems. Biosystems **90**, 48–60 (2007)
12. Păun, G.: Membrane Computing: An Introduction. Springer, New York (2002)
13. Păun, G., Rozenberg, G., Salomaa, A.: The Oxford Handbook of Membrane Computing. Oxford University Press, New York (2009)
14. Song, T., Pan, L., Păun, G.: Asynchronous spiking neural P systems with local synchronization. Inf. Sci. **219**(10), 197–207 (2013)
15. Wang, J., Hoogeboom, H.J., Pan, L., Păun, G., Pérez-Jiménez, M.J.: Spiking neural P systems with weights. Neural Comput. **22**(10), 2615–2646 (2010)

Expressive Power of Non-deterministic Evolving Recurrent Neural Networks in Terms of Their Attractor Dynamics

Jérémie Cabessa[1]([✉]) and Jacques Duparc[2]

[1] Laboratory of Mathematical Economics,
University of Paris 2 – Panthéon-Assas, 4 Rue Blaise Desgoffe,
75006 Paris, France
jeremie.cabessa@u-paris2.fr
[2] Department of Information Systems, Faculty of Business and Economics,
University of Lausanne, CH-1015 Lausanne, Switzerland

Abstract. We introduce a model of nondeterministic hybrid recurrent neural networks – made up of Boolean input and output cells as well as internal sigmoid neurons, and equipped with the possibility to have their synaptic weights evolve over time, in a nondeterministic manner. When subjected to some infinite input stream and some specific synaptic evolution, the networks necessarily exhibit some attractor dynamics in their Boolean output cells, and accordingly, recognize some specific neural ω -languages. The expressive power of these networks is measured via the topological complexity of their underlying neural ω-languages. In this context, we prove that the two models of rational-weighted and real-weighted nondeterministic hybrid neural networks are computationally equivalent, and recognize precisely the set of all analytic neural ω-languages. They are therefore strictly more expressive than the nondeterministic Büchi and Muller Turing machines.

Keywords: Recurrent neural networks · Neural computation · Analog computation · Evolving systems · Attractors · Turing machines · Expressive power

1 Introduction

The understanding of the computational and dynamical capabilities of brain-like models of computation represents an issue of central importance. In this context, much attention has been focused on comparing the computational powers of various neural models to those of diverse abstract machines, see for instance [2,4, 13–16,18–20,23]. As a consequence, the computational power of neural networks has been shown to be intimately related to the nature of their synaptic weights and activation functions, and able to range from finite state automata [13–15] up to super-Turing capabilities [2,4,18–20].

  Following this global line of thought, the first author initiated the study of the expressive power of recurrent neural networks from the perspective of

C.S. Calude and M.J. Dinneen (Eds.): UCNC 2015, LNCS 9252, pp. 144–156, 2015.
DOI: 10.1007/978-3-319-21819-9_10

their attractor dynamics [7,10]. This approach is motivated by the fact that, in their model, the attractor dynamics of the neural networks are the precise phenomena that underly the arising of spatiotemporal patterns of discharges – a feature considered to be significantly involved in the processing and coding of information in the brain [24,25].

In this context, they proved that Boolean recurrent neural networks provided with some assignment of their attractors into two different kinds are computationally equivalent to Muller automata, and hence recognize precisely the so-called ω-regular neural languages. Consequently, the most refined topological classification of ω-languages [26] can be transposed from the automaton to the neural network context, and yields to some transfinite hierarchical classification of Boolean neural networks according to their attractor dynamics [6], which in turn represents a new attractor-based complexity measurement for Boolean recurrent neural networks [10].

More recently, they considered a model of so-called *hybrid recurrent neural networks* composed with Boolean input and output cells as well as internal sigmoid neurons. They showed that the rational and real-weighted hybrid neural networks are computationally equivalent to and strictly more powerful than deterministic Muller Turing machines, respectively [5]. Furthermore, the evolving hybrid neural nets are equivalent to the real-weighted ones, irrespective of whether their synaptic weights are modelled by rational or real numbers [5]. These results provide a generalization to this specific computational context of those obtained for the cases of classical [2,4] and interactive computation [1,3,9,11].

Here, we provide the nondeterministic counterpart of these results. We consider a model of *nondeterministic hybrid recurrent neural networks*, which consist of hybrid neural nets equipped with the possibility to have their synaptic weights evolve over time – in a nondeterministic manner. When subjected to some infinite input stream as well as to some specific evolution of their synaptic weights, the networks necessarily exhibit some attractor dynamics in their Boolean output cells, which is assumed to be of two possible kinds, either *meaningful* or *spurious*. The neural ω-language of a network corresponds to the set of all input streams which induce a meaningful attractor dynamics, for some possible evolution of its synaptic weights. The expressive power of the networks is then measured via the topological complexity of their underlying neural ω-languages. In this context, we prove that the two models of rational-weighted and real-weighted nondeterministic hybrid neural networks are computationally equivalent, and recognize precisely the set of all analytic neural ω-languages. They are therefore strictly more expressive than the nondeterministic Büchi and Muller Turing machines. These results are discussed in the last section.

2   Preliminaries

A *topological space* is a pair $(S, \mathcal{T})$ where S is a set and $\mathcal{T}$ is a collection of subsets of S such that $\emptyset \in \mathcal{T}$, $S \in \mathcal{T}$, and $\mathcal{T}$ is closed under arbitrary unions and finite intersections. The collection $\mathcal{T}$ is called a *topology* on S, and its members are called *open sets*. Given some topological space $(S, \mathcal{T})$, the class *Borel subsets* of S, denoted by $\boldsymbol{\Delta}_1^1$, consists of the smallest collection of subsets of S containing all open sets and closed under countable union and complementation. For every ordinal α, one defines by transfinite induction the following *Borel classes*:

- $\boldsymbol{\Sigma}_1^0 = \{X \subseteq S : X \text{ is open}\}$,
- $\boldsymbol{\Pi}_\alpha^0 = \{X \subseteq S : X^{\complement} \in \boldsymbol{\Sigma}_\alpha^0\}$,
- $\boldsymbol{\Sigma}_\alpha^0 = \{X \subseteq S : X = \bigcup_{n \geq 0} X_n,\ X_n \in \boldsymbol{\Pi}_{\alpha_n}^0,\ \alpha_n < \alpha,\ n \in \mathbb{N}\}$, for $\alpha > 1$,
- $\boldsymbol{\Delta}_\alpha^0 = \boldsymbol{\Sigma}_\alpha^0 \cap \boldsymbol{\Pi}_\alpha^0$.

The collection of all classes $\boldsymbol{\Sigma}_\alpha^0$, $\boldsymbol{\Pi}_\alpha^0$, and $\boldsymbol{\Delta}_\alpha^0$ provides a stratification of the whole class of Borel sets known as *the Borel hierarchy*. The *rank* of a Borel set $X \subseteq S$ is the smallest ordinal α such that $X \in \boldsymbol{\Sigma}_\alpha^0 \cup \boldsymbol{\Pi}_\alpha^0 \cup \boldsymbol{\Delta}_\alpha^0$, and represents the minimal number of complementation and countable union operations that are needed in order to obtain X from an initial collection of open sets. It is commonly considered as a relevant measure of the topological complexity of Borel sets.

Besides, given any set A, we let A^*, A^+ and A^ω denote respectively the sets of finite sequences, non-empty finite sequences and infinite sequences of elements of A. For any $x \in A^* \cup A^\omega$, the *length* of x is denoted by $|x|$, the $(i+1)$-th element of x will be denoted by $x(i)$ for any $0 \leq i < |x|$, and the subsequence of the n-th first elements of x is denoted by $x[0{:}n]$, with the convention that $x[0{:}0] = \lambda$, the empty sequence. Hence, any $x \in A^+$ and $y \in A^\omega$ can be written as $x = x(0)x(1) \cdots x(|x|-1)$ and $y = y(0)y(1)y(2) \cdots$, respectively. The fact that x is a *prefix* (resp. *strict prefix*) of y will be denoted by $x \sqsubseteq y$ (resp. $x \sqsubsetneq y$). The concatenation of x and y is denoted $x \cdot y$, and for any $X \subseteq A^*$ and $Y \subseteq A^* \cup A^\omega$, one sets $X \cdot Y = \{z \in A^* \cup A^\omega : z = x \cdot y \text{ for some } x \in X \text{ and } y \in Y\}$. A set of the form $\{x\} \cdot A^\omega$ is generally denoted $x \cdot A^\omega$. Finally, a sequence of $A^* \cup A^\omega$ will also be called a *word*, and a subset of A^ω is generally called an *ω-language*.

In the sequel, the spaces of N-dimensional Boolean, rational and real vectors will be denoted by $\mathbb{B}^N$, $\mathbb{Q}^N$ and $\mathbb{R}^N$, respectively. The space $(\mathbb{B}^N)^\omega$ is naturally assumed to be equipped with the product topology of the discrete topology on $\mathbb{B}^N$. Accordingly, the basic open sets are of the form $p \cdot (\mathbb{B}^N)^\omega$, for some $p \in (\mathbb{B}^N)^*$. The general open sets are countable unions of basic open sets. This space is Polish (i.e., separable and completely metrizable) [12]. The spaces $(\mathbb{Q}^N)^\omega$ and $(\mathbb{R}^N)^\omega$ are assumed to be equipped with the product topologies of the usual topologies on $\mathbb{Q}^N$ and $\mathbb{R}^N$, respectively. Accordingly, the basic open sets are of the form $X_0 \cdot \ldots \cdot X_n \cdot (\mathbb{Q}^N)^\omega$ or $X_0 \cdot \ldots \cdot X_n \cdot (\mathbb{R}^N)^\omega$, for some $n \geq 0$, where each X_i is an open set of $\mathbb{Q}^N$ or $\mathbb{R}^N$ for their usual topologies, respectively. The general open sets are arbitrary unions of basic open sets. These two spaces are also Polish [12].

An ω-language $L \subseteq (\mathbb{B}^N)^\omega$ is *analytic* iff there exists some $\boldsymbol{\Pi}_2^0$-set $X \subseteq (\mathbb{B}^N)^\omega \times \{0,1\}^\omega$ such that $L = \pi_1(X) = \{s \in (\mathbb{B}^N)^\omega : \exists\, e \in \{0,1\}^\omega \text{ s.t. } (s, e) \in X\}$ [12, Exercise 14.3]. This fact will be used in forthcoming Proposition 1. Equivalently, $L \subseteq (\mathbb{B}^N)^\omega$ is *analytic* iff there exists some Polish space E and some Borel set $X \subseteq (\mathbb{B}^N)^\omega \times E$ such that $L = \pi_1(X)$ [12, Exercise 14.3]. This fact will be used in forthcoming Proposition 2. The class of analytic sets, denoted by $\boldsymbol{\Sigma}_1^1$, strictly contains that of Borel sets, namely $\boldsymbol{\Delta}_1^1 \subsetneq \boldsymbol{\Sigma}_1^1$ [12, Theorem 14.2].

3   Büchi and Muller Turing Machines

The study of the behavior of reactive systems has led to the emergence of a theory of automata working on infinite objects [17,22]. In this context, a *Büchi* (resp. a *Muller*) *Turing machine* can be defined as a pair $(\mathcal{M}, \mathcal{F})$ (resp. a pair $(\mathcal{M}', \mathcal{T})$), where $\mathcal{M}$ (resp. $\mathcal{M}'$) is a classical Turing machine and $\mathcal{F}$ is a subset of the states of $\mathcal{M}$ (resp. $\mathcal{T}$ is a collection of subsets of the states of $\mathcal{M}'$). In the case of $\mathcal{M}$ (resp. $\mathcal{M}'$) being deterministic, an infinite input stream s is said to be recognized by $\mathcal{M}$ (resp. by $\mathcal{M}'$) if the set of states visited infinitely often by $\mathcal{M}$ (resp. by $\mathcal{M}'$) during the processing of s intersects the set $\mathcal{F}$ (resp. belongs to the collection $\mathcal{T}$). In the non-deterministic case, s is said to be *recognized* by each such machine if there exists a computational path which satisfies the required condition. The ω-language associated with each such machine consists of the set of all words that it recognizes.

The deterministic Büchi Turing machines are strictly less powerful than the deterministic Muller ones. Indeed, every ω-language recognized by some deterministic Büchi Turing machine belongs to the topological class $\mathbf{\Pi_2^0}$, whereas the ones recognized by Muller Turing machine belong to the topological class $BC(\mathbf{\Pi_2^0})$, i.e., the finite Boolean combinations of $\mathbf{\Pi_2^0}$-sets [21, Corollaries 3.3 and 3.4]. Moreover, one can easily show the existence of infinitely many ω-languages which are recognizable by some Muller Turing machines but by no Büchi Turing machine. In the non-deterministic case, Büchi and Muller Turing machines are computationally equivalent. They recognize precisely the class of *effectively analytic* ω-languages [21, Theorem 3.5].

The class of effectively analytic sets is usually denoted by Σ_1^1 (lightface), and for the sequel, we recall that the relation $\Sigma_1^1 \subsetneq \mathbf{\Sigma_1^1}$ trivially holds [12].

4   The Model

We introduce a model of so-called *hybrid evolving recurrent neural network*. The term *hybrid* refers to the fact that the network involves both Boolean and sigmoid cells. The term *evolving* refers to the fact that the synaptic weights are able to evolve over time. The expressive power of the networks will be related to the attractor dynamics of their Boolean output cells.

A *hybrid (or Boolean/sigmoid) evolving recurrent neural network* (denoted by Ev-RNN) consists of a synchronous network of neurons related together in a general architecture. The network contains N internal sigmoid neurons $(x_i)_{i=1}^N$, M Boolean input cells $(u_i)_{i=1}^M$, and P Boolean output cells $(y_i)_{i=1}^P$. The dynamics of the network is computed as follows: given the activation values of the internal and input neurons $(x_j)_{j=1}^N$ and $(u_j)_{j=1}^M$ at time t, the activation values of each internal neuron x_i and each output neuron y_i at time $t+1$ are updated by the following equations, respectively:

$$x_i(t+1) = \sigma \left(\sum_{j=1}^N a_{ij}(t) \cdot x_j(t) + \sum_{j=1}^M b_{ij}(t) \cdot u_j(t) + c_i(t) \right) \text{ for } i = 1, \ldots, N \quad (1)$$

$$y_i(t+1) = \theta \left(\sum_{j=1}^{N} a_{ij}(t) \cdot x_j(t) + \sum_{j=1}^{M} b_{ij}(t) \cdot u_j(t) + c_i(t) \right) \text{ for } i = 1, \ldots, P \quad (2)$$

Here, $a_{ij}(t)$, $b_{ij}(t)$, and $c_i(t)$ are time dependent values describing the evolving weighted synaptic connections and weighted bias of the network, and σ and θ are the classical sigmoid-linear and hard-threshold activation functions respectively defined by:

$$\sigma(x) = \begin{cases} 0 & \text{if } x < 0, \\ x & \text{if } 0 \leq x \leq 1, \\ 1 & \text{if } x > 1 \end{cases} \quad \text{and} \quad \theta(x) = \begin{cases} 0 & \text{if } x < 1, \\ 1 & \text{if } x \geq 1. \end{cases}$$

We further assume that the synaptic weights $a_{ij}(t)$, $b_{ij}(t)$, $c_i(t)$ might evolve between two designated bounds S and S' imposed by the biological constitution of the synapses.

Throughout this paper, two models of Ev-RNNs are considered according to the nature of their synaptic weights. In fact, an Ev-RNN will be called *rational* (denoted by Ev-RNN[$\mathbb{Q}$]) or *real* (denoted by Ev-RNN[$\mathbb{R}$]) if its synaptic weights $a_{ij}(t), b_{ij}(t), c_i(t)$ are modelled by rational or real numbers at any time step t, respectively. Note that any Ev-RNN[$\mathbb{Q}$] is also an Ev-RNN[$\mathbb{R}$] by definition.

Let $\mathcal{N}$ be some Ev-RNN $\mathcal{N}$. For each time step $t \geq 0$, the Boolean vector

$$\boldsymbol{u}(t) = (u_1(t), \ldots, u_M(t)) \in \mathbb{B}^M$$

describing the activation values of the M input units of $\mathcal{N}$ at time t is the *input* submitted to $\mathcal{N}$ at time t. The pair

$$\langle \boldsymbol{x}(t), \boldsymbol{y}(t) \rangle \in [0,1]^N \times \mathbb{B}^P$$

describing the activation values of the internal and output cells at time t is the *state* of $\mathcal{N}$ at time t. The second element of this pair, namely $\boldsymbol{y}(t)$, is the *Boolean state* of $\mathcal{N}$ at time t.

Assuming the initial state of the network to be $\langle \boldsymbol{x}(0), \boldsymbol{y}(0) \rangle = \langle \boldsymbol{0}, \boldsymbol{0} \rangle$, any infinite input stream

$$s = (\boldsymbol{u}(t))_{t \in \mathbb{N}} = \boldsymbol{u}(0)\boldsymbol{u}(1)\boldsymbol{u}(2) \cdots \in (\mathbb{B}^M)^\omega$$

induces via Eqs. (1) and (2) an infinite sequence of consecutive states

$$c_s = (\langle \boldsymbol{x}(t), \boldsymbol{y}(t) \rangle)_{t \in \mathbb{N}} = \langle \boldsymbol{x}(0), \boldsymbol{y}(0) \rangle \langle \boldsymbol{x}(1), \boldsymbol{y}(1) \rangle \cdots \in ([0,1]^N \times \mathbb{B}^P)^\omega$$

called the *computation* of $\mathcal{N}$ induced by s. The corresponding infinite sequence of Boolean states

$$c'_s = (\boldsymbol{y}(t))_{t \in \mathbb{N}} = \boldsymbol{y}(0)\boldsymbol{y}(1)\boldsymbol{y}(2) \cdots \in (\mathbb{B}^P)^\omega$$

is the *Boolean computation* of $\mathcal{N}$ induced by s.

Note that any Ev-RNN $\mathcal{N}$ (with P Boolean output cells) can only have 2^P – i.e., finitely many – possible distinct Boolean states. Consequently, for any infinite Boolean computation c'_s, there necessarily exists at least one Boolean state that recurs infinitely often in c'_s. In fact, any Boolean computation c'_s necessarily consists of a finite prefix of Boolean states followed by an infinite suffix of Boolean states that repeat infinitely often – yet not necessarily in a periodic manner. The non-empty set of all the Boolean states that repeat infinitely often in c'_s will be denoted by $inf(c'_s)$. According to these considerations, a set of states of the form $inf(c'_s)$ for some computation c'_s will be called an *attractor* for $\mathcal{N}$. A precise definition can be given as follows [10]:

Definition 1. Let $\mathcal{N}$ be some Ev-RNN. A set $A = \{\boldsymbol{y}_0, \ldots, \boldsymbol{y}_k\} \subseteq \mathbb{B}^P$ is an *attractor* for $\mathcal{N}$ if there exists some infinite input stream s such that the corresponding Boolean computation c'_s satisfies $inf(c'_s) = A$.

In words, an attractor of $\mathcal{N}$ is a set of Boolean states into which the computation of the network could become forever trapped – yet not necessarily in a periodic manner –, for some infinite input stream s.

In this work, we suppose that attractors can be of two distinct types, namely either *meaningful* or *spurious*. The type of each attractor could be determined by its neurophysiological significance with respect to measurable observations, e.g. associated with certain behaviors or sensory discriminations. The classification of these attractors into meaningful or spurious types is not the subject of this paper. Hence, from this point onwards, we assume any Ev-RNN to be equipped with a corresponding classification of all of its attractors into meaningful and spurious types.

According to these considerations, an infinite input stream $s \in (\mathbb{B}^M)^\omega$ of $\mathcal{N}$ is called *meaningful* if $inf(c'_s)$ is a meaningful attractor, and it is called *spurious* if $inf(c'_s)$ is a spurious attractor. The set of all meaningful input streams of $\mathcal{N}$ is called the *neural ω-language* of $\mathcal{N}$ and is denoted by $L(\mathcal{N})$. An arbitrary set of input streams $L \subseteq (\mathbb{B}^M)^\omega$ is said to be *recognizable* by some Ev-RNN if there exists a network $\mathcal{N}$ such that $L(\mathcal{N}) = L$.

We now introduce a natural notion of a nondeterministic Ev-RNN, where the nondeterminism is expressed as a set of possible infinite evolving patterns of the synaptic weights. At the beginning of a computation, the network chooses one such possible evolution in a nondeterministic manner, and sticks to it throughout its whole computational process.

A *nondeterministic* Ev-RNN consists of a pair $(\mathcal{N}, E)$, where $\mathcal{N}$ is an Ev-RNN with K evolving synaptic connections, and $E \subseteq ([S, S']^K)^\omega$ is a set of infinite sequences of K-dimensional vectors – describing the possible infinite evolutions for the K synaptic connections of $\mathcal{N}$. Every element e of E is called a possible *evolution* for $\mathcal{N}$, and if the evolution $e = \boldsymbol{e}(0)\boldsymbol{e}(1)\boldsymbol{e}(2)\cdots \in E$ is followed by $\mathcal{N}$, each vector $\boldsymbol{e}(t)$ describes the values of the K synaptic weights of $\mathcal{N}$ at time step t.[1] In this context, the Boolean computation produced by $(\mathcal{N}, E)$ when it

---

[1] By contrast, a deterministic Ev-RNN has only one possible evolution for its synaptic weights, and hence corresponds to a nondeterministic Ev-RNN where the set E is reduced to a singleton.

receives the input stream $s \in (\mathbb{B}^M)^\omega$ and follows the evolution $e \in E$ is denoted by $c'_{(s,e)}$.

According to these considerations, a *nondeterministic* Ev-RNN[$\mathbb{Q}$] is a pair $(\mathcal{N}, E)$ such that $E \subseteq ((\mathbb{Q} \cap [S, S'])^K)^\omega$, and a *nondeterministic* Ev-RNN[$\mathbb{R}$] is a pair $(\mathcal{N}, E)$ such that $E \subseteq ((\mathbb{R} \cap [S, S'])^K)^\omega$. We assume from now on that $(\mathbb{Q} \cap [S, S'])^K$ and $(\mathbb{R} \cap [S, S'])^K$ are equipped with the induced topologies of $\mathbb{Q}^K$ and $\mathbb{R}^K$, and that $((\mathbb{Q} \cap [S, S'])^K)^\omega$ and $((\mathbb{R} \cap [S, S'])^K)^\omega$ are equipped with the product topologies of these induced topologies, respectively. Moreover, E is always assumed to be a closed subset of these Polish subspaces, and hence is also Polish [12].[2]

Finally, given some nondeterministic Ev-RNN $\mathcal{N}$, an infinite input stream $s \in (\mathbb{B}^M)^\omega$ is called *meaningful* if there exists some evolution $e \in E$ such that $inf(c'_{(s,e)})$ is a meaningful attractor, and it is called *spurious* otherwise, i.e., if for all evolution $e \in E$, the set $inf(c'_{(s,e)})$ is a spurious attractor. The set of all meaningful input streams of $\mathcal{N}$ is called the *neural ω-language* of $\mathcal{N}$ and is denoted by $L(\mathcal{N})$. An arbitrary set of input streams $L \subseteq (\mathbb{B}^M)^\omega$ is said to be *recognizable* by some nondeterministic Ev-RNN if there exists a nondeterministic network $(\mathcal{N}, E)$ such that $L(\mathcal{N}) = L$.

5 Results

Following considerations from ω-languages and automata theory [17], the expressive power of hybrid neural networks is characterized as the topological complexity of their underlying neural ω-language. For the sake of clarity, we first recall the results obtained in the deterministic context [5]. In this case, the static rational-weighted hybrid neural networks are computationally equivalent to deterministic Muller Turing machines, hence recognize neural ω-languages inside the class of finite Boolean combinations of $\mathbf{\Pi}_2^0$-sets ($BC(\mathbf{\Pi}_2^0)$). The other models of static real-weighted, evolving rational-weighted, and evolving real-weighted hybrid networks are all computationally equivalent. They recognize precisely all the $BC(\mathbf{\Pi}_2^0)$ neural ω-languages and, therefore, are strictly more powerful than deterministic Büchi and Muller Turing machines, since these later cannot recognize the whole class of $BC(\mathbf{\Pi}_2^0)$-sets (cf. Sect. 3).

Here, we show that both models of rational- and real-weighted nondeterministic hybrid neural networks are computationally equivalent, and recognize precisely the class of all analytic sets ($\mathbf{\Sigma}_1^1$ boldface). Therefore, their expressive powers strictly encompass those of Büchi and Muller Turing machines, which are restricted to the effectively analytic sets (Σ_1^1 lightface) (cf. Sect. 3).

We first show that any analytic neural ω-language L can be recognized by some nondeterministic rational Ev-RNN $\mathcal{N}$. The idea of the proof is the following. First, we note that the analytic set L can be written as the first projection π_1 of some $\mathbf{\Pi}_2^0$-set $X \subseteq (\mathbb{B}^M)^\omega \times \{0, 1\}^\omega$ (cf. Sect. 2). Next, we consider some recursive encoding of X by an infinite word $w_X \in \{0, 1\}^\omega$. Afterwards, we consider a

---

[2] The results of the paper hold equally true even with E taken as $\mathbf{\Pi}_2^0$.

nondeterministic Ev-RNN[$\mathbb{Q}$] $\mathcal{N}$ equipped with only two possible evolving synaptic connections: one which might follow any possible binary evolution $e \in \{0,1\}^{\omega}$, and the other one which always follows the same binary evolution $w_X \in \{0,1\}^{\omega}$. We then design the static part of $\mathcal{N}$ such that $\mathcal{N}$ visits a meaningful attractor iff the current input s and evolving synaptic pattern $e \in \{0,1\}^{\omega}$ are such that (s,e) belongs the set encoded by w_X, namely X. In this way, $L(\mathcal{N}) = \pi_1(X) = L$, and thus L is recognized by $\mathcal{N}$.

Proposition 1. *Let $L \subseteq (\mathbb{B}^M)^{\omega}$ such that $L \in \mathbf{\Sigma}_1^1$. Then there exists some nondeterministic Ev-RNN[$\mathbb{Q}$] $(\mathcal{N}, E)$ such that $L(\mathcal{N}) = L$.*

Proof. Since $L \in \mathbf{\Sigma}_1^1$, there exists some $X \subseteq (\mathbb{B}^M)^{\omega} \times \{0,1\}^{\omega}$ such that $X \in \mathbf{\Pi}_2^0$ and $L = \pi_1(X)$. Since $X \in \mathbf{\Pi}_2^0$, it can be written as $X = \bigcap_{i \geq 0} \bigcup_{j \geq 0} (p_{i,j} \cdot (\mathbb{B}^M)^{\omega} \times q_{i,j} \cdot \{0,1\}^{\omega})$, where each $(p_{i,j}, q_{i,j}) \in (\mathbb{B}^M)^* \times \{0,1\}^*$. Consequently, the set X (and hence also L) is completely determined by the countable sequence of pairs of finite prefixes $((p_{i,j}, q_{i,j}))_{i,j \geq 0}$. We can thus consider some encoding $w_X \in \{0,1\}^{\omega}$ of the sequence $((p_{i,j}, q_{i,j}))_{i,j \geq 0}$ such that, for any pair of indices $(i,j) \in \mathbb{N} \times \mathbb{N}$, the decoding procedure $(w_X, i, j) \mapsto (p_{i,j}, q_{i,j})$ is actually recursive.

We now consider the infinite procedure given by Algorithm 1 below. This procedure requires as input and auxiliary items the following three infinite sequences delivered step by step: an infinite input stream $s \in (\mathbb{B}^M)^{\omega}$, an infinite word $e \in \{0,1\}^{\omega}$ chosen arbitrarily, and the precise infinite word $w_X \in \{0,1\}^{\omega}$. Note that provided that these three items are correctly supplied by some external source, every instruction of the procedure is actually recursive. Farther note that, by construction, the procedure returns infinitely many 1's iff the pair of infinite sequences (s,e) belongs to X.

Based on the infinite procedure, we provide the description of a nondeterministic Ev-RNN[$\mathbb{Q}$] $(\mathcal{N}, E)$ such that $L(\mathcal{N}) = L$. The network $(\mathcal{N}, E)$ contains only two evolving synaptic weights $w_1(t)$ and $w_2(t)$ which evolve among only two possible values, 0 or 1. All other synaptic weights are static. The weight $w_1(t)$ might follow every possible evolution in $\{0,1\}^{\omega}$, while $w_2(t)$ always follows the same evolution, which are the successive letters of w_X. Formally, one has the following *closed* set of possible evolutions:

$$E = \{\tilde{e} \in (\{0,1\}^2)^{\omega} : (\tilde{e}(t))_0 \in \{0,1\} \text{ and } (\tilde{e}(t))_1 = w_X(t), \text{ for any } t \geq 0\}.$$

We then consider a neural circuit which stores the incoming values of the input stream $s \in (\mathbb{B}^M)^{\omega}$ into M designated neurons, as well as two neural circuits which store the successive bits of $w_1(t)$ and $w_2(t)$ into two designated neurons (see [20] for further technical details). Afterwards, according to the real time computational equivalence between static RNN[$\mathbb{Q}$] and Turing machines [20], we consider a static RNN[$\mathbb{Q}$] which is suitably designed and connected to the above mentioned circuits in order to simulate all the recursive instructions of Algorithm 1. We finally add a single Boolean output neuron y and update the whole construction in order that y takes an activation value of 1 precisely when the simulation of Algorithm 1 by our network enters the instruction "returns 1".

In this way, one has the description of a nondeterministic Ev-RNN[$\mathbb{Q}$] $(\mathcal{N}, E)$ which suitably simulates the behavior of Algorithm 1.

Besides, the single output cell y leads to the existence of only three possible attractors, namely $\{(0)\}, \{(0), (1)\}$, and $\{(1)\}$. We set $\{(0)\}$ as spurious, and $\{(0), (1)\}$ and $\{(1)\}$ as meaningful. This means that $(\mathcal{N}, E)$ visits a meaningful attractor iff the simulation of Algorithm 1 returns infinitely many 1's.

According to all the previous considerations, one has that $s \in L(\mathcal{N})$ iff, by definition, there exists some $\tilde{e} \in E$ such that $inf(c'_{(s,\tilde{e})})$ is meaningful, iff there exists $e \in \{0,1\}^\omega$ such that the simulation of Algorithm 1 returns infinitely many 1's, iff there exists $e \in \{0,1\}^\omega$ such that the pair $(s, e) \in X$, iff, by definition, $s \in \pi_1(X) = L$. In other words, $L(\mathcal{N}) = L$, showing that L is recognized by the nondeterministic Ev-RNN[$\mathbb{Q}$] $(\mathcal{N}, E)$. $\qquad\square$

Algorithm 1. Infinite procedure

Require:

1. Input $s = s(0)s(1)s(2) \cdots \in (\mathbb{B}^M)^\omega$ supplied step by step at successive time steps $t = 0, 1, 2, \ldots$
2. some auxiliary infinite word $e = e(0)e(1)e(2) \cdots \in \{0,1\}^\omega$ supplied step by step at successive time steps $t = 0, 1, 2, \ldots$
3. the specific auxiliary infinite word $w_X = w_X(0)w_X(1)w_X(2) \cdots \in \{0,1\}^\omega$ supplied step by step at successive time steps $t = 0, 1, 2, \ldots$

1: **SUBROUTINE 1**
2: $c \leftarrow 0$ // c counts the number of letters provided so far
3: **for all** time step $t \geq 0$ **do**
4:     store each incoming Boolean vector $s(t) \in \mathbb{B}^M$
5:     store each incoming bit $e(t) \in \{0,1\}$
6:     store each incoming bit $w_X(t) \in \{0,1\}$
7:     $c \leftarrow c + 1$
8: **end for**
9: **END SUBROUTINE 1**

10: **SUBROUTINE 2**
11: $i \leftarrow 0, j \leftarrow 0$
12: **loop**
13:     wait until $c \geq \max\{|p_{i,j}|, |q_{i,j}|\}$
14:     wait until $w_X[0{:}c]$ becomes long enough to contain the encoding of $(p_{i,j}, q_{i,j})$
15:     decode $(p_{i,j}, q_{i,j})$ from $w_X[0{:}c]$ // recursive procedure
16:     **if** $p_{i,j} \subseteq s[0{:}c]$ and $q_{i,j} \subseteq e[0{:}c]$ **then**   // $(s, e) \in p_{i,j} \cdot (\mathbb{B}^M)^\omega \times q_{i,j} \cdot \{0,1\}^\omega$
17:        **return** 1   // $\exists\, j$ s.t. $(s, e) \in p_{i,j} \cdot (\mathbb{B}^M)^\omega \times q_{i,j} \cdot \{0,1\}^\omega$
18:        $i \leftarrow i+1, j \leftarrow 0$ // test if $(s, e) \in p_{i+1,0} \cdot (\mathbb{B}^M)^\omega \times q_{i+1,0} \cdot \{0,1\}^\omega$
19:     **else**   // $(s, e) \notin p_{i,j} \cdot (\mathbb{B}^M)^\omega \times q_{i,j} \cdot \{0,1\}^\omega$
20:        **return** 0   // $\neg \exists j' \leq j$ s.t. $(s, e) \in p_{i,j'} \cdot (\mathbb{B}^M)^\omega \times q_{i,j'} \cdot \{0,1\}^\omega$
21:        $i \leftarrow i, j \leftarrow j+1$ // test if $(s, e) \in p_{i,j+1} \cdot (\mathbb{B}^M)^\omega \times q_{i,j+1} \cdot \{0,1\}^\omega$
22:     **end if**
23: **end loop**
24: **END SUBROUTINE 2**

We now conversely show that every ω-language recognized by some nondeterministic Ev-RNN is analytic.

Proposition 2. *Let* $(\mathcal{N}, E)$ *be some nondeterministic Ev-RNN[$\mathbb{R}$]. Then* $L(\mathcal{N}) \in \mathbf{\Sigma}_1^1$.

Proof. First of all, note that the dynamics of $(\mathcal{N}, E)$ can naturally be associated with the function $f_{(\mathcal{N},E)} : (\mathbb{B}^M)^\omega \times E \to (\mathbb{B}^P)^\omega$ defined by $f_{(\mathcal{N},E)}(s, e) = c'_{(s,e)}$. The nature of our dynamics ensures that this function is sequential, i.e., for any time step $t \geq 0$, the vectors $s(t)$, $e(t)$ and $y(t)$ are generated simultaneously. Therefore, given any basic open set $w \cdot (\mathbb{B}^P)^\omega$, with $w \in (\mathbb{B}^P)^*$, one has that $f_{(\mathcal{N},E)}^{-1}(w \cdot (\mathbb{B}^P)^\omega)$ is of the form $\Theta_w = \bigcup_{i \in I} \left[u_i \cdot (\mathbb{B}^M)^\omega \times (v_{\mathbb{R},i} \cdot ([S, S']^K)^\omega \cap E)\right]$ with each $u_i \in (\mathbb{B}^M)^{|w|}$ and $v_{\mathbb{R},i} \in ([S, S']^K)^{|w|}$. Notice that for each $i \in I$, $v_{\mathbb{R},i} \cdot ([S, S']^K)^\omega \cap E$ is closed (inside E) and $u_i \cdot (\mathbb{B}^M)^\omega$ is clopen, and hence $(u_i \cdot (\mathbb{B}^M)^\omega) \times (v_{\mathbb{R},i} \cdot ([S, S']^K)^\omega \cap E)$ is closed. By [4, Lemma 9], it follows that given any u_i and $v_{\mathbb{R},i}$ as above, there exists $I_{\mathbb{Q},i} = (\prod_{k=1}^K \,]a_{j,k}, b_{j,k}[)_{j<|w|}$, where each $a_{j,k}, b_{j,k} \in \mathbb{Q}$ and $v_{\mathbb{R},i} \in I_{\mathbb{Q},i}$, and such that

$$f_{(\mathcal{N},E)}\left[u_i \cdot (\mathbb{B}^M)^\omega \times (I_{\mathbb{Q},i} \cdot ([S, S']^K)^\omega \cap E)\right] \subseteq w \cdot (\mathbb{B}^P)^\omega.$$

One thus has $\Theta_w = \bigcup_{i \in I} \left[u_i \cdot (\mathbb{B}^M)^\omega \times (I_{\mathbb{Q},i} \cdot ([S, S']^K)^\omega \cap E)\right]$. Since there exist only countably many u_i and $I_{\mathbb{Q},i}$, it turns out that Θ_w is a countable union of closed sets, i.e. a $\mathbf{\Sigma}_2^0$ set, which shows that $f_{(\mathcal{N},E)}$ is of Baire class 1, cf. [12].[3]

Furthermore, note that since $\mathcal{N}$ contains finitely many output cells, is also has finitely many possible Boolean states, and therefore also finitely many possible attractors. This feature is independent from the nondeterministic behavior associated with the set of possible evolutions E. Hence, suppose that $\mathcal{N}$ contains the I meaningful attractors $A_i = \{b_{i_1}, \dots, b_{i_{k(i)}}\}$, for $i = 1, \dots, I$, where $1 \leq i_1 < \dots < i_{k(i)} \leq 2^P$, and where b_n denotes the n-th Boolean vector of $\mathbb{B}^P$ according to the lexicographic order.

According to these considerations, the ω-language $L(\mathcal{N})$ can be expressed by the following sequence of equalities:

$$L(\mathcal{N}) = \{s \in (\mathbb{B}^M)^\omega : \text{there exists } e \in E \text{ s.t. } \inf(c'_{(s,e)}) \text{ is a meaningful attractor}\}$$
$$= \{s \in (\mathbb{B}^M)^\omega : \text{there exists } e \in E \text{ s.t. } \inf(c'_{(s,e)}) = A_i, \text{ for some } i = 1, \dots, I\}$$
$$= \pi_1\Big(\{(s, e) \in (\mathbb{B}^M)^\omega \times E : \inf(c'_{(s,e)}) = A_i, \text{ for some } i = 1, \dots, I\}\Big)$$
$$= \pi_1\Big(\bigcup_{i=1}^I \{(s, e) \in (\mathbb{B}^M)^\omega \times E : \inf(c'_{(s,e)}) = A_i\}\Big)$$
$$= \pi_1\Big(\bigcup_{i=1}^I \{(s, e) \in (\mathbb{B}^M)^\omega \times E : \forall j \in \{i_1, \dots, i_{k(i)}\}, f_{(\mathcal{N},E)}(s, e) \text{ has } \infty\text{-many } b'_j s$$
$$\text{and } \forall j \in \{1, \dots, 2^P\} \backslash \{i_1, \dots, i_{k(i)}\}, f_{(\mathcal{N},E)}(s, e) \text{ has finitely many } b'_j s\}\Big)$$

---

[3] We recall that the preimage by a Baire class 1 function of a set in $\mathbf{\Sigma}_n^0$ (resp. $\mathbf{\Pi}_n^0$) is in $\mathbf{\Sigma}_{n+1}^0$ (resp. $\mathbf{\Pi}_{n+1}^0$).

$$= \pi_1 \Big(\bigcup_{i=1}^{I} \Big[\bigcap_{j \in \{i_1,\dots,i_{k(i)}\}} \{(s,e) \in (\mathbb{B}^M)^\omega \times E :$$

$$f_{(\mathcal{N},E)}(s,e) \in \underbrace{\bigcap_{n \geq 0} \bigcup_{m \geq 0} (\mathbb{B}^P)^{n+m} \cdot b_j \cdot (\mathbb{B}^P)^\omega}_{\substack{c'_{(s,e)} \text{ contains infinitely many } b'_j \text{ s, i.e.} \\ \forall n \geq 0 \; \exists m \geq n \; y(n+m) = b_j, \text{ thus in } \mathbf{\Pi}_2^0}} \} \cap$$

$$\bigcap_{j \in \{1,\dots,2^P\} \setminus \{i_1,\dots,i_{k(i)}\}} \{(s,e) \in (\mathbb{B}^M)^\omega \times E :$$

$$f_{(\mathcal{N},E)}(s,e) \in \underbrace{\Big(\bigcap_{n \geq 0} \bigcup_{m \geq 0} (\mathbb{B}^P)^{n+m} \cdot b_j \cdot (\mathbb{B}^P)^\omega \Big)^{\complement}}_{\substack{c'_{(s,e)} \text{ contains only finitely many } b'_j \text{ s, i.e.} \\ \text{complement of a } \mathbf{\Pi}_2^0 \text{-set, thus in } \mathbf{\Sigma}_2^0}} \} \Big] \Big)$$

$$= \pi_1 \Big(\bigcup_{i=1}^{I} \Big[\bigcap_{j \in \{i_1,\dots,i_{k(i)}\}} \underbrace{f_{(\mathcal{N},E)}^{-1} \Big(\bigcap_{n \geq 0} \bigcup_{m \geq 0} (\mathbb{B}^P)^{n+m} \cdot b_j \cdot (\mathbb{B}^P)^\omega \Big)}_{\text{preimage by a Baire class 1 function of a } \mathbf{\Pi}_2^0 \text{-set, thus in } \mathbf{\Pi}_3^0 [12]} \cap$$

$$\bigcap_{j \in \{1,\dots,2^P\} \setminus \{i_1,\dots,i_{k(i)}\}} \underbrace{f_{(\mathcal{N},E)}^{-1} \Big(\Big(\bigcap_{n \geq 0} \bigcup_{m \geq 0} (\mathbb{B}^P)^{n+m} \cdot b_j \cdot (\mathbb{B}^P)^\omega \Big)^{\complement} \Big)}_{\text{preimage by a Baire class 1 function of a } \mathbf{\Sigma}_2^0 \text{-set, thus in } \mathbf{\Sigma}_3^0 [12]} \Big] \Big)$$

It follows that $L(\mathcal{N})$ is a projection of a finite union and intersection of $\mathbf{\Pi}_3^0$ and $\mathbf{\Sigma}_3^0$ subsets of the Polish space $(\mathbb{B}^M)^\omega \times E$, and therefore, $L(\mathcal{N}) \in \mathbf{\Sigma}_1^1$. $\qquad \square$

Finally, Propositions 1 and 2 allow to conclude that nondeterministic evolving neural networks recognize precisely the set of all analytic sets, irrespective of whether their synaptic weights are modelled by rational or real numbers.

Theorem 1. *Let* $L \subseteq (\mathbb{B}^M)^\omega$*. The following conditions are equivalent:*

1. $L \in \mathbf{\Sigma}_1^1$;
2. *L is recognizable by some nondeterministic Ev-RNN[ℚ]* $(\mathcal{N}, E)$;
3. *L is recognizable by some nondeterministic Ev-RNN[ℝ]* $(\mathcal{N}, E)$.

Proof. (1) → (2) is provided by Proposition 1. (2) → (3) holds by definition. (3) → (1) is provided by Proposition 2. $\qquad \square$

6   Discussion

We have introduced a model of nondeterministic hybrid recurrent neural networks. The nondeterminism is expressed as a set of possible synaptic evolutions associated with each neural network. The network chooses one of these in a nondeterministic manner, and then sticks to it throughout its whole computational process. In this context, we have proven that the two models of rational-weighted and real-weighted nondeterministic hybrid neural networks are computationally equivalent, and recognize precisely the class of all $\mathbf{\Sigma}_1^1$ neural ω-languages.

They are therefore strictly more expressive than the nondeterministic Büchi and Muller Turing machines, which recognize the Σ_1^1 (lighface) ω-languages.

These results together with those of [5] show that nondeterminism injects an extensive amount of computational power – from $BC(\Pi_2^0)$ to Σ_1^1 – to the hybrid neural systems. Besides, as opposed to the deterministic case, the consideration of real synaptic weights in the present nondeterministic context does actually not add any additional computational power to the neural networks. The added value of the power of the continuum is somehow absorbed by the nondeterminism, and any kind of analog assumption can therefore be dropped without compromising the achievement of a maximal computational power. More generally, these achievements support the idea that the nondeterminism plays a crucial role in neural information processing. They also support the claim that recurrent neural networks represent a natural model of computation beyond the Turing limits [8].

For future work, the study of the computational capabilities of more biologically-oriented neural models involved in more bio-inspired paradigms of computation is expected to be pursued.

Finally, we hope that such comparative studies between the computational capabilities of neural models and abstract machines might eventually bring further insight to the understanding of the intrinsic natures of both biological as well as artificial intelligences.

References

1. Cabessa, J.: Interactive evolving recurrent neural networks are super-Turing. In: Filipe, J., Fred, A.L.N. (eds.) Proceedings of ICAART, pp. 328–333. SciTePress (2012)
2. Cabessa, J., Siegelmann, H.T.: Evolving recurrent neural networks are super-Turing. In: Proceedings of IJCNN 2011, pp. 3200–3206. IEEE (2011)
3. Cabessa, J., Siegelmann, H.T.: The computational power of interactive recurrent neural networks. Neural Comput. **24**(4), 996–1019 (2012)
4. Cabessa, J., Siegelmann, H.T.: The super-Turing computational power of plastic recurrent neural networks. Int. J. Neural. Syst. **24**(8), 1450029 (2014)
5. Cabessa, J., Villa, A.E.P.: Computational capabilities of recurrent neural networks based on their attractor dynamics. In: Proceedings of IJCNN 2015. IEEE (to appear, 2015) (accepted)
6. Cabessa, J., Villa, A.E.P.: A hierarchical classification of first-order recurrent neural networks. In: Dediu, A.-H., Fernau, H., Martín-Vide, C. (eds.) LATA 2010. LNCS, vol. 6031, pp. 142–153. Springer, Heidelberg (2010)
7. Cabessa, J., Villa, A.E.P.: The expressive power of analog recurrent neural networks on infinite input streams. Theor. Comput. Sci. **436**, 23–34 (2012)
8. Cabessa, J., Villa, A.E.P.: Recurrent neural networks - a natural model of computation beyond the Turing limits. In: Rosa, A.C., et al., (ed.) Proceedings of IJCCI 2012, pp. 594–599. SciTePress (2012)
9. Cabessa, J., Villa, A.E.P.: The super-turing computational power of interactive evolving recurrent neural networks. In: Mladenov, V., Koprinkova-Hristova, P., Palm, G., Villa, A.E.P., Appollini, B., Kasabov, N. (eds.) ICANN 2013. LNCS, vol. 8131, pp. 58–65. Springer, Heidelberg (2013)

10. Cabessa, J., Villa, A.E.P.: An attractor-based complexity measurement for boolean recurrent neural networks. PloS ONE **9**(4), e94204+ (2014)
11. Cabessa, J., Villa, A.E.P.: Interactive evolving recurrent neural networks are superturing universal. In: Wermter, S., Weber, C., Duch, W., Honkela, T., Koprinkova-Hristova, P., Magg, S., Palm, G., Villa, A.E.P. (eds.) ICANN 2014. LNCS, vol. 8681, pp. 57–64. Springer, Heidelberg (2014)
12. Kechris, A.S.: Classical Descriptive Set Theory. Graduate Texts in Mathematics, vol. 156. Springer-Verlag, New York (1995)
13. Kleene, S.C.: Representation of events in nerve nets and finite automata. In: Shannon, C., McCarthy, J. (eds.) Automata Studies, pp. 3–41. Princeton University Press, Princeton, NJ (1956)
14. McCulloch, W.S., Pitts, W.: A logical calculus of the ideas immanent in nervous activity. Bull. Math. Biophys. **5**, 115–133 (1943)
15. Minsky, M.L.: Computation: Finite and Infinite Machines. Prentice-Hall Inc., Englewood Cliffs (1967)
16. Neumann, J.V.: The Computer and the Brain. Yale University Press, New Haven (1958)
17. Perrin, D., Pin, J.-E.: Infinite Words - Automata, Semigroups, Logic and Games. Pure and Applied Mathematics, vol. 141. Elsevier, San Diego (2004)
18. Siegelmann, H.T.: Neural Networks and Analog Computation: Beyond the Turing Limit. Birkhauser Boston Inc., Cambridge (1999)
19. Siegelmann, H.T., Sontag, E.D.: Analog computation via neural networks. Theor. Comput. Sci. **131**(2), 331–360 (1994)
20. Siegelmann, H.T., Sontag, E.D.: On the computational power of neural nets. J. Comput. Syst. Sci. **50**(1), 132–150 (1995)
21. Staiger, L.: ω-languages. In: Rozenberg, G., Salomaa, A. (eds.) Handbook of Formal Languages: Beyond Words, vol. 3, pp. 339–387. Springer-Verlag, New York (1997)
22. Thomas, W.: Automata on infinite objects. In: van Leeuwen, J. (ed.) Handbook of Theoretical Computer Science: Formal Models and Semantics, vol. B, pp. 133–192. Elsevier and MIT Press, Amsterdam (1990)
23. Turing, A.M.: Intelligent machinery. Technical report, National Physical Laboratory, Teddington, UK (1948)
24. Vaadia, E., Haalman, I., Abeles, M., Bergman, H., Prut, Y., Slovin, H., Aertsen, A.: Dynamics of neuronal interactions in monkey cortex in relation to behavioural events. Nature **373**(6514), 515–518 (1995)
25. Villa, A.E.P., Tetko, I.V., Hyland, B., Najem, A.: Spatiotemporal activity patterns of rat cortical neurons predict responses in a conditioned task. Proc. Natl. Acad. Sci. U.S.A. **96**(3), 1106–1111 (1999)
26. Wagner, K.: On ω-regular sets. Inf. Control **43**(2), 123–177 (1979)

Duplications and Pseudo-Duplications

Da-Jung Cho[1], Yo-Sub Han[1]([✉]), Hwee Kim[1],
Alexandros Palioudakis[1], and Kai Salomaa[2]

[1] Department of Computer Science, Yonsei University, 50 Yonsei-Ro,
Seodaemum-Gu, Seoul 120–749, Republic of Korea
{dajung,emmous,kimhwee,alex}@cs.yonsei.ac.kr
[2] School of Computing, Queen's University, Kingston, ON K7L 3N6, Canada
ksalomaa@cs.queensu.ca

Abstract. A duplication is basic phenomenon that occurs through molecular evolution on a biological sequence. A duplication on a string copies any substring of the string. We define k-pseudo-duplication of a string w that consists, roughly speaking, of all strings obtained from w by inserting after a substring u another substring obtained from u by at most k edit operations. We consider three variants of duplication operations, duplication, k-pseudo-duplication and reverse-duplication. First, we give the necessary and sufficient number of states that a nondeterministic finite automaton needs to recognize duplications on a string. Then, we show that regular languages and context-free languages are not closed under the duplication, k-pseudo-duplication and reverse-duplication operations. Furthermore, we show that the class of context-sensitive languages is closed under duplication, pseudo-duplication and reverse-duplication.

Keywords: Bio-inspired operations · State complexity · Finite automata · Context-free grammars · Context-sensitive grammars

1 Introduction

A DNA sequence undergoes various transformations from the primitive sequence through several biological operations such as insertion, deletion, substitution, inversion, translocation and duplication. This phenomena on DNA sequence lead many researchers to study theoretical properties of them [4,5,15,16,18]. Some researchers considered string matching problems with bio-inspired operations [3,5,25]. Moreover, one of the important problems in biology is sequence comparison and there are several tools for sequence searching such that BLAST and FASTA [22,23]. This leads some researchers to consider finite state methods that are useful for the sequence searching problems to improve search times in the face of exponentially increasing size of DNA sequences [2,13].

A duplicated segment of a chromosome occurs as a result of genetic recombination named *chromosomal crossover* [8] (see Fig. 1 for an example). Depending on the position of cutting somewhere within two chromosomes, the first segment of the first sequence and the last segment of the second sequence combine and

© Springer International Publishing Switzerland 2015
C.S. Calude and M.J. Dinneen (Eds.): UCNC 2015, LNCS 9252, pp. 157–168, 2015.
DOI: 10.1007/978-3-319-21819-9_11

Fig. 1. An example of chromosomal crossover between two sequences. The last segment BCDE of the second sequence is attached to the first segment ABC of the first sequence. As a consequence of this crossing over, a subsequence BC occurs twice.

a new sequence with duplicated region may be obtained. Moreover, duplication of gene sequence may cause *replication slippage* during DNA replication and this phenomenon is closely linked with hereditary human diseases [12,28]. Kong et al. [19] indeed considered 736 complete chromosomes and showed that inverse segmental duplications are an important mechanism in the growth and evolution of genomes.

From a formal language theoretic framework, duplication leads a string $w_1w_2w_3$ to transform to the string $w_1w_2w_2w_3$, and this is one of the well-studied operations in both DNA computing and formal language theory. Many researchers have considered a variant of duplication operations. For other variants of duplication we refer the reader to the literature [9,10,17,20,26,30]. Searls [26] introduced linguistic formulations of rearrangement that occur in evolution such as duplication, inversion, transposition and deletion. Yokomori and Kobayashi [30] showed new representation for duplication using a set of basic operations, primitive language operation and mapping operations. Dassow et al. [9] defined an iterated duplication and considered closure properties of iterated version of duplication languages in the Chomsky hierarchy. Moreover, Dassow et al. [10] considered several operations arising from the genome evolution and noticed the result that a family of languages in the Chomsky hierarchy is closed under duplication. Leupold et al. [20] considered two types of languages defined by a string through iterated duplications and showed the formal language theoretical properties concerning two types of iterated duplications. Ito et al. [17] showed closure properties for bounded iterative duplication over alphabets of several sizes. Furthermore, some researchers considered duplication grammars [11,21].

For the DNA evolutionary analysis, an iterated version of duplication is regarded as multiple steps of evolutions, thus concerning the operation is natural to study their linguistic properties. We consider general duplication operation that occurs only once within a generation. Moreover, we introduce a new operation *k-pseudo-duplication* that copies any part of an input sequence allowing a certain amount of errors. We also consider *reverse-duplication*, and establish their properties. Note that Dassow et al. [10] presented similar closure properties for inversion, transposition and duplication: They considered a pre-specified set, and a operation works when a language contains a string in the pre-specified set. Recently, Cho et al. [4,6] showed similar results for the pseudo-inversion operation defined as an incomplete inversion, and estimated state complexity of inversion operations.

In Sect. 2, we briefly recall several notations. Then, we introduce the definitions of duplication and reverse-duplication and we define the k-pseudo-duplication in Sect. 3. Moreover, we give tight upper and lower bounds for the number of states that finite automaton needs to recognize the set of (pseudo-) duplications of a given string in Sect. 3.1. We establish some closure properties for three variants of duplication operation in Sect. 3.2. We mention a possible future direction and conclude the paper in Sect. 4.

2   Preliminaries

We briefly give definitions and notations used throughout the paper. The reader may refer to the textbooks [14,27,29] for more details on formal language theory.

Let Σ be a finite alphabet and Σ^* be the set of all strings over Σ. For any positive integer n we use $[n]$ to denote the set $\{1, 2, \ldots, n\}$. The symbol $\emptyset$ denotes the empty language, the symbol λ denotes the empty string and Σ^+ denotes $\Sigma^* \setminus \{\lambda\}$. Given a string w, we denote the reversal of w by w^R and the length of w by $|w|$.

A *nondeterministic finite automaton* (NFA) is a five tuple $A = (Q, \Sigma, \delta, S, F)$, where Q is a finite set of states, Σ is a finite alphabet, δ is a multi-valued transition function from $Q \times (\Sigma \cup \{\lambda\})$ into 2^Q, $S \subseteq Q$ is the set of initial states and $F \subseteq Q$ is the set of final states. Our definition of NFAs allows the use of λ-transitions. It is well known [29] that an NFA with λ-transitions can be converted to an equivalent NFA without λ-transitions and having the same number of states. The automaton A is *deterministic* (DFA) if S is a singleton set and δ is a single-valued transition function from $Q \times \Sigma \to Q$. It is well known the NFAs and DFAs recognize the regular language [24,27].

A *context-free grammar* (CFG) is four tuple $G = (V, T, P, S)$, where V a set of non-terminal symbols, Σ is a set of final symbols, P is a set of production rules of the form $N \to \alpha$ for $N \in V$ and $\alpha \in (V \cup T)^*$, and S is the initial symbol. A language L generated by CFG is known as *context-free language*.

A grammar $G = (V, T, P, S)$ is *context-sensitive* (CSG) if P has a set of production rules of the form $\alpha N \beta \to \alpha \gamma \beta$ for $\alpha, \beta \in (V \cup \Sigma)^*, \gamma \in (V \cup T)^+$ and $N \in V$. A language L generated by CSG is said to be *context-sensitive language*.

The edit-distance between two strings x and y is the smallest number of basic operations that transform x to y [1,7]. We use three operations insertion, deletion and substitution: Given an alphabet Σ, an insertion operation that inserts $a \in \Sigma$ is denoted as $(\lambda \to a)$, a deletion operation that deletes $a \in \Sigma$ is denoted as $(a \to \lambda)$ and a substitution operation that substitutes b for a is denoted as $(a \to b)$. We denote the edit-distance between two string x and y by $d(x, y)$. The Hamming distance is the number of positions in which two strings of same length differ. Note that we use only a substitution operation for computing Hamming distance. We denote the Hamming distance between two strings x and y by $d_H(x, y)$.

For finding the nondeterministic state complexity of given languages, we use a technique called the *extended fooling set technique*. This technique gives us a lower bound on the size of any NFA recognizing a given language.

Proposition 1 (Extended Fooling set technique [27]). *Let $L \subseteq \Sigma^*$ be a regular language. Suppose that there exists a set $P = \{(x_i, w_i) \mid 1 \leq i \leq n\}$ of pairs such that*

(i) $x_i w_i \in L$ for $1 \leq i \leq n$,
(ii) if $i \neq j$, then $x_i w_j \notin L$ or $x_j w_i \notin L, 1 \leq i, j \leq n$.

Then, a minimal NFA for L has at least n states.

Note that a set P satisfying the conditions (i) and (ii) of Proposition 1 is called *fooling set* for the language L.

3   Duplication and Pseudo-duplication

The duplication operation occurs in a bio sequence w when a substring of w is copied abnormally. We give the formal definition of the duplication operation.

Definition 1 (Searls [26]). Let $w \in \Sigma^*$ be a string over the alphabet Σ, the *duplication* of w is the set

$$\mathbb{D}(w) = \{x_1 x_2 x_2 x_3 \mid w = x_1 x_2 x_3, x_1, x_2, x_3 \in \Sigma^*.\}$$

Furthermore, Dassow et al. [9] considered the iterated duplication operation

$$\mathbb{D}^*(L) = \bigcup_{i \geq 0} \mathbb{D}^i(L).$$

Note that Dassow et al. [9] considered a duplication operation (defined by a duplication scheme) that is, roughly speaking, as in Definition 1 except that the repeated substring is restricted to belong to a pre-specified finite set. The language theoretic properties for the operation defined by a duplication scheme as in Dassow et al. [9] are significantly different from our results.

We define the *k-pseudo-duplication* that allows k errors on the resulting sequence. Note that during the process of DNA replication in practice some mutations such as insertion, deletion and substitution may occur.

Definition 2. Let $w \in \Sigma^*$ be a string and $k \geq 0$ a non-negative integer, we define the *k-pseudo-duplication* of w to be

$$\mathbb{PD}_k(w) = \{x_1 x_2 x_2' x_3 \mid w = x_1 x_2 x_3, x_1, x_2, x_3 \in \Sigma^*, d(x_2, x_2') \leq k\}.$$

When the value of k is known from the context, or is not important, we sometimes call the operation simply pseudo-duplication.

We also consider the *reverse-duplication* operation.

Definition 3 (Dassow et al. [9]). Let $w \in \Sigma^*$ be a string, we define the *reverse-duplication* of w to be

$$\mathbb{RD}(w) = \{x_1 x_2 x_2^R x_3 \mid w = x_1 x_2 x_3, x_1, x_2, x_3 \in \Sigma^*\}.$$

The *duplication* operation, the *pseudo-duplication* operation and the *reverse-duplication* operation are extended to languages in the following way:

(i) $\mathbb{D}(L) = \bigcup_{w \in L} \mathbb{D}(w),$

(ii) $\mathbb{PD}_k(L) = \bigcup_{w \in L} \mathbb{PD}_k(w),$

(iii) $\mathbb{RD}(L) = \bigcup_{w \in L} \mathbb{RD}(w).$

3.1   State Complexity of Duplication Operations

As we will see that the regular languages are not closed under the duplication, pseudo-duplication or reverse-duplication operation, here we consider the state complexity of the sets of (pseudo-) duplications of an individual string. For a string $w \in \Sigma^*$, it is obvious that the languages $\mathbb{D}(w)$, $\mathbb{PD}_k(w)$, and $\mathbb{RD}(w)$ are regular, since all are finite. Thus we focus on the nondeterministic state complexity of duplication, pseudo-duplication, and reverse-duplication operations. We give a matching upper and lower bound for the duplication operation of a string w.

Theorem 1. *Let $w \in \Sigma^*$ be a string of length n, for a positive integer n. Then, $\mathbb{D}(w)$ is recognized by a DFA with $2n+1$ states.*

Moreover, any NFA recognizing the language $\mathbb{D}(w)$ needs at least $2n+1$ states.

Proof. Let a string $w = w_1 \ldots w_n$, where $w_i \in \Sigma$, for $1 \leq i \leq n$. We can also assume than $n \geq 2$, since, if $n = 1$ we can check easily that the claim is true. Then, we can construct the NFA $A_w = (Q, \Sigma, \delta, p_1, F)$ that recognizes the language $\mathbb{D}(w)$. We first define the set of states Q.

$$Q = \{p_i' \mid 1 \leq i \leq n\} \cup \{p_i \mid 1 \leq i \leq n + 1\}$$

Now the transitions of the NFA A_w are as follows; $\delta(p_i, w_i) = p_{i+1}$ for all $1 \leq i \leq n$, $\delta(p_i', w_{i+1}) = p_{i+1}'$ for all $1 \leq i \leq n - 1$, and $\delta(p_i, w_j) = p_j'$ for all $1 \leq j < i \leq n$. The final states of A_w are the states p_{n+1} and p_n'. We give an example in Fig. 2, in the case where $w = x_1 x_2 x_3 x_4$.

Now, we easily verify the lower bound for the state complexity of duplication. We note that $\mathbb{D}(w)$ is a finite language where the length of the longest string is $2n$. This implies that any NFA recognizing the language $\mathbb{D}(w)$ needs at least $2n+1$ states.   □

With similar ideas we can find the state complexity bounds for the pseudo-duplication and reverse-duplication of a given word. We formalize these bounds in the next two theorems.

Theorem 2. *Let $w \in \Sigma^*$ be a string of length n, for a positive integer n. Then, the language $\mathbb{PD}_k(w)$, for $k \geq 1$, is recognized by an NFA with $k \cdot \frac{(n+1)(n+2)}{2} + n + 1$ states.*

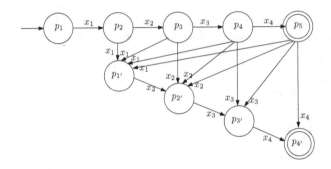

Fig. 2. An illustrative example of constructing an NFA recognizing $\mathbb{D}(w)$, where $w = x_1 x_2 x_3 x_4$ for $x_1, x_2, x_3, x_4 \in \Sigma$.

Moreover, for every n_0 positive integer, there is a word w_0 over an alphabet Σ with $|w_0| = n_0$ and $|\Sigma| = |w_0|$, such that any NFA recognizing the language $\mathbb{PD}_k(w_0)$, needs at least $k \cdot \frac{(|w_0|+1)(|w_0|+2)}{2} + |w_0| + 1$ states.

Proof. Let a string $w = x_1 \ldots x_n$, where $x_i \in \Sigma$, for $1 \le i \le n$. We can also assume than $n \ge 2$, since, if $n = 1$ we can check easily that the claim is true. Then, we can construct the NFA, with λ-transitions, $B_w = (Q, \Sigma, \delta, p_{(0,0,k)}, F)$ that recognizes the language $\mathbb{PD}_k(w)$. We first define the set of states Q.

$$Q = \{p_i \mid 0 \le i \le n\} \cup \{p_{(j,i,h)} \mid 0 \le i \le n, 0 \le j \le i, \text{ and } 1 \le h \le k\}$$

Now the transitions of the NFA B_w are as follows;

(i) $p_{(0,i,k)} \in \delta(p_{(0,i-1,k)}, x_i)$, for all $1 \le i \le n$,

(ii) $p_{(j,i,k)} \in \delta(p_{(j-1,i,k)}, x_j)$, for all $1 \le i \le n$, $1 \le j \le i$, and $1 \le h \le k$,

(iii) $p_{(j,i,k)} \in \delta(p_{(0,i,k)}, x_j)$, for $2 \le i \le n$, and $2 \le j \le i$,

(iv) $p_{(j,i,k-1)} \in \delta(p_{(0,i,k)}, *)$, for $* \in \Sigma \cup \{\lambda\}$, $1 \le i \le n$, and $1 \le j \le i$, if $k \ge 2$,
(if $k = 1$, then we have $p_j \in \delta(p_{(0,i,k)}, *)$, for $* \in \Sigma \cup \{\lambda\}$, $1 \le i \le n$, and $1 \le j \le i$)

(v) $p_{(j,i,h-1)} \in \delta(p_{(j,i,h)}, *)$, for $* \in \Sigma \cup \{\lambda\}$, $0 \le i \le n$, $0 \le j \le i$, and $2 \le h \le k$,

(vi) $p_{(j+1,i,h-1)} \in \delta(p_{(j,i,h)}, *)$, for $* \in \Sigma \cup \{\lambda\}$, $1 \le i \le n$, $0 \le j < i$, and $2 \le h \le k$,

(vii) $p_j \in \delta(p_{(j,i,1)}, *)$, for $* \in \Sigma \cup \{\lambda\}$, $0 \le i \le n$, $0 \le j \le i$, and $2 \le h \le k$,

(viii) $p_{j+1} \in \delta(p_{(j,i,1)}, *)$, for $* \in \Sigma \cup \{\lambda\}$, $1 \le i \le n$, $0 \le j < i$, and $2 \le h \le k$.

The final state of B_w is the states p_n. Additionally, it is not hard to transform the λ-NFA B_w to an equivalent NFA B'_w without λ transitions which has the same states as B_w. We give an example of the NFA B_w in Fig. 3, in the case where $w = x_1 x_2 x_3$ and $k = 2$.

Now we will give an informal explanation of how the transitions of the NFA B_w work. A state $p_{(j,i,h)}$ represents that the pseudo-duplication appears in the

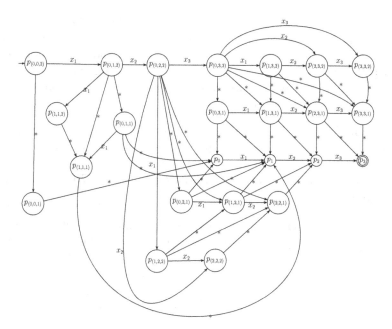

Fig. 3. An illustrative example of constructing an NFA recognizing $\mathbb{PD}_k(w)$, where $w = x_1x_2x_3$ for $x_1, x_2, x_3 \in \Sigma$ and $k = 2$.

i-th position of w, there are $i-j$ characters left from the inserted word, and that h errors remain. In more details from the definition of pseudo-duplication of w, we have all the words $x_1x_2x_2'x_3$ where $w = x_1x_2x_3$, for some $x_1, x_2, x_3 \in \Sigma^*$ and $d(x_2, x_2') \leq k$. The transitions that appear in (i) read the prefix of w x_1x_2. The transitions in (iii) and (iv) nondeterministically split the string x_1x_2 to the strings x_1 and x_2. The transitions in (ii) read the parts of the word x_2' that do not differ from the word x_2. The transitions in (v) and (vii) introduce an inserted character, in (vi) and (viii) substitute or delete a character.

Similar we can work for the correctness of the above construction. We can prove that every word $x \in \mathbb{PD}_k(w)$, it is also in $L(B_w)$ from the construction of B_w. Moreover, we can easily prove that for every word $x \in L(B_w)$ we have that w also belongs in $\mathbb{PD}_k(w)$.

The number of states of the NFA B_w are $n+1$ from the states p_i, $0 \leq i \leq n$, and there are $k \cdot (1+2+\ldots+(n+1))$, then it has $k\frac{(n+1)(n+2)}{2}+n+1$ states.

For the lower bound, let as have a word w_0 over an alphabet Σ_0 with $|w_0|$ letters. Let assume also that every letter of the alphabet Σ_0 appears in the word w_0. Then, let w_0 be the word $x_1x_2\ldots x_n$, for $|w_0| = n$. Now, for defining the extended fooling set, first let us have the following $n + 1$ pairs:

$$P' = \{(x_1x_2\ldots x_n(x_2)^k x_0 x_1 \ldots x_i, x_{i+1} \ldots x_n) \mid 0 \leq i \leq n \text{ and } x_0 = \lambda\}$$

Now, we want to transform any triple of numbers (j, i, h) to a pair of strings, for $0 \leq i \leq n$, $0 \leq j \leq i$, and $1 \leq h \leq k$. We associate the triple (j, i, h) to the pair $(x_1 x_2 \ldots x_i (x_n)^{k-h} x_1 \ldots x_j, (x_n)^h x_{j+1} \ldots x_n)$. The P'' be the set of pairs that we get by all triples (j, i, h) for $0 \leq i \leq n$, $0 \leq j \leq i$, and $1 \leq h \leq k$. Now, the fooling set will be the set of pairs $P = P' \cup P''$. We notice that for any two distinct pairs $(x, y), (x', y') \in P$ the string xy' or the string $x'y$ does not belong in $\mathbb{PD}_k(w_0)$, since the pseudo-duplication will appear in a different position or one of these strings will have more than k errors. $\square$

Theorem 3. *Let $w \in \Sigma^*$ be a string of length n, for a positive integer n. Then, the language $\mathbb{RD}(w)$ is recognized by an NFA with $\frac{n^2 + 3n + 2}{2}$ states.*

Moreover, for every $n \in \mathbb{N}$, there exists a string w of length n over an alphabet of size n such that any NFA recognizing the language $\mathbb{RD}(w)$ needs at least $\frac{n^2 + 3n + 2}{2}$ states.

We omit the proof of Theorem 3 due to the page limitation, but Fig. 4 gives an insight on how we compute the nondeterministic state complexity for reverse-duplication of a string.

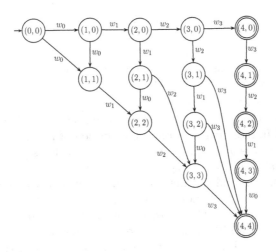

Fig. 4. An illustrative example of constructing an NFA recognizing $\mathbb{RD}(w)$, where $w = w_0 w_1 w_2 w_3$ for $w_i \in \Sigma$, $0 \leq i \leq 3$.

3.2   Closure Properties of Duplication Operations

Next, we study the closure properties of duplication and pseudo-duplication for regular and context-free languages. We first show that regular and context-free languages are not closed under the duplication operation.

Theorem 4. *Regular languages are not closed under the duplication operation.*

Theorem 5. *Context-free languages are not closed under the duplication operation.*

Before we consider the closure properties of the pseudo-duplication operation, we mention that regular languages and context-free languages over unary alphabet are closed under the duplication, pseudo-duplication and reverse-duplication operations.

Proposition 2. *The unary regular languages are closed under the duplication, pseudo-duplication and reverse-duplication operations.*

Theorem 6. *Regular languages are not closed under the pseudo-duplication operation.*

Theorem 7. *Context-free languages are not closed under the pseudo-duplication operation.*

Theorems 6 and 7 show that regular and context-free languages are not closed under the pseudo-duplication operation. On the other hand, regular and context-free languages are closed under the pseudo-duplication operation when Σ is a unary alphabet.

Theorem 8. *Regular languages are not closed under the reverse-duplication operation.*

Theorem 9. *Context-free languages are not closed under the reverse-duplication operation.*

Now, we show that the class of context-sensitive languages is closed under the operations of duplication, pseudo-duplication and reverse-duplication. For clarity, we start with the following example.

Example 1. There is a context-sensitive grammar G recognizing the copy language $L = \{ww \mid w \in \Sigma^+\}$ over the alphabet $\Sigma = \{a, b\}$. We now give a grammar with the following rules:

$$
\begin{aligned}
S &\to A_1 A_2^S S^E \mid B_1 B_2^S S^E \mid aa \mid bb & B_2 B_1^E &\to B_1^E B_2 \\
S^E &\to A_1 A_2 S^E \mid B_1 B_2 S^E \mid A_1^E A_2 \mid B_1^E B_2 & A_2^S A_1^E &\to A_1^E A_2^S \\
A_2 A_1 &\to A_1 A_2 & B_2^S A_1^E &\to A_1^E B_2^S \\
B_2 A_1 &\to A_1 B_2 & A_2^S B_1^E &\to B_1^E A_2^S \\
A_2 B_1 &\to B_1 A_2 & B_2^S B_1^E &\to B_1^E B_2^S \\
B_2 B_1 &\to B_1 B_2 & A_1^E A_2^S &\to aa \\
A_2^S A_1 &\to A_1 A_2^S & B_1^E A_2^S &\to ba \\
B_2^S A_1 &\to A_1 B_2^S & A_1^E B_2^S &\to ab \\
A_2^S B_1 &\to B_1 A_2^S & B_1^E B_2^S &\to bb \\
B_2^S B_1 &\to B_1 B_2^S & \gamma A_2 &\to \gamma a, \ \gamma \in \{a, b\} \\
A_2 A_1^E &\to A_1^E A_2 & \gamma B_2 &\to \gamma b, \ \gamma \in \{a, b\} \\
B_2 A_1^E &\to A_1^E B_2 & A_1 \gamma &\to a\gamma, \ \gamma \in \{a, b\} \\
A_2 B_1^E &\to B_1^E A_2 & B_1 \gamma &\to b\gamma, \ \gamma \in \{a, b\}
\end{aligned}
$$

Where the symbols $S, S^E, A_1, A_1^S, A_1^E, B_1, B_1^S$, and B_1^E are the non-terminal symbols of the grammar.

Now for the correctness of the grammar, we notice that in the grammar the non-terminal symbol A corresponds to the final symbol a and the non-terminal symbol B corresponds to the final symbol b. Every time that the grammar produces a non-terminal symbol A for the first string, represented by A_1, A_1^S, or A_1^E, it also produces a non-terminal symbol A for the second string, A_2, A_2^S, or A_2^E, and vice versa. From the third rule of the first column up to the fifth rule of the second column, the grammar makes sure that the symbols corresponding to letters of the first string to be followed be symbols corresponding to letters of the second string. Notice that the grammar does not change the order of symbols which correspond to the same string. Finally, before any non-terminal transforms into a final symbol the grammar makes sure that all non-terminal symbols are in their correct positions. We do that by checking that the symbol corresponding to the last letter of the first string to be before the symbol corresponding to the first letter of the second string. This happens with the sixth to ninth rules of the second column and by these rules being the only rules who can start the transformation of non-terminals to final symbols.

The careful reader may notice that in Example 1, occasionally, we use rules of the form $AB \rightarrow BA$ which strictly speaking, they do not follow the definition of context-sensitive grammars. Such rules could be replaced with the rules $AB \rightarrow NB, NB \rightarrow NA$, and $NA \rightarrow BA$ by adding a new non-terminal symbol N. We allow rules of the above form in order to keep the number of rules low and increase readability.

Proposition 3. *Let G be a context-sensitive grammar. There is a context-sensitive grammar G' recognizing the copy language $L = \{ww \mid w \in L(G)\}$.*

Proposition 3 shows that given a context-sensitive grammar G we build a new context-sensitive grammar that recognizes the copy language $L = \{ww \mid w \in L(G)\}$. Based on the grammar of Proposition 3 we can construct a context-sensitive grammar that recognizes the language $\mathbb{D}(L(G))$.

Theorem 10. *The class of context-sensitive languages is closed under the duplication operation.*

With a similar technique with Theorem 10, we have the following theorem.

Theorem 11. *The class of context-sensitive languages is closed under the reverse-duplication and pseudo-duplication operations.*

4   Conclusions

We have considered biologically inspired operations called the duplication and reverse-duplication. The duplication operation on a string copies a substring and the reverse-duplication operation copies a substring in reverse. We have defined the pseudo-duplication operation as an extended variant of duplication where a substring can be repeated with some errors, and the number of errors is specified by an integer parameter. Then, we have estimated state complexity for these operations of a string and showed closure properties.

We have shown that the state complexity for duplication, pseudo-duplication and reverse-duplication of a string are $2n+1$, $k \cdot \frac{(n+1)(n+2)}{2}+n+1$ and $\frac{n^2+3n+2}{2}$ respectively, where n is length of a string and $k \geq 1$. Moreover, we have obtained the closure properties of the families of languages in the Chomsky hierarchy under three variants of duplication: Regular languages and context-free languages are not closed under duplication, pseudo-duplication and reverse-duplication whereas context-sensitive languages are closed under these operations.

A problem for further research is the complexity of determining whether or not a given language L has a string that belongs to the duplication, pseudo-duplication and reverse-duplication of another string in L. Moreover, it is also our future work to look for deterministic, nondeterministic state complexity of duplication and pseudo-duplication on unary regular languages.

Acknowledgements. We wish to thank the referees for valuable suggestions that improve proofs for several results.

This research was supported by the Basic Science Research Program through NRF funded by MEST (2012R1A1A2044562), the International Cooperation Program managed by NRF of Korea (2014K2A1A2048512), the Yonsei University Future-leading Research Initiative of 2014 and the Natural Sciences and Engineering Research Council of Canada Grant OGP0147224.

References

1. Calude, C., Salomaa, K., Yu, S.: Additive distances and quasi-distances between words. Univ. Comput. Sci. **8**(2), 141–152 (2002)
2. Cameron, M., Williams, H.E., Cannane, A.: A deterministic finite automaton for faster protein hit detection in blast. Comput. Biol. **13**(4), 965–978 (2006)
3. Cantone, D., Cristofaro, S., Faro, S.: Efficient string-matching allowing for non-overlapping inversions. Theor. Comput. Sci. **483**, 85–95 (2013)
4. Cho, D.J., Han, Y.S., Kang, S.D., Kim, H., Ko, S.K., Salomaa, K.: Pseudo-inversion on formal languages. In: Ibarra, O.H., Kari, L., Kopecki, S. (eds.) UCNC 2014. LNCS, vol. 8553, pp. 93–104. Springer, Heidelberg (2014)
5. Cho, D.J., Han, Y.S., Kim, H.: Alignment with non-overlapping inversions and translocations on two strings. Theor. Comput. Sci. **575**, 90–101 (2015)
6. Cho, D.J., Han, Y.S., Ko, S.K., Salomaa, K.: State complexity of inversion operations. Theor. Comput. Sci. (in press)
7. Choffrut, C., Pighizzini, G.: Distances between languages and reflexivity of relations. Theor. Comput. Sci. **286**(1), 117–138 (2002)
8. Creighton, H.B., McClintock, B.: A correlation of cytological and genetical crossing-over in zea mays. Nat. Acad. Sci. U.S.A. **17**(8), 492–497 (1931)
9. Dassow, J., Mitrana, V., Paun, G.: On the regularity of duplication closure. Bull. EATCS **69**, 133–136 (1999)

10. Dassow, J., Mitrana, V., Salomaa, A.: Operations and language generating devices suggested by the genome evolution. Theor. Comput. Sci. **270**(1), 701–738 (2002)
11. Dassow, J., Mitrana, V., Salomaa, A.: Context-free evolutionary grammars and the structural language of nucleic acids. Biosystems **43**(3), 169–177 (1997)
12. Djian, P.: Evolution of simple repeats in dna and their relation to human disease. Cell **94**(2), 155–160 (1998)
13. Herrmannsfeldt, G.: A highly parallel finite state automaton processor for biological pattern matching. In: Stringology, pp. 58–72 (1998)
14. Hopcroft, J., Ullman, J.: Introduction to Automata Theory, Languages, and Computation, 2nd edn. Addison-Wesley, Reading (1979)
15. Hussini, S., Kari, L., Konstantinidis, S.: Coding properties of DNA languages. Theor. Comput. Sci. **290**(3), 1557–1579 (2003)
16. Ibarra, O.H.: On decidability and closure properties of language classes with respect to bio-operations. In: Murata, S., Kobayashi, S. (eds.) DNA 2014. LNCS, vol. 8727, pp. 148–160. Springer, Heidelberg (2014)
17. Ito, M., Leupold, P., Shikishima-Tsuji, K.: Closure of language classes under bounded duplication. In: Ibarra, O.H., Dang, Z. (eds.) DLT 2006. LNCS, vol. 4036, pp. 238–247. Springer, Heidelberg (2006)
18. Kari, L., Mahalingam, K.: DNA codes and their properties. In: Mao, C., Yokomori, T. (eds.) DNA12. LNCS, vol. 4287, pp. 127–142. Springer, Heidelberg (2006)
19. Kong, S.G., Fan, W.L., Chen, H.D., Hsu, Z.T., Zhou, N., Zheng, B., Lee, H.C.: Inverse symmetry in complete genomes and whole-genome inverse duplication. PLoS One **4**(11), e7553 (2009)
20. Leupold, P., Mitrana, V., Sempere, J.M.: Formal languages arising from gene repeated duplication. In: Jonoska, N., Păun, G., Rozenberg, G. (eds.) Aspects of Molecular Computing. LNCS, vol. 2950, pp. 297–308. Springer, Heidelberg (2003)
21. Mitrana, V., Rozenberg, G.: Some properties of duplication grammars. Acta Cybernetica **14**(1), 165–177 (1999)
22. Mount, D.W.: Using the basic local alignment search tool (blast). Cold Spring Harbor Protoc. **2007**(7), pdb-top17 (2007)
23. Pearson, W.R., Lipman, D.J.: Improved tools for biological sequence comparison. Nat. Acad. Sci. **85**(8), 2444–2448 (1988)
24. Rozenberg, G., Salomaa, A. (eds.): Handbook of Formal Languages. Beyond Words, vol. 3. Springer-Verlag New York Inc., New York (1997)
25. Schöniger, M., Waterman, M.S.: A local algorithm for DNA sequence alignment with inversions. Bull. Math. Biol. **54**(4), 521–536 (1992)
26. Searls, D.B.: The computational linguistics of biological sequences. Artif. Intell. Mol. Biol. **2**, 47–120 (1993)
27. Shallit, J.: A Second Course in Formal Languages and Automata Theory. Cambridge University Press, Cambridge (2009)
28. Viguera, E., Canceill, D., Ehrlich, S.D.: Replication slippage involves DNA polymerase pausing and dissociation. EMBO J. **20**(10), 2587–2595 (2001)
29. Wood, D.: Theory of Computation. Harper & Row, New York (1987)
30. Yokomori, T., Kobayashi, S.: DNA evolutionary linguistics and RNA structure modeling: a computational approach. In: Neural and Biological Systems, pp. 38–45 (1995)

Going Beyond Turing with P Automata: Partial Adult Halting and Regular Observer ω-Languages

Rudolf Freund[1]([⊠]), Sergiu Ivanov[2], and Ludwig Staiger[3]

[1] Technische Universität Wien, Vienna, Austria
rudi@emcc.at
[2] Université Paris Est, Paris, France
sergiu.ivanov@u-pec.fr
[3] Martin-Luther-Universität Halle-Wittenberg, Halle, Germany
staiger@informatik.uni-halle.de

Abstract. In this paper we investigate several variants of P automata having infinite runs on finite inputs. By imposing specific conditions on the infinite evolution of the systems, it is easy to find ways for going beyond Turing if we are watching the behavior of the systems on infinite runs. As specific variants we introduce a new halting variant for P automata which we call *partial adult halting* with the meaning that a specific predefined part of the P automaton does not change any more from some moment on during the infinite run. In a more general way, we can assign ω-languages as observer languages to the infinite runs of a P automaton. Specific variants of regular ω-languages then, for example, characterize the red-green P automata.

1 Introduction

Various possibilities how one may "go beyond Turing" are discussed in [11], for example, the definitions and results for red-green Turing machines can be found there. In [2] the notion of red-green automata for register machines with input strings given on an input tape (often also called *counter automata*) was introduced and the concept of *red-green P automata* for several specific models of membrane systems was explained. Via red-green counter automata, the results for acceptance and recognizability of finite strings by red-green Turing machines were carried over to red-green P automata. The basic idea of red-green automata is to distinguish between two different sets of states (red and green states) and to consider infinite runs of the automaton on finite input objects (strings, multisets); allowed to change between red and green states more than once, red-green automata can recognize more than the recursively enumerable sets (of strings, multisets), i.e., in that way we can "go beyond Turing". In the area of P systems, first attempts to do that can be found in [4] and [18]. Computations with infinite words by P automata were investigated in [9].

In this paper, we also consider infinite runs of P automata, but in a more general way take into account the existence/non-existence of a recursive feature of

© Springer International Publishing Switzerland 2015
C.S. Calude and M.J. Dinneen (Eds.): UCNC 2015, LNCS 9252, pp. 169–180, 2015.
DOI: 10.1007/978-3-319-21819-9_12

the current sequence of configurations. In that way, we obtain infinite sequences over $\{0, 1\}$ which we call "observer languages" where 1 indicates that the specific feature is fulfilled by the current configuration and 0 indicates that this specific feature is not fulfilled. The recognizing runs of red-green automata then correspond with ω-regular languages over $\{0, 1\}$ of a specific form ending with 1^{ω} as observer languages. A very special observer language is $\{0, 1\}^* \{1\}^{\omega}$ which corresponds with a very special acceptance condition for P automata which we call "partial adult halting". This special acceptance variant for P automata with infinite runs on finite multisets is motivated by an observation we make for the evolution of time lines described by P systems – at some moment, a specific part of the evolving time lines, for example, the part describing time 0, shall not change any more.

2   Definitions

We assume the reader to be familiar with the underlying notions and concepts from formal language theory, e.g., see [17], as well as from the area of P systems, e.g., see [13–15]; we also refer the reader to [25] for actual news.

2.1   Prerequisites

The set of integers is denoted by $\mathbb{Z}$, and the set of non-negative integers by $\mathbb{N}$. Given an alphabet V, a finite non-empty set of abstract symbols, the free monoid generated by V under the operation of concatenation is denoted by V^*. The elements of V^* are called strings, the empty string is denoted by λ, and $V^* \setminus \{\lambda\}$ is denoted by V^+. For an arbitrary alphabet $V = \{a_1, \ldots, a_n\}$, the number of occurrences of a symbol a_i in a string x is denoted by $|x|_{a_i}$, while the length of a string x is denoted by $|x| = \sum_{a_i \in V} |x|_{a_i}$. A (finite) multiset over a (finite) alphabet $V = \{a_1, \ldots, a_n\}$ is a mapping $f : V \to \mathbb{N}$ and can be represented by $\left\langle a_1^{f(a_1)}, \ldots, a_n^{f(a_n)} \right\rangle$ or by any string x for which $(|x|_{a_1}, \ldots, |x|_{a_n}) = (f(a_1), \ldots, f(a_n))$. The families of regular and recursively enumerable string languages are denoted by REG and RE, respectively.

2.2   The Arithmetical Hierarchy

The Arithmetical Hierarchy (e.g., see [3]) is usually developed with the universal ($\forall$) and existential ($\exists$) quantifiers restricted to the integers. Levels in the Arithmetical Hierarchy are labeled as Σ_n if they can be defined by expressions beginning with a sequence of n alternating quantifiers starting with $\exists$; levels are labeled as Π_n if they can be defined by such expressions of n alternating quantifiers that start with $\forall$. Σ_0 and Π_0 are defined as having no quantifiers and are equivalent. Σ_1 and Π_1 only have the single quantifier $\exists$ and $\forall$, respectively. We only need to consider alternating pairs of the quantifiers $\forall$ and $\exists$ because two quantifiers of the same type occurring together are equivalent to a single quantifier.

3   Time Travel P Systems

In the most general case, we can think of P systems as devices manipulating multisets in a hierarchical membrane structure. The membranes can have labels and polarizations both eventually changing with the application of rules. Membranes may be divided, generated or deleted. Together with the division or the generation of a new membrane the whole contents of another membrane may be copied. For a general framework of P systems we refer to [7].

Usually, configurations in P systems (and other systems like Turing machines) evolve step by step through time, see Fig. 1.

Time configurations

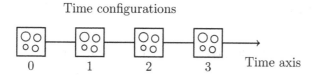

Fig. 1. Standard time line evolution.

Without time travel option, we need only consider the evolution of the system on one time axis from time n to time $n+1$. The situation becomes more difficult if we follow the idea of parallel worlds (*time axes*), which means that we have another time dimension, described by the vertical evolution in Fig. 2, i.e., the time configurations at time n may be altered depending on future evolutions.

Time configurations

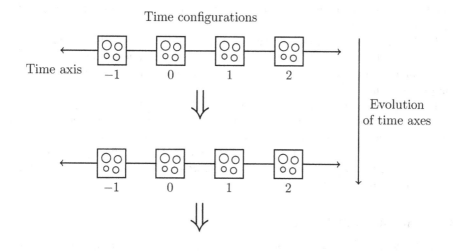

Fig. 2. Time lines evolution.

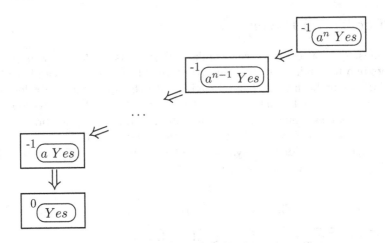

Fig. 3. Sending back an answer from time n to time 0.

For example, we can consider membrane systems with polarizations assigned to the membranes. The usual polarization of the whole time configuration in the normal case is $+1$, indicating that the evolution of the membrane(s) goes from time configuration n to time configuration $n + 1$. Now assume we allow polarization -1 indicating that the corresponding membrane evolves from time configuration n to time configuration $n - 1$. Having kept trace of the number of computation steps, e.g., by the multiplicity of a specific object a, we are able to send back information – like the answer *yes* to a question we have posed at time 0 which then is sent back to time configuration 0, i.e., to the time we have posed the question. In that way, on a specific time line we can have answers to questions in zero time, see Fig. 3.

During its travel through the time back, the time capsule with polarization -1 can be assumed not to be affected by the other membranes in the intermediate time configurations. Obviously, this restriction can be alleviated for even more complex systems.

Putting a new skin membrane around all the current time configurations of one time axis, we again obtain a conventional evolution model, yet now with a vertical time evolution as depicted in Fig. 4. The only assumption we have to do for making this variant possible is that at the beginning only a finite number of time configurations exists (in fact, we usually will start with the time configuration at time 0).

3.1 Partial Adult Halting

Going back to the time travel model of Fig. 2 the question that arises is what kind of results we may obtain and how. For example, given a specific input in time configuration 0, we may request that from some moment on this time configuration becomes stable, i.e., it is not changed any more (by time capsules arriving there).

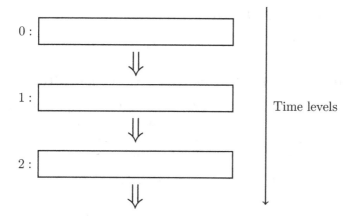

Fig. 4. Conventional evolution model.

So the specific feature an external observer would see is that the time configuration at time 0 is not changing any more starting from some specific time line at level tl_0 on, i.e., for all time levels $tl \geq tl_0$ the *time configuration at time 0 stays stable*.

With respect to the situation described in Fig. 4 this means that one specific part (one membrane and all its contents) does not change any more.

In that way we obtain a new variant of a halting condition in P systems which we call *partial adult halting*:

Adult halting:

   means that the configuration does not change any more

Partial:

   we only look at some part of the configuration

3.2   Partial Adult Halting for Turing Machines

The idea of partial adult halting can also be applied to Turing machines:

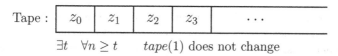

On tape cell 1 we want to obtain an "answer" whether the given input word is accepted – 1 – or not – 0. We first put 0 there, and if the computation ends saying "accept" we go back to tape cell 1 and write 1 there. Hence, with looking to infinity in that way we obtain a "decider" for recursively enumerable languages.

4   Variants of P Automata

In this section, we shortly describe some variants of P automata.

4.1   The Basic Model of P Automata with Antiport Rules

The basic model of P automata as introduced in [6] and in a similar way in [8] is based on antiport rules, i.e., on rules of the form u/v, which means that the multiset u goes out through the membrane and v comes in instead.

A *P automaton (with antiport rules)* is a construct

$$\Pi = (O, T, \mu, w_1, \ldots, w_m, R_1, \ldots, R_m) \text{ where}$$

- O is the alphabet of *objects*;
- $T \subset O$ is the alphabet of *terminal objects*;
- μ is the hierarchical membrane structure, with the membranes uniquely labeled by the numbers from 1 to m;
- $w_i \in (O \setminus T)^*$, $1 \le i \le m$, is the *initial multiset* in membrane i;
- R_i, $1 \le i \le m$, is a finite set of *antiport rules* assigned to membrane i.

Given a multiset of terminal symbols in the skin membrane 1, it is usually accepted by Π via a halting computation.

Now consider the situation of partial adult halting for a P automaton

$$\Pi = (O, T, [_1[_2\ ]_2]_1, q_0, n, R_1, R_2)$$

which – with the input multiset in addition given in the skin membrane – simulates, in a deterministic way, a register machine defining a recursively enumerable set L of multisets (see [12]), by the rules in R_1. If the computation stops in the final state q_h, i.e., the multiset is accepted, we add the rules q_h/y and n/n in R_1. R_2 only contains the rule n/y. In case the multiset is accepted, n in the second membrane is replaced by y, while the rule n/n in R_1 guarantees an infinite computation. In case the input multiset is not accepted, the register machine already guarantees an infinite computation by the simulating P automaton, too. Hence, as in the case of the Turing machine with partial adult halting we get a "decider" for L, with the result from some moment on to be found in membrane 2.

4.2   P Automata with Anti-Matter

In *P automata with anti-matter*, for each object a we may have its anti-matter object a^-. If an object a meets its anti-matter object a^-, then these two objects annihilate each other, which corresponds to the application of the cooperative erasing rule $aa^- \to \lambda$. In the following, we shall only consider the variant where these annihilation rules have weak priority over all other rules, which allows for a deterministic simulation of deterministic register machines, see [1].

A *P automaton with anti-matter* is a construct

$$\Pi = (O, T, \mu, w_1, \ldots, w_m, R_1, \ldots, R_m) \text{ where}$$

- O is the alphabet of *objects*;
- $T \subset O$ is the alphabet of *terminal objects*;
- μ is the hierarchical membrane structure, with the membranes uniquely labeled by the numbers from 1 to m;
- $w_i \in (O \setminus T)^*$, $1 \leq i \leq m$, is the *initial multiset* in membrane i;
- R_i, $1 \leq i \leq m$, is a finite set of

Non-cooperative Rules: are rules of the form $u \to v$ where $u \in O$ and $v \in (O \times \{here, in, out\})^*$;

Matter/Anti-matter Annihilation Rules: are cooperative rules of the form $aa^- \to \lambda$, i.e., the matter object a and its anti-matter object a^- annihilate each other, and these annihilation rules have weak priority over all other rules.

With the target indications $\{here, in, out\}$ we can leave an object in the current membrane ($here$), whereas with $\{in\}$ we send it into an inner membrane and with $\{out\}$ we send it into the surrounding membrane region.

In a similar way as in the preceding subsection we may consider the situation of partial adult halting for a P automaton

$$\Pi = (O, T, [_1 [_2]_2]_1, q_0, n, R_1, R_2)$$

where following the proof from [1] the register machine actions are simulated in the skin membrane; if the input multiset is accepted, by using the rules $q_h \to (f, here)(n^-, in)$, $f \to f$, we obtain an infinite computation with the contents of membrane 2 being empty indicating the acceptance, as by the annihilation rule $nn^- \to \lambda$ the original object n is annihilated.

5   Red-Green Automata

In general, a red-green automaton M is an automaton whose set of internal states Q is partitioned into two subsets, Q_{red} and Q_{green}, and M operates without halting. Q_{red} is called the set of "red states", Q_{green} the set of "green states". Moreover, we shall assume M to be deterministic, i.e., for each configuration there exists exactly one transition to the next one.

5.1   Red-Green Turing Machines

Red-green Turing machines, see [11], can be seen as a type of ω-Turing machines on finite inputs with a recognition criterion based on some property of the set(s) of states visited (in)finitely often, in the tradition of ω-automata (see [9]), i.e., we call an infinite run of the Turing machine M on input w *recognizing* if and only if

- no red state is visited infinitely often and
- some green states (one or more) are visited infinitely often.

A set of strings $L \subset \Sigma^*$ is said to be *accepted* by M if and only if the following two conditions are satisfied:

(a) $L = \{w \mid w$ is recognized by $M\}$.
(b) For every string $w \notin L$, the computation of M on input w eventually stabilizes in red; in this case w is said to be *rejected*.

The phrase "mind change" is used in the sense of changing the color, i.e., changing from red to green or vice versa.

The following results were established in [11]:

Theorem 1. *A set of strings L is recognized by a red-green Turing machine with one mind change if and only if $L \in \Sigma_1$, i.e., if L is recursively enumerable.*

Theorem 2. *(Computational power of red-green Turing machines)*

(a) Red-green Turing machines recognize exactly the Σ_2-sets of the Arithmetical Hierarchy.
(b) Red-green Turing machines accept exactly those sets which simultaneously are Σ_2- and Π_2-sets of the Arithmetical Hierarchy.

In [2], similar results were shown for red-green counter automata and register machines, respectively.

5.2   Red-Green P Automata

As it was shown in [2], P automata with antiport rules and with anti-matter can simulate the infinite computations of any red-green register machine, even with a clearly specified finite set of "states" having the same color as the corresponding labels ("states") of the instructions of the red-green register machine.

Hence, as a consequence, similar results as for red-green Turing machines also hold for red-green P automata with antiport rules and with anti-matter. From the results shown in [2] we therefore infer:

Theorem 3. *(Computational power of red-green P automata)*

(i) A set of multisets L is recognized by a red-green P automaton (with antiport rules, with anti-matter) with one mind change if and only if L is recursively enumerable.
(ii) Red-green P automata (with antiport rules, with anti-matter) recognize exactly the Σ_2-sets.
(iii) Red-green P automata (with antiport rules, with anti-matter) accept exactly those sets which simultaneously are Σ_2- and Π_2-sets of the Arithmetical Hierarchy.

6   Observer Languages

An observer language for infinite computations is an ω-language over $\{0, 1\}$ where 1 indicates that a specific feature of the current configuration in the infinite computation sequence is fulfilled and 0 indicates that this specific feature of the current configuration is not fulfilled.

6.1 Expressing Partial Adult Halting as Observer Language

If we define the specific feature to be that no rule is applicable in the specified "observed" membrane, then acceptance by partial adult halting can be described by the (regular) ω-language $\{0,1\}^*\{1\}^\omega$.

6.2 Expressing Recognition by Red-Green P Automata Using Observer Languages

As observer languages for infinite computations in red-green P automata we again use ω-languages over $\{0,1\}$ where now 1 indicates that we will have to apply a green multiset of rules to the current configuration in the infinite computation sequence and 0 indicates that we will have to apply a red multiset of rules to the current configuration.

So for recognizing a language from RE we use the the ω-language $\{0\}^+\{1\}^\omega$, for a language from co-RE we use the the ω-language $\{0\}\{1\}^\omega$.

The corresponding regular ω-languages for the recognition by red-green automata (Turing machines, P automata) with multiple mind-changes are described as follows:

exactly $2k+1$ mind-changes, $k \geq 0$: $\{0\}^+\big(\{1\}^+\{0\}^+\big)^k\{1\}^\omega$

at most $2k+1$ mind-changes, $k \geq 0$: $\bigcup_{i=0}^k\{0\}^+\big(\{1\}^+\{0\}^+\big)^i\{1\}^\omega$

The upper bound for languages recognized by red-green P automata (with antiport rules, with anti-matter) with k mind-changes for some $k \geq 0$ is Σ_2, see [2].

These results will be refined in the next section.

7 Recognition Using Regular Observer Languages

In this section we investigate which languages are recognized by red-green P automata using observer languages defined by finite automata. This class of ω-languages defined by finite automata is well-understood and has widely been investigated (see [16,21,23,24]). We follow the line of [20] where for Turing machines infinite computations accepting finite words were investigated in detail (see also [5]). In this paper a word w was accepted by a Turing machine when the sequence $(s_i)_{i\in\mathbb{N}}$ of states the machine runs through during its accepting process fulfills certain simple conditions known from the acceptance of ω-languages. This can be seen as w to be accepted if the observed state sequence $(s_i)_{i\in\mathbb{N}}$ belongs to a certain (regular) observer language. We have to point out that usually the notion *acceptance* is used here instead of the notion *recognition* as used by van Leeuwen and Wiedermann for the red-green Turing machines.

7.1   Observer Languages of the Form $W \cdot \{1\}^\omega$ with $W \in REG$

The observer languages in Sect. 6 all were of the form $W \cdot \{1\}^\omega$ where $W \subseteq \{0,1\}^*$ is a regular language. In this section we investigate which languages can be accepted by red-green P automata using observer languages of this form. Here we follow the line of the papers [20] and [11] where the influence of regular observer languages on the acceptance and recognition, respectively, behavior of Turing machines was investigated.

To this end we use the following theorem which follows from a general classification of regular ω-languages (see [19, 22] and also the survey [21]).

Theorem 4. *If $F \subseteq \{0,1\}^\omega$ is a regular ω-language, then*

1. *F is in the Boolean closure of Σ_2, and*
2. *if $F \in \Sigma_2 \cap \Pi_2$, then F is in the Boolean closure of Σ_1.*

Since every regular $F \subseteq \{0,1\}^* \cdot \{1\}^\omega$ as a countable set is in Σ_2, we immediately obtain the following.

Corollary 1. *If $W \subseteq \{0,1\}^*$ is a regular language then $W \cdot \{1\}^\omega$ satisfies one of the following conditions:*

1. *$W \cdot \{1\}^\omega \in \Sigma_2 \setminus \Pi_2$, or*
2. *$W \cdot \{1\}^\omega$ is a Boolean combination of ω-languages in Σ_1.*

Remark 1. In the second case we can obtain an even sharper result:

$$W \cdot \{1\}^\omega = \bigcup_{i=0}^{k} (W_i \cdot \{0,1\}^\omega \setminus V_i \cdot \{0,1\}^\omega)$$

for suitable $k \in \mathbb{N}$ and *regular* languages $W_i, V_i \subseteq \{0,1\}^*$, $0 \leq i \leq k$. In particular, this is true for the ω-languages representing a bounded number of mind-changes from Subsect. 6.2:

$$\bigcup_{i=0}^{k} \{0\}^+ (\{1\}^+ \{0\}^+)^i \{1\}^\omega =$$
$$\bigcup_{i=0}^{k} \left(\{0\}^+ (\{1\}^+ \{0\}^+)^i \{1\} \cdot \{0,1\}^\omega \setminus \{0\}^+ (\{1\}^+ \{0\}^+)^i \{1\}^+ \{0\} \cdot \{0,1\}^\omega \right)$$

From Corollary 1 we immediately infer:

Theorem 5. *Let L be recognized by a red-green P automaton (with antiport rules, with anti-matter) using an observer language $W \cdot \{1\}^\omega$ where $W \subseteq \{0,1\}^*$ is regular.*

1. *Then $L \in \Sigma_2$.*

2. *If $W \cdot \{1\}^\omega = \bigcup_{i=0}^{k}(F_i \setminus E_i)$ is a Boolean combination of ω-languages $F_i, E_i \in \Sigma_1$, $0 \leq i \leq k$, then $L = \bigcup_{i=0}^{k}(K_i \setminus L_i)$ where $K_i, L_i \in RE$, $0 \leq i \leq k$.*

The converse of Theorem 5 is also true. In particular, it shows that we can restrict ourselves to the observer languages of Subsects. 6.1 and 6.2.

Theorem 6. *Let* $L \in \Sigma_2$.

1. *Then* L *is recognized by a red-green P automaton* Π *using the observer language* $\{0,1\}^* \cdot \{1\}^\omega$, *i.e.,* L *is accepted by* Π *by partial adult halting.*

2. *Let* $L = \bigcup_{i=0}^{k}(K_i \setminus L_i)$ *where* $K_i, L_i \in RE$, $0 \le i \le k$. *Then there exists a red-green P automaton which recognizes* L *using an observer language with a bounded number of mind-changes.*

7.2   Regular Observer Languages

Admitting all regular ω-languages as observer languages extends the range of recognizable languages. In view of Theorem 4 we obtain a result extending what was shown in Theorem 5.

Theorem 7. *Let* L *be recognized by a red-green P automaton using an observer language* $F \subseteq \{0,1\}^\omega$. *Then*

1. *if* F *is a Boolean combination of* ω-*languages* $F_i, E_i \in \Sigma_2$, $0 \le i \le k$, *then* $L = \bigcup_{i=0}^{k}(K_i \setminus L_i)$ *where* $K_i, L_i \in \Sigma_2$, $0 \le i \le k$,

2. *if* $F \in \Sigma_2$, *then* $L \in \Sigma_2$,

3. *if* $F \in \Pi_2$, *then* $L \in \Pi_2$, *and*

4. *if* F *is regular and* $F \in \Sigma_2 \cap \Pi_2$, *then* $L = \bigcup_{i=0}^{k}(K_i \setminus L_i)$ *where* $K_i, L_i \in RE$, $0 \le i \le k$.

The converse of Theorem 7 is also true:

Theorem 8. *Let* L *be a Boolean combination of languages in* Σ_2. *Then* L *is recognized by a red-green P automaton using a regular observer language* $F \subseteq \{0,1\}^\omega$.

8   Conclusion

In this paper we have investigated the computational power of P automata working with infinite runs on finite input multisets. With regular observer languages $W \cdot \{1\}^\omega$, $W \in REG$, we obtain the Σ_2-sets, the same as with red-green P automata. Moreover, the Σ_2-sets are already obtained by the special observer language $\{0,1\}^* \cdot \{1\}^\omega$, which corresponds to the special acceptance condition of *partial adult halting*.

References

1. Alhazov, A., Aman, B., Freund, R.: P systems with anti-matter. In: [10], pp. 66–85
2. Aman, B., Csuhaj-Varjú, E., Freund, R.: Red–green P automata. In: [10], pp. 139–157

3. Budnik, P.: What Is and What Will Be. Mountain Math Software, Los Gatos (2006)
4. Calude, C.S., Păun, Gh.: Bio-steps beyond Turing. Biosystems **77**, 175–194 (2004)
5. Calude, C.S., Staiger, L.: A note on accelerated Turing machines. Math. Struct. Comput. Sci. **20**(6), 1011–1017 (2010)
6. Csuhaj-Varjú, E., Vaszil, Gy.: P automata or purely communicating accepting P systems. In: Păun, Gh., Rozenberg, G., Salomaa, A., Zandron, C. (eds.) Membrane Computing. Lecture Notes in Computer Science, vol. 2597, pp. 219–233. Springer, Heidelberg (2003)
7. Freund, R., Pérez-Hurtado, I., Riscos-Núñez, A., Verlan, S.: A formalization of membrane systems with dynamically evolving structures. Int. J. Comput. Math. **90**(4), 801–815 (2013)
8. Freund, R., Oswald, M.: A short note on analysing P systems. Bull. EATCS **78**, 231–236 (2002)
9. Freund, R., Oswald, M., Staiger, L.: ω-P automata with communication rules. In: Martín-Vide, C., Mauri, G., Păun, Gh., Rozenberg, G., Salomaa, A. (eds.) WMC 2003. LNCS, vol. 2933, pp. 203–217. Springer, Heidelberg (2004)
10. Pérez-Jiménez, M.J.: A bioinspired computing approach to model complex systems. In: Gheorghe, M., Rozenberg, G., Salomaa, A., Sosík, P., Zandron, C. (eds.) CMC 2014. LNCS, vol. 8961, pp. 20–34. Springer, Heidelberg (2014)
11. van Leeuwen, J., Wiedermann, J.: Computation as an unbounded process. Theor. Comput. Sci. **429**, 202–212 (2012)
12. Minsky, M.L.: Computation: Finite and Infinite Machines. Prentice Hall, Englewood Cliffs (1967)
13. Păun, Gh.: Computing with membranes. J. Comput. Syst. Sci. **61**(1), 108–143 (2000). (and Turku Center for Computer Science-TUCS Report 208, November 1998. http://www.tucs.fi)
14. Păun, Gh.: Membrane Computing: An Introduction. Springer, Heidelberg (2002)
15. Păun, Gh., Rozenberg, G., Salomaa, A. (eds.): The Oxford Handbook of Membrane Computing. Oxford University Press, Oxford (2010)
16. Perrin, D., Pin, J.-É.: Infinite Words. Pure and Applied Mathematics, vol. 141. Elsevier, Amsterdam (2004)
17. Rozenberg, G., Salomaa, A. (eds.): Handbook of Formal Languages: 3 volumes. Springer, Heidelberg (1997)
18. Sosík, P., Valík, O.: On evolutionary lineages of membrane systems. In: Freund, R., Păun, Gh., Rozenberg, G., Salomaa, A. (eds.) WMC 2005. LNCS, vol. 3850, pp. 67–78. Springer, Heidelberg (2006)
19. Staiger, L.: Finite-state ω-languages. J. Comput. Syst. Sci. **27**(3), 434–448 (1983)
20. Staiger, L.: ω-computations on Turing machines and the accepted languages. In: Lovász, L., Szemerédi, E. (eds.) Theory of Algorithms (Colloquia Mathematica Societatis Janos Bolyai), vol. 44, pp. 393–403. North Holland, Amsterdam (1986)
21. Staiger, L.: ω-languages. In: [17], vol. 3, pp. 339–387
22. Staiger, L., Wagner, K.: Automatentheoretische und automatenfreie Charakterisierungen topologischer Klassen regulärer Folgenmengen. Elektron. Informationsverarb. Kybernetik **10**(7), 379–392 (1974)
23. Thomas, W.: Automata on infinite objects. In: van Leeuwen, J. (ed.) Handbook of Theoretical Computer Science, vol. B, pp. 133–192. North Holland, Amsterdam (1990)
24. Wagner, K.: On ω-regular sets. Inf. Control **43**(2), 123–177 (1979)
25. The P Systems Website. http://www.ppage.psystems.eu

DiSCUS: A Simulation Platform for Conjugation Computing

Angel Goñi-Moreno[1] and Martyn Amos[2]($^{\boxtimes}$)

[1] Systems Biology Program, Centro Nacional de Biotecnología, Madrid, Spain
[2] Informatics Research Centre, School of Computing,
Mathematics and Digital Technology,
Manchester Metropolitan University, Manchester, UK
m.amos@mmu.ac.uk

Abstract. In bacterial populations, cells are able to cooperate in order to yield complex *collective* functionalities. Interest in population-level cellular behaviour is increasing, due to both our expanding knowledge of the underlying biological *principles*, and the growing range of possible *applications* for engineered microbial consortia. The ability of cells to interact through small signalling molecules (a mechanism known as *quorum sensing*) is the basis for the majority of existing engineered systems. However, horizontal gene transfer (or *conjugation*) offers the possibility of cells exchanging messages (using DNA) that are much more information-rich. The potential of engineering this conjugation mechanism to suit specific goals will guide future developments in this area. Motivated by a lack of computational models for examining the specific dynamics of conjugation, we present a simulation framework for its further study.

(This paper was first presented at the Spatial Computing Workshop of the 13th International Conference on Autonomous Agents and Multi-agent Systems (AAMAS), Paris, France, May 5–9 2014. There were no published proceedings).

1 Introduction

"Imagine a discipline of cellular engineering that tailor-makes biological cells to function as sensors and actuators, as programmable delivery vehicles for pharmeceuticals, or as chemical factories for the assembly of nanoscale structures" (Abelson, *et al.*, talking about *amorphous computing*, in the year 2000 [1]).

This growing discipline is now known as *synthetic biology* [3,12,22], and researchers in the field have successfully demonstrated the construction of several types of device based on populations of engineered microbes [29]. Recent work has focussed attention on the combination of *single-cell* intracellular devices [5,17] with *intercellular* engineering, in order to build increasingly complex systems [6,11]. As Beal argues, "Biological systems can often be viewed as spatial computers: space-filling collections of computational devices with strongly localized communication." [9] This is *precisely* the view of living cells that we

© Springer International Publishing Switzerland 2015
C.S. Calude and M.J. Dinneen (Eds.): UCNC 2015, LNCS 9252, pp. 181–191, 2015.
DOI: 10.1007/978-3-319-21819-9_13

take here; that is, microbes may be engineered to both implement some "program", *and* share information with other cells in order to implement distributed computations. This concept has already been successfully demonstrated in the laboratory (see [2] for a review), with applications including programmed pattern formation [8], edge detection [35], distributed evaluation of Boolean logic [32,36], and a synthetic "predator-prey" ecosystem [7]. These papers (and many others) clearly demonstrate how engineered living cells extend, beyond traditional silicon-based machines, the definition of what it means to "compute".

To date, most work on engineered cell-cell communication has focussed on quorum-sensing (QS) [4], which may be thought of as a communication protocol to facilitate inter-bacterial communication via the generation and receiving of small *signal molecules*. However, recent studies on DNA messaging [31] highlight the importance and utility of transferring whole sets of DNA molecules from one cell (the so-called donor) to another (the recipient). Bacterial *conjugation* is a cell-to-cell communication mechanism [13,14] that enables such transfers to occur. We have recently proposed the notion of *conjugation computing*: multicellular computation that uses conjugation as its fundamental mode of information transfer [19]. In this paper, we expand on this result, and present full implementation details of our simulation platform for conjugation computing. DiSCUS (Discrete Simulation of Conjugation Using Springs) realistically simulates (in a modular fashion) both intracellular genetic networks and intercellular communication via conjugation. To our knowledge, this is the *first* such platform to offer both of these facilities. We first review previous work on cell simulation, before presenting the details of our model. We validate it against previous experimental work, and then discuss possible applications of our method.

2   Previous Work

The rapid development of bacterial-based devices is accompanied by a need for computational simulations and mathematical modelling to facilitate the characterisation and design of such systems. A number of platforms and methods are available for this purpose. Agent-based models (AbMs) are widely used [20], and were first used to study microbial growth in *BacSim* [26]. Continuous models have also been proposed [30], and recent developments make use of hardware optimisation, by using GPUs (Graphics Processing Units) in order to scale up the number of cells simulated [33].

Because of the complexity of the system under study, several computational platforms focus on either specific cellular behaviours (e.g., bacterial chemotaxis [15], morphogenesis of dense tissue like systems [24]) , or on specific organisms (e.g., *Myxococcus xanthus* [23]). Platforms that incorporate cell-cell communication generally focus their attention on quorum-sensing. Simulations of conjugation do exist, but these consider cells as abstracted *circular objects* [27,34]. We demonstrate in this paper how a consideration of the *shape* of cells is an essential feature for understanding the conjugation behaviour of the population. We now describe our model for bacterial growth, in which conjugation is handled explicitly.

3   Methods

We apply an *individual-based modelling* approach [28] to the study of conjugation dynamics. This models each cell as an individual, mobile entity, each of which is subject to physical forces arising from contact with other cells and the environment (e.g., surfaces). Each cell has a number of different *attributes*, listed in Table 1, which correspond to various physiological states and characteristics.

Table 1. Cell attributes.

Attribute	Type	Definition
shape	*pymunk*.Shape	Shape of the cell
program	$[m_0 \ldots m_i]$	List of the i regulatory network molecules (m)
elongation	[int,int]	Elongation values (one per cell pole)
position	[x,y]	Coordinates of centre point, x and y
speed	float	Velocity
conjugating	Boolean	Conjugation state
plasmid	Boolean	Program state (present/not present)
role	int	Donor (0), recipient (1) or transconjugant (2)
partner	int	Role of plasmid transfer cell

Bacteria are modelled as rod-shaped cells with a constant radius (parameter width in Table 2). Elongation processes occur along the longitudinal axis, which has a minimum dimension of length, and division takes place whenever the cell measures 2*length. The division of a cell into two new daughter cells is also controlled by max_overlap, which monitors the physical *pressure* affecting each cell; if the pressure exceeds this parameter value, the cell delays its growth and division. Thus, a cell with pressure grows slower than without it. The global parameter growth_speed (Table 2) also helps us simulate cell flexibility in a realistic fashion. This parameter defines a "cut off" value for the number of iterations in which the physics engine must resolve *all* the current forces and collisions. Thus, smaller values will cause the solver to be effectively "overloaded", and some collisions may, as a result, be partially undetected. This means that cells behave as flexible shapes, which gives the simulation a more realistic performance.

Horizontal genetic transfer (or conjugation) is modelled using an *elastic spring* to connect donor and recipient cells [25]. Parameter c_time defines the duration of that linkage, which determines the time in which the DNA is transferred. The springs are constantly monitored to ensure that they physically connect both cells during conjugation. Importantly, during conjugation, the resolution of collisions involving relevant cells considers the forces produced by the spring connection, in order to calculate the final movement of the bacteria. By coupling cells in this way, we obtain realistic population-level physical patterns that emerge as a result of large numbers of conjugation events. This agent-based

Table 2. Global simulation parameters.

Parameter	Definition
screenview	Size of the simulated *world*
width	Width of each cell (lattice squares)
network_steps	Number of steps of the ODEs per Gt
number_donors	Initial number of donor cells
real_Gt	Real doubling time of the studied cells (minutes)
Gt	Doubling time of the simulated cells (iterations)
number_recipients	Initial number of recipient cells
length	Length of each cell (lattice squares)
max_overlap	Pressure tolerance of cells
bac_friction	Friction coefficient (Coulomb friction model)
spring_damping	The amount of viscous damping to apply
bac_mass	Mass of the cell (for calculating the moment)
c_time	Duration of the conjugation process
p_d	Probability of conjugation event (donors)
p_t1	Probability of conjugation event (transconj.1)
p_t2	Probability of conjugation event (transconj.2)
spring_rest_length	Natural sprint expansion/contraction
growth_speed	Iterations between elongation processes
spring_stiffness	The tensile modulus of the spring
cell_infancy	Time lag (percentage)
pymunk_steps	Update the space for the given time step
pymunk_clock_ticks	Frame frequency (FPS - frames per second)

algorithm has an iteration-driven structure, where - after initialisation of the main global parameters - it repeatedly performs the following steps for each cell: (1) Update springs (position and timing); (2) Perform cell division (if cell is ready); (3) Elongate cell (every growth_speed steps); (4) Handle conjugation; (5) Update physical position.

Conjugation decisions (step 4) made by cells are driven by three sequential steps: (1) *Decide*, following a probability distribution, whether or not to conjugate (one trial per iteration); (2) If conjugating, randomly select a mate from surrounding bacteria (if present); (3) If valid mate is found, effect conjugation transfer.

The discrete probability distribution used for the conjugation process is $C(N, p, \texttt{c\_time})$, where N is the number of trials in a cell lifetime (width * length), p is the success probability in each trial (with $p \in [0\ldots 1]$) and c_time is the time interval during $p = 0.0$ (i.e., when the cell is already conjugating). As stated in [34], p can vary, depending on whether the cell is a donor (p_d), a transconjugant that received the DNA message from a donor (p_t1), or a transconjugant that received the DNA from another transconjugant (p_t2).

Intracellular circuits (that is, any new genetic components that are introduced into the cells in order to implement a computation) are modelled separately, and then held in each cell by storing the state (i.e., protein concentrations, etc.) of the circuit in an attribute of the cell (program). Thus, there are effectively as many copies of the circuit as cells in the simulation (the number of cells we currently handle can range from single digits to around two thousand before we hit significant performance issues). This circuit simulation is implemented in a modular fashion, so that the internal cellular "program" may be easily replaced with any other. In this paper we demonstrate the principle using a two-component genetic oscillator as the DNA message that is exchanged through conjugation. The ordinary differential equations (ODEs) for this circuit are:

$$\frac{dx}{dt} = \Delta \left(\beta \frac{1 + \alpha x^2}{1 + x^2 + \sigma y^2} - x \right) \tag{1}$$

$$\frac{dy}{dt} = \Delta \gamma \frac{1 + \alpha x^2}{1 + x^2} - y \tag{2}$$

which are detailed in [21], as well as the meaning and value of the parameters (we use the same values in the code provided). We recently used our software platform to investigate the spatial behaviour of a *reconfigurable* genetic logic circuit (without conjugation) [18], which demonstrates (1) how it may easily be modified to accommodate different sets of equations, and (2) how it may be used as a "general purpose" cell simulation platform, with conjugation "turned off". The actions controlling the growth rates of cells occur on a longer time scale than the integration steps that control molecular reactions (as Eqs. 1 and 2). In order to ensure synchronisation, the parameter network_steps defines the number of integration steps of the ODEs that run per Gt. Thus, a number of network_steps/Gt integration steps will update the attribute network of each cell every iteration. Other important physical parameters listed in Table 2 are spring_rest_length, spring_stiffness and spring_damping; these are three parameters to model the material and behaviour of the bacterial pilus (i.e. the spring) during conjugation. Parameter cell_infancy is a delay period, during which a cell is considered to be too young to conjugate (as observed experimentally [34]). Parameters pymunk_steps and pymunk_clock_ticks are used by the physics engine to update the world, and may be adjusted by the user in order to alter the performance of the simulation (machine dependent). Parameters bac_mass and bac_friction play a role in collision handling. Our platform is written in *Python*, and makes use of the physics engine *pymunk* (www.pymunk.org) as a wrapper for the 2D physics library Chipmunk, which is written in C (www.chipmunk-physics.net/). As cells are represented as semi-rigid bodies in a 2D lattice, pymunk handles the physical environment on our behalf. For monitoring purposes, parameters Gt and real_Gt allow us to stablise the relation between iterations and clock minutes: *minute* =Gt/real_Gt (units: iterations).

4   Results

We now describe the results of experiments to validate our conjugation model, using three sets of simulations. We first validate individual conjugation dynamics; then we validate the biomechanical properties of the simulation; the final set of experiments studies the effects of mixing on conjugation dynamics.

4.1   Conjugation Dynamics

The objective of the first set of experiments is to validate the software in terms of *conjugation dynamics*. For that purpose, we first focus on conjugation, using images of a *Pseudomonas putida* population (Fig. 1A) extracted, with permission, from [34]. These show donor cells (dark red) growing in contact with recipients (yellow). The DNA information they share after conjugation makes the

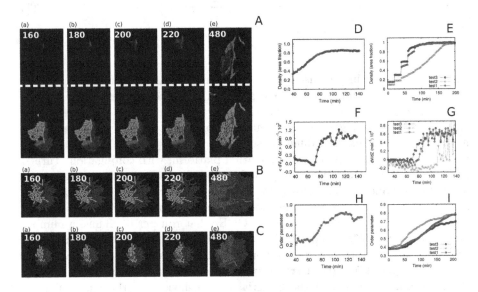

Fig. 1. Validation of cell movement and conjugation dynamics using real data. (A): Figure extracted from [34] where a colony of *Pseudomonas putida* is divided into dark red donor cells (DsRed), yellow recipient cells (YFP) and transconjugants, expressing both yellow and green light (YFP and GFP). The upper row shows the transconjugant signal, and the bottom row shows the whole community. (B and C): Simulation results. Two simulations of similar colonies are recorded over exactly the same time intervals (min). The colours of the cells match the colours observed in (A). Graphs (D), (F) and(H) are extracted from [37], and show **experimental results** of *Escherichia Coli* growth regarding density, velocity and ordering (respectively). Graphs (E), (G) and (I) correspond to our **simulation results**, using similar conditions to [37], for the same parameters (density, velocity and ordering respectively). Tests 1, 2 and 3 in graphs correspond to different spatial distribution of cells inside the microfluidic chanel (details in text). This figure first appeared as Supporting Information Figure S7 in [19] (i.e., not as part of the main paper) (Color figure online).

transconjugant cells display GFP (green fluorescent protein). We adjusted the parameters of our simulations until the behaviour matched the images of real cells (two simulations shown: Figures 1B and C), in terms of both time-series behaviour and the type of physical pattern displayed. The algorithm for this adjustment used information on the number of transconjugants, donors and recipients at a particular time (taken from images of actual colonies), and then explored (in the simulation) the space of conjugation probabilities until values were found that gave rise to the observed numbers). It is important to note that the differential probabilities of conjugation of donors and transconjugants (higher in the latter) causes directional spreading of the DNA information. After the first transconjugant appears (160 min), the newly-formed transconjugants appear - most probably - in the immediate neighbourhood. The final parameter values used to reproduce this experiment are: `width=5`, `length=15`, `growth_speed=30`, `p_d=0.001`, `p_t1=0.02`, `p_t2=0.05` and `c_time=450` (the rest of the parameters are as defined in the DiSCUS distribution). Movie *DemoConjugation1* (found in the project repository) shows a simulation of a similar experiment where the transconjugants do not act as new donors.

4.2   Biomechanical Properties

The second set of validation experiments focuses on *biomechanical movement*. We use experimental data from [37], which describe an *Escherichia coli* colony growing in a microfluidic channel ($30 * 50 * 1 \ \mu m^3$) (Figs. 1D, F and H). Using exactly the same setup (`width=5`, `length=24`, `growth_speed=30`) we highlight how different initial positioning of cells inside the channel can affect the final result (*test1*, with more cells observed in the centre than at the edges; *test2* with all cells initially in the centre; *test3* with all cells homogeneously spread along the channel). Density graphs (Figs. 1D and E) show the increasing curve as the channel becomes more populated (results vary depending on which area is considered for monitoring). Velocity gradients (Figs. 1F and G) depict the differential velocity across the longitudinal axis of the channel with respect to the centre (we see negative values when the cells in the centre move faster than the rest). The difference in the y axis is due to our considering different spacial intervals in the velocity gradient calculation. Ordering graphs (Figs. 1H and I) are based on calculating the cosine of a cell's angle with respect to the longitudinal axis of the channel (e.g. angle 0, $\cos(0)=1$, completely aligned). As time increases, we see that the cells tend to align themselves.

4.3   Effects of Mixing

Conjugation behaviour within a population may be altered in different ways to achieve different behaviours, depending on the desired application. For example, in the previous experiments described in this paper, transconjugants are unable to act as recipients (simulating a *radical* entry exclusion [16]). That is to say, they will not receive more plasmids (genetic circuits) from either donors or transconjugants. Furthermore, we may also engineer the transconjugants to

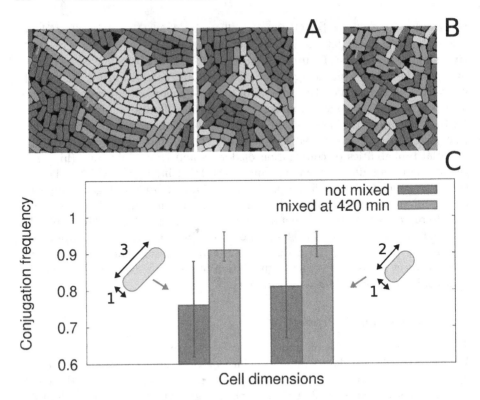

Fig. 2. Effects of manual mixing on conjugation frequency. (A): Recipient-trapping behaviour of a population with donors (red), transconjugants (green) and recipients (yellow). Two snapshots depict clearly-observed clusters. (B): Population after random mixing, where the clusters are automatically dissolved. (C): Graph showing conjugation frequencies ($Y = T/(R + T)$) of 560-minute experiments (ratio D/R = 50 %). Blue bars represent Y on an untouched population, while red bars represent Y when the population is mixed at 420 min. The two sets of bars correspond to experiments with different cell dimensions (1x3 -left- and 1x2 -right). Error bars show variation across 15 experiments of each class. This figure first appeared as Supporting Information Figure S8 in [19] (i.e., not as part of the main paper) (Color figure online).

stop acting as *new donors* [14], so that only the original donors have the ability to transfer the DNA message. *Mixing* of the cell population becomes essential in this last scenario, in order to ensure maximal contact between donors and recipients.

Investigations of how manual mixing can affect conjugation frequencies are described in in [14], using an *Escherichia coli* population. We now reproduce those results using our software, and give valuable insight into the reasons for that behaviour: the *isolation* of the recipients. For that purpose (Fig. 2) we grow a population of donors (D, red) and recipients (R, yellow) in which the ratio D/R is 50 % and the transconjugants (T, green) are unable to act as new donors.

The frequency of conjugation, Y, is measured as $Y = T/(R + T)$. The graph in Fig. 2C shows the frequency after 560 min of *untouched* populations (not mixed, blue bars) and populations that have been *manually mixed* at 420 min (red bars). The difference that the mixing produces is based on the isolation of the recipients in untouched populations. Figure 2A shows two different occasions in which clusters of recipients are formed, where the transconjugants do not allow donors to reach new possible mates. After the population is completely "shuffled" (Fig. 2B), the clusters are dissolved, and new pairs of donor-recipient can arise in the new topology.

An interesting result from Fig. 2C is the fact that the smaller the size of the cell, the higher results we observe for conjugation frequencies. This may be due to the fact that smaller cells are able to slip through physical gaps, and the biomechanical ordering of the population becomes more "fuzzy". This underlines the importance of considering the physical shape of cells, since circle-shaped cells would not give valid results. Importantly, all of these results are *entirely consistent* with the behaviour observed in the laboratory study [14].

5   Discussion

The conjugation model presented here is the first agent-based model to explicitly simulate conjugation processes with growing rod-shaped cells. Full validation against real data is performed, which shows the capacity of the software to reproduce observed behaviour. In addition, the mixing study offers valuable insights into the design of multi-strain populations. The software also allows for genetic *programs* to be *installed* inside cells; the potential for horizontal gene transfer to recreate distributed information processing within a microbial consortium is of significant interest in synthetic biology/spatial computing [10], and the software presented will aid the design and testing of systems before their *wet-lab* implementation. Possible future work may focus on further validation of the model through (1) studying the frequency of conjugation in different bacterial strains, and under different conditions, (2) studying the effect of the cell's shape and/or doubling (reproduction) time, and (3) investigating mixing effects caused by the topology of the region(s) bounding the cell colony. The computational cost of the simulations may also prove to be a limiting factor, so it may be useful to investigate parallelisation of the code (either on GPUs, or by using a platform such as MPI). This may, in the future, open up the possibility of using the code for three-dimensional biofilm studies.

Simulation code and movies are available at http://www.bactocom.eu.

Acknowledgments. This work was supported by the European Commission FP7 Future and Emerging Technologies Proactive initiative: Bio-chemistry-based Information Technology (CHEM-IT, ICT-2009.8.3), project reference 248919 (BACTOCOM).

References

1. Abelson, H., Allen, D., Coore, D., Hanson, C., Homsy, G., Knight Jr, T.F., Nagpal, R., Rauch, E., Sussman, G.J., Weiss, R.: Amorphous computing. Commun. ACM 43(5), 74–82 (2000)
2. Amos, M.: Population-based microbial computing: a third wave of synthetic biology? Int. J. Gen. Syst. 43(7), 770–782 (2014)
3. Andrianantoandro, E., Basu, S., Karig, D.K., Weiss, R.: Synthetic biology: new engineering rules for an emerging discipline. Mol. Syst. Biol. 2, 0028 (2006)
4. Atkinson, S., Williams, P.: Quorum sensing and social networking in the microbial world. J. R. Soc. Interface 6(40), 959–978 (2009)
5. Ausländer, S., Ausländer, D., Müller, M., Wieland, M., Fussenegger, M.: Programmable single-cell mammalian biocomputers. Nature 487(7405), 123–127 (2012)
6. Bacchus, W., Fussenegger, M.: Engineering of synthetic intercellular communication systems. Metab. Eng. 16, 33–41 (2013)
7. Balagaddé, F.K., Song, H., Ozaki, J., Collins, C.H., Barnet, M., Arnold, F.H., Quake, S.R., You, L.: A synthetic Escherichia coli predator-prey ecosystem. Mol. Syst. Biol. 4, 187 (2008)
8. Basu, S., Gerchman, Y., Collins, C.H., Arnold, F.H., Weiss, R.: A synthetic multicellular system for programmed pattern formation. Nature 434(7037), 1130–1134 (2005)
9. Beal, J.: Bridging biology and engineering together with spatial computing. In: Gheorghe, M., Păun, G., Rozenberg, G., Salomaa, A., Verlan, S. (eds.) CMC 2011. LNCS, vol. 7184, pp. 14–18. Springer, Heidelberg (2012)
10. Beal, J., Bachrach, J.: Cells are plausible targets for high-level spatial languages. In: 2008 Second IEEE International Conference on Self-Adaptive and Self-Organizing Systems Workshops. SASOW 2008, pp. 284–291. IEEE (2008)
11. Brenner, K., You, L., Arnold, F.H.: Engineering microbial consortia: a new frontier in synthetic biology. Trends Biotechnol. 26(9), 483–489 (2008)
12. Cheng, A.A., Timothy, K.L.: Synthetic biology: an emerging engineering discipline. Annu. Rev. Biomed. Eng. 14, 155–178 (2012)
13. de la Cruz, F., Frost, L.S., Meyer, R.J., Zechner, E.L.: Conjugative DNA metabolism in gram-negative bacteria. FEMS Microbiol. Rev. 34(1), 18–40 (2010)
14. del Campo, I., Ruiz, R., Cuevas, A., Revilla, C., Vielva, L., de la Cruz, F.: Determination of conjugation rates on solid surfaces. Plasmid 67(2), 174–182 (2012)
15. Emonet, T., Macal, C.M., North, M.J., Wickersham, C.E., Cluzel, P.: Agentcell: a digital single-cell assay for bacterial chemotaxis. Bioinformatics 21(11), 2714–2721 (2005)
16. Garcillán-Barcia, M.P., de la Cruz, F.: Why is entry exclusion an essential feature of conjugative plasmids? Plasmid 60(1), 1–18 (2008)
17. Gardner, T.S., Cantor, C.R., Collins, J.J.: Construction of a genetic toggle switch in Escherichia coli. Nature 403, 339–342 (2000)
18. Moreno, A.G., Amos, M.: A reconfigurable NAND/NOR genetic logic gate. BMC Syst. Biol. 6(1), 126 (2012)
19. Moreno, A.G., Amos, M., de la Cruz, F.: Multicellular computing using conjugation for wiring. PLoS ONE 8(6), e65986 (2013)
20. Gorochowski, T.E., Matyjaszkiewicz, A., Todd, T., Oak, N., Kowalska, K., Reid, S., Tsaneva-Atanasova, K.T., Savery, N.J., Grierson, C.S., di Bernardo, M.: BSim: an agent-based tool for modeling bacterial populations in systems and synthetic biology. PLoS ONE 7(8), e42790 (2012)

21. Guantes, R., Poyatos, J.F.: Dynamical principles of two-component genetic oscillators. PLoS Comput. Biol. **2**(3), e30 (2005). preprint(2006)
22. Heinemann, M., Panke, S.: Synthetic biology-putting engineering into biology. Bioinformatics **22**(22), 2790–279 (2006)
23. Holmes, A.B., Kalvala, S., Whitworth, D.E.: Spatial simulations of myxobacterial development. PLoS Comput. Biol. **6**(2), e1000686 (2010)
24. Izaguirre, J.A., Chaturvedi, R., Huang, C., Cickovski, T., Coffland, J., Thomas, G., Forgacs, G., Alber, M., Hentschel, G., Newman, S.A., Glazier, J.A.: Compucell, a multi-model framework for simulation of morphogenesis. Bioinformatics **20**(7), 1129–1137 (2004)
25. Jass, J., Schedin, S., Fällman, E., Ohlsson, J., Nilsson, U.J., Uhlin, B.E., Axner, O.: Physical properties of *Escherichia coli* p pili measured by optical tweezers. Biophys. J. **87**(6), 4271–4283 (2004)
26. Kreft, J.U., Booth, G., Wimpenny, J.W.T.: Bacsim, a simulator for individual-based modelling of bacterial colony growth. Microbiology **144**(12), 3275–3287 (1998)
27. Krone, S.M., Lu, R., Fox, R., Suzuki, H., Top, E.M.: Modelling the spatial dynamics of plasmid transfer and persistence. Microbiology **153**(Pt 8), 2803–2816 (2007)
28. Lardon, L.A., Merkey, B.V., Martins, S., Dötsch, A., Picioreanu, C., Kreft, J.-U.U., Smets, B.F.: idynomics: next-generation individual-based modelling of biofilms. Environ. Microbiol. **13**(9), 2416–2434 (2011)
29. Macía, J., Posas, F., Solé, R.V.: Distributed computation: the new wave of synthetic biology devices. Trends Biotechnol. **30**(6), 342–349 (2012)
30. Melke, P., Sahlin, P., Levchenko, A., Jönsson, H.: A cell-based model for quorum sensing in heterogeneous bacterial colonies. PLoS Comput. Biol. **6**(6), e1000819 (2010)
31. Ortiz, M.E., Endy, D.: Engineered cell-cell communication via DNA messaging. J. Biol. Eng. **6**(1), 16 (2012)
32. Regot, S., Macia, J., Conde, N., Furukawa, K., Kjellén, J., Peeters, T., Hohmann, S., de Nadal, E., Posas, F., Solé, R.: Distributed biological computation with multicellular engineered networks. Nature **469**(7329), 207–211 (2011)
33. Rudge, T.J., Steiner, P.J., Phillips, A., Haseloff, J.: Computational modeling of synthetic microbial biofilms. ACS Synthetic Biol. **1**, 345–352 (2012)
34. Seoane, J., Yankelevich, T., Dechesne, A., Merkey, B., Sternberg, C., Smets, B.F.: An individual-based approach to explain plasmid invasion in bacterial populations. FEMS Microbiol. Ecol. **75**(1), 17–27 (2011)
35. Tabor, J.J., Salis, H.M., Simpson, Z.B., Chevalier, A.A., Levskaya, A., Marcotte, E.M., Voigt, C.A., Ellington, A.D.: A synthetic genetic edge detection program. Cell **137**(7), 1272–1281 (2009)
36. Tamsir, A., Tabor, J.J., Voigt, C.A.: Robust multicellular computing using genetically encoded NOR gates and chemical 'wires'. Nature **469**(7329), 212–215 (2011)
37. Volfson, D., Cookson, S., Hasty, J., Tsimring, L.S.: Biomechanical ordering of dense cell populations. Proc. National Acad. Sci. **105**(40), 15346–15351 (2008)

A Cost/Speed/Reliability Tradeoff to Erasing

Manoj Gopalkrishnan[✉]

Tata Institute of Fundamental Research, Mumbai 400 005, India
manoj.gopalkrishnan@gmail.com
http://www.tcs.tifr.res.in/~manoj

Abstract. We present a KL-control treatment of the fundamental problem of erasing a bit. We introduce notions of **reliability** of information storage via a reliability timescale τ_r, and **speed** of erasing via an erasing timescale τ_e. Our problem formulation captures the tradeoff between speed, reliability, and the Kullback-Leibler (KL) cost required to erase a bit. We show that erasing a reliable bit fast costs at least $\log 2 - \log\left(1 - e^{-\frac{\tau_e}{\tau_r}}\right) > \log 2$, which goes to $\frac{1}{2}\log\frac{2\tau_r}{\tau_e}$ when $\tau_r >> \tau_e$.

1 Motivation

Szilard [24] and later Landauer [16] have argued from the second law of thermodynamics that erasing at temperature T requires at least $k_B T \log 2$ units of energy, where k_B is Boltzmann's constant. The **Szilard engine** is a simple illustration of this result. Imagine a single molecule of ideal gas in a cylindrical vessel. If this molecule is in the left half of the vessel, think of that as encoding the bit "0," and the bit "1" otherwise. Erasing this Brownian bit corresponds to ensuring that the molecule lies on the left half, for example by compressing the ideal gas to half its volume. For a heuristic analysis we may use the ideal gas law $PV = k_B T$, integrating the expression $dW = -PdV$ for work from limits V to $V/2$ to obtain $W = k_B T \log 2$. More rigorous and general versions of this calculation are known, which also clarify why this is a lower bound [8,11,19].

In practice, one finds that both man-made and biological instrumentation often require energy several orders of magnitude more than $k_B T \log 2$ to perform erasing [17,18]. John von Neumann remarked on this large gap in his 1949 lectures at the University of Illinois [29].

How does one explain this large gap? Note that the result of $k_B T \log 2$ holds only in the isothermal limit, which takes infinite time. In practice, we want erasing to be performed fast, which requires extra entropy production. For intuition, suppose one wants to compress a gas fast, it heats up, and pushes back, increasing the work required. One hypothesis is that part of this large gap can be addressed by explicitly introducing such a speed requirement.

Several groups [3,5,32] have recognized that rapid erasing requires entropy production which pushes up the cost of erasing beyond $k_B T \log 2$, and have obtained bounds for this problem. A grossly oversimplified, yet qualitatively accurate, sketch of these various results is obtained by considering the energy

© Springer International Publishing Switzerland 2015
C.S. Calude and M.J. Dinneen (Eds.): UCNC 2015, LNCS 9252, pp. 192–201, 2015.
DOI: 10.1007/978-3-319-21819-9_14

cost of compressing the Szilard engine fast. Specializing a result from finite-time thermodynamics [20] to the case of the Szilard engine, one obtains an energy cost $k_B T \log 2 \left(1 + \frac{k_B \log 2}{\sigma \tau_e - k_B \log 2}\right)$ where σ is the coefficient of heat conductivity of the vessel.

The bounds obtained by such considerations depend on technological parameters like the heat conductivity σ, and not just on fundamental constants of physics. If one varies over the technological parameters as well, e.g. allowing $\sigma \to \infty$, these bounds do not improve on $k_B T \log 2$.

Our Contribution: We follow up on von Neumann's suggestion [29] that the gap was "due to something like a desire for reliability of operation". Swanson [23] and Alicki [2] have also looked into issues of reliability. We introduce the notion of "reliability timescale", and explicitly consider the three-way trade-off between speed, reliability, and cost.

The other novelty of our approach is in bringing the tools of KL control [9, 27] to bear on the problem of erasing a bit. The intuitive idea is that the control can reshape the dynamics as it pleases, but pays for the deviation from the uncontrolled dynamics. The cost of reshaping the dynamics is a relative entropy or Kullback-Leibler divergence between the controlled and uncontrolled dynamics.

We find the optimal control for erasing a reliable bit fast, and argue that it requires cost of at least $\log 2 - \log\left(1 - e^{-\frac{\tau_e}{\tau_r}}\right) > \log 2$, which goes to $\frac{1}{2} \log \frac{2\tau_r}{\tau_e}$ when $\tau_r \gg \tau_e$. Importantly, our answer does not depend on any technological parameters, but only on fundamental constants and requirement specifications of the problem.

2   The Erasing Problem

As a model of a bit, consider a two-state continuous-time Markov chain with states 0 and 1 and the **passive** or uncontrolled dynamics given by transition rates k_{01} from state 0 to state 1 and k_{10} from state 1 to state 0.

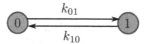

The transition rates k_{01} and k_{10} model spontaneous transitions between the states when no one is looking at the bit or trying to erase it. The time independence of these rates represents the physical fact that the system is not being driven.

Such finite Markov chain models often arise in physics by "coarse-graining." For example, for the case of the Szilard engine, the transition rate k_{10} models the rate at which the molecule enters the left side, conditioned on it currently being on the right side.[1]

Suppose the distribution at time t is $(p_0(t), p_1(t))$ with $p_1(t) = 1 - p_0(t)$. Then the time evolution of the bit is described by the ODE

$$\dot{p}_0(t) = -k_{01}p_0(t) + k_{10}(1 - p_0(t)). \tag{1}$$

Setting $\pi_0 = k_{10}/(k_{01} + k_{10})$ and the **reliability timescale** $\tau_r := 1/(k_{01} + k_{10})$, this admits the solution

$$p_0(t) = \pi_0 + e^{-t/\tau_r}(p_0(0) - \pi_0) \tag{2}$$

Here τ_r represents the time scale on which memory is preserved. The smaller the rates k_{01} and k_{10}, the larger is the value of τ_r, and the slower the decay to equilibrium, so that the system remembers information for longer.

Fix a **required erasing time** τ_e. Fix $p(0) = \pi_0$. We want to control the dynamics with transition rates $u_{01}(t)$ and $u_{10}(t)$ to achieve $p(\tau_e) = (1, 0)$, where

$$\dot{p}_0(t) = -u_{01}(t)p_0(t) + u_{10}(t)(1 - p_0(t)) \tag{3}$$

We want to find the cost of the optimal protocol $u_{01}^*(t)$ and $u_{10}^*(t)$ to achieve this objective, according to a cost function which we introduce next. In particular, when $k_{01} = k_{10}$, the equilibrium distribution $\pi = (\pi_0, 1 - \pi_0)$ takes the value $(1/2, 1/2)$ and we can interpret this task as erasing a bit of reliability $\tau_r = 1/(k_{01} + k_{10})$ in time τ_e.

2.1   Kullback Leibler Cost

Define the **path space** $\mathcal{P} := \{0, 1\}^{[0, \tau_e]}$ of the two-state Markov chain. This is the set of all paths in the time interval $[0, \tau_e]$ that jump between states 0 and 1 of the Markov chain. Each path can also be succinctly described by its initial state, and the times at which jumps occur. We can also effectively think of the path space as the limit as $h \to 0$ of the space $\mathcal{P}_h := \{0, 1\}^{\{0, h, 2h, \ldots, Nh = \tau_e\}}$ corresponding to the discrete-time Markov chain that can only jump at clock ticks of h units.

Once the rates $u_{01}(t), u_{10}(t)$ and the initial distribution $p(0) = p$ for the Markov chain are fixed, there is a unique probability measure $\mu_{u,p}$ on path space which intuitively assigns to every path the probability of occurrence of that path according to the Markov chain evolution (Eq. 3) with initial conditions p.

For pedagogic reasons, we first describe the discrete-time measure $\mu_{u,p}^h$ for a single path $i = (i_0, i_1, \ldots, i_N) \in \mathcal{P}_h$. First we describe the transition probabilities

---

[1] Apart from their importance in approximating the behavior of real physical systems, finite Markov chains are also important to thermodynamics from a logical point of view. They may be viewed as finite models of a mathematical theory of thermodynamics. The terms "theory" and "model" are to be understood in their technical sense as used in mathematical logic. We develop this remark no further here since doing so would take us far afield.

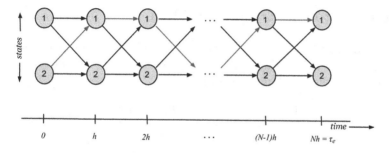

Fig. 1. The discrete-time path space $\mathcal{P}_h$. A specific path is labeled in red (Color figure online).

of the discrete-time Markov chain. For $a, b \in \{0, 1\}$ with $a \neq b$, for all times t, define $u_{aa}^h(t) := 1 - hu_{ab}(t)$ and $u_{ab}^h(t) := hu_{ab}(t)$ as the probability of jumping to a and to b respectively in the time step t, conditioned on being in state a. Then the probability of the path i under control u is given by:

$$\mu_{u,p}(i) := p_{i_0} \prod_{j=0}^{N-1} u_{i_j, i_{j+1}}^h(jh)$$

We describe the continous-time case now. We could obtain the measure $\mu_{u,p}$ from $\mu_{u,p}^h$ by sending $h \to 0$, but it can also be described more directly. Fix $i_0 \in \{0, 1\}$, and consider the set of paths $\mathcal{S} = \mathcal{S}_{i_0, t_1, t_2, \ldots, t_n}$ starting at i_0 with jumps occurring at times $t_1 < t_2 < \cdots < t_n$ within infinitesimal intervals $dt_1, dt_2, \ldots, dt_n$ and leading to the trajectory $(i_0, i_1, \ldots, i_n) \in \{0, 1\}^{n+1}$. Setting $t_0 = 0$:

$$\mu_{u,p}(\mathcal{S}) := p_{i_0} \prod_{j=0}^{n-1} e^{-\int_{t_j}^{t_{j+1}} u_{i_j i_{j+1}}(s) ds} u_{i_j i_{j+1}}(t_{j+1}) dt_{j+1}$$

where p_{i_0} is the probability of starting at i_0, $e^{-\int_0^{t_1} u_{i_0 i_1}(s) ds}$ is the probability of not jumping in the time interval $(0, t_1)$, $u_{i_0 i_1}(t_1) dt_1$ is the probability of jumping from i_0 to i_1 in the interval $(t_1, t_1 + dt_1)$ and so on.

Specializing to $u_{01}(t) = k_{01}$ and $u_{10}(t) = k_{10}$, we obtain the probability measure $\mu_{k,p}$ induced on $\mathcal{P}$ by the passive dynamics (Eq. 1) with initial conditions p.

We declare the Kullback Leibler (KL) cost $D(\mu_{u,p} \| \mu_{k,p})$ as the cost for implementing the control u. More generally, for a physical system with path space $\mathcal{P}$, passive dynamics corresponding to a measure ν on $\mathcal{P}$, and a controlled dynamics with a control corresponding to a measure μ on $\mathcal{P}$, we declare $D(\mu \| \nu)$ as the cost for implementing the control. This cost function has been widely used in control theory [7,9,12–15,22,25–28,30]. In Sect. 4 we will explore some other interpretations of this cost function.

3   Solution to the Erasing Problem

Out of all controls $u(t)$, we want to find a control $u^*(t)$ that starts from $p(0) = \pi = (k_{10}/(k_{01} + k_{10}), k_{01}/(k_{01} + k_{10}))$, and achieves $p(\tau_e) = (1, 0)$ while minimizing the relative entropy $D(\mu_{u^*,\pi} \| \mu_{k,\pi})$.

$$\text{To find: } u^* = \arg\inf_u D(\mu_{u,\pi} \| \mu_{k,\pi})$$

$$\text{Subject to: } \mu_{u,\pi}(\tau_e) = (1, 0)$$

Section 3 can be described within the framework of a well-studied problem in optimal control theory that has a closed-form solution [6,9,27]. Following Todorov [27], we introduce the **optimal cost-to-go** function $v(t) = (v_0(t), v_1(t))$. We intend $v_i(t)$ to denote the expected cumulative cost for starting at state i at time $t < \tau_e$, and reaching a distribution close to $(1, 0)$ at time τ_e.

To discourage the system from being in state 1 at time τ_e, define $v_1(\tau_e) = +\infty$ and $v_0(\tau_e) = 0$.

Suppose the control performs actions $u_{01}(t)$ and $u_{10}(t)$ at time t. Fix a small time $h > 0$. Define the transition probability $u_{ij}^h(t)$ as the probability that a trajectory starting in state i at time t will be found in state j at time $t + h$. When $i \neq j$, $u_{ij}^h(t) \approx h u_{ij}(t)$, where as $u_{ii}^h(t) \approx 1 - u_{ij}^h(t)$ ignoring terms of size $O(h^2)$. We define k_{ij}^h similarly.

Let log denote the natural logarithm. To derive the law satisfied by the optimal cost-to-go $v(t)$, we approximate $v(t)$ by the backward recursion relations:

$$v_0(t) = \min_{u_{01}(t)} \mathbb{E}\left[v_i(t + h) + \log \frac{u_{0i}^h(t)}{k_{0i}^h}\right]$$

$$v_1(t) = \min_{u_{10}(t)} \mathbb{E}\left[v_i(t + h) + \log \frac{u_{1i}^h(t)}{k_{1i}^h}\right]$$

where the first expectation is over $i \sim_{\text{law}} (u_{00}^h(t), u_{01}^h(t))$, and the second is over $i \sim_{\text{law}} (u_{10}^h(t), u_{11}^h(t))$, and the approximation ignores terms of size $O(h^2)$. As $h \to 0$ the second terms $\mathbb{E}\log \frac{u_{ji}^h(t)}{k_{ji}^h}$ approach the relative entropy cost in path space over the time interval $(t, t + h)$.

In words, Eq. 3 says that the cost-to-go from state 0 at time t equals the cost of the control $u(t)$ plus the expected cost-to-go in the new state i reached at time $t + h$. The cost of the control is measured by relative entropy of the control dynamics relative to the passive dynamics, over the time interval $(t, t + h)$.

Define the **desirability** $z_0(t) = e^{-v_0(t)}$ and $z_1(t) = e^{-v_1(t)}$. Define

$$G_0[z](t) = k_{00}^h z_0(t) + k_{01}^h z_1(t),$$

$$G_1[z](t) = k_{10}^h z_0(t) + k_{11}^h z_1(t).$$

We can rewrite (3) as

$$\log z_0(t) = \log G_0[z](t+h) - \min_{u_{01}(t)} \mathbb{E}\left[\log \frac{u_{0i}^h(t)G_0[z](t+h)}{k_{0i}^h z_i(t+h)}\right]$$

$$\log z_1(t) = \log G_1[z](t+h) - \min_{u_{10}(t)} \mathbb{E}\left[\log \frac{u_{1i}^h(t)G_1[z](t+h)}{k_{1i}^h z_i(t+h)}\right]$$

Since the last term is the relative entropy of $(u_{j0}^h(t), u_{j1}^h(t))$ relative to the probability distribution $(k_{j0}^h z_0(t+h)/G_j[z](t+h), k_{j1}^h z_1(t+h)/G_j[z](t+h))$, its minimum value is 0, and is achieved by the protocol u^* given by:

$$\frac{u_{ji}^*(t)}{k_{ji}} = \lim_{h\to 0} \frac{e^{-v_i(t+h)}}{G_j[z](t+h)} = \frac{e^{-v_i(t)}}{e^{-v_j(t)}} \tag{4}$$

when $i \neq j$.

It remains to solve for $z(t)$ and the optimal cost. From (3), at the optimal control u^* the desirability $z(t)$ must satisfy the equation $-\log z(t) = -\log G[z](t+h) + 0$, so that:

$$\begin{pmatrix} z_0(t) \\ z_1(t) \end{pmatrix} = \begin{pmatrix} 1 - k_{01}h & k_{01}h \\ k_{10}h & 1 - k_{10}h \end{pmatrix} \begin{pmatrix} z_0(t+h) \\ z_1(t+h) \end{pmatrix}$$

which simplifies to $\frac{dz}{dt} = -Kz$ in the limit $h \to 0$, where $K = \begin{pmatrix} -k_{01} & k_{10} \\ k_{10} & -k_{10} \end{pmatrix}$ is the infinitesimal generator of the Markov chain. This equation has the formal solution $z(\tau_e - t) = e^{Kt} z(\tau_e)$ where $z(\tau_e) = \begin{pmatrix} 1 \\ 0 \end{pmatrix}$ by (3).

In the symmetric case $k_{01} = k_{10}$,

$$z(t) = e^{H(0)}\left(\begin{pmatrix} 1/2 \\ 1/2 \end{pmatrix} + e^{-\frac{\tau_e - t}{\tau_r}} \begin{pmatrix} 1/2 \\ -1/2 \end{pmatrix}\right)$$

where $\tau_r = 1/(k_{01} + k_{10})$. Substituting $t = 0$ and taking logarithms, we find the cost-to-go function at time 0:

$$v(0) = \begin{pmatrix} \log 2 \\ \log 2 \end{pmatrix} - \begin{pmatrix} \log\left(1 + e^{-\tau_e/\tau_r}\right) \\ \log\left(1 - e^{-\tau_e/\tau_r}\right) \end{pmatrix}$$

When $v(0) = (1/2, 1/2)$ with $k_{01} = k_{10}$, the cost $C_{\text{erase}}(\tau_r, \tau_e, T)$ required for erasing a bit of reliability $\tau_r = 1/(k_{01} + k_{10})$ in time τ_e at temperature T is at least:

$$\log 2 - \frac{1}{2}\log\left(1 - e^{-2\tau_e/\tau_r}\right) \tag{5}$$

Note that $C_{\text{erase}} \geq \log 2$ with equality when $\tau_e/\tau_r \to \infty$, since $1 - e^{-2\tau_e/\tau_r} \leq 1$. From Eq. 5, $C_{\text{erase}} \geq \frac{1}{2}\log\frac{2\tau_r}{\tau_e}$ when $\tau_r \gg \tau_e$.

4   Other Meanings to the KL Cost

The motivation for our cost function comes from the field of KL control theory. We now compare other possible meanings to this cost function.

1. The relative entropy $D(\mu\|\nu)$ counts the number of nats[2] erased by the control in path space, relative to the passive dynamics. Since the Szilard-Landauer principle asserts that erasing one bit requires at least $k_B T \log 2$ units of energy, our cost function may be viewed as a formal extension of this principle to path space.

2. We wish to compare the cost $D(\mu\|\nu)$ with the usual thermodynamic expected work. Before doing so, we will find it convenient to define the time reversal Markov chain. Given a distribution q at time τ_e, the time reversal Markov chain of the Markov chain in Eq. 3 evolves backward in time according to the ODE:

$$\dot{q}_0(t) = u_{01}(t)q_0(t) - u_{10}(t)(1 - q_0(t))$$
$$q(\tau_e) = q. \tag{6}$$

The measure $\mu_{u,q}^{\mathrm{rev}}$ is the measure on path space described by Eq. 6.

The usual thermodynamic expected work can be defined as follows. Run the control dynamics Eq. 3 forward from initial condition $p(0)$ upto time τ_e to obtain the distribution $p(\tau_e)$. Now consider the measure $\mu_{u,p(\tau_e)}^{\mathrm{rev}}$. By the First Law of Thermodynamics,

$$\Delta W = \Delta F + k_B T D(\mu_{u,p}\|\mu_{u,p(\tau_e)}^{\mathrm{rev}}) \tag{7}$$

where the increase in free energy of the system

$$\Delta F = k_B T \left(D(p(\tau_e)\|\pi) - D(p(0)\|\pi) \right)$$

and $D(\mu_{u,p}\|\mu_{u,p(\tau_e)}^{\mathrm{rev}})$ is the total entropy production during the time interval $[0, \tau_e]$.

Now to compare our cost function with ΔW. We first recognize the time reversal $\mu_{k,q}^{\mathrm{rev}}$ as a specialization of $\mu_{u,q}^{\mathrm{rev}}$. After some algebra, we obtain

$$D(\mu_{u,p} \| \mu_{k,p}) = \frac{\Delta F}{k_B T} + D(\mu_{u,p}\|\mu_{k,p(\tau_e)}^{\mathrm{rev}}) \tag{8}$$

where $p(\tau_e)$ is — as in Eq. 7 — the solution to the control dynamics Eq. 3 at time τ_e. Comparing 7 and 8, a KL control treatment replaces the total entropy production $D(\mu_{u,p}\|\mu_{u,p(\tau_e)}^{\mathrm{rev}})$ in 7 by $D(\mu_{u,p}\|\mu_{k,p(\tau_e)}^{\mathrm{rev}})$.

---

[2] A nat is the unit of information when logarithms are taken to the base of Euler's constant. 1 bit $= \log 2$ nats.

3. Our cost function $D(\mu\|\nu)$ also admits a large deviation interpretation which was, remarkably, already noted by Schrödinger in 1931 [1,4,10,21]. Motivated by quantum mechanics, Schrödinger asked: conditioned on a more or less astonishing observation of a system at two extremes of a time interval, what is the least astonishing way in which the dynamics in the interval could have proceeded? Specializing to our problem of erasing, suppose an ensemble of two-state Markov chain with passive dynamics given by Eq. 1 was observed at time 0 and at time τ_e. Suppose the empirical state distribution over the ensemble was found to be the equilibrium distribution π at time 0, and $(1,0)$ at time τ_e respectively. This would be astonishing because no control has been applied, yet the ensemble has arrived at a state of higher free energy. Conditioned on this rare event having taken place, what is the least unlikely measure μ^* on path space via which the process took place?

   By a statistical treatment of multiple single particle trajectories, Schrödinger found that the likelihood of an empirical measure μ on path space falls exponentially fast with the relative entropy $D(\mu\|\nu)$ where ν is the measure induced by the passive dynamics. In particular, the least unlikely measure μ^* is that measure which — among all μ whose marginals at time 0 and time τ_e respect the observations — minimizes $D(\mu\|\nu)$. So for the problem of erasing where $k_{01} = k_{10}$, the measure μ varies over all measures that have marginal $(1/2, 1/2)$ at time 0 and marginal $(1,0)$ at time τ_e, and μ^* is that measure among all such μ that minimizes $D(\mu\|\mu_{k,(1/2,1/2)})$. Thus our optimal control produces in expectation the least surprising trajectory among all controls that perform rapid erasing.

4. Eq. 4 is not accidental for this example, but is in fact a general feature when the cost function is relative entropy [6]. More abstractly, the Radon-Nikodym derivative (i.e., "probability density") $\frac{d\mu^*}{d\nu}$ of the measure μ^* induced on path space by the optimal control u^* with respect to the measure ν induced by the passive dynamics is a **Gibbs measure**, with the cost-to-go function $v(t)$ playing the role of an energy function. In other words, mathematically our problem is precisely the free energy minimization problem so familiar from statistical mechanics. There is also a possible physical interpretation: we are choosing paths in $\mathcal{P}$ as microstates, instead of points in phase space. The idea of paths as microstates has occurred before [31].

5   Concluding Remarks

Since charging a battery can also be thought of as erasing a bit [11], our result may also hold insights into the limits of efficiencies of batteries that must be rapidly charged, and must hold their energy for a long time.

So long as the noise is Markovian, we conjecture that the KL cost for erasing the two-state Markov chain is a lower bound for more general cases – for example for bits with Langevin dynamics [33], which is a stochastic differential equation expressing Newton's laws of motion with Brownian noise perturbations.

Acknowledgements. I thank Sanjoy Mitter, Vivek Borkar, Nick S. Jones, Mukul Agarwal, and Krishnamurthy Dvijotham for helpful discussions. I thank Abhishek Behera for drawing Fig. 1.

References

1. Aebi, R.: Schrödinger Diffusion Processes. Springer, Heidelberg (1996)
2. Alicki, R.: Information is not physical. arXiv preprint arXiv:1402.2414 (2014)
3. Aurell, E., Gawędzki, K., Mejía-Monasterio, C., Mohayaee, R., Muratore-Ginanneschi, P.: Refined second law of thermodynamics for fast random processes. J. Stat. Phys. **147**(3), 487–505 (2012)
4. Beurling, A.: An automorphism of product measures. Ann. Math. **72**(1), 189–200 (1960)
5. Diana, G., Bagci, G.B., Esposito, M.: Finite-time erasing of information stored in fermionic bits. Phys. Rev. E **87**(1), 012111 (2013)
6. Dupuis, P., Ellis, R.S.: A Weak Convergence Approach to the Theory of Large Deviations, vol. 902. Wiley, New York (2011)
7. Dvijotham, K., Todorov, E.: A unified theory of linearly solvable optimal control. In: Artificial Intelligence (UAI), p. 1 (2011)
8. Esposito, M., Van den Broeck, C.: Second law and Landauer principle far from equilibrium. EPL (Europhys. Lett.) **95**(4), 40004 (2011)
9. Wendell, H.F., Mitter, S.K.: Optimal control and nonlinear filtering for nondegenerate diffusion processes. Stoch. Int. J. Probab. Stoch. Processes **8**(1), 63–77 (1982)
10. Föllmer, H.: Random fields and diffusion processes. In: Hennequin, P.-L. (ed.) École d'Été de Probabilités de Saint-Flour XV-XVII, 1985–87, vol. 1362, pp. 101–203. Springer, Heidelberg (1988)
11. Gopalkrishnan, M.: The Hot Bit I: the Szilard-Landauer correspondence. CoRR, abs/1311.3533 (2013)
12. Horowitz, M.B.: Efficient methods for stochastic optimal control. PhD thesis, California Institute of Technology (2014)
13. Kappen, H.J.: Linear theory for control of nonlinear stochastic systems. Phys. Rev. Lett. **95**(20), 200201 (2005)
14. Kappen, H.J.: Path integrals and symmetry breaking for optimal control theory. J. Stat. Mech. Theor. Exp. **2005**(11), P11011 (2005)
15. Kappen, H.J., Gómez, V., Opper, M.: Optimal control as a graphical model inference problem. Mach. Learn. **87**(2), 159–182 (2012)
16. Landauer, R.: Irreversibility and heat generation in the computing process. IBM J. Res. Dev. **5**, 183–191 (1961)
17. Laughlin, S.B., de Ruyter van Steveninck, R.R., Anderson, J.C.: The metabolic cost of neural information. Nat. Neurosci. **1**(1), 36–41 (1998)
18. Mudge, T.: Power: a first-class architectural design constraint. Computer **34**(4), 52–58 (2001)
19. Reeb, D., Wolf, M.M.: An improved Landauer principle with finite-size corrections. New J. Phys. **16**(10), 103011 (2014)
20. Salamon, P., Nitzan, A.: Finite time optimizations of a Newton's law carnot cycle. J. Chem. Phys. **74**, 3546 (1981)
21. Schrödinger, E.: Uber die umkehrung der naturgesetze, sitzung ber preuss. Akad. Wissen. Berlin Phys. Math., 144 (1931)

22. Stulp, F., Theodorou, E.A., Schaal, S.: Reinforcement learning with sequences of motion primitives for robust manipulation. IEEE Trans. Rob. **28**(6), 1360–1370 (2012)

23. Swanson, J.A.: Physical versus logical coupling in memory systems. IBM J. Res. Dev. **4**(3), 305–310 (1960)

24. Szilard, L.: On the reduction of entropy in a thermodynamic system by the interference of intelligent beings. Z Phys. **53**, 840–856 (1929)

25. Theodorou, E., Todorov, E.: Relative entropy and free energy dualities: connections to path integral and KL control. In: CDC, pp. 1466–1473 (2012)

26. Theodorou, E.A.: Iterative path integral stochastic optimal control: Theory and applications to motor control. PhD thesis, University of Southern California (2011)

27. Todorov, E.: Efficient computation of optimal actions. Proc. National Acad. Sci. **106**(28), 11478–11483 (2009)

28. van den Broek, B., Wiegerinck, W., Kappen, B.: Graphical model inference in optimal control of stochastic multi-agent systems. J. Artif. Intell. Res. (JAIR) **32**, 95–122 (2008)

29. von Neumann, J.: Theory of Self-reproducing Automata. University of Illinois Press, Urbana (1966). lecture delivered at University of Illinois in December (1949)

30. Wiegerinck, W., van den Broek, B., Kappen, H.: Stochastic optimal control in continuous space-time multi-agent systems. arXiv preprint arXiv:1206.6866 (2012)

31. Wissner-Gross, A.D., Freer, C.E.: Causal entropic forces. Phys. Rev. Lett. **110**(16), 168702 (2013)

32. Zulkowski, P.R., DeWeese, M.R.: Optimal finite-time erasure of a classical bit. Physical Review E **89**(5), 052140 (2014)

33. Zwanzig, R.: Nonequilibrium Statistical Mechanics. Oxford University Press, USA (2001)

Replication of Arbitrary Hole-Free Shapes via Self-assembly with Signal-Passing Tiles

Jacob Hendricks, Matthew J. Patitz$^{(\boxtimes)}$, and Trent A. Rogers

Department of Computer Science and Computer Engineering,
University of Arkansas, Fayetteville, AR, USA
{jhendric,tar003}@uark.edu, mpatitz@self-assembly.net

Abstract. In this paper, we investigate the abilities of systems of self-assembling tiles which can each pass a constant number of signals to their immediate neighbors to create replicas of input shapes. Namely, we work within the Signal-passing Tile Assembly Model (STAM), and we provide a universal STAM tile set which is capable of creating unbounded numbers of assemblies of shapes identical to those of input assemblies. The shapes of the input assemblies can be arbitrary 2-dimensional hole-free shapes at scale factor 2. This improves previous shape replication results in self-assembly that required models in which multiple assembly stages and/or bins were required, and the shapes which could be replicated were more constrained.

1 Introduction

As a process by which molecular systems can organize themselves, autonomously forming complex structures and even performing computations, self-assembly has been shown both theoretically [5,11,15,16,19,21] and experimentally [2,6,10,12,18,20] to be an extremely powerful process. In fact, it is even the basis of many natural, especially biological, systems. In an effort to further understand the capabilities of self-assembling systems, computational theory has been applied to design systems which perform *algorithmic* self-assembly, namely self-assembly in which the constituent components are intrinsically guided by algorithmic behavior. The systems developed have been capable of everything from extremely efficient (in terms of the numbers of unique building blocks necessary) building of shapes [15,21], Turing machine simulations [11,16,22], and intrinsically universal constructions [5]. In fact, those examples were all developed in a very simple model of self-assembling systems known as the abstract Tile Assembly Model (aTAM) [22], in which the basic components are square *tiles* which bind together, one at a time via *glues* on their edges, to form assemblies.

Jacob Hendricks and Matthew J. Patitz—This author's research was supported in part by National Science Foundation grant CCF-1422152.

Trent A. Rogers—This author's research was supported by the National Science Foundation Graduate Research Fellowship Program under Grant No. DGE-1450079, and National Science Foundation grant CCF-1422152.

© Springer International Publishing Switzerland 2015
C.S. Calude and M.J. Dinneen (Eds.): UCNC 2015, LNCS 9252, pp. 202–214, 2015.
DOI: 10.1007/978-3-319-21819-9_15

However, in order to gain more insight into various properties of self-assembling systems, models have been developed which are extensions of the aTAM and which allow behaviors like combinations of arbitrarily large assemblies [3], glues with repulsive forces [14], and many others.

In this paper, we work in one such (relatively new) model, the Signal-passing Tile Assembly Model (STAM) [13]. This model allows for the individual tiles, rather than being static and unchanging as in the aTAM, to each perform a constant number of operations which change the glues with which they can bind. With these changes being spurred by binding events of the tiles, the changes of glues on individual tiles can be propagated across entire assemblies, which can be thought of as analogous to sending *signals* which help direct the self-assembly process. While the STAM has been shown to be quite powerful by previous results [13], here we apply the strength of the model to a problem which has been previously studied in other models, namely the replication of shapes [1], and we prove yet more aspects of its power. (Note that, additionally, the replication of 2-D patterns of symbols encoded onto rectangular assemblies using the STAM was studied in [9].)

In this paper, we show how sets of arbitrary 2-dimensional hole-free shapes can be provided (at scale factor 2) to self-assembling systems within the STAM, using a single universal replicator tile set, and the resulting system will perform the parallel and exponentially increasing, unbounded replication of those shapes. This is a dramatic improvement over previous results [1,4] which required a model where multiple standalone stages and multiple assembly *bins* are required, since these STAM systems are single stage, single bin systems. Furthermore, these previous results placed significant restrictions on the shapes which could be replicated. As a significant additional result which we use to produce our replication result, we provide a construction which is able to perform a complicated form of distributed leader election, namely it is able to take as input an arbitrary 2-dimensional, hole-free shape with perfectly uniform glues on its exterior and produce an assembly which surrounds it but does so in a way in which all the portions of the shape's perimeter are covered and exactly one location on the perimeter is uniquely marked, or identified as the "leader". This is especially difficult given the distributed, parallel, and asynchronous nature of tile assembly in the STAM combined with the fact that absolutely no assumptions can be made about the input shapes. The techniques of this construction, as well as several other gadgets used in the full shape replication result, are likely to be useful in future work with the STAM.

We first present a high-level introduction to the models used in this paper, then provide our leader election construction (which we refer to as *frame building*, and finally present the shape replication result. Due to space constraints, many of the technical details of the constructions and proofs are located in the appendix.

2   Preliminaries

Here we provide informal descriptions of the models and terms used in this paper. Due to space limitations, the formal definitions can be found in [7].

2.1   Informal Description of the STAM

The STAM, as formulated, is intended to provide a model based on experimentally plausible mechanisms for glue activation and deactivation. A detailed, technical definition of the STAM model is provided in [7].

(Note that the STAM is an extension of the 2HAM, and an informal description of the 2HAM can be found in the appendix.) In the STAM, tiles are allowed to have sets of glues on each edge (as opposed to only one glue per side as in the TAM and 2HAM). Tiles have an initial state in which each glue is either "on" or "latent" (i.e. can be switched on later). Tiles also each implement a transition function which is executed upon the binding of any glue on any edge of that tile. The transition function specifies, for each glue g on a tile, a set of glues (along with the sides on which those glues are located) and an action, or *signal* which is *fired* by g's binding, for each glue in the set. The actions specified may be to: 1. turn the glue on (only valid if it is currently latent), or 2. turn the glue off (valid if it is currently on or latent). This means that glues can only be on once (although may remain so for an arbitrary amount of time or permanently), either by starting in that state or being switched on from latent (which we call *activation*), and if they are ever switched to off (called *deactivation*) then no further transitions are allowed for that glue. This essentially provides a single "use" of a glue (and the signal sent by its binding). Note that turning a glue off breaks any bond that glue may have formed with a neighboring tile. Also, since tile edges can have multiple active glues, when tile edges with multiple glues are adjacent, it is assumed that all matching glues in the on state bind (for a total binding strength equal to the sum of the strengths of the individually bound glues). The transition function defined for a tile type is allowed a unique set of output actions for the binding event of each glue along its edges, meaning that the binding of any particular glue on a tile's edge can initiate a set of actions to turn an arbitrary set of the glues on the sides of the same tile on or off.

As the STAM is an extension of the 2HAM, binding and breaking can occur between tiles contained in pairs of arbitrarily sized supertiles. It was designed to model physical mechanisms which implement the transition functions of tiles but are arbitrarily slower or faster than the average rates of (super)tile attachments and detachments. Therefore, rather than immediately enacting the outputs of transition functions, each output action is put into a set of "pending actions" which includes all actions which have not yet been enacted for that glue (since it is technically possible for more than one action to have been initiated, but not yet enacted, for a particular glue). Any event can be randomly selected from the set, regardless of the order of arrival in the set, and the ordering of either selecting some action from the set or the combination of two supertiles is also completely arbitrary. This provides fully asynchronous timing between the initiation, or firing, of signals (i.e. the execution of the transition function which puts them in the pending set) and their execution (i.e. the changing of the state of the target glue), as an arbitrary number of supertile binding events may occur before any signal is executed from the pending set, and vice versa.

An STAM system consists of a set of tiles and a temperature value. To define what is producible from such a system, we use a recursive definition of producible assemblies which starts with the initial tiles and then contains any supertiles which can be formed by doing the following to any producible assembly:
1. executing any entry from the pending actions of any one glue within a tile within that supertile (and then that action is removed from the pending set),
2. binding with another supertile if they are able to form a τ-stable supertile, or
3. breaking into 2 separate supertiles along a cut whose total strength is $< \tau$.

Throughout this paper, we will use the following definitions and conventions. We define a *shape* as a finite, connected subset of $\mathbb{Z}^2$. Following [17], we say that a shape s is *hole-free* if the complement of s is an infinite connected subset of $\mathbb{Z}^2$. We say that an assembly α is hole-free if (α) is hole-free. Then, an *input assembly* is a non-empty, τ-stable, hole-free assembly α such that every glue on the perimeter of α is strength 1 and of the same type. Throughout this section, we denote an input assembly by α and the type of the glue exposed on the perimeter of α by x. Furthermore, a *side* of a shape is any segment of the perimeter which connects two vertices (each of which can be convex or concave).

3   Frame Building

Throughout this paper, we provide constructions which take as input assemblies of arbitrary 2D hole-free shapes. For the frame building construction described in this section, no scale factor is necessary. For the replication construction of Sect. 4, the shapes require a scale factor of 2. All input assemblies have completely uniform perimeters in terms of glue labels, meaning that no location on a perimeter is marked any differently from the others. Given the local nature of the self-assembly process, namely that tiles bind based only on local interactions of matching glues, and also with the order and locations of tile attachments being nondeterministic and growth of assemblies massively in parallel, a distributed problem such as "leader election" can be quite difficult, and similarly so is the problem of uniquely identifying exactly one point on the perimeter of an input assembly when no assumptions can be made about the shape other than the facts that it (1) is connected and (2) has no interior holes which are completely surrounded by the assembly. Therefore, in this section we provide a construction which is a single universal STAM system capable of forming *frames*, or simply borders composed of tiles, completely surrounding input assemblies in such a way that the growth of the frames performs a distributed algorithm which uniquely identifies exactly one perimeter location on each input shape. While this algorithm and STAM system, as well as several of the novel techniques, are of independent interest, they also play integral roles in the remaining constructions of this paper and will potentially also provide a useful toolkit for future constructions in others.

At a very high-level, the frame building construction can be broken into three main components. First, a series of layers of tiles attach to the input assembly α, each slowly helping to fill in the openings to any concavities, until eventually

α is enclosed in an assembly which has a rectangular outer layer. Second, that rectangular layer is able to detach after its unique southeast corner tile "gadget" initiates the propagation of a signal inward through all of the layers to the easternmost of the southernmost tiles which have attached directly to α. The tile that is immediately to the left of this tile is elected the "leader" of the frame. Third, the leader initiates a signal which propagates in a counterclockwise direction around α, carefully ensuring that the entire perimeter of α is surrounded by tiles which have bound to it and made a complete "mold" of the shape. After this is accomplished, the entire frame detaches from α. The result is a perfect mold of α, with generic glues exposed around its entire interior surface except for one specific location, the leader, which exposes a unique glue. It is from this unique glue that the frame assembly will then be able to initiate the growth which fills it in and makes a replica of α.

3.1   Building Layers of the Frame

We now give an extremely high-level sketch of the formation of the *frame*. (See [8] for more details.) Essentially, the frame grows as a series of layers of tiles which begin on (possibly many) southeast convex corners of α (depending on its shape) and grow counterclockwise (CCW) around α. A greatly simplified example of the basic tiles which can form a layer of the frame can be seen in Fig. 1. Each path which forms a layer can grow only CCW, and therefore, depending on α's shape, may crash into a concavity of α (or one formed by a previous layer that the current is growing on top of). Such *collisions* are detected by a specialized set of *collision detection* tiles, and an example of a collision and its detection is shown in Fig. 2. The need for collision detection tiles is technical and related to the need for the exposed glues on all parts of the growing frame assembly to be minimized and carefully controlled so that multiple shapes and copies of shapes can be replicated in parallel, without separate assemblies interfering with each other.

The growth of frame layers is carefully designed so that it is guaranteed to proceed until all external openings to concavities of α have been filled in by partially completed layers, resulting in layers which are more and more rectangular, and eventually an exactly rectangular layer. At this point, and only at this point, we are guaranteed to have a layer which has exactly one convex southeast corner. Due to the distributed and asynchronous nature of the assembly process, and the fact that each tile only has local information, throughout layer formation it is necessary for some layers to make local "guesses" that they are rectangular, and in order for that not to cause errors, a mechanism of layer detachment is used. Basically, layers which guess they may be rectangular attempt to disconnect, but only the first truly rectangular layer can successfully detach. At this point it activates glues on the layer immediately interior of it, which it has *primed* to receive a signal from a tile which will now be free to attach since the covering exterior layer dissociates. This is then used in the unique leader election. It is by the careful use of the "global" information provided by the layer detachment that the construction can proceed correctly.

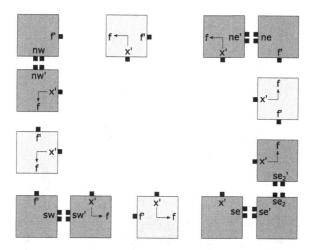

Fig. 1. A simplified version of the tile set which grows layer 1 of the frame around α. The darker grey tiles represent *corner gadgets* (CG) which form as duples (or a triple for the southeast corner gadget, CG_{SE}). Growth begins with the initial attachment of a CG_{SE} and proceeds CCW. There is also an analogous set with $x2'$ glues instead of x' glues to form layer 2 (and all subsequent layers). Note that this is a basic, beginning tile set to which we will add additional signals and tiles throughout the construction.

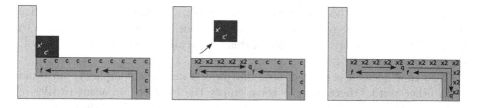

Fig. 2. Depiction of a path colliding into a concavity, which is detected by the attachment of a collision detection tile. Upon connecting, the collision detection tile initiates a q message which causes all outward c glues to deactivate and $x2$ glues to turn on. This also causes the collision detection tile to fall off.

3.2   Electing a Leader and Casting a Mold of α

In this section, we assume that the last added layer F of the frame has completed growth and is rectangular. Here we give a high-level description of what it means to elect a leader tile of layer 1 and how this is achieved. (See [8] for more details.) When F completes the growth of a rectangle, it will pass a *detach* message CW through each tile of F back to the only CG_{SE} belonging to F, which we denote by CG_F. When the d message is received along the north edge of the northernmost tile of CG_F, it initiates a series of signals so that after F detaches, the remaining assembly exposes a strength-2 glue. This strength-2 glue is exposed so that a singleton tile can bind to it. This binding event initiates the signals that "scan"

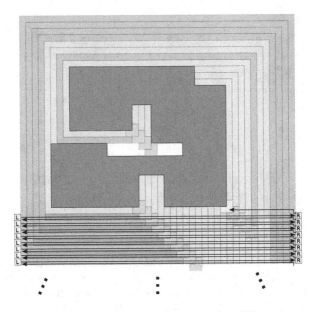

Fig. 3. An example of electing a CG_{SE}. The particular CG_{SE} that is elected has a corner tile that is the easternmost tile of the southernmost tiles of layer 1.

from right to left for the first corner tile of a CG_{SE} belonging to layer 1. Notice that this will be the easternmost tile of the southernmost tiles belonging to layer 1. The tile directly to the west of this tile is called the *leader tile* of layer 1. For an overview see Fig. 3.

Now that a leader is elected, note that layer 1 need not completely surround α. In other words, there may be some empty tile locations adjacent to tiles of α. In the next section, we show how to "complete" layer 1 so that for every tile location adjacent to a tile of α, this location contains a tile of layer 1. At a high-level, we describe signals and tiles that "extend" layer 1 of the frame to completely surround α by passing a g message CCW around α. Starting with the leader tile, as this message is passed, it activates glues which we use to replicate α. The leader tile exposes a unique glue.

Once we have exposed glues that will allow for the replication of α, we propagate a br message through layer 1 of the frame that deactivates all of the x' glues of layer 1 except for the x' glue on the north edges of the leader tile. This will allow α to disassociate from the frame and allow the frame to be used to replicate α.

3.3 Correctness of the Frame Construction

The goal of the frame construction is to result in an assembly which completely encases α, making a perfect mold of its shape, and then detaches. Furthermore, and extremely importantly, that mold must have uniquely identified exactly one tile on its interior (i.e. its "elected leader"). We now state the properties which are guaranteed by the frame construction. Their proofs can be found in [8].

First, for notation we will refer to the collision detections tiles as $T_{CD} \subset T$, the tile type(s) which make up α as T_α, and the remaining tiles as $T_{frame} = (T - T_{CD})\text{-}T_\alpha$.

Lemma 1. *For each STAM system $\mathcal{T} = (T, \alpha, 2)$ with tile set T (i.e. the frame building tile set) and input assembly α, there exists some constant c_α such that regardless of the assembly sequence, after c tile attachments a rectangular frame layer of tiles in T_{frame} will have grown around α.*

Lemma 2. *For each STAM system $\mathcal{T} = (T, \alpha, 2)$ with tile set T (i.e. the frame building tile set) and input assembly α, as a frame assembly grows, no subassembly containing tiles of T_{frame} can completely detach from the assembly unless it consists of a path which forms a complete and exact rectangle. Furthermore, the first such rectangular path will detach and then no further layers will grow.*

Lemma 3. *For each STAM system $\mathcal{T} = (T, \alpha, 2)$ with tile set T (i.e. the frame building tile set) and input assembly α, as a frame assembly grows, the eventual detachment of the rectangular layer will result in a single tile of the frame (the leader), which is adjacent to a location of α, activating a z glue.*

Lemma 4. *The leader tile will initiate a message which will propagate around α and guarantee that for every location directly or diagonally adjacent to a tile in α, layer 1 contains a tile in this location. Moreover, after all pending signals of the br message have fired, the entire frame assembly detaches from α exposing on its interior a unique glue activated on only the leader.*

Lemma 5. *Let β and γ be distinct producible assemblies of $\mathcal{T}$ that each have an input assembly as a subassembly. Then β and γ cannot bind.*

In Theorem 1, let $\mathcal{T} = (T, \sigma, 2)$ be a STAM system such that T is the frame building tile set given by the construction in Sect. 3 and σ is a set of input shape assemblies. Given an input shape assembly α, and a TAS $\mathcal{T}$, we say that a terminal assembly β is a *completed frame assembly for α that exposes a unique glue, z say*, if (after some translation of the locations in dom (β)) there is a single finite connected component of the complement of dom (β) in $\mathbb{Z}^2$ that is equal to dom (α), and moreover, the tiles of β at locations adjacent to locations of dom (α) expose glues on the perimeter of β such that there is a single tile (a leader tile) which exposes z on a single edge of the perimeter of β.

Theorem 1. *For any finite set σ of input shape assemblies, if $\beta \in \mathcal{A}_\square[\mathcal{T}]$, then either β is in σ, β is a completed frame assembly for α that exposes a unique glue, which we denote by z, or β does not expose z on its perimeter (for example, the rectangular frame layer that detaches in our frame construction).*

Proof. This follows directly from the Lemmas 1, 2, 3, 4, and 5.

4 Replication

In this section, we provide a construction in the STAM which is capable of replicating the shapes of a given set of input assemblies with the restriction that the shapes of the input assembly cannot be disconnected by removing a single tile, i.e. shapes with minimum width (*min-width*) 2. Furthermore, we show this replication can be done in an exponential manner.

4.1 Exponential, Unbounded Replication

We now define what it means for an STAM system to replicate a shape P. In the following definition, we assume that the input assemblies $\sigma_1, \sigma_2, ..., \sigma_n$ all have the same glue on each edge of their perimeter and there is only one of each in the system. We say that an STAM system $\mathcal{T} = (T, \{\sigma_1, \sigma_2, ..., \sigma_n\}, \tau)$ infinitely replicates the shapes $P_1, P_2, ..., P_n$ provided that 1) dom $\sigma_i = P_i$ for all i, 2) there are a bounded number of different terminal assemblies, and 3) there are an infinite number of assemblies of shape P_i for all i. We call assemblies $\sigma_1, \sigma_2, ..., \sigma_n$ replicable supertiles. In general, a replicable supertile in a system $\mathcal{T}$ is a supertile which can be "replicated".

In the replication process for a shape P, we consider a time step to be producing a new assembly α with dom $\alpha = P$. We say that an STAM system $\mathcal{T}$ *exponentially replicates without bound* the shapes $P_1, P_2, ..., P_n$ provided that (1) the system $\mathcal{T}$ infinitely replicates the shapes $P_1, P_2, ..., P_n$, (2) the number of (super)tile attachment and/or detachments required in the creation of a copy of shape P_i (i.e. one time step) is bounded by $poly(|P_i|)$, (3) every (super)tile attachment involves a singleton tile or a two tile assembly and an existing assembly that is replicating P_i for some i (i.e. tiles either attach to a frame layer or attach as filler tiles); and moreover, all supertile detachment involves either a single tile wide rectangle detaching from a frame, a completed frame detaching from a seed shape assembly P_i for some i, or a completed frame detaching from a replicated shape assembly P_i for some i, and (4) if there are n copies of the shape P_i at time step t, then there are $2n$ copies of the shape P_i at time step $t + 1$. Though this definition is specific to the replication technique given by our construction, it is motivated by the observation that for a single shape P, if a system $\mathcal{T}$ exponentially replicates without bound the shape P, then $\mathcal{T}$ exponentially replicates the shape P according to the more general definition of exponential replication given in [9] (Definition 3).

Theorem 2. *For any finite set of hole-free, min-width 2 shapes $P = \{P_1, P_2, ..., P_n\}$, there exists an STAM system $\mathcal{T} = (T, \sigma_P, 2)$, with σ_P a set of n assemblies, one of each shape in P, and $\mathcal{T}$ exponentially replicates without bound all shapes in P.*

We now provide a high level overview of the construction. Let P be a connected, hole-free, min-width 2 shape. Our construction begins with designing a tile set that builds a frame around σ where dom $(\sigma) = P$ which detaches upon completion. Next, we design tiles so that an inner ring forms within the completed ring.

Once this ring within a ring is complete, it detaches and fills in its interior. The outer ring is then free to make another copy while the interior of the inner ring can host the growth of another frame.

Our construction begins with adding tiles to our tile set which build a frame around σ using the machinery from the previous sections. We design our tile set for this frame system so that once the frame completes, it detaches from σ with (1) exactly one south east corner of the frame which exposes a z glue on the north of the west most tile and a y glue on the west side of the north most tile of that corner, and (2) on every other interior side of the frame, a y glue is exposed. We refer to this frame as the outer frame.

To construct the set of tiles which forms an inner ring inside the outer frame, we begin by adding to our tile set the tiles shown in Fig. 4.

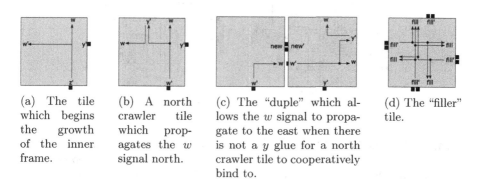

(a) The tile which begins the growth of the inner frame.

(b) A north crawler tile which propagates the w signal north.

(c) The "duple" which allows the w signal to propagate to the east when there is not a y glue for a north crawler tile to cooperatively bind to.

(d) The "filler" tile.

Fig. 4. The partial tile set which builds an inner frame and fills it.

To complete the tile set for the inner frame, we add rotated versions of each of the tiles discussed so far to T (except for the start tile) so that the w signal may be propagated to the north, east, west, and south of the frame in a counterclockwise fashion.

We now modify the tiles discussed above, so that (1) the inner frame separates from the outer frame, (2) the inner frame fills its interior with tiles and (3) the inner frame exposes x glues along its border like the original shape. To allow the inner frame to detach, we overlay signals on all of the tiles which turn off all of the y' glues on the inner frame. We add these signals so that this cascade of signals is triggered once the w signal reaches the start tile. To ensure we do not have any extra exposed glues after our frame detaches, we add these signals so that they follow the w signal (see [8] for signal following gadgetry). To fill in the shape, we once again overlay signals on the existing tile set so that when the signal returns to the initial tile, it initiates a signal which exposes strength 2 *fill* glues allowing for the attachment of "filler tiles" on the interior of the inner frame. These filler tiles simply attach and trigger signals on all 3 remaining sides which allow for the attachment of more filler tiles. Next, we add signals to the

y' glues on the tiles in the inner frame so that when a y' glue attaches to a y glue on the outer frame, it activates an x glue on the same side.

Frame Example. Figure 5 shows a schematic diagram of the propagation of the w signal. Notice that the w signal always attempts to take the counterclockwise most path. It does this by "bouncing" off of glues of existing tiles until it finds an edge which does not have a tile abutting it.

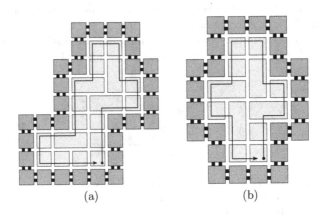

(a)   (b)

Fig. 5. A schematic view of how the w signal is passed through the inner frame. The darkly shaded tiles represent the outer frame and the lightly shaded tiles represent the tiles composing the inner frame. The path through the tiles indicates the flow of the w signals through the inner frame.

Exponential, Unbounded Replication of Shapes at Scale Factor 2. Since all shapes at scale factor 2 are min-width 2 shapes, Theorem 2 yields the following corollary.

Corollary 1. *For any finite set of hole-free shapes $P = \{P_1, P_2, ..., P_n\}$, let $P' = \{P'_1, P'_2, ..., P'_n\}$ be the shapes of P at scale factor 2. Then, there exists an STAM system $\mathcal{T} = (T, \sigma'_P, 2)$, with σ'_P a set of n assemblies, one of each shape in P', and $\mathcal{T}$ exponentially replicates without bound all shapes in P'.*

References

1. Abel, Z., Benbernou, N., Damian, M., Demaine, E., Demaine, M., Flatland, R., Kominers, S., Schweller, R.: Shape replication through self-assembly and RNase enzymes. In: SODA 2010 Proceedings of the Twenty-first Annual ACM-SIAM Symposium on Discrete Algorithms (Austin, Texas), Society for Industrial and Applied Mathematics (2010)
2. Barish, R.D., Schulman, R., Rothemund, P.W., Winfree, E.: An information-bearing seed for nucleating algorithmic self-assembly. Proc. Nat. Acad. Sci. **106**(15), 6054–6059 (2009)

3. Demaine, E.D., Patitz, M.J., Rogers, T.A., Schweller, R.T., Summers, S.M., Woods, D.: The two-handed assembly model is not intrinsically universal. ICALP 2013. LNCS, pp. 400–412. Springer, Heidelberg (2013)

4. Demaine, E.D., Patitz, M.J., Schweller, R.T., Summers, S.M.: Self-assembly of arbitrary shapes using RNAse enzymes: meeting the kolmogorov bound with small scale factor (extended abstract). In: Schwentick, T., Dürr, C. (eds.) (STACS 2011), vol. 9, pp. 201–212. Schloss Dagstuhl-Leibniz-Zentrum fuer Informatik, Dagstuhl, Dortmund (2011)

5. Doty D., Lutz JH., Patitz MJ., Schweller RT., Summers SM.: Woods D The tile assembly model is intrinsically universal. In: Proceedings of the 53rd Annual IEEE Symposium on Foundations of Computer Science, FOCS 2012, pp. 302–310 (2012)

6. Evans, C.G.: Crystals that count! physical principles and experimental investigations of DNA tile self-assembly, Ph.D. thesis, California Institute of Technology (2014)

7. Fochtman, T., Hendricks, J., Padilla, J.E., Patitz, M.J., Rogers, T.A.: Signal transmission across tile assemblies: 3D static tiles simulate active self-assembly by 2D signal-passing tiles, Technical report 1306.5005, Computing Research Repository (2013)

8. Hendricks, J., Patitz, M.J., Rogers, T.A.: Replication of arbitrary hole-free shapes via self-assembly with signal-passing tiles (extended abstract), ArXiv e-prints (2015)

9. Keenan, A., Schweller, R., Zhong, X.: Exponential replication of patterns in the signal tile assembly model. In: Soloveichik, D., Yurke, B. (eds.) DNA 2013. LNCS, vol. 8141, pp. 118–132. Springer, Heidelberg (2013)

10. LaBean, T.H., Winfree, E., Reif, J.H.: Experimental progress in computation by self-assembly of DNA tilings. DNA Based Comput. **5**, 123–140 (1999)

11. Lathrop, J.I., Lutz, J.H., Patitz, M.J., Summers, S.M.: Computability and complexity in self-assembly. Theory Comput. Syst. **48**(3), 617–647 (2011)

12. Mao, C., LaBean, T.H., Relf, J.H., Seeman, N.C.: Logical computation using algorithmic self-assembly of DNA triple-crossover molecules. Nature **407**(6803), 493–6 (2000)

13. Padilla, J.E., Patitz, M.J., Schweller, R.T., Seeman, N.C., Summers, S.M., Zhong, X.: Asynchronous signal passing for tile self-assembly: fuel efficient computation and efficient assembly of shapes. Int. J. Found. Comput. Sci. **25**(4), 459–488 (2014)

14. Patitz, M.J., Schweller, R.T., Summers, S.M.: Exact shapes and turing universality at temperature 1 with a single negative glue. In: Cardelli, L., Shih, W. (eds.) DNA 17 2011. LNCS, vol. 6937, pp. 175–189. Springer, Heidelberg (2011)

15. Patitz, M.J., Scott, M.: Summers, Self-assembly of discrete self-similar fractals. Nat. Comput. **1**, 135–172 (2010)

16. Patitz, M.J., Scott, M.: Summers, self-assembly of decidable sets. Nat. Comput. **10**(2), 853–877 (2011)

17. Patitz, M.J., Summers, S.M.: Identifying shapes using self-assembly. Algorithmica **64**(3), 481–510 (2012)

18. Rothemund, P.W.K., Papadakis, N., Winfree, E.: Algorithmic self-assembly of DNA Sierpinski triangles. PLoS Biol. **2**(12), e424–436 (2004)

19. Rothemund, P.W.K., Winfree, E.: The program-size complexity of self-assembled squares (extended abstract), STOC 2000: Proceedings of the Thirty-second Annual ACM Symposium on Theory of Computing (Portland, Oregon, United States), pp. 459–468 ACM (2000)

20. Schulman, R., Winfree, E.: Synthesis of crystals with a programmable kinetic barrier to nucleation. Proc. Nat. Acad. Sci. **104**(39), 15236–15241 (2007)
21. Soloveichik, D., Winfree, E.: Complexity of self-assembled shapes. SIAM J. Comput. **36**(6), 1544–1569 (2007)
22. Winfree, E: Algorithmic self-assembly of DNA, Ph.D. thesis, California Institute of Technology, June 1998

Efficient Card-Based Protocols for Generating a Hidden Random Permutation Without Fixed Points

Rie Ishikawa[1], Eikoh Chida[1], and Takaaki Mizuki[2]([✉])

[1] Electrical and Computer Engineering, National Institute of Technology,
Ichinoseki College, Takanashi, Hagisho, Ichinoseki 021–8511, Japan
{g10205,chida}@g.ichinoseki.ac.jp
[2] Cyberscience Center, Tohoku University, 6–3 Aramaki-Aza-Aoba,
Aoba-ku, Sendai 980–8578, Japan
tm-paper+cardperm@g-mail.tohoku-university.jp

Abstract. Consider the holiday season, where there are n players who would like to exchange gifts. That is, we would like to generate a random permutation having no fixed point. It is known that such a random permutation can be obtained in a hidden form by using a number of physical cards of four colors with identical backs, guaranteeing that it has no fixed point (without revealing the permutation itself). This paper deals with such a problem and improves the known result: whereas the known protocol needs $O(n^2)$ cards of four colors, our efficient protocol uses only $O(n \log n)$ cards of two colors.

1 Introduction

Consider the holiday season, where there are n players who would like to exchange gifts. We wish to avoid the undesirable situation in which a player must buy a present for himself/herself. That is, we need to produce a random permutation $\pi \in S_n$ that has no fixed point, where S_n denotes the symmetric group of degree n (throughout this paper). There is an unconventional solution to the "no fixed point" problem, i.e., it is known that such a random permutation can be obtained in a hidden form by using a number of physical cards of four colors, say $\clubsuit$, $\heartsuit$, $\diamondsuit$, and $\spadesuit$,[1] with identical backs $\boxed{?}$, guaranteeing that it has no fixed point (without revealing the permutation itself) [3]. This paper deals with such a problem and proposes an efficient approach that improves the known result.

1.1 Known Method for Generating a Random Permutation

In 1993, Crépeau and Kilian gave a card-based protocol for generating a random permutation $\pi \in S_n$ without any fixed point [3]. Their protocol produces a pile

---

[1] Throughout this paper, we say that a card has the same "color" as another one if they have the same pattern on their face sides.

© Springer International Publishing Switzerland 2015
C.S. Calude and M.J. Dinneen (Eds.): UCNC 2015, LNCS 9252, pp. 215–226, 2015.
DOI: 10.1007/978-3-319-21819-9_16

of n cards that consists of $(n-1)$ ♣s and one ♡ with their faces down (on the table) for every player $p_i, 1 \le i \le n$:

$$p_i : \boxed{?}\boxed{?} \cdots \boxed{?} \cdots \boxed{?}.$$

The position of card ♡ corresponds to the value of $\pi(i)$ when all the n cards are revealed:

$$p_i : \underset{1}{\boxed{♣}}\underset{2}{\boxed{♣}} \cdots \underset{\pi(i)}{\boxed{♡}} \cdots \underset{n}{\boxed{♣}}.$$

Thus, if player p_i looks at his/her pile privately, then the information about who p_i is going to buy a present for will be kept secret.

Because the protocol produces a pile of such cards for each of the n players, as seen above, it uses $n(n-1)$ ♣s and n ♡s. In addition, it requires a number of cards of different colors, namely $n^2/2$ ♢s and $n^2/2$ ♠s. Thus, the known method needs $2n^2$ cards of four colors in total[2]. Further details are given in Sect. 2.

1.2   Our Results and Related Work

Table 1 summarizes both the known result and our results. As mentioned above, to generate a random permutation without fixed points, the known method [3] requires $2n^2$ cards of four colors. In this paper, we reduce the number of required colors and cards. First, we devise a new shuffling operation called a "pile-scramble shuffle" in Sect. 3. Using this new shuffle, we can enhance the efficiency of the known protocol, and consequently, we can show that n^2 cards of two colors are sufficient. We then show in Sect. 4 that $(2n\lceil \log n \rceil + 6)$ cards[3] of two colors are sufficient to solve the "no fixed point" problem by considering another expression of each player's index.

Table 1. Performance of each protocol

	No. of colors	No. of cards
Known protocol [3] (§2)	4	$2n^2$
Improvement with pile-scramble shuffle (§3)	2	n^2
Our main protocol (§4)	2	$2n\lceil \log n \rceil + 6$

Before presenting our protocols, we present a complete description of the known protocol [3] in Sect. 2. Section 5 concludes this paper with some discussion.

Card-based cryptography allows us not only to generate a random permutation, but also to have various kinds of cryptographic protocols such as secure multiparty computations and zero-knowledge proof. For example, there are known

---

[2] Note that we cannot use a standard deck of playing cards because each of them has a unique pattern on its face side.

[3] All logarithms are base 2 throughout this paper.

protocols for securely computing AND [1,3,7,8,10,13], XOR [3,8,9], adder [6], 3-variable symmetric functions [12], and so on. Furthermore, the relationship between playing cards and cryptography has been explored in the literature (e.g., [2,4,5,14]).

2 Known Protocol

In this section, we present a complete description of the Crépeau-Kilian protocol [3] that generates a hidden random permutation having no fixed point.

Assume that n players $p_1, p_2, \ldots, p_n$ would like to produce a random permutation $\pi \in S_n$ without any fixed point. Their protocol consists of two phases, the Random-Permutation Generating phase and the Fixed-Point Checking phase, as follows.

[Random-Permutation Generating phase]

1-1. Using $n(n-1)$ ♣s and n ♡s, arrange the cards as below (putting each ♡ on the diagonal), and insert a "marker" after each row, where a marker consists of $n/2$ ◇s and $n/2$ ♠s (for simplicity, n is assumed to be an even number):

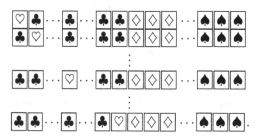

1-2. Turn over the cards so that they are all face down, and apply a random cut, i.e., a cyclic shuffle, to the sequence of $2n^2$ cards (obtained by row-wise concatenation).

1-3. Reveal the first card. If the face-up card is either ♣ or ♡, go back to step (1-2). If it is either ◇ or ♠, i.e., a marker, then proceed to the next step. Note that the probability of returning to step (1-2) is exactly 1/2.

1-4. Assume that the face-up card is ◇:

$$\boxed{◇}\boxed{?} \cdots \boxed{?} \cdots \boxed{?}\boxed{?}\boxed{?}\boxed{?}\boxed{?} \cdots \boxed{?}\boxed{?}\boxed{?}$$
$$\boxed{?}\boxed{?} \cdots \boxed{?} \cdots \boxed{?}\boxed{?}\boxed{?}\boxed{?}\boxed{?} \cdots \boxed{?}\boxed{?}\boxed{?}$$
$$\vdots$$
$$\boxed{?}\boxed{?} \cdots \boxed{?} \cdots \boxed{?}\boxed{?}\boxed{?}\boxed{?}\boxed{?} \cdots \boxed{?}\boxed{?}\boxed{?} .$$

Its right-hand card must also be a marker. Reveal the markers right next to it one by one. After all the makers on the right side (which are ℓ ◇s for some ℓ

and $n/2$ $\boxed{\spadesuit}$s) are face up, reveal the remaining markers on the left side (where the first card's "left" is the last card), namely $(n/2 - \ell - 1)$ $\boxed{\diamondsuit}$s.

For the case where the first card is $\boxed{\spadesuit}$, we manipulate the sequence of cards similarly to the $\boxed{\diamondsuit}$ case. Note that in this case, we start revealing the markers toward the left side first.

Remove all of the (face-up) n markers.

1-5. After all of the n markers are removed, we regard the first n cards as the value of $\pi(1)$. That is, the pile of these n cards is assigned to player p_1 and corresponds to $\pi(1)$:

$$p_1 : \boxed{?}\boxed{?} \cdots \boxed{?} \cdots \boxed{?}.$$

1-6. Similarly, for the remaining cards, repeat steps (1-2)–(1-4) so that we obtain piles corresponding to $\pi(2), \pi(3), \ldots, \pi(n)$.

[Fixed-Point Checking phase]

2-1. To verify that the generated permutation π has no fixed point, arrange the piles of cards assigned to $p_1, p_2, \ldots, p_n$ as below:

$$p_1 : \boxed{?}\boxed{?} \cdots \boxed{?} \cdots \boxed{?}\boxed{?}$$
$$p_2 : \boxed{?}\boxed{?} \cdots \boxed{?} \cdots \boxed{?}\boxed{?}$$
$$\vdots$$
$$p_n : \boxed{?}\boxed{?} \cdots \boxed{?} \cdots \boxed{?}\boxed{?}.$$

2-2. Reveal all the cards on the diagonal to determine if they are all $\boxed{\clubsuit}$. If so, π has no fixed point. If one of them is $\boxed{\heartsuit}$, then the pile corresponds to a fixed point and in this case, we must return to the Random-Permutation Generating phase.

Thus, the first phase of this protocol produces a random permutation $\pi \in S_n$, and then the second phase checks that π has no fixed point. In the first phase, we need to repeat the steps until markers are found, and hence it is a Las Vegas algorithm taking $2n$ trials on average. With respect to the second phase, note that in general, the probability that a random permutation $\pi \in S_n$ has no fixed point is $\sum_{i=0}^{n}(-1)^i/i!$, which is approximately $1/e$, where e is the base of the natural logarithm [3]. Therefore, the average number of how many times we need to execute the Fixed-Point Checking phase is approximately $e \approx 2.7$.

This is the existing protocol for solving the "no fixed point" problem. It uses $2n^2$ cards of four colors, as detailed above. We improve on this efficiency in the succeeding sections.

3   Pile-Scramble Shuffle

In this section, we focus on the process of producing a random permutation and propose an efficient method for achieving this.

Remember that the known protocol [3] uses random cuts and markers to generate a random permutation, as shown in the preceding section. That is, in order to shuffle n piles (each of which consists of n cards and is assigned to a player), we repeatedly apply a random cut to create each value of $\pi(i)$ one by one, while markers are used as "delimiters." Here, instead of using markers, we consider a somewhat more direct way of shuffling piles.

Assume that there are a number of face-down cards that are divided into n piles of the same size. We denote each pile by $pile_i$, $1 \leq i \leq n$. Given a sequence of piles $(pile_1, pile_2, pile_3, ..., pile_n)$, consider a shuffle operation that outputs $(pile_{\pi(1)}, pile_{\pi(2)}, pile_{\pi(3)}, ..., pile_{\pi(n)})$, where $\pi \in S_n$ is a random permutation. As we now have n piles, a permutation is randomly chosen from the $n!$ possibilities. We call such a shuffling operation a *pile-scramble shuffle*. We believe that the pile-scramble shuffle can be easily implemented by human beings using rubber bands, clips, envelopes, or something similar.

If steps (1-2)–(1-6) in the Random-Permutation Generating phase of the known protocol [3] introduced in Sect. 2 are replaced with the pile-scramble shuffle, it is obvious that n^2 cards of two colors are sufficient to produce a random permutation. That is, we can generate a random permutation without any marker, meaning that we do not require any trials, and hence can output a random permutation after exactly one pile-scramble shuffle. Therefore, taking the Fixed-Point Checking phase into account, such an improved protocol needs only n^2 cards of two colors and takes an average number of about 2.7 trials to generate a random permutation having no fixed point. Thus, we are able to reduce the numbers of required cards and colors by half (see Table 1 again).

In the next section, we further reduce the number of required cards.

4 Our Main Protocol

In this section, we propose a more efficient method than those mentioned previously. Our main protocol requires only $(2n\lceil \log n \rceil + 6)$ cards to generate a random permutation having no fixed point.

First, in Sect. 4.1, we show that considering a binary representation of players' indices dramatically reduces the number of required cards. Next, in Sect. 4.2, we present a sub-protocol to check for fixed points under such a binary representation. Finally, in Sect. 4.3, by combining these components, we present a complete description of our protocol.

4.1 Binary Representation

In the Crépeau-Kilian protocol [3] presented in Sect. 2, each player's index $i \in \{1, 2, \ldots, n\}$ and its permuted position $\pi(i)$ are represented by a pile of n cards, i.e., $(n-1)$ ♣s and one ♡, say

$$p_i : \underset{1}{\clubsuit}\,\underset{2}{\clubsuit} \cdots \underset{i}{\heartsuit} \cdots \underset{n}{\clubsuit} \text{ or } \underset{1}{\clubsuit}\,\underset{2}{\clubsuit} \cdots \underset{\pi(i)}{\heartsuit} \cdots \underset{n}{\clubsuit}.$$

In contrast, we represent this information using a binary representation with $2\lceil \log n \rceil$ cards as follows.

To deal with Boolean values, following the previous studies (e.g., [1,3,10,13]), we use the encoding rule with a pair of cards:

$$\boxed{\clubsuit}\boxed{\heartsuit} = 0, \quad \boxed{\heartsuit}\boxed{\clubsuit} = 1. \tag{1}$$

For a bit $x \in \{0,1\}$, when two face-down cards $\boxed{?}\boxed{?}$ have a value equaling x according to encoding (1) above, the pair of these face-down cards is called a *commitment* to x, and is written as

$$\underbrace{\boxed{?}\boxed{?}}_{x}.$$

Under such an encoding rule, each player's index can be represented by $\lceil \log n \rceil$ commitments, namely $2\lceil \log n \rceil$ cards. Therefore, n players' indices are represented naturally by $2n\lceil \log n \rceil$ cards. Thus, we can greatly reduce the number of required cards to express players' indices.

It is obvious that we can easily produce a random permutation by applying a pile-scramble shuffle (explained in Sect. 3) to these n piles that are based on this binary expression.

4.2   How to Check for Fixed Points

In this subsection, we present a sub-protocol to check that a random permutation in the form of binary representation has no fixed point.

Assume that a random permutation $\pi \in S_n$ has been generated by a pile-scramble shuffle, as shown in Sect. 3, based on the binary representation shown in Sect. 4.1. That is, a pile of $\lceil \log n \rceil$ commitments is assigned to each player p_i:

$$p_i : \underbrace{\boxed{?}\boxed{?}}_{a_{\log n}} \cdots \underbrace{\boxed{?}\boxed{?}}_{a_2} \underbrace{\boxed{?}\boxed{?}}_{a_1},$$

where and hereafter, $\log n$ in the subscript means $\lceil \log n \rceil$. Because the pile above corresponds to $\pi(i)$, we have

$$(\pi(i) - 1)_{10} = (a_{\log n} \cdots a_2 a_1)_2.$$

In order to verify that the pile is not a fixed point, namely $\pi(i) \neq i$, we check whether the equation below holds:

$$(a_1 \oplus \overline{b_1}) \wedge (a_2 \oplus \overline{b_2}) \wedge \cdots \wedge (a_{\log n} \oplus \overline{b_{\log n}}) = 0, \tag{2}$$

where $\oplus$ denotes the exclusive-or (XOR) operation and bits $b_1, b_2, \cdots, b_{\log n}$ are defined as

$$(i - 1)_{10} = (b_{\log n} \cdots b_2 b_1)_2.$$

Aiming to compute Eq. (2) efficiently without revealing values a_i, $1 \leq i \leq \lceil \log n \rceil$, we first introduce the existing copy protocol [8], and then present a "one-input-preserving" AND protocol. Finally we describe a sub-protocol for checking that Eq. (2) holds.

Copy Protocol. Give a commitment to a bit x together with four additional cards, the known copy protocol [8] generates two copied commitments to x, as follows.

1. Arrange two commitments to 0:

2. Rearrange the order of the sequence as:

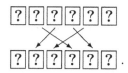

3. Bisect the sequence of six cards and switch the two portions randomly (we call this a random bisection cut [8] and denote it by $[\,\cdot\,|\,\cdot\,]$):

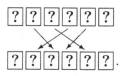

4. Rearrange the order of the sequence as:

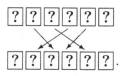

We then have

where r is a (uniformly distributed) random bit because of the random bisection cut.

5. Reveal the first two cards from the left. We then have

Thus, we obtain two copied commitments to x. In the latter case, we can easily convert $\bar{x}$ to x using the NOT operation that swaps the left and right cards. In addition, the two face-up cards ♣♡ are available for another computation.

One-input-preserving AND Protocol. We present a *one-input-preserving AND protocol* that can keep one of input commitments after the AND computation. The protocol can be constructed immediately based on two known ideas: the AND protocol [8] and the half-adder protocol [6].

First, we present some notation. For a pair of bits (x, y), define operations get and shift as

$$\mathsf{get}^0(x,y) = x; \quad \mathsf{get}^1(x,y) = y,$$
$$\mathsf{shift}^0(x,y) = (x,y); \quad \mathsf{shift}^1(x,y) = (y,x).$$

Note that

$$a \wedge b = \mathsf{get}^{a \oplus r}(\mathsf{shift}^r(0,b)) \qquad (3)$$

for an arbitrary bit $r \in \{0,1\}$. In addition, for two bits x and y, the expression

$$\underbrace{\boxed{?}\,\boxed{?}\,\boxed{?}\,\boxed{?}}_{(x,y)}$$

means

$$\underbrace{\boxed{?}\,\boxed{?}}_{x}\,\underbrace{\boxed{?}\,\boxed{?}}_{y}.$$

The following is a one-input-preserving AND protocol that produces not only a commitment to $a \wedge b$ but also a commitment to the input a using eight cards.

1. In addition to the input commitments to a and b, arrange two commitments to 0 as follows:

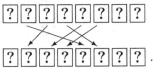

2. Rearrange the order of the sequence as:

$$\boxed{?}\,\boxed{?}\,\boxed{?}\,\boxed{?}\,\boxed{?}\,\boxed{?}\,\boxed{?}\,\boxed{?}$$

$$\boxed{?}\,\boxed{?}\,\boxed{?}\,\boxed{?}\,\boxed{?}\,\boxed{?}\,\boxed{?}\,\boxed{?}.$$

3. Apply a random bisection cut:

$$\left[\,\boxed{?}\,\boxed{?}\,\boxed{?}\,\boxed{?}\,\middle|\,\boxed{?}\,\boxed{?}\,\boxed{?}\,\boxed{?}\,\right] \rightarrow \boxed{?}\,\boxed{?}\,\boxed{?}\,\boxed{?}\,\boxed{?}\,\boxed{?}\,\boxed{?}\,\boxed{?}.$$

4. Rearrange the order of the sequence as:

$$\boxed{?}\,\boxed{?}\,\boxed{?}\,\boxed{?}\,\boxed{?}\,\boxed{?}\,\boxed{?}\,\boxed{?}$$

$$\boxed{?}\,\boxed{?}\,\boxed{?}\,\boxed{?}\,\boxed{?}\,\boxed{?}\,\boxed{?}\,\boxed{?}.$$

We then have

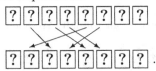

where r is a (uniformly distributed) random bit.

5. Reveal the first two cards. If they are ♣♥, we have $a \oplus r = 0$, i.e., $r = a$. Therefore, the output is (see Eq. (3)):

$$\boxed{♣}\boxed{♥}\underbrace{\boxed{?}\boxed{?}}_{a}\underbrace{\boxed{?}\boxed{?}\boxed{?}\boxed{?}}_{a \wedge b}.$$

If they are ♥♣, we have $a \oplus r = 1$, i.e., $r = \bar{a}$. Therefore, the output is:

$$\boxed{♥}\boxed{♣}\underbrace{\boxed{?}\boxed{?}}_{\bar{a}}\underbrace{\boxed{?}\boxed{?}\boxed{?}\boxed{?}}_{a \wedge b}.$$

In this way, we can obtain commitments to both $a \wedge b$ and a. The two face-up cards ♣♥ are still available for another computation. In addition, the two cards of the remaining commitment can also be available after they are shuffled.

Sub-protocol for Checking Eq. (2). Given the discussion above, we are ready to present a procedure for checking Eq. (2) to determine if there are fixed points. Given a pile

$$p_i : \underbrace{\boxed{?}\boxed{?}}_{a_{\log n}}\cdots\underbrace{\boxed{?}\boxed{?}}_{a_2}\underbrace{\boxed{?}\boxed{?}}_{a_1},$$

the following sub-protocol computes the value of

$$(a_1 \oplus \overline{b_1}) \wedge (a_2 \oplus \overline{b_2}) \wedge \cdots \wedge (a_{\log n} \oplus \overline{b_{\log n}}),$$

where

$$(i - 1)_{10} = (b_{\log n} \cdots b_2 b_1)_2.$$

1. Arrange $\lceil \log n \rceil$ input commitments and six additional cards as follows:

$$\underbrace{\boxed{?}\boxed{?}}_{a_{\log n}}\cdots\underbrace{\boxed{?}\boxed{?}}_{a_3}\underbrace{\boxed{?}\boxed{?}}_{a_2}\underbrace{\boxed{?}\boxed{?}}_{a_1}\boxed{♣}\boxed{♥}\boxed{♣}\boxed{♥}\boxed{♣}\boxed{♥}.$$

2. Copy the commitment to a_1 using the copy protocol [8] mentioned above:

$$\underbrace{\boxed{?}\boxed{?}}_{a_{\log n}}\cdots\underbrace{\boxed{?}\boxed{?}}_{a_3}\underbrace{\boxed{?}\boxed{?}}_{a_2}\underbrace{\boxed{?}\boxed{?}}_{a_1}\underbrace{\boxed{?}\boxed{?}}_{a_1}\boxed{♣}\boxed{♥}\boxed{♣}\boxed{♥}.$$

3. Apply the NOT computation depending on the values of b_1 and b_2 so that we have

$$\underbrace{\boxed{?}\boxed{?}}_{a_{\log n}}\cdots\underbrace{\boxed{?}\boxed{?}}_{a_3}\underbrace{\boxed{?}\boxed{?}}_{a_2 \oplus \overline{b_2}}\underbrace{\boxed{?}\boxed{?}}_{a_1 \oplus \overline{b_1}}\underbrace{\boxed{?}\boxed{?}}_{a_1}\boxed{♣}\boxed{♥}\boxed{♣}\boxed{♥}.$$

Note that each value of b_i is public.

4. Apply the one-input-preserving AND protocol presented above to obtain commitments to $(a_1 \oplus \overline{b_1}) \wedge (a_2 \oplus \overline{b_2})$ and $(a_2 \oplus \overline{b_2})$. Furthermore, apply the NOT computation to the latter commitment depending on the value of b_2. We then have

5. Similarly, obtain commitments to $(a_1 \oplus \overline{b_1}) \wedge (a_2 \oplus \overline{b_2}) \wedge (a_3 \oplus \overline{b_3})$ and a_3:

Repeat this until we have

6. Reveal the commitment to $(a_1 \oplus \overline{b_1}) \wedge (a_2 \oplus \overline{b_2}) \wedge \cdots \wedge (a_{\log n} \oplus \overline{b_{\log n}})$. If the value is 1, then this is a fixed point. Otherwise, it is not a fixed point. It should be noted that in either case, any commitments to $a_1, a_2, \ldots, a_{\log n}$ are not lost.

4.3 Description of Our Proposed Protocol

We are now ready to present an efficient protocol for generating a random permutation having no fixed point. Our protocol uses $(2n\lceil \log n \rceil + 6)$ cards to produce n piles corresponding to this random permutation.

1. Using $n\lceil \log n \rceil$ ♣s and $n\lceil \log n \rceil$ ♡s, arrange $n\lceil \log n \rceil$ commitments according to players' indices based on the binary representation:

2. Regarding each row as a pile, apply a pile-scramble shuffle to the n piles; we then obtain a random permutation π in which the i-th pile corresponds to $\pi(i)$:

$$p_1 : \boxed{?}\boxed{?}\cdots\boxed{?}\boxed{?}\boxed{?}\boxed{?}$$
$$p_2 : \boxed{?}\boxed{?}\cdots\boxed{?}\boxed{?}\boxed{?}\boxed{?}$$
$$\vdots$$
$$p_n : \boxed{?}\boxed{?}\cdots\boxed{?}\boxed{?}\boxed{?}\boxed{?}.$$

3. Using six additional cards, apply the sub-protocol presented in Sect. 4.2 to confirm that π has no fixed point, that is, to verify that p_i is not a fixed point for every i, $1 \le i \le n$, in turns. If we find a fixed point, then we go back to step (2). If we confirm that there is no fixed point, the permutation π is a desired one.

This is our main protocol for solving the "no fixed point" problem with $O(n \log n)$ cards.

5   Conclusions

The known protocol [3] requires $2n^2$ cards of four colors to generate a random permutation having no fixed point. In this paper, we first devised a new shuffle operation called a pile-scramble shuffle that immediately enabled us to achieve the same task using only n^2 cards of two colors. Furthermore, we showed that using a binary representation dramatically reduces the number of required cards, that is, $(2n\lceil\log n\rceil + 6)$ cards of two colors are sufficient.

In our protocol, the $2n\lceil\log n\rceil$ cards are used to hold each players' index, and the remaining six cards correspond to the additional cards $\boxed{\clubsuit}\boxed{\heartsuit}\boxed{\clubsuit}\boxed{\heartsuit}\boxed{\clubsuit}\boxed{\heartsuit}$ required to execute the sub-protocol for checking fixed points. This comes from the fact that the one-input-preserving AND protocol given in Sect. 4.2 requires four additional cards. Recently, it was shown that such a one-input-preserving AND computation can be done with only two additional cards [11]. Therefore, applying this recently invented protocol [11], we can reduce the number of required cards to $2n\lceil\log n\rceil + 4$.

In addition to the protocol solving the "no fixed point" problem, Crépeau and Kilian designed a general protocol for producing a random permutation that satisfies a predetermined condition such as having no short cycle of length at most k, and showed that it can be applied to the "Discreet Solitary Games" [3]. Thus, it is intriguing future work to design an efficient way to determine whether a given permutation based on our binary representation has k-cycles.

Although the card-based protocol is an unconventional way to secure multiparty computations, this approach has many advantages. The most important feature is that even nonspecialists are able to easily understand why the computation is secure.

Acknowledgments. We thank the anonymous referees whose comments helped us to improve the presentation of the paper. This work was supported by JSPS KAKENHI Grant Number 26330001.

References

1. den Boer, B.: More efficient match-making and satisfiability. In: Quisquater, J.J., Vandewalle, J. (eds.) EUROCRYPT 1989. LNCS, vol. 434, pp. 208–217. Springer, Heidelberg (1990)
2. Cordón-Franco, A., Van Ditmarsch, H., Fernández-Duque, D., Soler-Toscano, F.: A colouring protocol for the generalized Russian cards problem. Theor. Comput. Sci. **495**, 81–95 (2013)
3. Crépeau, C., Kilian, J.: Discreet solitary games. In: Stinson, D.R. (ed.) CRYPTO 1993. LNCS, vol. 773, pp. 319–330. Springer, Heidelberg (1994)
4. Duan, Z., Yang, C.: Unconditional secure communication: a Russian cards protocol. J. Comb. Optim. **19**(4), 501–530 (2010)
5. Fischer, M.J., Wright, R.N.: Bounds on secret key exchange using a random deal of cards. J. Cryptology **9**(2), 71–99 (1996)
6. Mizuki, T., Asiedu, I.K., Sone, H.: Voting with a logarithmic number of cards. In: Mauri, G., Dennunzio, A., Manzoni, L., Porreca, A.E. (eds.) UCNC 2013. LNCS, vol. 7956, pp. 162–173. Springer, Heidelberg (2013)
7. Mizuki, T., Kumamoto, M., Sone, H.: The five-card trick can be done with four cards. In: Wang, X., Sako, K. (eds.) ASIACRYPT 2012. LNCS, vol. 7658, pp. 598–606. Springer, Heidelberg (2012)
8. Mizuki, T., Sone, H.: Six-card secure AND and four-card secure XOR. In: Deng, X., Hopcroft, J.E., Xue, J. (eds.) FAW 2009. LNCS, vol. 5598, pp. 358–369. Springer, Heidelberg (2009)
9. Mizuki, T., Uchiike, F., Sone, H.: Securely computing XOR with 10 cards. Australas. J. Comb. **36**, 279–293 (2006)
10. Niemi, V., Renvall, A.: Secure multiparty computations without computers. Theor. Comput. Sci. **191**(1–2), 173–183 (1998)
11. Nishida, T., Hayashi, Y., Mizuki, T., Sone, H.: Card-based protocols for any Boolean function. In: Jain, R., Jain, S., Stephan, F. (eds.) TAMC 2015. LNCS, vol. 9076, pp. 110–121. Springer, Heidelberg (2015)
12. Nishida, T., Mizuki, T., Sone, H.: Securely computing the three-input majority function with eight cards. In: Dediu, A.-H., Martín-Vide, C., Truthe, B., Vega-Rodríguez, M.A. (eds.) TPNC 2013. LNCS, vol. 8273, pp. 193–204. Springer, Heidelberg (2013)
13. Stiglic, A.: Computations with a deck of cards. Theor. Comput. Sci. **259**(1–2), 671–678 (2001)
14. Swanson, C.M., Stinson, D.R.: Combinatorial solutions providing improved security for the generalized Russian cards problem. Des. Codes Crypt. **72**(2), 345–367 (2014)

Simulation of the 2JLP Gene Assembly Process in Ciliates

Md. Sowgat Ibne Mahmud and Ian McQuillan$^{(\boxtimes)}$

University of Saskatchewan, Saskatoon, SK, Canada
mdm179@mail.usask.ca, mcquillan@cs.usask.ca

Abstract. The gene assembly process in ciliates consists of a massive amount of DNA excision from the micronucleus and sometimes the rearrangement of the rest of the DNA sequences. Several models exist that describe certain parts of this process. In this research, a simulation is created and tested with real data to test the feasibility of the 2JLP model. Several parameters are introduced in the model that are used to test ambiguities or edge cases of the biological model. Parameters are systematically varied within the simulation to try to find their optimal values. Interestingly, a negative correlation is found between the degree to which the simulation successfully descrambles genes, and a parameter that is used to filter out scnRNAs that are similar to IES specific sequences from the macronucleus. This provides *in silico* evidence that if a scnRNA consists of both a portion of MDS and IES, then from the perspective of maximizing the accuracy of the descrambling, it is desirable to filter out this scnRNA. The simulator successfully performs the gene assembly process whether the inputs are scrambled or unscrambled DNA sequences. On average, before the proof checking stage that is in the model, the descrambling intermediate genes are 91.1 % similar to the descrambled genes. After the proof checking stage, the intermediate genes are 99.4 % similar. We hope that this work and further simulations can serve as a foundation for future computational and mathematical study of descrambling, and to help inform and refine the biological model.

Keywords: Biological simulation · Template guided recombination · Scan RNAs · Scrambled genes · Gene assembly · Ciliates · Natural computing

1 Introduction

Ciliates are a group of unicellular protozoa characterized by the presence of hair-like organelles called cilia. Worldwide, 4,500 different species of ciliates are known [1]. Two distinct types of nuclei are present in each cell, called the *micronucleus* and the *macronucleus* [14]. The macronucleus produces all the RNA

This research was supported by a grant from the Natural Sciences and Engineering Research Council of Canada.

C.S. Calude and M.J. Dinneen (Eds.): UCNC 2015, LNCS 9252, pp. 227–238, 2015.
DOI: 10.1007/978-3-319-21819-9_17

and proteins needed for day-to-day operations, and the micronucleus remains silent functionally, except after conjugation when certain micronucleus specific genes get expressed [3]. During the period of conjugation, ciliates destroy their macronuclei and exchange haploid micronuclei. Each then constructs a fully functional macronucleus from the micronuclear genome by doing a massive quantity of DNA excision and rearrangement [6,8,13].

Micronuclear genes have two classes of DNA sequences— non-coding DNA segments that get excised in the conversion, known as *IESs* (internal eliminated sequences) and segments that are retained, known as *MDSs* (macronuclear destined DNA sequences). A functional macronucleus can be constructed by deleting IESs and merging MDSs from the micronucleus. Different ciliates perform the gene assembly process in different ways. In the case of two genera of ciliates *Tetrahymena* and *Euplotes*, the MDSs of the micronucleus are interrupted by IESs but the MDSs occur in the same order as in the macronucleus. But in the case of stichotrichs (containing genera *Stylonychia* and *Oxytricha*), the MDSs are not only interrupted by IESs, but the MDSs can also occur in a scrambled order.

Figure 1 shows a diagram of a scrambled micronuclear gene, and the descrambled variant.

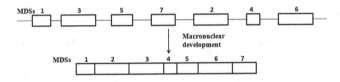

Fig. 1. During macronuclear development, IESs (the lines between the boxes) are excised from the micronucleus and the MDSs are joined in the correct order to yield a macronuclear gene.

In stichotrichous ciliates, IESs are flanked by repeat sequences called *pointers* [18]. These pointers are less than 20 bp in size with one copy of the pointer at the 3′-end of one MDS and the other copy at the 5′-end of the next MDS (next MDS according to the correct ordering in the macronucleus) [15,17]. IESs are excised between two adjacent MDSs along with one copy of the pointer.

There are a variety of biological models and hypotheses that have been created to model the gene assembly process in ciliates, such as the intramolecular model [16], the intermolecular model [7], the *scnRNA model* [9], the *template guided model* [17], and the *2JLP model* [5] (to be described in Sect. 2). And from a number of those, formal models have been created in an attempt to capture the biological models. All the existing models appear to capture at least part of the gene assembly process, even though some have experimentally verified limitations in scope [10]. More recently, the 2JLP model [5] was created, and involves a combination of the scnRNA model for excising IESs from the micronucleus, and the template-guided model for removing the remaining IESs, for rearranging MDSs, and for a proofreading process.

This paper briefly describes existing formal and biological models as well as known limitations in Sect. 2. Then, a simulation is presented together with the algorithms to capture and analyze the 2JLP model. The implemented algorithms are provided and discussed in Sect. 3. Later on, the outcome of the simulation is discussed based on its use with real micronuclear and macronuclear genes. In the simulator, some important parameters are considered such as the minimum value needed for sufficient similarity between scnRNAs (small RNAs) and MDSs, and the minimum value to needed for sufficient similarity between filtered scnRNAs and the new micronucleus in order to identify subwords for deletion. These parameters are used to deal with ambiguities in the biological model and to determine optimal values according to the simulation. Indeed, the primary motivation of the work lies in its potential towards:

- unifying existing models and new aspects into well-defined algorithms while capturing the biological 2JLP model, thereby establishing which aspects of existing models are compatible with each other,
- building simulations to test the feasibility of the model and its consistency with real micronuclear and macronuclear genes,
- and testing and resolving ambiguities of existing models through systematic variation of parameters.

Furthermore, as far as the authors are aware, the use of computer simulations to test a gene assembly model is novel, and may contribute techniques towards new biological models such as the more recent piRNA model [1] for *Oxytricha*, which has some similar aspects.

2   Existing Models

A variety of biological and formal models have emerged that attempt to explain different parts of the gene assembly process. In this section, we briefly describe some of the models, as they relate to the 2JLP model.

Landweber and Kari proposed a model for gene assembly known as the *intermolecular model* [7]. It consists of one unary intramolecular and two binary intermolecular operations of DNA recombination on pointers. Another model for gene assembly was introduced by Prescott et al. [16] and Ehrenfeucht et al. [4] called the *intramolecular model*. It consists of three unary molecular operations based on pointers. One of the major limitations in scope of these models is that they do not discuss the process of pointer identification, as pointers are too short to uniquely identify their other copy.

A model for the gene assembly process was proposed by Mochizuki et al. in 2002 based on small RNAs, called the *scan RNA* (scnRNA) model [9]. They proposed that during the early conjugation period, a RNAi-related pathway starts with a bi-directional transcription of the micronucleus. From that, it generates small RNAs of size $28 - 29$ bp also known as *scnRNAs*. These localize to the parental macronucleus where all scnRNAs that are similar to some segment of the parental macronucleus degrades. The rest of the scnRNAs that fail to degrade are therefore likely similar to IES-specific sequences. Then these IES-specific scnRNAs travel to the developing macronucleus where they eliminate subsequences that are similar. A limitation of this model is that it does not address MDS reordering. Moreover, the model does not easily explain IES removal for cases where IESs are smaller than scnRNAs.

In a key experiment on the ciliate *Paramecium tetraurelia* (that does not have scrambling, but does have IESs), an *IES* was injected into a macronucleus before mating (so that a portion of the macronuclear gene "looked like" the micronuclear version, with two MDSs separated by an IES) [15]. Then, the ciliate was allowed to traverse into the sexual cycle, after which it was found that this particular *IES* was present in the structure of the new macronucleus. As a result of this experiment, it was thought that some sequence-specific information must be transferred from the parental macronucleus to the new macronucleus. Hence, a biological model of gene assembly was introduced by Prescott et al. in 2003 and is known as the *template guided model* [17]. In this model a molecule (later determined to be RNA [12]) that has been generated from the parental macronucleus is used as a template to guide both IES removal and MDS reordering in the developing macronucleus. A limitation of this model can be seen by examining the notion of *cryptic pointers*, which are direct repeats of length 1–8 that are in proximity to real pointers. In fact, despite not being the real pointers, ciliates frequently use cryptic pointers for splicing. It was observed in an experiment [10] that IESs are deleted randomly and sometimes imprecisely (when IESs are removed based on cryptic pointers) at the middle-late stage of macronuclear development. These become corrected at a later stage.

Despite the limitations of these models, there is indeed evidence that the *scnRNA* model does filter out IESs from the new micronucleus. There is also other evidence that some parts of the template model must also be true, with template molecules being present, and influencing the resulting macronucleus. Based on this, a biological model of gene assembly was proposed by Jönsson et al. [5]. It is known as the *2JLP* model, and it unifies portions of the previous models, which all occur within a temporal procedure (Fig. 2) summarized as follows:

Definition 1 (2JLP Model). *This model can be defined by the following steps:*

1. *During the early period after conjugation, each ciliate generates scnRNAs. The genome of the micronucleus is transcribed bi-directionally and the resulting transcripts generate double-stranded RNA molecules which are eventually processed into scnRNAs.*

2. *These scnRNAs travel to the parental macronucleus and any scnRNAs similar to DNA sequences in the parental macronucleus are degraded.*

3. *In the late conjugation stages, the remaining portion of the scnRNAs (that are similar to IESs) are transferred to the developing new macronucleus, where they target and identify IESs to be eliminated by base pairing between repeats (either real or cryptic pointers).*

4. *At the same time, the template guided model generates template RNAs from the parental macronucleus to guide the alignment of MDSs and their pointer sequences, and produces the new macronucleus.*

5. *In the case of scrambled genes, the template RNAs perform unscrambling of MDSs according to their order in the macronuclear chromosomes. Homologous recombination between the aligned pointers splice out IESs. For IES excision, if cryptic pointers are used instead of real pointers, a proofreading mechanism guided by the template ensures the missing sequences are filled in and the extra sequences are removed to create full-length chromosomes.*

More recently the procedure has been discovered to be different between *Tetrahymena* and *Oxytricha*, where *Tetrahymena* uses scnRNAs from the old micronucleus as in the 2JLP model, whereas *Oxytricha* uses 27bp small RNAs (called piRNAs) from the old macronucleus to mark MDS regions in the developing macronucleus. A simulation involving the latter model is left as future work.

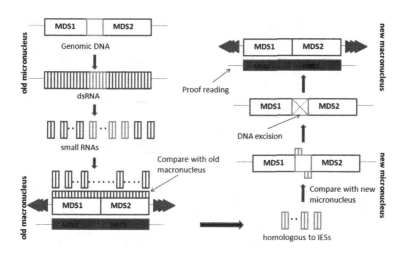

Fig. 2. The 2JLP model combines aspects from the scanRNA model and the template-guided model to explain the gene assembly in ciliates: the whole micronuclear genome is transcribed early in macronuclear development into long double-stranded transcripts, which are processed into small RNAs (scnRNAs). These invade the old macronucleus. There, scnRNAs similar to macronuclear sequences (dark blue) degrade. The rest of the scnRNAs (red) are sent to the new micronucleus for marking and excision of IESs by recruiting chromatin-modifying proteins to the micronuclear-specific sequences. Imprecisely processed sequences will be corrected by a proofreading mechanism that is guided by template RNAs (gray). These template RNAs originate from the old macronucleus. In scrambled genes, the template RNAs guide alignment of micronuclear MDSs in the correct order of the template, creating a new macronucleus (Color figure online).

3   Simulation

This section describes the implementation for the simulation of the 2JLP model. The purpose of developing the simulation is to test the model's feasibility, and determine additional important aspects regarding the gene assembly process by analysing the results with real data. These findings can be helpful for refining the 2JLP model. For example, in the algorithm, certain values are parameterized that were left ambiguous or not described in the biological model of Definition 1. Then, it can be tested which values for the parameters give optimal results.

Figure 3 shows the flow diagram of the pipeline used to simulate the 2JLP model (each part explained in Sect. 3.1). Global sequence alignment and semi-global alignment are used within, which are the standard Needleman-Wunsch algorithm to compute the optimal global sequence alignment and its semi-global variant [11]. For scoring alignments, a match score of 1, mismatch score of −1, and gap penalty of −2 are used.

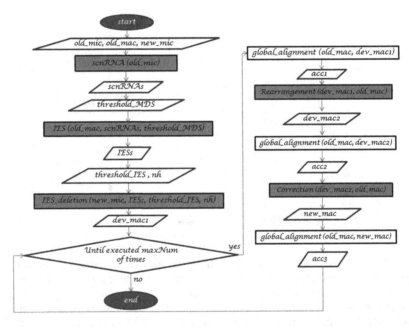

Fig. 3. Flow diagram of the simulator. Major functions of the simulator are represented by green shaded rectangles. The parameters are explained in Table 1. Each part of the pipeline will be explained in Sect. 3.1 (Color figure online).

From Fig. 3, it is shown that the simulator has five major functions (green shaded rectangles). These are *scnRNA, IES, IES_deletion, rearrangement,* and *correction.* Among these, the scnRNA function closely simulates the construction process of scnRNAs (first step of Definition 1). The IES function simulates the mechanism of finding putative IESs (second step of Definition 1).

The *IES_deletion* function simulates the mechanism of deleting IESs from the new micronucleus (third step of Definition 1). For simulating the construction process of the new macronucleus (forth and fifth steps of Definition 1), both the *rearrangement* and the *correction* (simulating the proof-checking step) functions are used.

3.1 Important Parameters, Algorithms, and Methods of Evaluation

Three important parameters, *threshold_MDS*, *threshold_IES*, and *nh* are considered. They can take on a range of possible values, and all integer values within the range are simulated for each. Their meaning and ranges are described below.

It is possible to determine "how much" of the gene has been descrambled after each stage of the simulation by computing the similarity of the developing gene to the macronuclear gene. If the percent similarity (computed from a global sequence alignment) between the string computed thus far shows similarity to the fully descrambled variant, then it has been largely descrambled. Hence, three percentages are calculated throughout the simulation: *acc1* is computed after deleting IESs from the micronucleus (*dev_mac1*), *acc2* is computed after rearrangment based on templates (*dev_mac2*), and *acc3* is computed after proof checking (*new_mac*).

Table 1. List of the important parameters

Parameter name	Range	Purpose of parameter
threshold_MDS	1 to 28	The minimum score of the semi-global alignment needed for sufficient similarity between scnRNAs and *old_mac*.
threshold_IES	1 to 28	The minimum score of the semi-global alignment needed for sufficient similarity between filtered scnRNAs and *new_mic*.
nh	1 to 20	The size of the neighbourhood indicates the area around where filtered scnRNAs match the developing macronucleus

The implemented algorithm takes three input strings: *old_mic*, *old_mac*, and *new_mic*. Of these, *old_mic* and *old_mac* are a single matching micronuclear gene and macronuclear gene, respectively.

The *scnRNA* function generates all possible scnRNAs through a "sliding window" technique. In the *scnRNA* function, *old_mic* is divided into all subwords of length 28, as is done in step 1 of Definition 1. The output, an array called *scnRNAs* is taken along with *old_mac* as inputs to the *IES* function to generate an array called *IESs*. This function compares each element from *scnRNAs* with the parental macronucleus, and if there is a match that is "similar enough", it gets filtered out as it will largely be MDS specific. However, "similar enough" is ambiguous, and therefore a semi-global alignment between the scnRNA of length 28

and the macronuclear gene is used with the parameter *threshold_MDS*. This is
the parameter representing the minimum score needed to classify as "similar".
Ultimately, the simulation is tested for all values of this parameter between 1
and 28, as there is no indication in the model as to what degree of similarity is
needed.

Then, *new_mic*, *IESs*, and *threshold_IES* are inputs to the *IES_deletion* function to generate *dev_mac1* (the gene obtained after IES removal in step 3 of
Definition 1). This function has two parts. In the first part, it compares all
strings of *IESs* with *new_mic* and performs a "marking of matched subwords"
(simulated by keeping track of the start and end positions in *new_mic* of where
it matches any string in *IESs*). In the second part, it removes each subword from
new_mic if it has a repeated segment of length between 2 and 20 "close to" the
ends of the marked portion. The range of between 2 and 20 is chosen as these are
the allowable lengths of pointers. An important aspect of this simulation is that
these repeated strings do not need to be the real pointers. Indeed, Möllenbeck
et al. [10] show that often cryptic pointers are used for splicing in proximity to
the MDS-IES junctions (see Definition 1 and the preceding discussion). Also, it
is possible that the repeated sequence is a part of an IES (which would result
in a portion of the IES remaining after deletion), but it is also possible that
the repeated sequence could be part of an MDS as well (which would result in
part of that MDS being missing). That is why in the algorithm, a parameter
named "neighbourhood (nh)" is taken to address the range of possible distances
of cryptic or real pointers to the marked portion. The model dictates that this is
close to the MDS-IES junctions and thus the parameter nh represents the largest
distance allowed, which is simulated for all values up to 20. As the selection of
repeats used for splicing is not always the same, we select repeats randomly
within the neighbourhood. However, the final descrambled gene will depend on
the random values chosen. Therefore, this step is simulated four times (represented by *maxNum* in Fig. 3) for each pointer, and for each value of nh to select
different repeats from *new_mic*, eventually generating many different values of
dev_mac1. The value *acc1* measuring the percent similarity is stored at this
stage, for each value of *dev_mac1*.

Then, the *rearrangement* function is used to generate *dev_mac2* by taking *dev_mac1*, and *old_mac* as inputs. The main purpose of this function is to
rearrange MDSs from *dev_mac1* based on the old macronucleus (*old_mac*). A precise method to predict the order in which MDSs descramble is not known, and
therefore, our simulation of this stage is a simplification of the actual biological procedure. Indeed, our method randomly picks a locus from the template
(which is the same as the parental macronuclear gene), finds a similar segment
in *dev_mac1* (on either the sense or antisense strand), extends in both directions, and repeats until all segments of the template are matched, and then the
matched segments are rearranged, creating *dev_mac2*. At this stage, the second
percent identity *acc2* is calculated to quantify the degree to which the gene has
been descrambled.

At this point, the *correction* function is applied. In this function, the final macronucleus (*new_mac*) is generated by comparing *dev_mac2* and the template, simulated with a sequence alignment. Based on the alignment, extra characters are removed from *dev_mac2* (from gaps along the template) and missing characters are inserted (from gaps in *dev_mac2*) into *dev_mac2*. Then, the final percent identity *acc3* is calculated from the resulting descrambled gene *new_mac*.

4   Results and Analysis

In the simulation, for each set of fixed parameters for *threshold_MDS*, *threshold_IES*, and neighbourhood, results are calculated at three different stages to measure the change from the new micronucleus to the new macronucleus. These three different stages are after the *IES_deletion* function, after the *rearrangement* function, and finally after the *correction* function. The term *accuracy* is defined to represent the degree to which descrambling has occurred at the various stages.

Input data was collected from the IES MDS Database [2]. From there, 13 real micronucleus and macronucleus matching gene pairs of the ciliate *Oxytricha trifallax* are used in the simulation. Although this is a limited number of pairs of genes, the micronuclear data contains 40,844 base pairs and the macronuclear data contains 32,770 base pairs, and also the simulation is run many times randomly choosing different repeats within each neighbourhood, and by trying all combinations of parameters.

Among these 13 input pairs, pair number 7 (the Actin I gene) has a smaller micronuclear sequence (989 bp) than its macronuclear sequence (1553 bp) due to incomplete data. This pair will indeed appear differently in the results. There is a very recent paper [3] on the sequencing and analysis of the micronuclear genome of the ciliate *Oxytricha trifallax*. However, as it is still in draft status, has not been used as further verification of the simulation.

For each input pair, the 15,680 different parameter combination are tested, each generating an average value for *acc1*, *acc2*, and *acc3* across all micronucleus and macronucleus gene pairs. The combination of three parameters that gives the maximum average *acc2* score is considered to be the optimal parameters. The reason the *acc2* accuracy value (after the *rearrangement* function) is used to define and to determine the optimal parameter values is because using the accuracy after the *IES_deletion* function (*acc1*) always gives low accuracies in the case of scrambled genes, as rearrangement has not yet occurred, and taking the accuracies after the *correction* function (*acc3*) often can fix otherwise bad alignments as the templates are used in this stage. Ideally, one would expect that for scrambled genes, *acc2* (used to determine optimal parameters) be "quite high" to account for cryptic pointers occurring in proximity of MDS-IES junctions, but not perfect as cryptic pointers do indeed occur (recall Definition 1 and preceding discussion on cryptic pointers, as sometimes IESs are eliminating around repeats nearby to the real pointers instead of the pointers themselves). Further, *acc3* should be almost perfect to account for proof checking from templates. Thus, using the accuracy after the *rearrangement* function seems to be the best way to calculate the optimal parameters and success of the simulation.

The maximum accuracy values using *acc2*, occurs when the parameters of *threshold_MDS* is 5, *threshold_IES* is 9, and *nh* is 15 (these are the values of the parameters for which the average *acc2* output is maximized across all data). For these optimal parameters, the simulation is run multiple times (at step 3 of Definition 1 was simulated *maxNum* times for each pointer selection) to calculate the average and standard deviation of the accuracies. Table 2 shows, on average over all gene pairs, the *acc1* value is 60.5 %, *acc2* value is 88.5 %, and *acc3* value is 99.5 %. Removing gene pair number 7 (due to having incomplete data) increases the average *acc2* value to 91.1 %. Indeed, this number is "quite high" but not perfect as was desirable.

Table 2. For each gene pair (indexed by the first column), the average (Avg) and standard deviation (STD) of *acc1*, *acc2*, and *acc3* are shown for the optimal parameters. The final two rows summarize the average over all 13 genes, and over the 12 genes without gene 7 that has incomplete data, respectively.

pair_no	Avg acc1	STD acc1	Avg acc2	STD acc2	Avg acc3	STD acc3
1	43	1.4	92.9	1.9	99.9	0.1
2	87.2	1.6	94.4	0.4	99.8	0.2
3	53.5	1	84.6	0.4	98.8	0.2
4	61.2	0.8	93.5	0.7	99.6	0.4
5	61.9	0.9	89.4	0.7	99.7	0.3
6	70.1	1	93.3	0.6	99.9	0.1
7	57.6	1.6	58.2	1.8	99.9	0.1
8	43.1	1.5	90.3	1.2	98.9	0.5
9	69.9	0.9	92.6	0.4	99.9	0.1
10	62.4	1	93.3	0.6	99.8	0.3
11	73.1	0.8	89.8	0.3	99.8	0.2
12	46.5	0.5	94.4	0.3	99.8	0.3
13	56.8	1.9	84.4	1.9	97.3	1.5
average	60.5	0.41	88.5	0.61	99.5	0.39
average-7	60.7	0.41	91.1	0.57	99.4	0.4

From the 2JLP model, it can be seen that the macronucleus is generated from the micronucleus in a successive manner. Table 2 shows that *acc2* is greater than *acc1* and *acc3* is greater than *acc2* for all input pairs, and the values of acc2 are quite high, but not perfect, which is exactly what we expect given the nature of cryptic pointers. And indeed, the values of acc3 are almost perfect as proof checking can add in missing, or remove excessive information.

Of interest, in Fig. 4, a scatter plot is shown that shows the relationship between *threshold_MDS* and average alignment scores between the descrambled and parental macronucleus. Here, an alignment score is calculated by dividing it by the size of *old_mac* and multiplying it by 100. Average alignment scores are calculated by the scores after the *rearrangement* function for all input pairs. In the same way, the average alignment scores are calculated for each value of *threshold_MDS* (from 1 to 28) where *threshold_IES* and neighbourhood (*nh*) are fixed with their optimal values. The scatter plot is generated by plotting *threshold_MDS* on the x-axis and average alignment scores on the y-axis. The trend-line equation is $y = -1.3576x + 76.105$ and the square of the correlation coefficient (R^2) value is 0.7435. The slope value is negative which indicates that there is a negative correlation present in between these two variables. If the value of *threshold_MDS* is increased it eventually degrades the value of the alignment score. As the R^2 value is 0.7435, this indicates approximately 74 % of the variation in accuracy can be explained by *threshold_MDS*.

Figure 4 shows that a lower value of *threshold_MDS* is good from the perspective of maximizing the alignment score for the simulation. These lower scores for *threshold_MDS* occur when shorter pieces of scnRNAs are matched to the old macronucleus at the time of filtering, similar to IES specific sequences from the set of scnRNAs. Thus, if a scnRNA contains part of an MDS and part of an IES, from the perspective of maximizing the alignment score of the simulation, it is desirable to filter out this scnRNA at this stage. This is because if it does not get filtered out then the simulation may discard the matching portion of that scnRNA from the new micronucleus. This may result in an erroneous deletion of an MDS from the micronucleus.

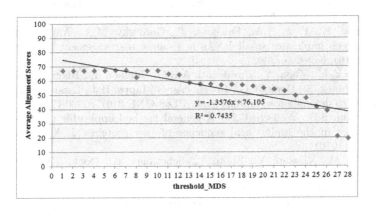

Fig. 4. Relationship between *threshold_MDS* and average alignment scores (*acc2*, after the *rearrangement* function, for all 13 input pairs). Here, *threshold_IES* and *nh* are fixed with the optimal values of *threshold_IES* as 9 and *nh* as 15.

5   Future Directions

Currently, the simulator has been tested only for thirteen pairs of real genes. After the assembly of the micronuclear genome emerges from draft status, a more extensive analysis will be possible. As mentioned is Sect. 3, a new simulation to capture piRNAs is desirable for *Oxytricha*. Furthermore, a simulation using scnRNAs as done in this paper using *Tetrahymena* data would help to validate the hypothesized model.

References

1. Bracht, J.R., Fang, W., Goldman, A.D., Dolzhenko, E., Stein, E.M., Landweber, L.F.: Genomes on the edge: programmed genome instability in ciliates. Cell **152**(3), 406–416 (2013)
2. Cavalcanti, A.: Ciliate nuclear dimorphism pages. http://oxytricha.princeton.edu/dimorphism/ (2004)
3. Chen, X., Bracht, J.R., Goldman, A.D., Dolzhenko, E., Clay, D., Swart, E., Perlman, D., Doak, T., Stuart, A., Amemiya, C., Sebra, R., Landweber, L.: The architecture of a scrambled genome reveals massive levels of genomic rearrangement during development. Cell **158**(5), 1187–1198 (2014)
4. Ehrenfeucht, A., Prescott, D.M., Rozenberg, G.: Computational aspects of gene (un)scrambling in ciliates. In: Evolution as Computation, pp. 216–256. Natural Computing Series, Springer, Berlin Heidelberg (2002)
5. Jönsson, F., Postberg, J., Lipps, H.J.: The unusual way to make a genetically active nucleus. DNA Cell Biol. **28**(2), 71–78 (2009)
6. Keil, J.M., Liu, J., McQuillan, I.: Algorithmic properties of ciliate sequence alignment. Theor. Comput. Sci. **411**(6), 919–925 (2010)
7. Landweber, L.F., Kari, L.: The evolution of cellular computing: nature's solution to a computational problem. Biosystems **52**, 3–13 (1999)
8. Landweber, L.F., Kuo, T.C., Curtis, E.A.: Evolution and assembly of an extremely scrambled gene. Proc. Natl. Acad. Sci. USA **97**(7), 3298–3303 (2000)
9. Mochizuki, K., Fine, N.A., Fujisawa, T., Gorovsky, M.A.: Analysis of a piwi-related gene implicates small RNAs in genome rearrangement in Tetrahymena. Cell **110**(6), 689–699 (2002)
10. Möllenbeck, M., Zhou, Y., Cavalcanti, A.R.O., Jönsson, F., Higgins, B.P., Chang, W.J., Juranek, S., Doak, T.G., Rozenberg, G., Lipps, H.J., Landweber, L.F.: The pathway to detangle a scrambled gene. PLoS ONE **3**(6), e2330 (2008)
11. Needleman, S.B., Wunsch, C.D.: A general method applicable to the search for similarities in the amino acid sequence of two proteins. J. Mol. Biol. **48**(3), 443–453 (1970)
12. Nowacki, M., Vijayan, V., Zhou, Y., Schotanus, K., Doak, T.G., Landweber, L.F.: RNA-mediated epigenetic programming of a genome-rearrangement pathway. Nature **451**, 153–158 (2008)
13. Prescott, D.M.: The unusual organization and processing of genomic DNA in hypotrichous ciliates. Trends Genet. **8**(12), 439–445 (1992)
14. Prescott, D.M.: The DNA of ciliated protozoa. Microbiol. Rev. **58**(2), 233–267 (1994)
15. Prescott, D.M.: Genome gymnastics: unique modes of DNA evolution and processing in ciliates. Nat. Rev. Genet. **1**(3), 191–198 (2000)
16. Prescott, D.M., Ehrenfeucht, A., Rozenberg, G.: Molecular operations for DNA processing in hypotrichous ciliates. Eur. J. Protistology **37**(3), 241–260 (2001)
17. Prescott, D.M., Ehrenfeucht, A., Rozenberg, G.: Template-guided recombination for IES elimination and unscrambling of genes in stichotrichous ciliates. J. Theor. Biol. **222**(3), 323–330 (2003)
18. Verlan, S., Alhazov, A., Petre, I.: A sequence-based analysis of the pointer distribution of stichotrichous ciliates. Biosystems **101**(2), 109–116 (2010)

A Uniform Family of Tissue P Systems with Protein on Cells Solving 3-Coloring in Linear Time

T. Mathu[1], Hepzibah A. Christinal[1]([✉]), and Daniel Díaz-Pernil[2]

[1] Karunya University, Coimbatore, Tamilnadu, India
{tometilda,christyhep}@gmail.com
[2] Research Group on Computational Topology and Applied Mathematics,
University of Sevilla, Avda. Reina Mercedes s/n, 41012 Sevilla, Spain
sbdani@gmail.com

Abstract. A new variant of tissue P systems called tissue P system with protein on cells is used in this paper. It has the ability to move proteins between cells. It is inspired from the biology that the cells communicate by sending and receiving signals. Signals most often move through the cell by passing from protein to protein. In tissue P systems with protein on cells, multisets of objects together with proteins between cells are exchanged. We present in this paper a linear solution of the 3-coloring problem, a well known NP-complete problem. In this new variant, these objects called proteins are used to obtain a new solution where the number of rules is lesser than that appears in the original solution with tissue P systems. The number of steps to obtain the solution is lesser than the conventional tissue P system. This is a strong point when someone wants to implement a solution in a practical way.

1 Introduction

Membrane computing is an emergent cross-disciplinary branch of Natural Computing, introduced by Paun in [16]. It has received important attention from the scientific community since then, with contributions from computer scientists, biologists, formal linguists and complexity theoreticians, enriching each other with results, open problems and promising new research lines.

The distinct feature of membrane computing is its distributed parallel computing models in the form of membrane systems, also called P systems. The main ingredients of a P system are the structure of the membrane, multisets of objects and the rules that cause the objects to evolve and pass through membranes from time to time. The three variants of P-systems considered mainly are known as cell-like P systems [16], tissue-like P systems [14] and neural-like P systems [17].

From the seminal definition of Tissue P systems [14,15], several research lines have been developed and other variants have been defined(see, for example, [1,4,6,10]). One of the most interesting variants of Tissue P systems was presented in [18]. In that paper, the definition of Tissue P systems is combined with

C.S. Calude and M.J. Dinneen (Eds.): UCNC 2015, LNCS 9252, pp. 239–249, 2015.
DOI: 10.1007/978-3-319-21819-9_18

the one of P systems with active membranes, yielding Tissue P systems with cell division.

A class of tissue P systems with protein on cells was proposed in [11] which abstracts the idea from the biological fact as follows: In addition to the lipid bilayer, the cell membrane also contains a number of proteins. While the lipid bilayer provides the structure for the cell membrane, membrane proteins allow for many of the interactions that occur between cells. Membrane proteins are free to move within the lipid bilayer and they perform various functions. They are generally classified as integral proteins or peripheral proteins. Integral proteins are embedded within the lipid bilayer and cannot be easily removed from the cell membrane. Peripheral proteins are attached to the exterior of the lipid bilayer and can be easily removed from the lipid bilayer, without harming the bilayer in any way. Tissue P systems with protein on cells contain one and only one copy of protein on each cell. The multisets of objects together with the proteins are exchanged if communication takes place between two cells and only proteins are exchanged if communication takes place between the cell and the environment.

In this paper we are going to present a NP-complete problem namely 3-coloring problem. This problem is related to the famous Four Color Conjecture (proved by Appel and Haken [2,3]. It is a special case of the problem of k−colorability of a graph, in which the range of C (color) is $\{1, \ldots, k\}$ with k being specified as part of the instance. The NP-completeness of the $3-$coloring problem was proved by Stockmeyer [21] (see [7]). The solution of this problem is already obtained using different variants of P systems like simple kernel P systems [9] and Tissue P system with cell division [5]. In [11], a polynomial-time solution to the **NP**-complete problem SAT is shown using tissue like P system with protein on cells and cell division. In this paper the same variant of tissue P system is used to find a linear-time solution to the 3−coloring problem.

This paper is organized as follows: First we recall some preliminaries and the definition of Tissue P systems with protein on cells and cell division. Next, recognizer of this variant of Tissue P systems is briefly described. A linear−time solution to the 3-coloring problem is presented in the following section, including a short overview of the computation and of the necessary resources. Finally, the main results and conclusion are presented.

2   Preliminaries

In this section, some of the concepts used in this paper are given briefly. The definitions are taken from [16,19].

An *alphabet*, Σ, is a non empty set, whose elements are called *symbols*. A finite sequence of symbols is a *string*. The number of symbols of a string u is the *length* of the string, and it is denoted by $|u|$. As usual, the empty string (with length 0) will be denoted by λ. The set of strings of length n built with symbols from the alphabet Σ is denoted by Σ^n and $\Sigma^* = \cup_{n \geq 0} \Sigma^n$. A *language* over Σ is a subset from Σ^*.

A *multiset* m over an alphabet A is a pair (A, f) where $f : A \to \mathbf{N}$ is a mapping. Given $m = (A, f)$ a multiset, its *support* is defined as $supp(m) = \{x \in A \mid f(x) > 0\}$ and its *size* is defined as $\sum_{x \in A} f(x)$. A multiset is *empty* (resp. *finite*) if its support is the empty set (resp. finite). The *union* of two multisets $m_1 = (A, f_1)$ and $m_2 = (A, f_2)$ is defined as $m_1 + m_2 = (A, f)$, where $f(a) = f_1(a) + f_2(a)$, for every $a \in A$. Given two multisets $m_1 = (A, f_1)$ and $m_2 = (A, f_2)$, m_1 is contained in m_2, $m_1 \leq m_2$, if and only if $f_1(a) \leq f_2(a)$, for every $a \in A$. If $m = (A, f)$ is a finite multiset over A, then it will be denoted as $m = a_1^{f(a_1)} a_2^{f(a_2)} \cdots a_k^{f(a_k)}$, where $supp(m) = \{a_1, \ldots, a_k\}$, and for each element a_i, $f(a_i)$ is called the *multiplicity* of a_i.

A *graph* G consists of a finite set V of objects called vertices, a finite set E of objects called edges and a function γ that assigns to each edge a subset $\{v, w\}$, where v and w are vertices. It is denoted by $G = (V, E, \gamma)$.

3   Formal Framework

Bosheng Song and Linqiang Pan introduced in [11] a new variant of Tissue P systems where a single protein is placed on each cell at the beginning of the computation. If a communication rule between two cells is applied then the multisets of objects together with the proteins are exchanged. If a communication rule between a cell and the environment is applied, then only the multisets of objects between the cell and the environment are exchanged. The following definitions are from [11].

Definition 1. *A tissue P system with protein on cells of degree $q \geq 1$ is a tuple* $\Pi = (\Gamma, P, \mathcal{E}, \mathcal{M}_1/p_1, \ldots, \mathcal{M}_q/p_q, \mathcal{R}, i_{out})$, *where:*

- Γ, P *are finite non–empty alphabets such that $\Gamma \cap P = \phi$;*
- $\mathcal{E}$ *is a finite alphabet such that $\mathcal{E} \subseteq \Gamma$;*
- $\mathcal{M}_i, 1 \leq i \leq q$, *are finite multisets over Γ;*
- $p_i, 1 \leq i \leq q$, *are elements in P;*
- $\mathcal{R}$ *is a finite set of rules of the following forms:*
    - *Communication Rules*
        - *(a) $(i, (p_i, u)/(p_j, v), j)$, for $i, j \in 1, \ldots, q, i \neq j, p_i, p_j \in P, u, v \in \Gamma^*$.*
        - *(b) $(i, (p_i, u)/v, 0)$, for $i \in 1, \ldots, q, p_i \in P, u, v \in \Gamma^*, |uv| > 0$*
- $i_{out} \in \{0, 1, \ldots, q\}$.

Definition 2. *A tissue P system with protein on cells and cell division of degree $q \geq 1$ is a tuple $\Pi = (\Gamma, P, \mathcal{E}, \mathcal{M}_1/p_1, \ldots, \mathcal{M}_q/p_q, \mathcal{R}, i_{out})$, where all components are as mentioned in previous definition and $\mathcal{R}$ is the finite set of rules, which contains communication rules of the forms mentioned in Definition 1 (a & b), and division rules of the form*

$$[p_i|a]_i \to [p_i'|b]_i \, [p_i''|c]_i, \quad for \quad i \in \{1, \ldots, q\}, \quad p_i, p_i', p_i'' \in P, \quad a, b, c \in \Gamma, \quad i \neq i_{out}$$

A tissue P system with protein on cells (and cell division) of degree $q \geq 1$ can be viewed as a set of q cells, labeled by $1, \ldots, q$, such that: (a) $\mathcal{M}_1, \ldots, \mathcal{M}_q$ represent the finite multisets of **objects** (symbols of the alphabet Γ) initially **placed** in the q cells of the system; (b) $p_1, \ldots, p_q$ represent one and only one copy of **protein** (symbols of the alphabet P) initially **placed on** the q cells of the system; (c) $\mathcal{E}$ is the set of objects initially located in the environment of the system, all of them available in an arbitrary number of copies; and (d) i_{out} represents a distinguished *zone* which will encode the output of the system. The term *zone* $i(0 \leq i \leq m)$ refers to cell i in the case of $1 \leq i \leq m$ and the environment in the case of $i = 0$. The length of a communication rule is the total number of objects and proteins involved in that rule.

A *configuration* of a tissue P system with protein on cells (and cell division) at any instant is described by all multisets of objects over Γ associated with all the cells present in the system, all the proteins presented on all cells, and the multiset of objects over $\Gamma \backslash \mathcal{E}$ associated with the environment at that moment. Bearing in mind the objects from $\mathcal{E}$ have infinite copies in the environment, they are not properly changed along the computation. The *initial configuration* is $(\mathcal{M}_1/p_1, \ldots, \mathcal{M}_q/p_q; \phi)$

A communication rule of type $(i, (p_i, u)/(p_j, v), j)$ is applicable to a configuration at an instant if cell i contains the protein p_i and the multiset u of objects, cell j contains the p_j and the multiset v of objects (multisets u,v may be empty). When applying such a rule, under the control of the proteins p_i on cell i and p_j on cell j, both the protein p_i and the multiset u of objects are sent from region i to region j, and simultaneously, the protein p_j and the multiset v of objects are sent from region j to region i; a particular case is $(i, (p_i, \lambda)/(p_j, \lambda), j)$, where only proteins change their places. A communication rule of type $(i, (p_i, u)/(v, 0))$ is applicable to a configuration at an instant if cell i contains the protein p_i and the multiset u of objects, the environment contains the multiset v of objects (at least one of multisets u,v is non-empty). When applying such a rule, under the control of the protein p_i on cell i, the multiset u of objects are sent from region i to the environment, and simultaneously, the multisets v of objects are sent from the environment to region i.

A division rule $[p_i|a]_i \rightarrow [p_i'|b]_i \ [p_i''|c]_i$ is applicable to a configuration at an instant if cell i contains the protein p_i and the object a. When applying such a rule, under the influence of protein p_i on cell i, the cell is divided into two cells with the same label; in the first copy the protein p_i is replaced by p_i' and the object a is replaced by b, in the second copy the protein p_i is replaced by p_i'' and the object a is replaced by c; all the remaining objects in the original cell are replicated and copied in each of the new cells.

Rules of a system like the above one are used in a maximally parallel way: at each step, all cells which can evolve must evolve (at each step we apply a multiset of rules which is maximal, no further rule can be added being applicable). This way of applying rules has only one restriction: when a cell is divided, the division rule is the only one which is applied to that cell at that step. In other words, division rule for that cell interrupts all its communication channels with the other cells and with the environment. The new cells resulting from division could participate in the interaction with other cells or the environment by means of communication rules at the next step - providing that they are not divided once again. The label of a cell precisely identifies the rules which can be applied to it.

Let us fix a tissue P system with protein on cells (and cell division) Π, we denote $\mathcal{C}_1 \Rightarrow_\Pi \mathcal{C}_2$ meaning that configuration $\mathcal{C}_1$ yields $\mathcal{C}_2$ in one transition step by a maximally parallel application of rules as described above. A configuration is a *halting configuration* if no rule of the system is applicable to it. A *computation* is a (finite or infinite) sequence of configurations such that: (1) the first term of the sequence is the initial configuration of the system; (2) each non–first term of the sequence is obtained from the previous configuration by applying rules of the system in a maximally parallel manner with the restrictions previously mentioned; and (3) if the sequence is finite (called *halting Computation* then the last term of the sequence is a halting configuration.

All the computations start from an initial configuration and proceed as stated above; only halting computations give a result, which is encoded by the objects present in the output zone i_{out} associated with the halting configuration.

3.1 Recognizer Tissue P Systems with Protein on Cells and Cell Division

In order to study the computational efficiency, the notions from classical computational complexity theory are adapted for membrane computing. A class of cell-like P systems, recognizer P systems, is introduced in [20]. With the same idea for recognizer cell-like P systems, recognizer tissue P systems are introduced in [18]. The following definitions follows from [11].

Definition 3. *A recognizer tissue P system with protein on cells and cell division of degree $q \geq 1$ is a tuple $\Pi = (\Gamma, P, \mathcal{E}, \mathcal{M}_1/p_1, \ldots, \mathcal{M}_q/p_q, \mathcal{R}, i_{in}, i_{out})$, where:*

- *the tuple $(\Gamma, P, \mathcal{E}, \mathcal{M}_1/p_1, \ldots, \mathcal{M}_q/p_q, \mathcal{R}, i_{out})$ is a tissue P system with protein on cells and cell division of degree $q \geq 1$;*
- *the working alphabet Γ has two distinguished objects yes and no, with at least one copy of them presents in some initial multisets $\mathcal{M}_1, \ldots, \mathcal{M}_q$, but none of them present in $\mathcal{E}$;*
- *Σ is an (input) alphabet strictly contained in Γ, and such that $\mathcal{E} \subseteq \Gamma \backslash \Sigma$;*
- *$\mathcal{M}_1, \ldots, \mathcal{M}_q$ are finite multisets over $\Gamma \backslash \Sigma$;*
- *$i_{in} \in \{1, \ldots, q\}$ is the input cell;*
- *the output zone i_{out} is the environment;*
- *all computations halt;*
- *if $\mathcal{C}$ is a computation of Π, then either object yes or object no (but not both) must have been released into the environment, and only at the last step of the computation.*

For each multiset w over Σ, the *computation of the system Π with input w* starts from the configuration of the form $(\mathcal{M}_1/p_1, \ldots, (\mathcal{M}_{in} + w)/p_{in}, \ldots, \mathcal{M}_q/p_q, \phi)$, that is, the input mutiset w has been added to the contents of the input cell $i_i n$. Therefore, we have an initial configuration associated with each input multiset w (over the input alphabet Σ) in this kind of systems.

We denote by **TPDC**(k) the class of recognizer tissue P systems with protein on cells and cell division with communication rules of length atmost k.

Definition 4. *We say that a decision problem* $X = (I_X, \theta_X)$ *is solvable in polynomial time by a family* $\mathbf{\Pi} = \{\Pi(n) : n \in \mathbb{N}\}$ *of recognizer tissue-like P systems with protein on cells and cell division in uniform way if the following conditions holds:*

- *The family* $\mathbf{\Pi}$ *is polynomially uniform by Turing machines, that is, there exists a deterministic Turing machine working in polynomial time which constructs the system* $\Pi(n)$ *from* $n \in \mathbb{N}$.
- *There exists a pair* (cod, s) *of polynomial-time computable functions over* I_X *(called a polynomial encoding of* I_X *in* $\mathbf{\Pi}$*) such that:*
  - *for each instance* $u \in I_X$, $s(u)$ *is a natural number and* $cod(u)$ *is an input multiset of the system* $\Pi(s(u))$;
  - *for each* $n \in \mathbb{N}, s^{-1}(n)$ *is a finite set;*
  - *the family* $\mathbf{\Pi}$ *is polynomially bounded with regard to* (X, cod, s), *that is, there exists* $k \in \mathbb{N}$ *a polynomial function, such that for each* $u \in I_X$ *every computation of* $\Pi(s(u))$ *with input* $cod(u)$ *is halting and, moreover, it performs at most* $k(|u|)$ *steps;*
  - *the family* $\mathbf{\Pi}$ *is sound with regard to* (X, cod, s), *that is, for each* $u \in I_X$, *if there exists an accepting computation of* $\Pi(s(u))$ *with input* $cod(u)$, *then* $\theta_X(u) = 1$;
  - *the family* $\mathbf{\Pi}$ *is complete with regard to* (X, cod, s), *that is, for each* $u \in I_X$, *if* $\theta_X(u) = 1$, *then every computation of* $\Pi(s(u))$ *with input* $cod(u)$ *is an accepting one.*

We denote by **PMC**$_{TPDC(k)}$ the set of all decision problems which can be solved by means of recognizer tissue-like P systems **TPDC(k)** in polynomial time. It is easy to prove that this class is closed under polynomial time reduction and under complement.

4   Solving the 3−coloring Problem by Using TPDC

Let G be a graph with $V(G)$ as set of vertices and $E(G)$ as set of edges. A k−coloring of a graph G is a function $C : V(G) \rightarrow \{1, \ldots, k\}$ such that for all $v, w \in V(G)$, if $C(v) = C(w)$, then $((v, w) \notin E(G))$. The k−coloring problem is to determine the number of such k-colorings for G.

Next, we will see that the 3-coloring problem can be solved by tissue P systems with protein on cells and cellular division in linear time. Let us consider a graph $G = (U, V)$, where $U = \{u_i | 1 \leq i \leq n\}$ is the set of vertices and $V = \{v_j | v_j = u_{j_1} u_{j_2} \wedge 1 \leq j \leq m \wedge 1 \leq j_1 < j_2 \leq n\}$ is the set of edges.

Let us consider $(n, (A_{ij})_n)$ in order to denote a generic instance of the problem, with n the size of the graph G, i.e., the number of vertices in G and let A be the set of the edges in the graph G, with

$$(A_{ij})_n = (A_{ij} : A_i A_j \in V \land 1 \leq i < j \leq n)$$

We will address the resolution via a brute force algorithm, which consists in the following stages:

- *Generation stage:* The initial cell labeled by 6 is divided into two new cells and the divisions are iterated until a cell has been produced for each possible candidate solution (3− colorings). Also cells 4 and 5 are divided to produce enough number of p_4 and p_5 proteins which are needed in the checking stage. Simultaneously, counter in the cell labeled by 1 that will be used for the output stage.
- *Pre-checking stage:* After obtaining all possible 3-colorings encoded in cells labeled by 6, in this stage we provide colors to the edges. So, from each object A_{ij}, we generate three objects R_{ij}, G_{ij} and B_{ij}.
- *Checking stage:* Objects R_i, G_i, B_i will be used in cells labeled by 6 to check if there exists a pair of adjacent vertices with the same color in the corresponding candidate solution. If this happens, the protein is changed to p_4 from cell 4.
- *Output stage:* The system sends to the cell labeled 2 the right answer according to the results of the previous stage.
    1. Answer **yes** : There exists a cell labeled 6 such that its protein is p_4 at the end of the step $4n + 4$. In this case, an object **yes** is sent to the cell 2.
    2. Answer **no**: It is the converse case. If all the cells labeled by 6 has p_5 as protein at the end of the step 4n+4, then the cell 1 does not receive any object T and an object **no** is sent to the cell 2.

Here, we present a family of recognizer tissue P systems with protein on cells and cell division where at the initial configuration each system of the family has 6 regions (labeled by 1, 2, 3, 4, 5 and 6).

For each $n \in \mathbb{N}$, we shall consider the system

$$\Pi = (\Gamma, P, \Sigma, \mathcal{E}, \mathcal{M}_1/p_1, \mathcal{M}_2/p_2, \mathcal{M}_3/p_3, \mathcal{M}_4/p_4, \mathcal{M}_5/p_5, \mathcal{M}_6/p_6, \mathcal{R}, i_{in}, i_{out}),$$

- $\Gamma = \Sigma \cup \{A_i, B_i, R_i, G_i, T_i, R'_i, G'_i, B'_i : 1 \leq i \leq n\}$
  $\cup \{a_i : 0 \leq i \leq 3n + 3\}$
  $\cup \{c_i : 1 \leq i \leq 2n + 3\}$
  $\cup \{d_i : 1 \leq i \leq 3n + 4\}$
  $\cup \{R_{ij}, B_{ij}, G_{ij}, T_{ij}\overline{R_{ij}}, \overline{G_{ij}}, \overline{B_{ij}}, T'_{ij}, T''_{ij}R'_{ij}, G'_{ij}, B'_{ij} : 1 \leq i < j \leq n\}$
  $\cup \{b, T, \text{yes, no}\}$
- $\Sigma = \{A_{ij} : 1 \leq i < j \leq n\}$
- $P = \{P_i : 1 \leq i \leq 2n + 6\}$
- $\mathcal{E} = \Gamma \backslash \Sigma$
- $\mathcal{M}_1 = \{a_1, \text{yes, no}\}$
- $\mathcal{M}_2 = \{b\}$

- $\mathcal{M}_3 = \{e_1\}$
- $\mathcal{M}_4 = \{c_1\}$
- $\mathcal{M}_5 = \{d_1\}$
- $\mathcal{M}_6 = \{T, A_1, \ldots, A_n\}$
- $\mathcal{R}$ is the following set of rules:
  1. *Division rules:*

  $r_{1,i} \equiv [p_k|A_i]_6 \longrightarrow [p_{k+1}|R_i]_6[p_{k+1}|T_i]_6$ for $i = 1, \ldots, n, k = 6, \ldots, 2n+6$

  $r_{2,i} \equiv [p_k|T_i]_6 \longrightarrow [p_{k+1}|G_i]_6[p_{k+1}|B_i]_6$ for $i = 1, \ldots, n, k = 6, \ldots, 2n+6$

  $r_{3,i} \equiv [p_4|c_i]_4 \longrightarrow [p_4|c_{i+1}]_4[p_4|c_{i+1}]_4$ for $i = 1 \ldots 2n$

  $r_{4,i} \equiv [p_5|d_i]_5 \longrightarrow [p_5|d_{i+1}]_5[p_5|d_{i+1}]_5$ for $i = 1 \ldots 2n$

  2. *Communication rules:*

  $r_{5,i} \equiv (1, (p_1, a_i)/a_{i+1}, 0)$ for $i = 1 \le 4n+4$

  $r_{6,i} \equiv (3, (p_3, e_i)/e_{i+1}, 0)$ for $i = 1 \le 4n+5$

  $r_{7,i,j} \equiv (6, (p_{2n+6}, A_{ij})/R_{ij}T_{ij}, 0)$ for $1 \le i < j \le n$

  $r_{8,i,j} \equiv (6, (p_{2n+6}, T_{ij})/G_{ij}T'_{ij}, 0)$ for $1 \le i < j \le n$

  $r_{9,i,j} \equiv (6, (p_{2n+6}, T'_{ij})/B_{ij}T''_{ij}, 0)$ for $1 \le i < j \le n$

  $r_{10,i,j} \equiv (6, (p_{2n+6}, T''_{ij})/(p_4, \lambda), 4)$ for $1 \le i < j \le n$

  $r_{11,i,j} \equiv (6, (p_4, K_iK_{ij})/\overline{K_{ij}}, 0)$ for $1 \le i < j \le n, K = R, G, B$

  $r_{12,i,j} \equiv (6, (p_4, \overline{K_{ij}}/K_iK'_j, 0)$ for $1 \le i < j \le n, K = R, G, B$

  $r_{13,i,j} \equiv (6, (p_4, K'_jK_j)/(p_5, \lambda), 5)$ for $1 \le i < j \le n, K = R, G, B$

  $r_{14} \equiv (1, (p_1, a_{4n+5})/(p_4, T), 6)$

  $r_{15} \equiv (1, (p_4, \mathbf{yes})/(p_2, b), 2)$

  $r_{16} \equiv (3, (p_3, e_{4n+6})/(p_1, a_{4n+5}), 1)$

  $r_{17} \equiv (1, (p_3, \mathbf{no})/(p_2, b), 2)$

- $i_{in} = 6$, is the input cell

- $i_{out} = 2$, is the output cell

4.1   An Overview of the Computation

A family of recognizer tissue P systems with protein on cells and cell division for solving 3-coloring problem is constructed above. Given an instance u of the problem, with size $s(u) = n$, and the codification of the instance will be the multiset $cod(u) = \{A_{ij}|1 \le i < j \le n\}$.

At the initial configuration, we have objects $\{a_1, \mathbf{yes}, \mathbf{no}\}$, $\{b\}$, $\{d_1\}$, $\{T, A_1, \ldots, A_n\}$, $\{N, c_1\}$ in cells $1, 2, 3, 4, 5$ and 6 respectively along with respective proteins p_1, p_2, p_3, p_4, p_5 and p_6.

The input of the above defined family of tissue P system with protein on cells and cell division for a graph with n vertices is encoded by its edges (objects A_{ij}). The input cell is labeled by 6.

The computation starts with two computational threads. On one hand we divide the cell 4 (rules $r_{3,i}$), cell 5 (rules $r_{4,i}$) and cell 6 (rules $r_{1,i}$ and $r_{2,i}$). Technical issues compel to divide cells 4, 5 and cell 6 is divided to generate all the possible solutions of our problem. The vertices with colors red, green and blue are codified by objects R_i, G_i and B_i . Moreover the protein of cell 6 evolves from p_6 to p_{2n+6} at the end of division phase.

We finish all the division rules in $2n$ steps. We proceed to change the color of the edges in the next steps using rules $r_{7,i,j}, r_{8,i,j}$ and $r_{9,i,j}$ in 3 steps. Then the protein p_4 arrives to cell 6 from cell 4 in $2n + 4$th step and the checking phase starts.

We use three rules $r_{11,i,j}, r_{12,i,j}$ and $r_{13,i,j}$ for checking. In the worst case (complete graph), we need $2n$ steps to complete the computation. It is not possible to apply the rules $r_{13,i,j}$ to all the cells labeled 4 without division on cell 5. So, we have two possible types of cells labeled 6 in the $4n + 4$th step. Some of these has the protein p_5 and the remaining cells conserve the protein p_4. The first type represents wrong 3−coloring (i.e. those cells containing p_5 protein) and the second type gives the affirmative coloring (i.e., the cells containing p_4 protein).

Consequently, we have two possible options. The first type implies all the colorings are wrong. Then the rules r_{16} and r_{17} are applied and the solution is sent to cell 2. The second type implies at least one 3−coloring is correct. So the rules r_{14} and r_{15} are applied and solution is sent to cell 2. In all possible cases, we need at most $4n + 7$ steps to complete the computation of the above system.

4.2 Necessary Resources

The presented family of tissue P systems solves the 3-coloring problem in polynomially uniform time by Turing machines. It can be observed that the definition of the family is done in a recursive manner from a given instance, in particular from the constant n. Furthermore the necessary resources to build an element of family are:

- Size of the alphabet: $6n^2 + 19n + 24 \in \theta(n^2)$
- Initial number of cells: $6 \in \theta(1)$,
- Initial number of objects: $n + m + 10 \in \theta(n)$
- Number of rules: $5n^2 + 14n + 13 \in \theta(n^2)$,
- Maximal length of a rule is 4.

4.3 Comparison with Other Variants

In the following table, we have compared our system with the tissue P system ([5]) and simple kernel P system ([9]). We can easily compare the values of the necessary resources.

Our solution presents a lesser number of rules with respect to the first solution but higher number with respect to the second. But, in this last case, our rules are shorter and the difference is really big. With respect to the size of the alphabet, our solution requires more of objects but this size has the same order than the other two solutions. There is no big difference in this case. If we see the initial number of objects, they are almost same in all the cases (Table 1).

Table 1. Comparison with other variants

	Tissue P systems	skP systems	Tissue P systems with Protein on cells
Size of the alphabet	$3n^2 + 9n + 2m + 3\lceil \log m \rceil + 28 \in \theta(n^2 + m)$	$n(n-1)/2 + 7n + 10$	$6n^2 + 19n + 24 \in \theta(n^2)$
Initial No. of cells	$2 \in \theta(1)$		$6 \in \theta(1)$
Initial No. of Objects	$n + m + 6 \in \theta(n+m)$		$n + m + 10 \in \theta(n)$
No. of Rules	$18n^2 - 9n + 2m + 3\lceil \log m \rceil + 24 \in \theta(n^2 + m)$	$2n, 2n + 7$	$5n^2 + 14n + 13 \in \theta(n^2)$
Max. length of a rule	4	$3n(n-1)/2$	4
No. of Steps	$2n + m + \lceil \log m \rceil + 11$	$2n + 3$	$4n + 7$

4.4 Main Results

From the discussion in the previous sections and according to the definition of solvability given in Sect. 3, we deduce the following result:

Theorem 1. *3-coloring* $\in$ **PMC**$_{TPDC}$.

As a consequence of this result we have:

Theorem 2. **NP** $\cup$ **co** $-$ **NP** $\subseteq$ **PMC**$_{TPDC}$.

Proof It suffices to make the following observations: the 3–coloring problem is **NP**-complete, 3–coloring $\in$ **PMC**$_{TPDC}$ and the class **PMC**$_{TPDC}$ is stable under polynomial-time reduction, and also closed under complement.

5 Conclusion

In this paper the system introduced by [11] has been used to solve the NP-complete 3−coloring problem and the overview of the computation is also given with needed resources. Also we propose here, a new solution to an NP-complete problem which can be used as a scheme for designing solutions to other problems from Graph Theory as the Vertex Cover Problem, Clique, etc. Moreover, the type of solution presented can be also adapted for solving numerical problems.

References

1. Alhazov, A., Freund, R., Oswald, M.: Tissue P systems with antiport rules and small numbers of symbols and cells. In: De Felice, C., Restivo, A. (eds.) DLT 2005. LNCS, vol. 3572, pp. 100–111. Springer, Heidelberg (2005)
2. Appel, K., Haken, W.: Every planar map is 4-colorable - 1: Discharging. Ill. J. Math. **21**, 429–490 (1977)
3. Appel, K., Haken, W.: Every planar map is 4-colorable - 2: Reducibility. Ill. J. Math. **21**, 491–567 (1977)
4. Bernardini, F., Gheorghe, M.: Cell communication in tissue P systems and cell division in population P systems. Soft Comput. **9**(9), 640–649 (2005)

5. Díaz-Pernil, D., Gutierrez-Naranjo, M.A., Perez-Jimenez, M.J., Riscos-Nunez, A.: A uniform family of tissue P systems with cell division solving 3-COL in a linear time. Theoret. Comput. Sci. **404**(1–2), 76–87 (2008)
6. Freund, R., Paun, G., Pérez-jiménez, M.J.: Tissue P systems with channel states. Theoret. Comput. Sci. **330**, 101–116 (2005)
7. Garey, M.R., Johnson, D.S.: Computers and Intractability A Guide to the Theory of NP-Completeness. W.H. Freeman and Company, New York (1979)
8. Linqiang, P., Pérez-Jiménez, M.J.: Computational complexity of tissue-like P systems. J. Complex. **26**(3), 296–315 (2010)
9. Gheorghe, M., Ipate, F., Lefticaru, R., Pérez-Jiménez, M.J., Turcanu, A., Valencia-Cabrera, L., Garcia-Quismondo, M., Mierla, L.: 3-Col problem modelling using simple kernel P systems. Int. J. Comput. Math. **90**(4), 816–830 (2013)
10. Krishna, S.N., Lakshmanan, K., Rama, R.: Tissue P systems with contextual and rewriting rules. In: Păun, G., Rozenberg, G., Salomaa, A., Zandron, C. (eds.) WMC-CdeA 2002, LNCS, vol. 2597, pp. 339–351. Springer, Heidelberg (2003)
11. Song, B., Pan, L., Pérez-Jiménez, M.J.: Tissue P systems with protein on cells. Fundamenta Informaticae **XXI**, 1001–1030 (2001)
12. Song, B., Song, T., Pan, L.: Time-free solution to SAT problem by P systems with active membranes and standard cell division rules. Natural Computing (2014). doi:10.1007/s11047-014-9471-4
13. Song, B., Pan, L.: Computational efficiency and universality of timed P systems with active membranes. Theoret. Comput. Sci. **567**, 74–86 (2015)
14. Martín-Vide, C., Pazos, J., Păun, G., Rodríguez-Patón, A.: Tissue P systems. Theoret. Comput. Sci. **296**(2), 295–326 (2003)
15. Martín-Vide, C., Pazos, J., Păun, G., Rodríguez-Patón, A.: A new class of symbolic abstract neural nets: tissue P systems. In: Ibarra, O.H., Zhang, L. (eds.) COCOON 2002. LNCS, vol. 2387, p. 290. Springer, Heidelberg (2002)
16. Păun, G.: Computing with membranes. J. Comput. Syst. Sci. **61**(1), 108–143 (2000)
17. Păun, G.: Membrane Computing: An Introduction. Springer-Verlag, Berlin (2002)
18. Păun, G., Pérez-Jiménez, M.J., Riscos-Nunez, A.: Tissue P system with cell division. Int. J. Comput. Commun. Control **3**(3), 295–303 (2008)
19. Păun, G., Rozenberg, G., Salomaa, A. (eds.): Handbook of Membrane Computing. Oxford University Press, Cambridge (2009)
20. Pérez-Jiménez, M.J., Romero-Jiménez, A., Sancho-Caparrini, F.: A polynomial complexity class in P systems using membrane division. J. Automata Lang. Comb. **11**(4), 423–434 (2006)
21. Stockmeyer, L.J.: Planar 3-colorability is NP-complete. SIGACT News **5**(3), 19–25 (1973)

Asynchronous Dynamics of Boolean Automata Double-Cycles

Tarek Melliti[1]([⊠]), Mathilde Noual[2], Damien Regnault[1],
Sylvain Sené[2,3], and Jérémy Sobieraj[1]

[1] IBISC, EA4526, Université d'Évry Val-d'Essonne, 91037 Évry, France
{tarek.melliti,damien.regnault}@ibisc.univ-evry.fr,
jeremy.sobieraj@gmail.com
[2] Aix-Marseille Université, CNRS, LIF UMR 7279, 13288 Marseille, France
{mathilde.noual,sylvain.sene}@lif.univ-mrs.fr
[3] IXXI, Institut Rhône-alpin des systèmes complexes, 69007 Lyon, France

Abstract. Because interaction networks occupy more and more space in our current life (social networks) and in our understanding of living systems(biological regulation networks), it seems necessary to develop the knowledge regarding them. By using Boolean automata networks as models of interaction networks, we present new results about the influence of cycles on their dynamics. Cycles in the architecture of boolean networks are known to be the primary engine of dynamical complexity. As a first particular case, we focus on cycle intersections and provide a characterisation of the dynamics of asynchronous Boolean automata networks composed of two cycles that intersect at one automaton. To do so, we introduce an efficient formalism inspired by algorithms to define long sequences of updates, which allows a more efficient description of their dynamics.

Keywords: Interaction networks · Boolean automata networks · Double-cycles · Asynchronous dynamics

1 Introduction

An increasing number of systems of our daily life is being understood as computational processes. At the foundation of these, *interactions* and *dynamics* combine in a fascinating, ever changing way. Our knowledge of these processes will condition our understanding of biological systems, such as gene regulatory networks or neural networks, and enable us to engineer a variety of things, from genetic cures to neuronal computers, or chemical computational devices. To tackle the overwhelming complexity of these challenges, we use a highly abstract model of interaction networks called *Boolean automata networks* (BANs). Despite its (deliberate) simplicity, this model is adequate for the computational study of interaction networks, as it can at the same time simulate Turing machines operating in constant space, and properly model interaction dynamics as observed in actual networks. The origins of this model are to be found in computer science

© Springer International Publishing Switzerland 2015
C.S. Calude and M.J. Dinneen (Eds.): UCNC 2015, LNCS 9252, pp. 250–262, 2015.
DOI: 10.1007/978-3-319-21819-9_19

and some variants have been applied to physics, biology and sociology [5,8,20]. Moreover, although it has also been studied from a computational point of view since the original work of McCulloch and Pitts [10], lots of its algorithmic properties are yet to be understood.

The present work takes place exactly at the frontier of theoretical computer science and *fundamental bio-informatics*, that aims at analysing and explaining formally the dynamics of biological regulations, that are at the core of molecular biology [6,7]. Since the seminal works of Kauffman [8,9] and Thomas [21,22] in theoretical biology, computer scientists have been trying to formalise the intuitions coming from biology. One of the most fundamental questions raised by these studies was formulated by Thomas and addressed the role of interacting cycles in BANs on their dynamics. Recent studies [16–18] have started to produce formal answers to this question. Their main results, first envisioned by Robert [19], are necessary conditions on the architectures of networks to generate complex dynamics, *i.e. syntactic* conditions for the appearance of complex *semantics*. However, even though interacting cycles are well identified as the primary engine of complex dynamics, we are far from a full understanding of these phenomena. This explains why many recent studies focused on these specific patterns. Among them, [1] provided a complete characterisation of the dynamical behaviours of Boolean automata cycles (BACs), under the parallel updating mode. Once the cycle dynamics were finely understood, it seemed natural to divide them into networks in order to make a step towards generality. But to obtain general results for any kind of network remains an open problem that seems intractable for the moment. So, following a constructive approach and as a first step, studies have been led on specific patterns combining cycles, such as the parallel double-cycles [1] and the asynchronous flower-graphs [2] for instance. In addition, other studies have dealt with the convergence time of specific classes of BANs, like circulant XOR networks [15] and networks without negative cycles [12].

This paper follows the same lines and solves a question that remained open until now: *how do Boolean automata double-cycles that evolve asynchronously over time behave?* We give here an answer by means of original methods relating algorithmic complexity to natural dynamical systems. We show that every kind of double-cycle admits a very limited number of attractors, either one or two. Also, we prove that recurrent configurations are not all similar in the sense that some of them have peculiar features in terms of reachability. Some of them can be reached by following paths of linear size according to the network sizes whereas other need quadratic sequences of updates to be reached.

The paper is organised as follows: Sect. 2 gives the main definitions and notations used in the paper, in particular those related to the double-cycles and the asynchronous updating mode; Sect. 3 gives the definition of the tools and methods developed here; finally, Sect. 4 is dedicated to the main contributions of this paper. Notice that, due to lack of space, the proofs (that reveal the intricacies of this work) are not given in the paper but are detailed in arXiv:1310.5747 [11].

2   Definitions and Notations

BANs. Consider $\mathbb{B} = \{0,1\}$ and $V = \{0,\ldots,n-1\}$ a set of n Boolean automata so that $\forall i \in V$, $x_i \in \mathbb{B}$ denotes the *state* of i. A *configuration* of a BAN $\mathcal{N}$ of size n instantiates the state of any i of V and is classically denoted as a vector, such that $x \in \mathbb{B}^n$, or as a binary word. Formally, a BAN $\mathcal{N}$, whose automata set is V, is a set of n Boolean functions, which means that $\mathcal{N} = \{f_i : \mathbb{B}^n \to \mathbb{B} \mid i \in V\}$. Given $i \in V$, f_i is the *local transition function* of i that predetermines its evolution for any configuration x. Actually, that means that if i is updated in x, its state switches from x_i to $f_i(x)$. Let us define now the *sign of an interaction* from j to i $(i,j \in V)$ in configuration $x \in \mathbb{B}^n$ with $\mathrm{sign}_x(j,i) = s(x_j) \cdot (f_i(x) - f_i(\bar{x}^j))$, where $s : \mathbb{B} \to \mathbb{1}$, with $\mathbb{1} = \{-1,1\}$, is defined as $s(b) = b - \neg b$, and $\forall i \in V$, $\bar{x}^i = (x_0,\ldots,x_{i-1},\neg x_i,x_{i+1},\ldots,x_{n-1})$. Interactions that are *effective* in x belongs to the set $A(x) = \{(j,i) \in V^2 \mid \mathrm{sign}_x(j,i) \neq 0\}$. From this is derived the *interaction graph* of $\mathcal{N}$ that is the digraph $G = (V,A)$, where $A = \bigcup_{x \in \mathbb{B}^n} A(x)$ is the set of interactions.

In this paper, the focus is put on BANs associated with *simple* interaction graphs: if there exists $(i,j) \in A$ such that $\mathrm{sign}_x(i,j) \neq 0$ for configuration x then $\nexists y \neq x$ such that $\mathrm{sign}_y(i,j) = -\mathrm{sign}_x(i,j)$. Thus, $\mathrm{sign}(i,j) \in \mathbb{1}$. If $\mathrm{sign}(i,j) = +1$ (resp. $\mathrm{sign}(i,j) = -1$), (i,j) is an activating (resp. inhibiting) interaction so that the state of j tends to mimic (resp. negate) that of i. We call the *signed interaction graph* of $\mathcal{N}$ the digraph obtained by labelling each arc $(i,j) \in A$ with $\mathrm{sign}(i,j)$. In order not to burden the reading, we also denote it by G. Abusing notations, a *cycle* C of G is said to be *positive* (resp. *negative*) if the product of the signs of the interactions that compose it equals $+1$ (resp. -1).

Asynchronous Transition Graphs. In a BAN $\mathcal{N}$, a pair of configurations $(x,y) \in \mathbb{B}^n \times \mathbb{B}^n$, such that y is obtained by updating the state of a single automaton of x is an *asynchronous transition*, and is denoted by $x \longrightarrow y$ (the Hamming distance $d(x,y) \leq 1$). If $x \neq y$, $x \longrightarrow y$ is said to be *effective*. Let $T = \{x \longrightarrow y \mid x,y \in \mathbb{B}^n\}$ be the set of asynchronous transitions of $\mathcal{N}$. Digraph $\mathcal{G} = (\mathbb{B}^n, T)$ is then the *asynchronous transition graph* (abbreviated simply by *transition graph*) of $\mathcal{N}$, which actually represents the *non-deterministic "perfectly" asynchronous discrete dynamical system* related to $\mathcal{N}$.

Consider an arbitrary BAN $\mathcal{N}$, its transition graph $\mathcal{G} = (\mathbb{B}^n,T)$ and $x \in \mathbb{B}^n$ any of its possible configurations. A *trajectory* of x is any path in $\mathcal{G}$ that starts in x. A strongly connected component of $\mathcal{G}$ that admits no outgoing asynchronous transitions is a *terminal strongly connected component*. Such a component of $\mathcal{G}$ represents an asymptotic behaviour of $\mathcal{N}$, i.e. one of its *attractors*. A configuration that belongs to an attractor is a *recurrent configuration* and, for a given attractor, the number of its configurations is said to be its *size*. An attractor of size 1 (resp. of size greater than 1) is a *stable configuration* (resp. *a stable oscillation*). We conclude this paragraph by defining the *convergence time of a configuration* x as the length of the shortest trajectory that leads it to an attractor and the *convergence time of a BAN* as the highest convergence time of all configurations in $\mathbb{B}^n$.

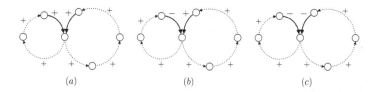

Fig. 1. Interaction graphs of the three kinds of canonical BADCs: (*a*) a canonical positive BADC, (*b*) a canonical mixed BADC, and (*c*) a canonical negative BADC.

Boolean Automata Double-cycles. The literature has put the emphasis on BACs. The reason comes from the three following results (theorems) which show that cycles are necessary for BANs to admit complex asymptotic dynamics.

Theorem 1. *Consider $\mathscr{G}$ as the asynchronous transition graph of a BAN $\mathscr{N}$.*

- *In [19] Whatever the updating mode is, if $\mathscr{N}$ does not contain any cycle, then it admits a unique attractor, that is a stable configuration.*
- *In [16,18,22] If $\mathscr{G}$ admits two stable configurations then the interaction graph of $\mathscr{N}$ contains a positive cycle.*
- *In [16,17,22] If $\mathscr{G}$ admits a stable oscillation then the interaction graph of $\mathscr{N}$ contains a negative cycle.*

On the basis of the theorems above, we propose in this paper to study Boolean automata double-cycles (BADCs) when updated asynchronously. Note that, synchronous (parallel) updated BADCs have already been studied in [1,13]. Informally, a *BADC* $\mathscr{D}$ of size $n+m-1$ is composed of two BACs $\mathscr{C}^\ell$ (of size n) and $\mathscr{C}^r$ (of size m) that intersect tangentially at one automaton that will be denoted specifically, for the sake of clarity in proofs, by c (resp. c_0^ℓ, c_0^r) when considering $\mathscr{D}$ (resp. $\mathscr{C}^\ell$, $\mathscr{C}^r$). Notice that in $\mathscr{D}$, every automaton admits a unary function as its local transition function that is either id or neg, except automaton c that admits a binary function. In this paper, we focus on monotone functions and enforce f_c to be the AND-function without loss of generality for our concern. Also, note that there exist three different kinds of BADCs: *positive BADCs* made of two positive BACs, *negative BADCs* made of two negative BACs, and *mixed BADCs* made of one positive and one negative cycles. An interesting point is that the study of BADCs of size $n+m-1$ in general can be reduced to that of three *canonical* BADCs of size $n+m-1$ [13,14], presented in Fig. 1, because of the isomorphism between their transition graphs. A canonical positive BADC $\mathscr{D}^+$ is composed only of positive interactions. A canonical negative BADC $\mathscr{D}^-$ is composed only of positive interactions, except the two that have c as their destination. A canonical mixed BADC $\mathscr{D}^\pm$ is composed only of positive interactions, except one of those that have c as their destination (we suppose that this interaction belongs to $\mathscr{C}^\ell$). To finish, for easing the proofs, we denote a BADC configuration x by a pair of two binary words, in which the first symbol represents x_c. For instance, the configuration in which all automata are at state $\mathbf{0}$ is denoted by $(\mathbf{0}^n, \mathbf{0}^m)$. Also, we denote by x^ℓ (resp. x^r) the projection of x on cycle $\mathscr{C}^\ell$ (resp. $\mathscr{C}^r$).

Thus, $x = (x^\ell, x^r)$ and the state of automaton c_i^ℓ in configuration x is x_i^ℓ. Note that $x_0 = x_0^\ell = x_0^r$ since these three notations stand for the state of automaton c in configuration x.

3   Algorithmic Tools

In this section, we introduce the tools that will be used further to study the dynamics of BADCs. We introduce first the *expressiveness* of a configuration, which counts the number of its **01** patterns. This notion is inspired by works on asynchronous cellular automata that have shown that the occurrence number of this pattern is crucial to understand their behaviour [3]. Then are introduced *instructions* to represent sequences of updates as classical algorithms. Instructions are used to express long sequences of updates with few lines of code.

3.1   Expressiveness

Definition 1. *Let x be a configuration of a BAC $\mathscr{C}$ of size n. The* expressiveness *of x is the number of* **01** *patterns in x, i.e. $|\{i \mid 0 \leq i \leq n-1, x_i = 0$ and $x_{i+1 \mod n} = 1\}|$.*

From Definition 1, we derive easily the expressiveness of a configuration x of a BADC $\mathscr{D}$ as the sum of the expressivenesses of x^ℓ and x^r. The least expressive configurations are $(\mathbf{0}^n, \mathbf{0}^m)$ and $(\mathbf{1}^n, \mathbf{1}^m)$ and the most expressive ones are $((\mathbf{10})^{\frac{n}{2}}, (\mathbf{10})^{\frac{m}{2}})$ and $((\mathbf{01})^{\frac{n}{2}}, (\mathbf{01})^{\frac{m}{2}})$ (if n and m are even). In the sequel, we will see that: *(i)* the lowly expressive configurations generally are recurrent and can be reached in linear time by most configurations; *(ii)* the highly expressive configurations either are not recurrent or can only be reached through very specific update sequences, and they can quickly reach any other configuration. So, for a BADC $\mathscr{D}$ that admits an attractor of exponential size made of lowly expressive and highly expressive configurations, we will show that: (1) *the shortest path from a highly expressive configuration to any other configuration is linear in n and m*; (2) *the shortest path from a lowly expressive configuration to a highly expressive one is quadratic in n and m.*

3.2   Elementary Instructions

In this article, many proofs of our results [11] rely on exhibiting update sequences between two configurations. However, the length of such sequences is problematic and a human reader would not manage to extract directly from these sequences the general proof ideas. Thus, we propose to view update sequences as *instructions* that allow us to define them and understand their effect on configurations easily.

Let $\mathscr{D}$ be a BADC, $\mathscr{C}$ be one of the BACs of $\mathscr{D}$, x the current configuration of $\mathscr{C}$, and c_i and c_j be two automata of $\mathscr{C}$ different from c and such that $i < j$. In the sequel, we will make particular use of the following elementary instructions:

- sync: $x_c \leftarrow f_c(x)$ # update of c
  sync is the only instruction that updates automaton c and where both BACs interact with each other. This (key)-instruction will always be called when c can change its state. sync can be used either to set c at a desired state or to increase the expressiveness from a configuration. Notice that sync is the only way to switch a **111** (resp. **000**) pattern into a **101** (resp. **010**) pattern and, thus, to increase the expressiveness. Remark that the BAC sub-configurations have to be specific for c to switch its state.
- update(c_i): $x_{c_i} \leftarrow f_{c_i}(x)$ # update of c_i
  update updates an automaton distinct from c.
- incUp($\mathscr{C}, i, j$): for $k = i$ to j do update(c_k)   # incremental updates
  incUp updates consecutive automata in increasing order. In fact, incUp propagates the state of c_{i-1} along $\mathscr{C}$. Notice that if $j < i$ then no automata are updated. Moreover, since $i \neq 0$, c cannot be updated with incUp.
  Property 1. Let x' be the result of applying incUp($\mathscr{C}, i, j$) on configuration x. Then we have: $\forall k \in \{i, \ldots, j\}$, $x'_k = x_{i-1}$ and $\forall k \notin \{i, \ldots, j\}$, $x'_k = x_k$.
- erase($\mathscr{C}$): incUp($\mathscr{C}, 1, \text{size}(\mathscr{C}) - 1$)
  erase is a particular case of incUp, it propagates the state of c_0 along $\mathscr{C}$. As a consequence, using erase on $\mathscr{C}$ decreases it expressiveness to 0.
  Property 2. Let x' be the result of applying erase($\mathscr{C}$) on configuration x. Then we have: $\forall k \in \{0, \ldots, \text{size}(\mathscr{C}) - 1\}$, $x'_k = x_0$.
- expand($\mathscr{C}$): incUp($\mathscr{C}, 1, \kappa - 1 \in \mathbb{N}$) with

$$\kappa = \min_{1 \leq k \leq \text{size}(\mathscr{C}-1)} \left\{ k \mid \begin{cases} (x_k = 0) \text{ and } (x_{k+1 \text{ mod size}(\mathscr{C})} = 1) & \text{if } x_c = 1 \\ (x_k = 1) \text{ and } (x_{k+1 \text{ mod size}(\mathscr{C})} = 0) & \text{if } x_c = 0 \end{cases} \right\}.$$

  expand is another particular case of incUp that aims at propagating the state of c_0 along $\mathscr{C}$ while neither **01** nor **10** patterns are destroyed.
- decUp($\mathscr{C}, i, j$): for $k = j$ down to i do update(c_k)   # decremental updates
  decUp updates consecutive automata by decreasing order. Once decUp($\mathscr{C}, i, j$) executed, the information of c_j is lost and that of c_{i-1} is possessed by both c_{i-1} and c_i. In fact, decUp aims at shifting partially a BAC section. As for incUp, if $j < i$ then no automata are updated and c cannot be updated with decUp.
  Property 3. Let x' be the result of applying decUp($\mathscr{C}, i, j$) on configuration x. Then we have: $\forall k \in \{i, \ldots, j\}$, $x'_k = x_{k-1}$ and $\forall k \notin \{i, \ldots, j\}$, $x'_k = x_k$.
- shift($\mathscr{C}$): decUp($\mathscr{C}, 1, \text{size}(\mathscr{C}) - 1$)
  shift is a particular case of decUp. Once executed, every automaton of $\mathscr{C}$ takes the state of its predecessor, except c whose state does not change. Automaton $c_{\text{size}(\mathscr{C}-1)}$ excluded, all the information contained along $\mathscr{C}$ is kept safe. shift is useful to propagate information along a BAC without losing too much expressiveness (at most one **01** pattern is destroyed).

Table 1. The sequences copy_c, copy and copy_p.

copy_c$(x, x', \mathscr{C}^s)$
01. $n \leftarrow$ size$(\mathscr{C}^s)$;
02. if $(x_{n-1}^s = x_{n-2}^s$ and $x_{n-1}^s \neq x_{n-1}'^s)$ then
03. $j \leftarrow \max\{k \mid k < n-1$ and $x_k^s \neq x_k'^s\}$;
04. else $j \leftarrow n$;
05. end if
06. for $(k = n-1)$ down to $(j+1)$ do
07.   update(c_{k-1}^s);
08.   update(c_k^s);
09. done
10. for $(k = j-1)$ down to (1) do
11.   if $(x_k^s \neq x_k'^s)$ then update(c_k^s);
12.   end if
13. done

copy(x, x')
01. copy_c$(x, x', \mathscr{C}^\ell)$;
02. copy_c$(x, x', \mathscr{C}^r)$;

copy_p(x, x')
01. if $(x_0 \neq x_0')$ then
02.   shift$(\mathscr{C}^\ell)$;
03.   shift$(\mathscr{C}^r)$;
04.   sync;
05. end if
06. copy(x, x');

4   Results

4.1   More Complex Instructions

Now, consider a configuration x of BADC $\mathscr{D}$ and an algorithm made of instructions that defines a sequence of updates (abbreviated simply by "sequence" from now) from x, denoted by sequence(x). Abusing language, in the sequel, sequence(x) represents both the underlying sequence and its result, namely the configuration resulting from the execution of sequence(x). To end this section, we introduce three other sequences in Table 1, more complex, that will be important later. In particular, Lemma 1 states that copy allows to transform x into x' if x is expressive enough (highly expressive actually).

Lemma 1. *Let $\mathscr{D}$ be a BADC and x and x' two of its configurations such that $x_0 = x_0'$. If, for all $s \in \{\ell, r\}$, one of the following properties holds for x:*

1. *$\forall i \in \{1, \ldots, size(\mathscr{C}^s) - 1\}$, $x_i^s \neq x_{i-1}^s$,*
2. *$\forall i \in \{1, \ldots, size(\mathscr{C}^s) - 2\}$, $x_i^s \neq x_{i-1}^s$ and $x_{size(\mathscr{C}^s)-1}^s = x_{size(\mathscr{C}^s)-1}'^s$,*
3. *$\forall i \in \{1, \ldots, size(\mathscr{C}^s) - 2\}$, $x_i^s \neq x_{i-1}^s$ and $\exists p \in \{1, \ldots, size(\mathscr{C}^s) - 2\}, x_p^s \neq x_p'^s$,*

then copy$(x, x') = x'$ and this sequence consists in at most $2(n + m - 6)$ updates.

From this first result that gives strong insights about the power of instructions and sequences to reveal possible trajectories between configurations, let us now focus on the dynamical behaviours of double-cycles. Notice that for not burdening the reading, as for copy and copy_p, $\mathscr{D}$ is always considered as a global variable of the sequences that follow.

Table 2. The sequences fix0 and fix1.

fix0(x)	fix1(x)
01. **if** ($x_0 = 1$) **then**	01. **if** ($x_0 = 0$) **then**
02. $i \leftarrow \min\{k \mid x_k^\ell = 0\}$;	02. $i \leftarrow \min\{k \mid x_k^\ell = 1\}$;
03. incUp($\mathscr{C}^\ell, i+1, n-1$);	03. incUp($\mathscr{C}^\ell, i+1, n-1$);
04. sync;	04. $j \leftarrow \min\{k \mid x_k^r = 1\}$;
05. **end if**	05. incUp($\mathscr{C}^r, j+1, m-1$);
06. erase($\mathscr{C}^\ell$);	06. sync;
07. erase($\mathscr{C}^r$);	07. **end if**
	08. erase($\mathscr{C}^\ell$);
	09. erase($\mathscr{C}^r$);

4.2   Positive BADCs

Since results of [13,14] have shown that positive BADCs behave as positive BACs, and because stable configurations are conserved between distinct updating modes [4], it is easy to show that the asymptotic dynamics of positive BADCs consists in two stable configurations x and $\bar{x}$ (where $\bar{x}$ denotes the negation of x). In the case of canonical BADCs, these stable configurations are $(\mathbf{0}^n, \mathbf{0}^m)$ and $(\mathbf{1}^n, \mathbf{1}^m)$. Here, let us focus on an arbitrary positive BADC $\mathscr{D}^+$. We show that two new sequences fix0 and fix1 (cf. Table 2) can respectively transform any configuration with at least one automaton at state $\mathbf{0}$ into $(\mathbf{0}^n, \mathbf{0}^m)$, and any configuration with at least one automaton at state $\mathbf{1}$ in both cycles into $(\mathbf{1}^n, \mathbf{1}^m)$.

Theorem 2. *Let $\mathscr{D}^+$ be a canonical positive BADC and x one of its unstable configurations. If x admits one automaton at state $\mathbf{0}$, then $fix0(x) = (\mathbf{0}^n, \mathbf{0}^m)$. Also, if x admits one automaton at state 1 in both its cycles, then $fix1(x) = (\mathbf{1}^n, \mathbf{1}^m)$. The convergence time of $\mathscr{D}^+$ is at most $2(n+m) - 5$.*

4.3   Mixed BADCs

Now, we pay attention to mixed BADCs. From the same works [13,14] that showed also that asynchronism keeps only recurrent configurations of least global instability, we know that their asymptotic dynamics consists only in a stable configuration. In particular, the attractor of canonical mixed BADCs is $(\mathbf{0}^n, \mathbf{0}^m)$. Let us focus on their convergence time. To do so, we will make particular use of the new sequence simp (cf. Table 3) that gives a way of converging to this stable configuration from any initial configuration x, by reducing progressively its expressiveness.

Theorem 3. *Let $\mathscr{D}^\pm$ be a canonical mixed BADC. For any configuration x of $\mathscr{D}^\pm$, $simp(x) = (\mathbf{0}^n, \mathbf{0}^m)$ holds. The convergence time of $\mathscr{D}^\pm$ is at most $2n+m-2$.*

Table 3. The sequences simp, comp1 and comp1.

simp(x)
01. if $(x_0 = 1)$ then
02.   erase($\mathscr{C}^\ell$);
03.   sync;
04. end if
05. erase($\mathscr{C}^\ell$);
06. erase($\mathscr{C}^r$);

comp1(x)
01. for $(i = 1)$ to $(n-1)$ do
02.   sync;
03.   expand($\mathscr{C}^\ell$);
04.   erase($\mathscr{C}^r$);
05. done

comp2(x)
01. if $(x^r = 1^m)$ then
02.   sync;
03.   erase($\mathscr{C}^r$);
04. end if
05. sync;
06. expand($\mathscr{C}^r$);
07. for $(i = 1)$ to $(m - 2)$ do
08.   shift($\mathscr{C}^\ell$);
09.   sync;
10.   expand($\mathscr{C}^r$);
11. done

4.4 Negative BADCs

In this section, we are interested in negative BADCs. Contrary to BADCs of other sorts, the previous results of [1,13,14] obtained under the parallel updating mode are not helpful for dealing with the asynchronous updating mode. Indeed, in parallel, negative BADCs admit an exponential number of attractors. In our asynchronous framework, we will show that they admit a unique stable oscillation of exponential size that depends on the parity of underlying cycles. In particular, the study that follows is divided in two axes: the first one deals with BADCs made of two negative cycles of even sizes (abbreviated by $\mathscr{D}_e^-$), the second one with the others where at least one cycle of odd size (abbreviated by $\mathscr{D}_o^-$).

Both Cycles Are Even. Here, we show that any BADC $\mathscr{D}_e^-$ admits only one stable oscillation of size 2^{n+m-1}. In other terms, all configurations are recurrent and the convergence time is null. However, although all configurations are reachable from each other, those of high expressiveness are hard to reach. The proof of this result follows three points (they will be referred to Points 1, 2 and 3 later) in which it is respectively shown that:

1. Any configuration can reach the least expressive one $(\mathbf{0}^n, \mathbf{0}^m)$ in linear time;
2. Configuration $(\mathbf{0}^n, \mathbf{0}^m)$ can reach the highest expressive one $((\mathbf{10})^{\frac{n}{2}}, (\mathbf{10})^{\frac{m}{2}})$ in quadratic time;
3. Any configuration can be reached from $((\mathbf{10})^{\frac{n}{2}}, (\mathbf{10})^{\frac{m}{2}})$ in linear time.

Notice that Point 2 above is the hardest part. Indeed, to reach $((\mathbf{10})^{\frac{n}{2}}, (\mathbf{10})^{\frac{m}{2}})$ from $(\mathbf{0}^n, \mathbf{0}^m)$ needs $O(n^2 + m^2)$ updates. We will see that this upper bound is tight and that to increase a configuration expressiveness by δ requires at least δ^2 updates (cf. Theorem 5).

Let us consider Point 1. It is easy to see that sequence simp is still efficient to reach $(\mathbf{0}^n, \mathbf{0}^m)$ and thus, that the following Lemma holds.

Lemma 2. *For any configuration x of $\mathscr{D}_e^-$, $simp(x) = (\mathbf{0}^n, \mathbf{0}^m)$ holds and takes at most $2n + m - 2$ updates.*

Now, let us pay attention to Point 2 that asks for increasing the expressiveness of $(\mathbf{0}^n, \mathbf{0}^m)$. We characterise here a path from this configuration to $((\mathbf{10})^{\frac{n}{2}}, (\mathbf{10})^{\frac{m}{2}})$. To do so, let us proceed in two steps. The first one aims at increasing the expressiveness of $\mathscr{C}^\ell$ by means of sequence comp1 (cf. Lemma 3), the second at increasing that of $\mathscr{C}^r$ while ensuring not to decrease that of $\mathscr{C}^\ell$ by means of comp2 (cf. Lemma 4). Then, we get directly Lemma 5 with the composition comp = comp2 ∘ comp1.

Lemma 3. *In a BADC $\mathscr{D}_e^-$, comp1$((\mathbf{0}^n, \mathbf{0}^m)) = ((\mathbf{10})^{\frac{n}{2}}, \mathbf{1}^m)$ holds and takes at most $(n-1)(n+m-2)$ updates.*

Lemma 4. *In a BADC $\mathscr{D}_e^-$, comp2$(((\mathbf{10})^{\frac{n}{2}}, \mathbf{1}^m)) = ((\mathbf{10})^{\frac{n}{2}}, (\mathbf{10})^{\frac{m}{2}})$ holds and takes at most $(m-2)(n+m-2) + (2m-1)$ updates.*

Lemma 5. *In a BADC $\mathscr{D}_e^-$, comp$((\mathbf{0}^n, \mathbf{0}^m)) = ((\mathbf{10})^{\frac{n}{2}}, (\mathbf{10})^{\frac{m}{2}})$ holds and takes at most $(n+m)^2 - 5(n-1) - 3m$ updates.*

Point 3 is developed in Lemma 6, in which we make particular use of copy_p (cf. Table 1).

Lemma 6. *In a BADC $\mathscr{D}_e^-$, for any x', copy_p$(((\mathbf{10})^{\frac{n}{2}}, (\mathbf{10})^{\frac{m}{2}}), x')$ transforms configuration $((\mathbf{10})^{\frac{n}{2}}, (\mathbf{10})^{\frac{m}{2}})$ into x' in at most $3(n+m-4) - 1$ updates.*

By combining Lemmas 2, 5 and 6, for all configurations x and x', the composition copy_p(comp(simp(x)), x') = x' holds, which shows that there exists a unique attractor of size 2^{n+m-1}. From this is derived the following theorem.

Theorem 4. *A BADC $\mathscr{D}_e^-$ admits a unique attractor of size 2^{n+m-1}. In this stable oscillation, any configuration can be reached by any other one in $O(n^2 + m^2)$. However, some configurations are specific: $(\mathbf{0}^n, \mathbf{0}^m)$ and $(\mathbf{1}^n, \mathbf{1}^m)$ can be reached from any other one in $O(n+m)$, and configurations $((\mathbf{01})^{\frac{n}{2}}, (\mathbf{01})^{\frac{m}{2}})$ and $((\mathbf{10})^{\frac{n}{2}}, (\mathbf{10})^{\frac{m}{2}})$ can reach any configuration in $O(n+m)$.*

Now we show that the bound $O(n^2 + m^2)$ of Theorem 4 above is tight.

Theorem 5. *Let x be a configuration of a BADC $\mathscr{D}_e^-$. Increasing the expressiveness of x by $\delta \in \mathbb{N}$ needs $\Omega(\delta^2)$ updates.*

Corollary 1 is then directly derived from the two previous theorems, considering that $\delta = \frac{n}{2}$ for $\mathscr{C}^\ell$ and $\delta = \frac{m}{2}$ for $\mathscr{C}^r$.

Corollary 1. *In a BADC $\mathscr{D}_e^-$, to reach $((\mathbf{10})^{\frac{n}{2}}, (\mathbf{10})^{\frac{m}{2}})$ from $(\mathbf{0}^n, \mathbf{0}^m)$ requires $\Theta(n^2 + m^2)$ steps.*

At Least One Cycle Is Odd. Like BADCs $\mathscr{D}_e^-$, BADCs $\mathscr{D}_o^-$ admit only one attractor but contrary to the latter, they also admit a set I of specific non-recurrent configurations, from which updates are "irreversible". In the sequel, abusing language, these configurations are said to be *irreversible*. Lemma 7 below shows the irreversibility of some configurations.

Lemma 7. *Let us consider a BADC $\mathscr{D}_o^-$. The following properties hold:*

1. *If $\mathscr{C}^s$, $s \in \{\ell, r\}$, is of odd size $k > 1$, then configuration x such that $x^s = ((\mathbf{10})^{\frac{k-1}{2}} \mathbf{1})$ is irreversible.*
2. *If both $\mathscr{C}^\ell$ and $\mathscr{C}^r$ are of odd sizes $n > 1$ and $m > 1$, then configuration $((\mathbf{01})^{\frac{n-1}{2}} \mathbf{0}, (\mathbf{01})^{\frac{m-1}{2}} \mathbf{0})$ is irreversible.*

Let I be the set of irreversible configurations of a BADC $\mathscr{D}_o^-$ given by Lemma 7. Theorem 6 below proves that I contains in fact all the irreversible configurations and, from this set, generalises Theorem 4 for any sort of negative BADCs. Notice that the complexity bounds remain valid.

Theorem 6. *Let $\alpha : \mathbb{N} \to \{0,1\}$ with $\alpha(k) = \begin{cases} 0 & \text{if } k = 0 \text{ or } k \equiv 1 \mod 2 \\ 1 & \text{otherwise} \end{cases}$*

Any negative BADC $\mathscr{D}^-$ admits one attractor of size $2^{n+m-1} - |I|$, where $|I| = \alpha(n-1) \times 2^{m-1} + \alpha(m-1) \times 2^{n-1}$.

5   Conclusion and Perspectives

In this paper we focused on the dynamical properties of BADCs subject to the asynchronous updating mode. The general idea was to make a step further to achieve a better understanding of how interaction networks work, given the fact that they are ceaselessly more present in our daily life. Again, the focus on BADCs is explained by the fact that although cycles have been known to be the engines of complexity in interaction networks since the 1980s, their influence on network dynamics is not really understood. However, because of the intrinsic difficulties to bring such studies in general frameworks (in general BANs for instance), we needed to restrain the spectrum of intersections considered to the "simplest" kinds, the tangential ones. In this setting, our contribution was twofold: *(i)* we gave a complete characterisation of the dynamical behaviour of asynchronous BADCs by means of *(ii)* new algorithmic tools that bring a new way to view updates in networks and a nice understanding of how information is relayed. Obviously, these tools have been built for our purpose and their use is consequently limited. Nevertheless, we believe that they can be applied almost directly in some more complex networks, in particular those with tangential cycle intersections, such as flower graphs for which they will help to provide characterisation results regarding their behaviours that will generalise the existence results given in [2]. Furthermore, another perspective would consist of adapting these tools in order to apply them to more complex intersections. Beyond the dynamical aspects, notice that the algorithmic tools presents the benefit of representing concisely long sequences of updates. About this abstraction, we would like to understand to what extent we can characterise network architectures when update sequences (that represent only pieces of dynamics) are given. For instance, the latter could be very useful to find networks of specific dynamics complexity classes (in terms of convergence time for instance, or even in terms of number of attractors). To finish, this work together with that of [13] raises once again the matter of the fundamental differences between synchronism and asynchronism whose study deserves to be pursued.

References

1. Demongeot, J., Noual, M., Sené, S.: Combinatorics of Boolean automata circuits dynamics. Discrete Appl. Math. **160**, 398–415 (2012)
2. Didier, G., Remy, É.: Relations between gene regulatory networks and cell dynamics in Boolean models. Discrete Appl. Math. **160**, 2147–2157 (2012)
3. Fatès, N., Regnault, D., Schabanel, N., Thierry, É.: Asynchronous behavior of double-quiescent elementary cellular automata. In: Correa, J.R., Hevia, A., Kiwi, M. (eds.) LATIN 2006. LNCS, vol. 3887, pp. 455–466. Springer, Heidelberg (2006)
4. Goles, E., Martínez, S.: Neural and Automata Networks: Dynamical Behaviour and Applications. Kluwer Academic Publishers, Norwell (1990)
5. Ising, E.: Beitrag zur theorie des ferromagnetismus. Z. für Phys. **31**, 253–258 (1925)
6. Jacob, F., Monod, J.: Genetic regulatory mechanisms in the synthesis of proteins. J. Mol. Biol. **3**, 318–356 (1961)
7. Jacob, F., Perrin, D., Sanchez, C., Monod, J.: L'opéron: groupe de gènes à expression coordonnée par un opérateur. C. R. Hebdomadaires Acad. Sci. **250**, 1727–1729 (1960)
8. Kauffman, S.A.: Metabolic stability and epigenesis in randomly constructed genetic nets. J. Theor. Biol. **22**, 437–467 (1969)
9. Kauffman, S.A.: Gene regulation networks: A theory for their global structures and behaviors. In: Moscana, A., Monroy, A. (eds.) Current Topics in Development Biology, vol. 6, pp. 145–181. Elsevier, New York (1971)
10. McCulloch, W.S., Pitts, W.H.: A logical calculus of the ideas immanent in nervous activity. Bull. Math. Biophys. **5**, 115–133 (1943)
11. Melliti, T., Noual, M., Regnault, D., Sené, S., Sobieraj, J.: Full characterization of attractors for two intersected asynchronous Boolean automata cycles. Technical report Université d'Évry - Val d'Essonne (2013). arXiv:1310.5747
12. Melliti, T., Regnault, D., Richard, A., Sené, S.: On the convergence of Boolean automata networks without negative cycles. In: Kari, J., Kutrib, M., Malcher, A. (eds.) AUTOMATA 2013. LNCS, vol. 8155, pp. 124–138. Springer, Heidelberg (2013)
13. Noual, M.: Dynamics of circuits and intersecting circuits. In: Dediu, A.-H., Martín-Vide, C. (eds.) LATA 2012. LNCS, vol. 7183, pp. 433–444. Springer, Heidelberg (2012)
14. Noual, M.: Updating automata networks. Ph.D. thesis, École normale supérieure de Lyon (2012)
15. Noual, M., Regnault, D., Sené, S.: About non-monotony in Boolean automata networks. Theoret. Comput. Sci. **504**, 12–25 (2013)
16. Remy, É., Ruet, P., Thieffry, D.: Graphic requirement for multistability and attractive cycles in a Boolean dynamical framework. Adv. Appl. Math. **41**, 335–350 (2008)
17. Richard, A.: Negative circuits and sustained oscillations in asynchronous automata networks. Adv. Appl. Math. **44**, 378–392 (2010)
18. Richard, A., Comet, J.P.: Necessary conditions for multistationarity in discrete dynamical systems. Discrete Appl. Math. **155**, 2403–2413 (2007)

19. Robert, F.: Discrete Iterations: A Metric Study. Springer, Heidelberg (1986)
20. Schelling, T.C.: Dynamic models of segregation. J. Math. Sociol. **1**, 143–186 (1971)
21. Thomas, R.: Boolean formalization of genetic control circuits. J. Theor. Biol. **42**, 563–585 (1973)
22. Thomas, R.: On the relation between the logical structure of systems and their ability to generate multiple steady states or sustained oscillations. In: Dora, J.D., Demongeot, J., Lacolle, B. (eds.) Numerical Methods in the Study of Critical Phenomena. Springer Series in Synergetics, vol. 9, pp. 180–193. Springer, Heidelberg (1981)

Non-cooperative Algorithms in Self-assembly

Pierre-Étienne Meunier[(✉)]

Department of Information and Computer Science,
Aalto University, Espoo, Finland
`pierre-etienne.meunier@aalto.fi`

Abstract. Imagine you are left alone in a forest with ogres and wolves, with a paper, a pen and a supply of small stones as your only weapons. How far can you go using a deterministic escape strategy, if you also want to be back in time for dinner (i.e. avoid running periodically)?

The answer to this question has been known for some time (and called the "pumping lemma") in the simple case where the forest has exactly one self-avoiding trail: after at most 2^n steps (where n is the number of bits writable on your paper) you start running periodically.

However, geometry can sometimes allow for better strategies: in this work, we show the first non-trivial positive algorithmic result (i.e. programs whose output is larger than their size), in a model of self-assembly that has been the center of puzzling open questions for almost 15 years: the planar non-cooperative variant of Winfree's abstract Tile Assembly Model. Despite significant efforts, very little has been known on this model, until the first fully general results on its computational power, proven recently in SODA 2014.

In this model, tiles can stick to an existing assembly as soon as one of their sides matches the existing assembly. This feature contrasts with the general *cooperative* model, where it can be required that tiles match on *several* of their sides in order to bind.

Since the exact computational power of this model is still completely open, we also compare it with classical models from automata theory.

1 Introduction

Whenever you are left alone in an unknown geometric space peopled by ogres (and possibly wolves), you'd better have a sure (i.e. deterministic) strategy to escape. Moreover, fear will not help you remember everything precisely; laying stones along the path, and taking notes in a notebook is probably better. And of course, you want to be back in time for dinner: you must avoid loops (starting to run periodically in the same direction) at all costs!

P.-E. Meunier—Dept. of Information and Computer Science, Aalto University, PO Box 15400, FI-00076, Aalto, Finland and Aix Marseille Université, CNRS, LIF UMR 7279, 13288, Marseille, France. Part of this work was carried out while at California Institute of Technology, Pasadena, CA 91125, USA. Supported in part by National Science Foundation Grant CCF-1219274.

© Springer International Publishing Switzerland 2015
C.S. Calude and M.J. Dinneen (Eds.): UCNC 2015, LNCS 9252, pp. 263–276, 2015.
DOI: 10.1007/978-3-319-21819-9_20

This is in essence the question asked in several contexts in computer science: it is indeed a particular case of *self-avoiding walks*, a model introduced by Flory in 1953 [4] in the context of polymer chemistry, and since then studied by various scientists, such as Knuth [5] in the 1980 s, or Bousquet-Mélou [1] in more recent years.

The formalism that we use in this paper can be seen as an algorithmic, resource-bounded version of this problem, formulated in the context of tile self-assembly. Originally developed as a model of crystal growth [7,8], this model considers the assembly of small square tiles with glues on their borders, where a glue is a pair of a *color* and a *strength*, starting from an initial assembly called a *seed*. The dynamics of this model is asynchronous, and proceeds one tile at a time, not deterministically, subject to the following constraint: a tile can only be placed at a position when the sum of glue strengths, on its sides whose colors match their neighbors, is at least equal to a parameter of the model called the *temperature* $\tau = 1, 2, 3, \ldots$ We will only be concerned in this paper with *temperature 1* self-assembly, which is the model where tiles stick to the current assembly as soon as one of their sides matches their neighborhood.

1.1   Main Results

Here, we present the first efficient constructions in the fully general planar non-cooperative model. The generally accepted definition of an "efficient program", in this context, is a program whose output is larger than its size. Of course, a simple first result on this model shows that arbitrary shapes can be built with a number of tile types equal to the number of tiles in the shape, or (for simpler shapes) equal to the Manhattan diameter of the shape [6].

Surprisingly, our results show that there are tile assembly systems whose terminal assemblies are all larger (in Manhattan diameter) than their number of tile types. Although a number of terms have not been defined yet, we briefly introduce our two main constructions. The first construction can be proven easily by hand; we will demonstrate it first in Sect. 3.1, and then generalize it in Sect. 3.2, to get the following theorem:

Theorem 1. *For all integer n, there is a tile assembly system $\mathcal{T}_n = (T_n, \sigma_n, 1)$ such that $|T_n| = n$, and for all terminal assembly $a \in \mathcal{A}_\square[\mathcal{T}_n]$, a is finite and of height $2n + o(n)$.*

Intuitively, this construction works by preventing subpaths starting and ending with the same tile type to repeat completely.

Understanding the precise computational capabilities of temperature 1 self-assembly has been an open question for quite a long time. We show in Sect. 4 that this model cannot be predicted by pushdown automata, nor by tree automata. Previous work on the relations between self-assembly and formal languages were mostly focused on a variant of self-assembly called *staged self-assembly* [9]. It is known, however, that its 3d generalization can simulate arbitrary Turing machines; understanding the minimal geometric requirements to perform arbitrary computation is therefore one of the most fundamental questions raised by our positive constructions.

In Sect. 4, we define the *language* $\mathcal{L}(\mathcal{T})$ of a tile assembly system $\mathcal{T}$, and compare temperature 1 tile assembly systems to classical automata models:

Theorem 2. *Temperature 1 tile assembly systems without mismatches are equivalent to tree automata of arity at most 3 (Proposition 2).*

On the other hand, there is a (2D) temperature 1 tile assembly systems whose language is not context-free (Proposition 4).

1.2   Key Technical Ideas and Methods

A major challenge, when studying non-cooperative self-assembly, is to overcome the intuition given by the one-dimensional case (which is equivalent to finite automata), that any repetition of a tile type may allow to "pump" an assembly. Indeed, an easy observation shows that assemblies formed at temperature 1 are nothing more than a collection of paths growing from the seed: if a tile type is ever repeated along a path, it is tempting to try to repeat the subpath between these repetitions.

However, geometry makes things more complex. First, there are simple counter-examples to this pumping idea. Moreover, paths could first lay "blocking parts" out, and then come back and branch to check which type of blocker has been formed; this is for instance the primary mechanism used by the simulation of Turing machines in 3d shown in [3]. However, their construction "fakes cooperation" by laying a blocker out for all alternatives but one.

On the other hand, recent (unpublished) progresses tend to show that this kind of "bit reading" gadgets is not possible in two dimensions. This model thus asks a different question: can you write efficient programs without the ability to read your workspace?

Our results show that this is possible, at least to some extent. They do so by carefully considering the fact that paths that are monotonic in one dimension are pumpable; therefore, we must build "caves", i.e. subpaths that are non-monotonic in both dimensions. However, since these are more expensive to build than straight paths, we also need to reuse these extra tile types several times, either by making these subpaths self-blocking (in Sect. 3.2), and branching before the blocking.

These results are quite puzzling and counter-intuitive; however, they do not seem to make Turing computation possible. Therefore, a natural question is the exact power of this model, that depends strongly on geometry, and that no other "classical" model seems to capture, as shown in Sect. 4.

2   Definitions and Preliminaries

We begin by defining the abstract tile assembly model, in a slightly more general framework than usually.

A *tile type* is a unit square with $2n$ sides, each consisting of a glue *label* and a nonnegative integer *strength*. In the most common case where $n = 2$, we call a tile's sides north, east, south, and west, respectively, according to the following picture:

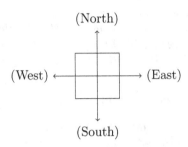

Also, we write these directions N, E, S and W, respectively. When there is no ambiguity, we also write N(t), E(t), S(t) and W(t), to mean the north, east, south and west glue of tile type t, respectively. Moreover, for each direction d, we write $-d$ its opposite direction. We assume a finite set T of tile types, but an infinite supply of copies of each type. An *assembly* is a positioning of the tiles on the grid graph G of $\mathbb{Z}^2$, that is, a partial function $\alpha : G \dashrightarrow T$. To simplify the notations, we will assume $G = \mathbb{Z}^2$ throughout the paper, unless explicitly mentioned.

We say that two tiles in an assembly *interact*, or are *stably attached*, if the glue labels on their abutting side are equal, and have positive strength. An assembly α induces a weighted *binding graph* $G_\alpha = (V_\alpha, E_\alpha)$, where $V_\alpha = \text{dom}(\alpha)$ (the domain of α), and there is an edge $(a, b) \in E_\alpha$ if and only if a and b interact, and this edge is weighted by the glue strength of that interaction. The assembly is said to be τ-stable if any cut of G_α has weight at least τ.

A *tile assembly system* is a triple $\mathcal{T} = (T, \sigma, \tau)$, where T is a finite tile set, σ is called the *seed*, and τ is the *temperature*. Throughout this paper, we will always have $\tau = 1$, and σ will always be an assembly with exactly one tile. Therefore, we can make the simplifying assumption that all glues have strength one without changing the behavior of the model.

Given two τ-stable assemblies α and β, we say that α is a *subassembly* of β, and write $\alpha \sqsubseteq \beta$, if $\text{dom}(\alpha) \subseteq \text{dom}(\beta)$ and for all $p \in \text{dom}(\alpha)$, $\alpha(p) = \beta(p)$. We also write $\alpha \to_1^{\mathcal{T}} \beta$ if we can get β from α by the binding of a single tile, that is, if $\alpha \sqsubseteq \beta$ and $|\text{dom}(\beta) \setminus \text{dom}(\alpha)| = 1$. We say that γ is *producible* from α, and write $\alpha \to^{\mathcal{T}} \gamma$ if there is a (possibly empty) sequence $\alpha = \alpha_1, \ldots, \alpha_n = \gamma$ such that $\alpha_1 \to_1^{\mathcal{T}} \ldots \to_1^{\mathcal{T}} \alpha_n$.

A sequence of $k \in \mathbb{Z}^+ \cup \{\infty\}$ assemblies $\alpha_0, \alpha_1, \ldots$ over $\mathcal{A}[\mathcal{T}]$ is a $\mathcal{T}$-*assembly sequence* if, for all $1 \leq i < k$, $\alpha_{i-1} \to_1^{\mathcal{T}} \alpha_i$.

The set of *productions* of a tile assembly system $\mathcal{T} = (T, \sigma, \tau)$, written $\mathcal{A}[\mathcal{T}]$, is the set of all assemblies producible from σ. An assembly α is called *terminal* if there is no β such that $\alpha \to_1^{\mathcal{T}} \beta$. The set of terminal assemblies is written $\mathcal{A}_\square[\mathcal{T}]$.

The *Manhattan distance* $\|\overrightarrow{AB}\|_1$ between two points $A = (x_A, y_A)$ and $B = (x_B, y_B)$ is $\|\overrightarrow{AB}\|_1 = |x_A - x_B| + |y_A - y_B|$. The *Manhattan diameter* of a connected assembly is the maximal Manhattan distance between two points in the assembly. We write $(u_n)_{n \in \mathbb{N}}$ to mean "the infinite sequence u_0, u_1, u_2, ...".

A *regular tree grammar* $G = (S, N, \mathcal{F}, R)$, according to [2], is given by an *axiom* S, a set N of *nonterminal symbols*, a set $\mathcal{F}$ of *terminal symbols*, and a set R of *production rules* of the form $A \to \beta$ where A is a nonterminal and β is a tree whose nodes are labeled by elements of $\mathcal{F} \cup N$. Moreover, it is required that $\mathcal{F} \cap N = \emptyset$. In this work, we write trees as "nested function applications": for instance, $f(x, g(y, z))$ is the following tree:

The classical example of a regular tree grammar is the grammar of lists of integers, with one axiom *List*, non-terminals *List* and *Nat*, terminals 0, *nil*, $s()$ and $cons(,)$, and the following rules:

$$List \to nil$$
$$List \to cons(Nat, List)$$
$$Nat \to 0$$
$$Nat \to s(Nat)$$

3 Efficient Algorithms

In this section, we show the main ideas of our efficient tileset.

3.1 A First Efficient Algorithm (Large Figures in Appendix A)

In this section, we call a tile assembly system $\mathcal{T} = (T, \sigma, 1)$ *efficient* if there is an integer r, such that the Manhattan diameter of all the terminal assemblies of $\mathcal{T}$ is strictly larger than $|T| + |\mathrm{dom}(\sigma)|$, and at most r.

A simple observation on paths, is that any path that is monotonic in one dimension (i.e. the sequence $(y_{P_i})_i$ of its y-coordinates, or the sequence $(x_{P_i})_i$ of its x-coordinates is monotonic), and repeats a tile type, is pumpable.

Therefore, the main ingredient of efficient paths is non-monotonicity: we call a *vertical cave* (respectively *horizontal cave*) a part of a path P between two indices i and j, such that (1) $y_{P_i} = y_{P_j}$, (2) for all $k < i$, $y_{P_k} \leq y_{P_i}$, and (3) for all $k \in \{i+1, i+2, \ldots, j-1\}$, $y_{P_k} < y_{P_i}$.

Theorem 3. *For all integer n, there is a tile assembly system $\mathcal{T}_n = (T_n, \sigma_n, 1)$ such that $|T_n| = n$, and for all terminal assembly $a \in \mathcal{A}_\square[\mathcal{T}_n]$, a is finite and of height $\frac{5(n+2)}{4} - 23$.*

Proof. Let T_0 be the set of tiles appearing on the lower right assembly of Fig. 1, and σ_0 be the upper left assembly of that figure.

This tileset has 38 tile types, and its terminal assemblies are of height 27; it is not efficient yet. But we will now add a number of new tile types to make it efficient. First replace the following glues (zoom in on Fig. 1 to see these glue numbers, or see the large version in Appendix A):

- glue 6 by $(6, 0)$ on the north, and $(6, n)$ on the south,
- glue 14 by $(14, 0)$ on the north, and $(14, n)$ on the south,
- glue 24 by $(24, 0)$ on the north, and $(24, n)$ on the south,
- glue 26 by $(26, 0)$ on the north, and $(26, n)$ on the south,

And then for all $i \in \{6, 14, 24, 26\}$ and $j \in \{0, 1, \ldots, n-1\}$, add a tile type to T, with south glue (i, j) and north glue $(i, j+1)$. In total, we have added $4n$ tile types, but the terminal assemblies of T grow $5n$ higher. See Fig. 2 for a larger example (saving tile type). $\qquad\square$

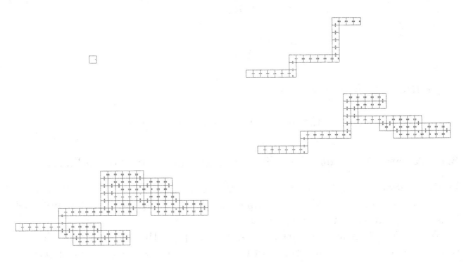

Fig. 1. Four successive stages of the construction: first the seed, then the main path grows, and finally, additional branches can also grow completely, along the main path.

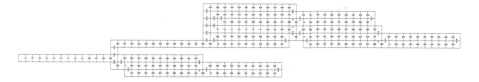

Fig. 2. An efficient tile assembly system, producing an assembly of width 112 with 106 tile types. This terminal assembly grew from a seed containing only its leftmost tile.

3.2 A More General Scheme

In the construction of Theorem 3, repetitions of a tile type are done at the expense of width of the assembly: indeed, in order to avoid collisions between repeated paths, each repetition needs to be more and more narrow. Generalizing this remark yields the following Theorem:

Theorem 1. *For all integer n, there is a tile assembly system $\mathcal{T}_n = (T_n, \sigma_n, 1)$ such that $|T_n| = n$, and for all terminal assembly $a \in \mathcal{A}_\square[\mathcal{T}_n]$, a is finite and of height $2n + o(n)$.*

Proof. The idea is to repeat the construction of Theorem 3 more than a constant number of times. A single cave, of height h (see Fig. 3), will be reused N times, and at each iteration $i \in \{0, 1, \ldots, N\}$, grow to height $2h - i$.

To do this, we use a sequence of assemblies as shown on Fig. 3, with different widths $(w_n)_n$. The general idea of this construction is: grow some construction starting with tile type t, then use some modification of the initial cave as a blocker, and then reuse t.

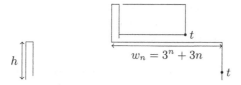

Fig. 3. The repeated part is shown on the left-hand side. The drawing on the right-hand side is a scheme of one step of the construction.

Then, we stack these parts on top of each other: on the Fig. 4, the next assembly, drawn in dashed line, is of width $w_{n-1} = 3^{n-1} + 3(n-1)$. In order to avoid making a pumpable path, we do not grow the full initial cave each time, but a smaller and smaller suffix of it at each iteration.

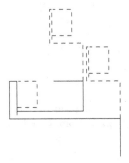

Fig. 4. Two successive iterations.

Because of this choice of widths, successive assemblies cannot collide with each other, and different repetitions of the same assembly cannot collide with each other either.

Let h be the height of the initial cave. For all integer n, the nth repetition requires $w_n + 2w_{n-1} \leq 2w_n$ new tiles horizontally, $h - n$ tiles vertically, and grows to a height of $2(h - n)$. If we decide to repeat the construction $N = \log h$ times, we need $|T| = 2\sum_{i=1}^{N} w_n + Nh + O(N^2)$ tile types, i.e. $h \log h + O(h)$ tile types.

Moreover, in this case, all terminal assemblies will have height $2h \log h + O(N^2)$, which is $2|T| + o(|T|)$.   □

4   Comparison with Automata

The constructions of Sect. 3 show the intricate connections between geometry and the computational power of temperature 1 self-assembly, raising the question of the exact characterization of the model, from the point of view of classical computational models. In this section, we show that we are far from understanding these relations.

When comparing tile assembly with automata theory, a first challenge is to find a mapping between tile assembly systems and languages. We introduce this mapping in the two definitions below, whose important length is due to the gap in formalisms between tile assembly and formal language theory.

In Proposition 1, we show an example of how to use these definitions. Also, remark in these definitions that the tree languages of the Turing machine simulations in [3] are not recognizable by tree automata.

Definition 1. *Let* $\mathcal{T} = (T, \sigma, 1)$ *be a temperature 1 tile assembly system where* σ *is single-tile seed assembly. We call* $\mathcal{L}(\mathcal{T})$, *the* language *of* $\mathcal{T}$, *the tree language recognized by the following tree grammar:*

– *For each tile* $t \in T$, *with glues* g_N *on the north,* g_E *on the east,* g_S *on the south, and* g_W *on the west,* $\mathcal{A}$ *has the four following production rules:*

$$N_{g_N} \rightarrow N(E_{g_E}, S_{g_S}, W_{g_W})$$
$$E_{g_E} \rightarrow E(S_{g_S}, W_{g_W}, N_{g_N})$$
$$S_{g_S} \rightarrow S(W_{g_W}, N_{g_N}, E_{g_E})$$
$$W_{g_W} \rightarrow W(N_{g_N}, E_{g_E}, S_{g_S})$$

– *Moreover, for each glue* g *appearing on the north (respectively south, west and east side) of some tile of* T, *add a terminal symbol* n_g *(respectively* s_g, w_g, e_g) *to the grammar, and the following rules:*

$$N_g \rightarrow n_g$$
$$E_g \rightarrow e_g$$
$$S_g \rightarrow s_g$$
$$W_g \rightarrow w_g$$

– *Finally, add a nonterminal symbol* S, *and the following rule:*

$$S \rightarrow \Sigma(N_{\sigma_N}, E_{\sigma_E}, S_{\sigma_S}, W_{\sigma_W})$$

Where σ_N, σ_E, σ_S *and* σ_W *are the north, east, south and west glues of the unique tile of* σ, *respectively.*

Definition 2. *Let* $\mathcal{T} = (T, \sigma, 1)$ *be a temperature 1 tile assembly system. A term* t *of* $\mathcal{L}(\mathcal{T})$ *describes the following assembly sequence:*

– *From* $\Sigma(N_{\sigma_N}, E_{\sigma_E}, S_{\sigma_S}, W_{\sigma_W})$, *concatenate the four assembly sequences obtained from* N_{σ_N}, E_{σ_E}, S_{σ_S}, W_{σ_W}, *successively.*
– *Let* $\alpha(x, y, n, N(E_{t_E}, S_{t_S}, W_{t_W}))$ *be concatenation of the following sequences:*
  • *the assembly of the unique tile type* $t \in T$ *with north glue* n, *east glue* t_E, *south glue* t_S *and west glue* t_W, *at position* (x, y).
  • *assembly sequence* $\alpha(x + 1, y, t_E, E_{t_E})$.
  • *assembly sequence* $\alpha(x - 1, y, t_W, W_{t_W})$.
  • *assembly sequence* $\alpha(x, y - 1, t_S, S_{t_S})$.
– *Similarly for* $\alpha(x, y, e, E(S_{t_S}, W_{t_W}, N_{t_N}))$, $\alpha(x, y, s, S(W_{t_W}, N_{t_N}, E_{t_E}))$, *and* $\alpha(x, y, w, W(N_{t_N}, E_{t_E}, S_{t_S}))$.
– *For terminals* t *of the form* n_g, s_g, e_g *or* w_g, *let* $\alpha(x, y, g, t)$ *be the empty assembly sequence.*

By extension, if this assembly sequence results in a producible assembly $a \in \mathcal{A}[\mathcal{T}]$, *we say that* t describes a. *Moreover, if all the terms of some tree language* L *describe a producible assembly of* $\mathcal{T}$, *and all producible assemblies of* $\mathcal{T}$ *are described by some term* $t \in L$, *we say that* L describes $\mathcal{A}[\mathcal{T}]$.

When all the nodes of terms of $\mathcal{L}(T)$ have at most one nonterminal child, this tree language is also a word language, over alphabet T.

As an example of these definitions, we re-prove a result from [8], using the formalism introduced in the above definitions[1].

Proposition 1. *Let A be a non-deterministic finite automaton on alphabet S. There is a (one-dimensional) tile assembly system $T_A = (T_A, \sigma_A, 1)$ such that $\mathcal{L}(A)$ describes $\mathcal{A}_\square[T_A]$.*

Proof. Let $A = (Q, \Sigma, \Delta, q_0, F)$ be any non-deterministic finite automaton, with Q its set of states, Σ its alphabet, $\Delta \in Q \times \Sigma \times Q$ its transition relation, q_0 its start state and F its set of final states.

We build an "equivalent" temperature 1 tile assembly system $T_A = (T_A, \sigma_A, 1)$, where T_A is a tileset with glue colors from Q, by letting:

- t_σ be a tile with exactly one non-zero strength glue, on its east side, with color q_0.
- for each $(q, s, q') \in \Delta$, $\delta_{(q,s,q')}$ be a tile with color q on its west side, q' on its east side, and s on its north side.
- for each $q \in F$, f_q be a tile with color q on its east side, and no other non-zero strength glue.

Then, let $T_a = \{t_\sigma\} \cup \{\delta_{(q,s,q')} | (q, s, q') \in \Delta\} \cup \{f_q | q \in F\}$, and σ_A be an assembly with exactly one tile of type t_σ, at position $(0, 0)$.

Clearly, the language $\mathcal{L}(A)$ recognized by A describes the terminal assemblies of $T_A = (T_A, \sigma_A, 1)$.   □

Proposition 2. *For any temperature 1 tile assembly system $T = (T, \sigma, 1)$ without mismatches, and such that σ is a connected assembly, there is a nondeterministic top-down tree automaton whose language describes $\mathcal{A}[T]$.*

Proof. Clearly, since there are no mismatches in the productions of T, every assembly described by $\mathcal{L}(T)$ is producible by T. The other direction (producible assemblies of T are described by $\mathcal{L}(T)$ is immediate.   □

When mismatches are allowed, the correspondance between tile assembly and the "1D languages" is not as clear, as exemplified by the following proposition:

Proposition 3. *There is a temperature 1 tile assembly system T such that $\mathcal{L}(T)$ describes assembly sequences not producible by T.*

---

[1] We would like to thank an anonymous reviewer for pointing out the equivalence with the known result.

Proof. Let T be the following tileset:

$$T = \left\{ t_0 = \boxed{}^{a}, t_1 = \boxed{}_{a}^{a}, t_2 = \boxed{}_{a}^{a\dashv}, t_3 = \vdash a \quad a \dashv, \right.$$

$$\left. t_4 = \vdash a \boxed{}_{b}, t_5 = \boxed{}_{b}^{b}, t_6 = \vdash c \boxed{}^{b}, t_7 = \vdash c \quad c \dashv \right\}$$

Let σ be the assembly with a single tile of type t_0.

We claim that for $\mathcal{T} = (T, \sigma, 1)$, $\mathcal{L}(\mathcal{T})$ describes assembly sequences not representing any assembly. First, since all the tiles of T can attach to at most two tiles, we can completely describe assembly sequences as words on T. Let L be the language of all assembly sequences (L is therefore a word language on alphabet T).

Since $\mathcal{L}(\mathcal{T})$ is a regular tree language, L is a regular language, and is therefore recognized by a deterministic finite automaton A. Let n be the number of states of A, and let $u = t_0 t_1^n t_2 t_4 t_5^{n+1} t_6 t_7^{10}$. Moreover, for $i \in \{0, 1, \ldots, |u| - 1\}$, let a_i be the state in which A is just before letter u_i. Since there are $n+1$ occurrences of t_5 in u, at least two distinct indices i and j, in subword t_5^{n+1} of u, are such that $a_i = a_j$.

This means that the following word, which does not described any production of $\mathcal{T}$, is recognized: $t_0 t_1^n t_2 t_4 t_5^{n+1-b+a} t_6 t_7^{10}$. $\qquad\square$

Proposition 4. *There is a temperature 1 tile assembly system $\mathcal{T} = (T, \sigma, 1)$ such that $\mathcal{L}(\mathcal{T})$ is a non-context-free word language on alphabet T.*

Proof. Let T be the following tileset:

$$T = \left\{ t_0 = \boxed{}^{a_0}, t_1 = \boxed{}_{a_0}^{a_1}, t_2 = \boxed{}_{a_1}^{b\dashv}, t_3 = \vdash b \quad b \dashv, t_4 = \vdash b \boxed{}_{c_2}, t_5 = \boxed{}_{c_1}^{c_2}, \right.$$

$$\left. t_6 = \vdash d \boxed{}^{c_1}, t_7 = \vdash d \quad d \dashv, t_8 = \boxed{}_{d}^{e}, t_9 = \boxed{}_{e}^{f\dashv}, t_{10} = \vdash f \quad f \dashv \right\}$$

Since all tiles of T have exactly two sides of non-zero strength, the tree language $\mathcal{L}(\mathcal{T})$ is actually also a word language, on alphabet T. However, the language L of the productions of T is the union of the language M describing the terminal assemblies of $\mathcal{T}$, with all the prefixes of these assemblies. Formally, M is the following language:

$$M = \{t_0 t_1 t_2 t_3^a t_4 t_5 t_6 t_7^b t_8 t_9 t_{10}^c | a > b \geq c\} \cup \{t_0 t_1 t_2 t_3^a t_4 t_5 t_6 t_7^a | a \in \mathbb{N}\}$$

Moreover, by the pumping Lemma on pushdown automata, this means if L were context-free, then it would also contain words of the form $t_0 t_1 t_2 t_3^a t_4 t_5 t_6 t_7^b$ $t_8 t_9 t_{10}^c$ in which either $c > b$ or $b \geq a$, which is not the case. Indeed, for all a, M contains the following word:

$$t_0 t_1 t_2 t_3^{a+1} t_4 t_5 t_6 t_7^a t_8 t_9 t_{10}^a$$

Therefore, the pumping lemma states that L were context-free, it would also contain:

- Either $t_0 t_1 t_2 t_3^{a+1-b} t_4 t_5 t_6 t_7^{a-b} t_8 t_9 t_{10}^a$ for some $b < a$. However, this word is not in L.
- Or $t_0 t_1 t_2 t_3^{a+1} t_4 t_5 t_6 t_7^{a+b} t_8 t_9 t_{10}^{a+b}$ for some $b > 0$, which is also not in L.
- Or $t_0 t_1 t_2 t_3^{a+1+b} t_4 t_5 t_6 t_7^a t_8 t_9 t_{10}^{a+b}$ for some $b > 0$, which is also not in L.   □

5   Open Problems and Discussion

Despite our efficient constructions, planar temperature 1 tile assembly model does not seem capable of Turing computation. Finding the limits of these constructions would give us a greater understanding of these processes, ubiquitous in natural systems:

Open Problem 1. *What is the largest integer s, such that all the terminal assemblies of a tile assembly system with n tiles and a single-tile seed, are of size s?*

Another question, left open by Sect. 4, is the exact characterization of this model, in terms of classical models.

Acknowledgements. The author thanks Damien Woods for insightful comments and discussions, and one of the anonymous reviewer whose expertise helped improved this paper quite a lot.

A   A Printable Version of Fig. 1

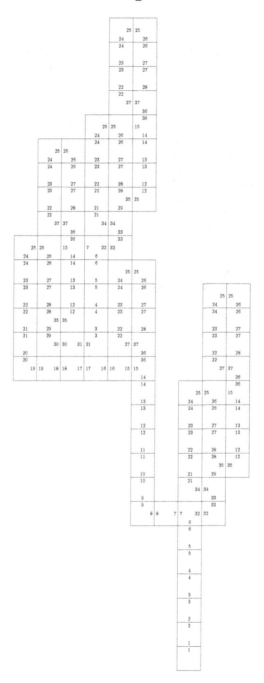

References

1. Bousquet-Mélou, M.: Families of prudent self-avoiding walks. J. Comb. Theory Ser. A **117**(3), 313–344 (2010)
2. Comon, H., Dauchet, M., Gilleron, R., Jacquemard, F., Lugiez, D., Löding, C., Tison, S., Tommasi, M.: Tree automata techniques and applications (2007). http://www.grappa.univ-lille3.fr/tata. Accessed 12 October 2007
3. Cook, M., Fu, Y., Schweller, R.T.: Temperature 1 self-assembly: deterministic assembly in 3D and probabilistic assembly in 2D. In: Proceedings of SODA 2011, pp. 570–589 (2011). Arxiv preprint: arXiv:0912.0027
4. Flory, P.J.: Principles of Polymer Chemistry. Cornell University, Ithaca (1953)
5. Knuth, D.E.: Mathematics and computer science: coping with finiteness. Math. People Prob. Results **2**, 210–211 (1984)
6. Rothemund, P.W.K., Winfree, E.: The program-size complexity of self-assembled squares (extended abstract). In: STOC 2000, Portland, Oregon, United States, pp. 459–468. ACM (2000)
7. Seeman, N.C.: Nucleic-acid junctions and lattices. J. Theor. Biol. **99**, 237–247 (1982)
8. Winfree, E.: Algorithmic self-assembly of DNA. Ph.D. thesis, California Institute of Technology, June 1998
9. Winslow, A.: Staged self-assembly and polyomino context-free grammars. In: Soloveichik, D., Yurke, B. (eds.) DNA 2013. LNCS, vol. 8141, pp. 174–188. Springer, Heidelberg (2013)

Tangle Machines

Daniel Moskovich and Avishy Y. Carmi[✉]

Faculty of Engineering Sciences,
Center for Quantum Information Science and Technology,
Ben-Gurion University of the Negev, 8410501 Beersheba, Israel
avcarmi@bgu.ac.il

Abstract. Tangle machines are topologically inspired diagrammatic models. The novel feature of tangle machines is their natural notion of equivalence. Equivalent tangle machines may differ locally, but globally they share the same information content. The goal of tangle machine equivalence is to provide a context-independent method to select, from among many ways to perform a task, the 'best' way to perform the task. The concept of equivalent tangle machines is illustrated through an example in which tangle machines represent networks for distributed information processing.

1 Introduction

1.1 The Idea in a Nutshell

This paper, which is a pared-down version of (Carmi and Moskovich 2015), introduces a diagrammatic formalism for computation and for information processing. Behind this endeavor is the observation that the combinatorial properties of knot diagrams mimic principles pertaining to conservation and to manipulation of information in networks.

We construct diagrammatic models called *tangle machines*, represented by labeled versions of diagrams such as those of Fig. 1, that represent entities and relationships between those entities. Unlike labeled graphs, in which edge e from vertex a to vertex b represents a transition from the label of a to the label of b, the basic building block of a tangle machine is an *interaction*, in which *agent* c causes a transition from colours of *input patients* $a_1, a_2, \ldots, a_k$ to colours of corresponding *output patients* $b_1, b_2, \ldots, b_k$. A machine makes explicit the *cause* of a transition. From one perspective, a machine is a computational scheme, a sort of "planar algorithm" wherein interactions simulate basic computations. From the dual perspective, a machine is a network within which information is manipulated at interactions and then transmitted further down to registers in other interactions. Information can be both a patient (*e.g.* an input data stream) and an agent (*e.g.* commands of a computer programme). This aspect of information is captured by tangle machines but not necessarily by labeled graphs.

The novel feature of tangle machines is their flexibility. Whereas competing graphical models are rigid, tangle machines admit a natural local notion of *equivalence*. Roughly speaking, two machines are equivalent if one can be perfectly

C.S. Calude and M.J. Dinneen (Eds.): UCNC 2015, LNCS 9252, pp. 277–289, 2015.
DOI: 10.1007/978-3-319-21819-9_21

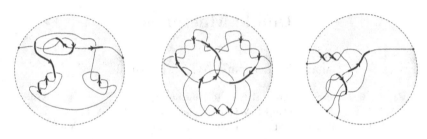

Fig. 1. Three different tangle machines with colours suppressed.

reproduced from the other. Machine equivalence parallels the notion of *ambient isotopy* in low dimensional topology. Local features such as implementation and performance of computations or information manipulations modeled by the tangle machine may be different for networks modeled by equivalent machines, but we consider their *information content* to be the same. We may thus use the tangle machine formalism to select, from among many equivalent models which 'perform the same task', the model (and thus the network) best suited for a specified application. This concept is illustrated in our examples.

In regard to the computational power of tangle machines, we prove elsewhere that tangle machines with a bounded number of interactions can decide any language in complexity class IP (Carmi and Moskovich 2014b).

We represent networks of distributed information processing in Sect. 3 using machines. In this example three equivalent machines are presented, one 'optimal', one 'suboptimal', and one 'abstract'. This illustrates the operational meaning of machine equivalence.

1.2   Scientific Context

Turing machines are the heart of theory of computation and complexity theory. They formalize the notion of an algorithm or of an effective procedure, and they define the class of computable functions. There are many profound interrelationships between Turing machines, and related notions of computation, and low dimensional topology, usually concerning computability of various topologically relevant functions.

The present paper suggests that coloured knots, tangles, spaces, and related structures can themselves be computers. Indeed, the term *tangle machine* imitates *Turing machine*. The *computation* of a tangle machine involves reading off colours of a chosen set of *output registers* given a colouring of a chosen set of *input registers* (assuming that the latter uniquely dictates the former). A tangle machine may thus capture a certain sort of network computation.

The idea to model computations using tangle diagrams and related structures from low dimensional topology was pioneered by Louis Kauffman. Kauffman used knot and tangle diagrams to study automata (Kauffman 1994), nonstandard set theory, and lambda calculus (Kauffman 1995, Buliga and Kauffman 2013). The diagrammatic calculus of braids (braids are a special class of tangles) also lies at the basis of topological quantum computing— see *e.g.* (Kauffman and Lomonaco 2004). In another direction, a different diagrammatic calculus, originating in higher category theory, has been used in the theory of quantum information— see *e.g.* (Abramsky and Coecke 2009, Baez and Stay 2011).

Despite many shared keywords, our approach is conceptually different from all of the above. We consider a 'crossing' (which we call an *interaction*) to represent a computation (in the sense of computer science or of automata) or a fusion of information whose basic symmetries are encapsulated by the three *Reidemeister moves* of Fig. 4 which generate machine equivalence. Topology suggests that these three local rewrite moves are in a sense different aspects of a single operation consisting of rotating a plane onto which an embedded object is projected. We call the reader's attention to the Reidemeister move R3 which manifests a distributivity axiom (Eq. 1). Tangle machines place primary emphasis on a distributive property of computation and of information (compare Roscoe 1990), as opposed to other approaches in which the lead role is played by associativity of a 'stacking' operation. Also, in contrast with other approaches, tangle machines are coloured. Colours of registers represent information and are a fundamental part of our structure. Interactions are coloured by binary operations representing fusion or computation schemes, which may differ for different interactions. A further difference is that our interactions cannot be merged or split. In addition, only our overstrands are oriented, and their orientations are independent of one another. For these reason we do not believe that it is possible to usefully reformulate tangle machines in the language of braided monoidal categories, that is the language of categorical quantum mechanics. Indeed, we have not yet found direct overlap between our applications and the applications of other low-dimensional topological approaches to computation.

2   Machines and Machine Equivalence

2.1   The Set of Labels of a Machine: A Quandle

We consider a set Q equipped with a set of binary operations $B\colon Q \times Q \to Q$. We think of elements of Q as representing *pieces of information* and of elements of B, which we call *updates*, as representing *information fusion*. An example of an information fusion operation is given in Sect. 3.

Our updates are required to satisfy three properties (Ishii 2013, Przytycki 2011):

Idempotence: $x \triangleright x = x$ for all $x \in Q$ and for all $\triangleright \in B$.

Reversibility: The map $\triangleright y\colon Q \to Q$ which send each $x \in Q$ to a corresponding element $x \triangleright y \in Q$ is a bijection for all $(y, \triangleright) \in (Q, B)$. In particular, if $x \triangleright y = z \triangleright y$ for some $x, y, z \in Q$ and for some $\triangleright \in B$, then $x = z$. We interpret this condition to mean that information fusion does not forget information, because x can uniquely be reconstructed from knowledge $x \triangleright y$, $\triangleright$, and y.

Distributivity: For all $x, y, z \in Q$ and for all $\triangleright, \blacktriangleright \in B$:

$$(x \triangleright y) \blacktriangleright z = (x \blacktriangleright z) \triangleright (y \blacktriangleright z) \tag{1}$$

We interpret this equation to mean that information fusion eliminates redundancy. Thus, information z which appeared once in $x \blacktriangleright z$ and once in $y \blacktriangleright z$ is not double-counted towards $(x \blacktriangleright z) \triangleright (y \blacktriangleright z)$.

We call (Q, B) a *B–family of quandles* or just a *quandle*. We list several archetypal examples of B–families of quandles.

Example 21 (Conjugation Quandle). Colours might be elements of a group Γ, and the operation might be conjugation:

$$x \blacktriangleright y \stackrel{\text{def}}{=} y^{-1}xy. \tag{2}$$

The pair $(\Gamma, \{\blacktriangleright\})$ is called a *conjugation quandle*. Such quandles feature in knot theory, *e.g.* Joyce (1982).

Example 22 (Linear Quandle). Colours might be elements of a real vector space Q and the operations might be convex combinations:

$$x \triangleright_s y \stackrel{\text{def}}{=} (1 - s)x + sy \qquad s \in \mathbb{R} \setminus \{1\}. \tag{3}$$

The pair $\left(Q, \{\triangleright_s\}_{s \in \mathbb{R} \setminus \{1\}}\right)$ is called a *linear quandle*. Our example in Sect. 3 involves linear quandles.

Example 23 (Loglinear quandle). In the same setting as Example 22, consider the operations:

$$x \bar{\triangleright}_s y \stackrel{\text{def}}{=} x^{1-s}y^s \qquad s \in \mathbb{R} \setminus \{1\}. \tag{4}$$

The pair $\left(Q, \{\bar{\triangleright}_s\}_{s \in \mathbb{R} \setminus \{1\}}\right)$ is called a *loglinear quandle*. In (Buliga and Kauffman 2014a) we have exhibited several standard information fusion operations, such as covariance intersection, as quandle operations of quotients of loglinear quandle.

2.2 Inductive Definition of Tangle Machines

The fundamental building block of a machine is an *interaction*. The simplest interaction is graphically depicted as

$$x \; -\!\!\!\left|\!\!\!\begin{array}{c} y \\ \\ \end{array}\right.\!\!\!- \; x \triangleright y$$

This describes initial information x (called the *input patient*) being updated by new information y (called the *agent*) to obtain updated information $x \triangleright y$ (called the *output patient*). The updating operation $\triangleright$ may differ for different interactions. The colours x, y, and $x \triangleright y$ are elements of a quandle (Q, B). We name the strands being coloured as *registers*. The assignments of colours to registers and of binary operations to interactions is called *colouring*.

One register in an interaction may update multiple registers. In this case the agent is drawn as a thick line. For example, with colours suppressed and with a dotted line to indicate that it may be a part of a larger machine:

$$(5)$$

A general tangle machine is obtained by concatenating a disjoint union of a finite number of interactions and building blocks which look like  Concatenation is the process of connecting endpoints of a tangle machine. See Fig. 2.

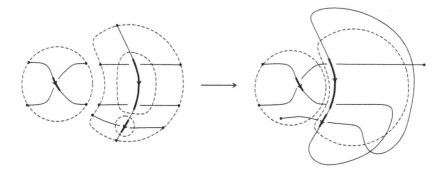

Fig. 2. Concatenation. Endpoints can be concatenated if they share the same colours (colours are suppressed in the above figure). At the third stage, note that in our formalism, only agents are oriented, and no compatibility requirement is imposed. The concatenation line chosen is arbitrary, and in particular it may intersect other concatenation lines.

Remark 24. Our diagrammatic model of machines as concatenations of interactions is inspired by diagrammatic formalisms in low dimensional topology. The field of *combinatorial knot theory* studies knots as planar diagrams instead of as embedded objects in 3–space. These diagrams are decomposed into *tangles* (Conway 1970). Knots and tangles are modified by *local moves*, which replace one tangle within a knot by another. Knots are thus revealed to be algebraic objects arising as concatenations of crossings (which are very simple tangles) in the plane (Jones 1999). Dropping the requirement that concatenation be planar, Kauffman defined *virtual tangles* (Kauffman 1999). A strengthening of the equivalence relation imposed on virtual tangles gives rise to w-tangles. Our diagrammatic construction is most similar to the diagrammatic calculus of w-tangles (Bar-Natan and Dancso 2013), which form an algebra over a *modular operad* (Getzler and Kapranov 1998). The differences are that our diagrams are coloured, that we allow multiple quandle operations, and also that our interactions cannot be split or merged. Also, no compatibility is required of orientations of concatenated agents, as in the theory of *disoriented tangles* (Clark et al. 2009).

For rigourous definitions, see (Carmi and Moskovich 2015). Examples of tangle machines are scattered throughout the paper.

2.3   Machine Equivalence

The main feature of machines is their a natural local notion of equivalence. First, we do not ascribe physical meaning to colours, but only to differences between colours. Thus, if change the colouring of a machine M by an action of an automorphism of (Q, B) inside a disc D, where M does not intersect the boundary of D, then the resulting machine M' is considered to be equivalent to M.

Secondly, as in graph theory, intersections between edges in diagrams of machines 'do not really exist', and can be added or taken away at will by one of the modifications $VR1$, $VR2$ and $VR3$ in Fig. 3. This amounts to choosing different concatenating lines when recursively building the machine out of interactions. Moves $I1$, $I2$, and $I3$ relate local pictures which express the same inputs changing to the same outputs as a result of the same agent. And move ST allows us to add and delete agents which do not act on anything.

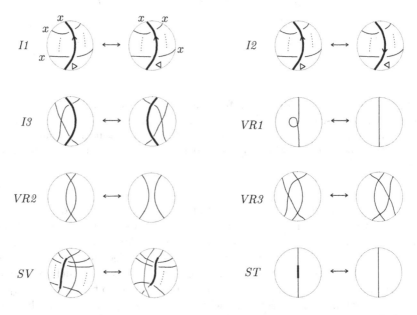

Fig. 3. Cosmetic Reidemeister moves for machines. Where directions are not indicated, the meaning is that the move is valid for any directions, and the same for colourings.

Third, updates performed by a single agent should be thought of as simultaneous. Thus, the two diagrams below, whose diagrams differ by permutation of input-output pairs (on the LHS the agent. indicated by the thick line, appears first to update process A and then process B, while on the RHS it appears first

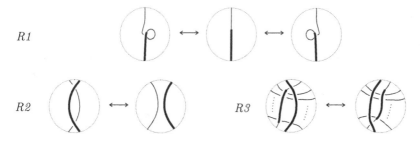

Fig. 4. Reidemeister moves for machines, valid for any directions of the agents and for any colouring.

to update process B and then process A), depict equivalent machine:

$$A \quad B \quad \longleftrightarrow \quad A \quad B \tag{6}$$

Fourth, the Reidemeister moves, R1, R2 and R3 of Fig. 4 embody the defining axioms of (Q, B). This is illustrated in Figures(7a), (7b), and (7c), which reflect idempotence, reversibility, and distibutivity respectively (in each equation designated colours on either sides of the arrow are equal). Note that reversibility implies the existence of an inverse operation $\triangleleft$ for each $\triangleright \in B$ such that $(x \triangleright y) \triangleleft y = x$ for all $x, y \in Q$. Machines related via a finite sequence of Reidemeister moves are considered equivalent.

$$\overline{x} \qquad \overline{x \triangleright x} \\ x \quad \longleftrightarrow \quad x \tag{7a}$$

$$y \quad \overline{x} \qquad y \quad \overline{(x \triangleright y) \triangleleft y} \\ y \quad x \quad \longleftrightarrow \quad y \quad x \tag{7b}$$

$$x \quad z \quad y \blacktriangleright z \qquad x \quad z \quad y \blacktriangleright z \\ y \quad z \quad (x \triangleright y) \blacktriangleright z \quad \longleftrightarrow \quad y \quad z \quad (x \blacktriangleright z) \triangleright (y \blacktriangleright z) \tag{7c}$$

To summarize:

Definition 25. *Tangle machines M and M' are considered* equivalent *if they (or rather their restrictions to a closed disk outside which they both consist only of rays to infinity) are related by an automorphism of (Q, B) together with planar isotopies and a finite number of the local moves of Figs. 3 and 4.*

For an example of equivalent machines see Fig. 5.

Fig. 5. An example of machine equivalence.

3   Machines and Information

The concept of computation is broad, and extends beyond calculating the answer to a prescribed problem. Perhaps the most general characterization of computation is that it is 'a manipulation or processing of information'. Computation and information are intertwined, and these two concepts rely heavily on one another.

In this section, machines are conceived of as a class of networks for distributed information processing. The colours represent information entropies. The information processing capacity associated with an interaction, called its *local capacity*, is defined to be the difference between initial and terminal colours. A machine M represents a network within which information is processed and sent further down to other interactions or registers. A machine equivalent to M is a network which, as a whole, exhibits an information processing capacity the same as M, but whose local capacities may be different.

Our definitions in this section follow (Cover and Joy 2006). We take note that the reader may not be fully acquainted with this field and hence maintain expositions as informal as possible.

We colour machines by the linear quandle (Q, B) whose elements are real numbers, with an operation

$$x \vartriangleright_s y \overset{\text{def}}{=} (1 - s)x + sy$$

for each $s \neq 1$. To recap, each register r is coloured by a real number $n_r \neq 1$, and it acts on each of its patients via either $\vartriangleright_{n_r}$ or $\vartriangleleft_{n_r}$. In this section, elements of Q represent entropies.

3.1   Preliminary Definitions

An *information channel* is an apparatus through which messages are transmitted from one location to another. In practical situations, a message entering the channel on one end will emerge corrupted on the other end. It is convenient to think of a message as a sequence of zeroes and ones. An information channel is characterized by its *capacity*, that is the maximal rate at which messages may be transmitted with a 'negligible' loss of information. Entropy is a measure of information, or rather, of uncertainty. If a message is constructed by sampling N independent identically distributed (iid) binary random variables, then Shannon's Source Coding Theorem tells us that, for *typical sequences*, the entropy times N is nearly the number of information units (*e.g.* bits) required to encode a message so that it can reliably be recovered by a receiver.

Compressible messages exhibit some kind of pattern ($H < 1$), and these admit shorter descriptions than the length of the message itself. This is the key principle underlying message compression. *Incompressible* messages are messages for which randomness inhibits descriptions shorter than the message own length (*i.e.* $H = 1$).

A general computing device (*e.g.* a universal Turing machine) requires two distinct inputs. The first input $\mathcal{X}_0$ is a stream of data that is read and manipulated by the machine according to instructions given by the second input $\mathcal{X}_1$. Both inputs $\mathcal{X}_0$ and $\mathcal{X}_1$ and the *result* of a computation $\mathcal{X}_{\text{out}}$ are all assumed to be typical binary sequences.

3.2   Information Processing by Machines

A machine describing an information processing network is a concatenation of interactions. Each of its registers is coloured by a real number representing an entropy. The colour of an agent register represents the entropy of a programme typical sequence, while colours of input registers represent entropies of data typical sequences. The agent register is equipped with a parameter $s \in (0,1)$, which may represent some (input-independent) property of the computing device itself. The colour of the output corresponding to input $H(\mathcal{X}_0)$ is:

$$H(\mathcal{X}_0) \rhd_s H(\mathcal{X}_1) \stackrel{\text{def}}{=} (1 - s)H(\mathcal{X}_0) + sH(\mathcal{X}_1). \tag{8}$$

If $H(\mathcal{X}_0) > H(\mathcal{X}_1)$ then the output entropy is strictly lower than the input entropy, *i.e.* $H(\mathcal{X}_0) \rhd_s H(\mathcal{X}_1) < H(\mathcal{X}_0)$.

Thus, the computing device computed $\mathcal{X}_{\text{out}}$ by applying the instruction data steam $\mathcal{X}_1$ to the input data stream $\mathcal{X}_0$, and the entropy of $\mathcal{X}_{\text{out}}$ is $H(\mathcal{X}_0) \rhd_s H(\mathcal{X}_1)$. See Fig. 6.

3.3   Capacity

In this section we describe various capacities associated to machines, which provide a measure of how 'good' a computation is. Our analysis of a computing

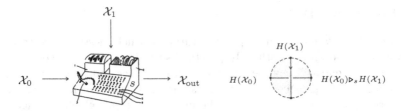

Fig. 6. The computation, and the corresponding interaction between entropies.

device whose internal workings are unknown to us focusses on discrepancies between its input and output streams. Suppose that we wish to know if the computation is meaningful in some sense. If no additional restrictions are made, then "meaningful" might mean that computations produce intelligible answers which could read off by a human operator. Translating this requirement into the language of preceding paragraphs, the output stream is expected to appear 'less random' than the input stream. According to this paradigm, computation and compression are literally the same thing. A 'good computation' is one which compresses $\mathcal{X}_0$ as much as possible, *given* $\mathcal{X}_1$. In the language of information theory, the optimal output $\mathcal{X}_{\text{out}}$ has entropy equal to the *conditional entropy* $H(\mathcal{X}_1 \mid \mathcal{X}_0)$. The *channel capacity* of the computing device is defined as the *mutual information*:

$$I(\mathcal{X}_1 : \mathcal{X}_0) \stackrel{\text{def}}{=} H(\mathcal{X}_1) - H(\mathcal{X}_1 \mid \mathcal{X}_0). \tag{9}$$

The *capacity* of a *process* (that is, a chain of registers connected by concatenation and by being input-output pairs of an interaction) is the entropy of its initial register minus the entropy of its terminal register. For example, for an interaction with a single input-output pair:

$$\text{Cap}_s \left(\text{In} \;\;\;\;\; \text{Out} \right) \stackrel{\text{def}}{=} \underbrace{H(\mathcal{X}_0)}_{\text{In}} - \underbrace{H(\mathcal{X}_0) \rhd_s H(\mathcal{X}_1)}_{\text{Out}} \tag{10}$$

An interaction is *optimal* if its capacity equals its the mutual information:

$$H(\mathcal{X}_0) - H(\mathcal{X}_0) \rhd_s H(\mathcal{X}_1) = I(\mathcal{X}_0 : \mathcal{X}_1) \tag{11}$$

which occurs when $H(\mathcal{X}_0) \rhd_s H(\mathcal{X}_1) = H(\mathcal{X}_0 \mid \mathcal{X}_1)$.

The *global capacity* of a machine is the set of all capacities of its processes.

3.4   Equivalent Machines

Consider the three equivalent machines in Fig. 7. As the three machines are equivalent, they have the same global capacities. But the capacities of their

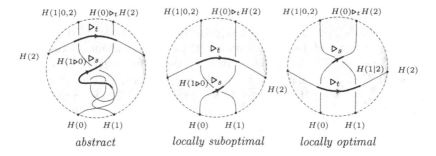

Fig. 7. Equivalent machines with the same global information processing capacities. The middle and right machines are feasible whereas the left machine is abstract. While all of them are globally optimal only the rightmost machine is also locally optimal.

interactions are quite different, and the leftmost machine represents an impossible, *abstract* computation.

Set the following values of t and s:

$$t \stackrel{\text{def}}{=} \frac{H(1) - H(1 \mid 2)}{H(1) - H(2)}, \quad s \stackrel{\text{def}}{=} \frac{H(1 \mid 2) - H(1 \mid 0, 2)}{H(1 \mid 2) - H(0) \triangleright_t H(2)}. \tag{12}$$

In order to assure that $t, s \in (0, 1)$, we choose our entropies so that:

$$H(1 \mid 2) > H(2), \quad H(1 \mid 0, 2) > H(0) \triangleright_t H(2) , \tag{13}$$

which essentially describe the extent to which the sources, $\mathcal{X}_0$, $\mathcal{X}_1$, and $\mathcal{X}_2$, are statistically dependent.

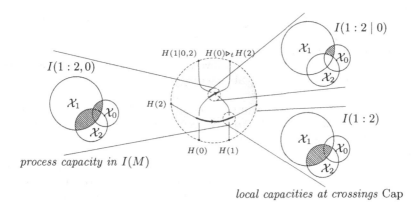

Fig. 8. Optimal information processing along a process P_1 in the rightmost (locally optimal) machine in Fig. 7.

All three machines are globally optimal, but the local capacities for the three machines in Fig. 7 are different. In the rightmost machine, by our choices of t

and s, each interaction is locally optimal— see Fig. 8. This is no longer true for the middle machine, which has a register labeled $H(1 \triangleright 0) \stackrel{\text{def}}{=} H(1) \triangleright_s H(0)$, which may not equal $H(1 \mid 0)$. In this case, the middle machine contains a non-optimal interaction. The left machine involves the inverse operation $\triangleleft_s$, so that its colour $H(1) \triangleleft_s H(0)$ might be negative. The idea of negative entropies may sound absurd, but nevertheless the leftmost machine in Fig. 7 is equivalent to a machine all of whose computations are feasible, and in fact even optimal. In view of this, we may think of this machine as a sort of *abstract* information processing scheme.

4   Conclusion

We have introduced tangle machines as a diagrammatic algebra uniting ideas in low-dimensional topology, information, and computation. There is a natural local notion of tangle machine equivalence. We have exhibited ways in which machine equivalence may represent networks with identical global properties, but with different local properties, within a certain paradigm of computation. Our vision is to model other complex real-world phenomena by machines, then to use machine equivalence to select a 'best' machine (whatever 'best' means in that context), and then to perform a computation for that 'best' machine which might not have been tractable for the machine that we started with.

References

Abramsky, S., Coecke, B.: Categorical quantum mechanics. In: Handbook of Quantum Logic and Quantum Structures, vol. 2, pp. 261–323 (2009). http://arxiv.org/abs/0808.1023

Baez, J., Stay, M.: Physics, topology, logic and computation: a Rosetta Stone. In: Coecke, B. (ed.) New Structures for Physics. LNP, vol. 813, pp. 95–172. Springer, Heidelberg (2011). arXiv:0903.0340

Bar-Natan, D., Dancso, S.: Finite type invariants of w-knotted objects i: w-knots and the Alexander polynomial. Manuscript submitted for publication (2013). arXiv:1405.1956

Buliga, M., Kauffman, L.: GLC actors, artificial chemical connectomes, topological issues and knots. In: ALIFE 14: Proceedings of the Fourteenth International Conference on the Synthesis and Simulation of Living Systems, pp. 490–497 (2013). arXiv:1312.4333v1

Carmi, A.Y., Moskovich, D.: Low dimensional topology of information fusion. In: BICT14: Proceedings of the 8th International Conference on Bio-inspired Information and Communications Technologies, ACM/EAI, pp. 251–258 (2014). arXiv:1409.5505

Carmi, A.Y., Moskovich, D.: Computing with coloured tangles. Manuscript submitted for publication (2014). arXiv:1408.2685

Carmi, A.Y., Moskovich, D.: Tangle machines. Proc. R. Soc. A **471**, 20150111 (2015). doi:10.1098/rspa.2015.0111

Clark, D., Morrison, S., Walker, K.: Fixing the functoriality of Khovanov homology. Geom. Topol. **13**(3), 1499–1582 (2009)

Conway, J.H.: An enumeration of knots and links, and some of their algebraic properties. In: Leech, J. (ed.) 1967 Proceedings Conference Computational Problems in Abstract Algebra, Oxford, pp. 329–358. Pergamon Press, Oxford, England (1970)

Cover, T.M., Joy, T.A.: Elements of Information Theory, 2nd edn. Wiley-Interscience, New York (1991)

Getzler, E., Kapranov, M.: Modular operads. Compos. Math. **110**(1), 65–126 (1998). arXiv:dg-ga/9408003

Ishii, A., Iwakiri, M., Jang, Y., Oshiro, K.: A G-family of quandles and handlebody-knots. Illinois J. Math. **57**, 817–838 (2013). arXiv:1205.1855

Jones, V.F.R.: Planar algebras I. Preprint (1999). arXiv:math/9909027

Joyce, D.: A classifying invariant of knots: the knot quandle. J. Pure Appl. algebra **23**, 37–65 (1982)

Kauffman, L.H.: Knot automata. In: Conference Proceedings of Twenty-Fourth International Symposium on Multiple-Valued Logic, 25-27 May 1994, pp. 328–333. IEEE Computer Society Press, Boston, Massachusetts (1994)

Kauffman, L.H.: Knot logic. In: Kauffman, L. (ed.) Knots and applications, Series of Knots and Everything, vol. 6, pp. 1–110. World Scientific Publications (1995)

Kauffman, L.H.: Virtual knot theory. Europ. J. Comb. **20**(7), 663–690 (1999). arXiv:math/9811028

Kauffman, L.H., Lomonaco Jr, S.J.: Braiding operators are universal quantum gates. New J. Phys. **6**(1), 134 (2004). arXiv:quant-ph/0401090

Przytycki, J.H.: Distributivity versus associativity in the homology theory of algebraic structures. Demonstr. Math. **44**(4), 823–869 (2011). arXiv:1109.4850

Roscoe, A.W.: Consistency in distributed databases. Oxford University Computing Laboratory Technical Monograph PRG-87 (1990)

Formalisation vs. Understanding
A Case Study in Isabelle

Declan Thompson[(✉)]

Department of Computer Science, University of Auckland, Auckland, New Zealand
declanthompsonnz@gmail.com

Abstract. We discuss how formalisation using proof assistants, an unconventional way of doing mathematics which seems to disregard Gödel's celebrated Incompleteness Theorems, interacts with ideas of understanding. Our experience is based on a formalisation carried out in the Isabelle generic proof assistant.

1 Introduction

Gödel's Incompleteness Theorems tell us that there are true but unprovable statements. No formal system is able to prove every true statement, and so automated proof assistants are guaranteed to never be wholly effective. Nonetheless, proof assistants are being used on larger and larger scales. This leads to a strange circumstance - we know proof assistants are ultimately doomed to fail, yet we still use them for formalisation. Conventionally, if something is proved impossible, we stop pursuing it. Formalisation leads to us putting aside Gödel's Theorems and testing how much we really can prove formally. It leads to a wholly unconventional way of doing mathematics.

Much thought is often given to the syntactical implications of Gödel's Theorems. While mathematics is syntactically limited by the Theorems, from a practical point of view we seem to be able to overcome this. However the difficulties arising in semantics are much harder to pin down. By its very nature, semantics is less conducive to formalisation than syntax, and so specific limitations are hard to describe. Related is the subjective notion of *understanding*, which is itself difficult to define. A less conventional view of proofs is that they serve not only to verify a statement, but also to provide some understanding as to why that statement is true.[1] In a 2009 paper by Calude and Müller [4], the authors propose a series of symptoms of understanding. These attempt to capture the idea of mathematical understanding, with reference to proofs and proof assistants.

Formalising a proof or concept involves ensuring that each step or notion is explicitly defined and explained, that no detail has been overlooked. In conventional mathematics proofs are not formalised, since much extra effort is required for what is perceived to be an uninformative task. A major objection to the use

---

[1] Our thanks to a reviewer for highlighting this unconventional view of proofs.

C.S. Calude and M.J. Dinneen (Eds.): UCNC 2015, LNCS 9252, pp. 290–300, 2015.
DOI: 10.1007/978-3-319-21819-9_22

of formal proofs is that they hinder understanding of the very concepts they are proving. If we take understanding to be fundamentally linked to proof, then this hindrance would preclude formal proofs from being proofs at all. The fundamental issue we seek to address in this paper is how the process of formalisation can help (or hinder) the process of understanding. We consider understanding in the context of Calude and Müller's symptoms.

We have undertaken a case study in formalisation in the Isabelle interactive proof assistant [1]. The area of formalisation was computability theory, specifically the formalisation of theorems appearing in [3]. Here we give impressions on the process undertaken and focus less on the formalisation itself than how it was achieved. Our findings are as follows.

- A discussion of the merits and difficulties of using Isabelle to formalise computability theory, including suggestions for improvements and additions to what is currently possible.
- Comments on the process of formalisation generally, and its relation to the concept of mathematical understanding.

This report has been written entirely within the Isabelle system.

2   The Isabelle Generic Proof Assistant

We begin with a brief discussion of the Isabelle generic proof assistant, upon which our experiences are based. Isabelle is derived from the Higher Order Logic (HOL) theorem proving software, which in turn is a descendant of Logic for Computable Functions (LCF) [5]. It is based on a small core set of logical principles from which theories can be built up. As such, the confidence with which we can claim any theorem proven in Isabelle to be true is the same confidence with which we can claim that small core is true.

Isabelle provides a formal language to work in, and a set of proof methods, which allow it to prove statements using logical rules, definitions, and axioms, as well as already proved statements. Proofs in Isabelle are essentially natural deduction style. A structured proof language, Isar, is provided which aims to make proofs more human readable, and which serves to greatly reduce the learning curve required to use Isabelle. Isabelle is developed jointly at the University of Cambridge, Technische Universität München and Université Paris-Sud [1].

The currently recommended interface for Isabelle is jEdit,[2] which is packaged with the distribution. This interface allows for correct parsing of special symbols in theories, and integrates well with Isabelle output. Syntax highlighting makes clear which statements are being processed, and when a proof is taking longer than might be expected. This results in a very useable interface, with a low learning curve.

---

[2] http://www.jedit.org/.

General Usage and Proof Methods. Isabelle provides a variety of tools for formalisation. Datatypes can be specified and built up from existing datatypes. Definitions for concepts can be expressed in a number of ways. Both recursive and non-recursive functions can be defined, and this can be inductive.

Propositions can be proved in Isabelle through the use of *lemmas, theorems* and *corollarys*. In keeping with general practice, these have no semantic difference in their use, and so distinctions can be arbitrarily made [2]. Proofs of propositions are given using any of a range of proof methods and, as with informal proofs, deductions can often be completed in a number of ways.

The *metis* proof method is supplied with previously proved propositions, and attempts to use these to prove the current goal. Metis can take some time as it searches for solutions to problems, but it is very useful when all the theorems needed to prove the goal are explicitly known. The more powerful *simp* proof method attempts to solve the goal by way of simplification rules and general reasoning. Any lemma can be marked as a simplification rule, which *simp* will make use of automatically. *simp* has access to far more resources than *metis* and will often run faster, though it is important to note that *simp* can be over zealous and fail where *metis* succeeds. *auto*, which calls *simp* as a subroutine, is more powerful still, and is adept at handling first-order logic applications, especially those involving quantifier rules. For even more advanced logic, *blast*, *fastforce* and *force* are provided. A wide variety of other proof methods exist, including *rule* for applications directly matching previously proved results and *ind-cases*, which is used for rule inversion with inductive definitions [6].

Proofs in Isabelle can be completed in two main ways: by applications of proof methods to the lemma, or through the Isar proof language. The latter of these closely models the style of informal proofs, and so allows for greater human readability as well as a reduction in the learning curve required for formalisation. As an example of the distinction, we give two proofs for the same result. First, we give a proof without Isar.

lemma $(x::nat) * (x - 1) \leq x\char`^2$
by (*metis comm-semiring-1-class.normalizing-semiring-rules*(29)
  comm-semiring-1-class.normalizing-semiring-rules(7) *diff-le-self mult-le-mono1*)

We simply supply *metis* with the required results to prove the statement. In many cases it is convenient and tidy to have a proof as short as this, however by way of exemplar, we give a fully detailed Isar proof.

lemma $(x::nat) * (x - 1) \leq x\char`^2$
proof (*induction x*)
case *0*
  show $(0::nat) * (0 - 1) \leq 0^2$ **by** *simp*
next case (*Suc x*)
  have $Suc\ x * (Suc\ x - 1) = (Suc\ x)*(Suc\ x) - (Suc\ x)$ **by** *simp*
  moreover have $(Suc\ x)*(Suc\ x) - (Suc\ x) \leq (Suc\ x)\char`^2$
    by (*metis diff-le-self power2-eq-square*)
  ultimately show *?case* **by** *simp*
qed

Isabelle actively interacts with the user during proofs such as that above, offering help as to what the current goals are, any counter examples it has found and information on why proof methods may have failed.

Sledgehammer is an incredibly useful tool built into Isabelle. Sledgehammer uses a number of external automated theorem provers and searches all available facts in an attempt to prove the current goal. The result is (generally) a *metis* command explicitly listing which facts are required. In this manner, sledgehammer provides an efficient means to search for the particular theorem needed to reach the goal.

3   Formalisation as a Tool for Understanding

A proof is "something that proves a statement; evidence or argument establishing a fact or the truth of anything" [7]. Mathematically, a proof is a "sequence of steps by which a theorem or other statement is derived from given premises" [7]. While informal proofs are the norm in most areas of mathematics and computer science, formal proofs such as those created in Isabelle are becoming more practical. It is readily apparent that a formal proof of a statement is more reliable than an informal proof - we need not appeal to any leaps of faith or intuition, and can (at least in principal) verify every step of the proof.

A question which naturally arises when discussing formal proof is that of understanding. Do formal proofs hinder understanding or help it? In their 2009 paper [4], Calude and Müller discuss this question, and more fundamentally the question of what understanding really means. They propose a series of symptoms of understanding, and discuss how these relate to formal theorem proving. Further, they envisage an *active proof environment* (APE), "in which users can write and check formal proofs as well as query them with reference to the symptoms of understanding".

In this section, we discuss the experience of formalisation from this perspective. We consider the interaction of formalisation and understanding and explore how well Isabelle matches the ideals of an APE, both from the perspective of a reader and a writer of proofs.

Formalisation in Isabelle immediately provides a number of the symptoms of understanding given in [4].

Symptom 1. Fill in simple details of the proof, like explication of notation and definitions.

Symptom 4. Cast the proof in different terms.

Symptom 7. Give natural examples and counter-examples for various notions used in the proof.

Symptom 20. Program (parts of) the proof in a programming language.

The last of these is clearly satisfied by formalisation in Isabelle, which uses a process very similar to programming. Since a formalisation requires all details to be complete, Symptom 1 is achieved. By rewriting an informal proof formally, we change radically the style of the proof, clearly an instance of Symptom 4.

Symptom 7 is provided by tools such as *AutoQuickcheck*, which searches for counterexamples to the current goal.

3.1   Facts and Assumptions

An important feature of formalisation we encountered was the explicit realisation of which facts and assumptions were required in order to deduce a proposition. In many cases, underlying assumptions not immediately obvious were uncovered. In other cases, assumptions that seemed necessary were in fact superfluous. These relate closely to the second, eighth and eleventh symptoms of understanding given in [4]:

Symptom 2. Justify other results implicitly used in the proof and inferences..
Symptom 8. Indicate where certain hypotheses are needed.
Symptom 11. Discuss interesting modifications of hypotheses and their corresponding modifications of conclusions.

A good example of the impact of unexpectedly required assumptions is the use of $\mathbb{N}$ for recursive functions, rather than $\mathbb{Z}^+$, which is what appeared in the source [3]. The addition of the number 0 changed a number of important properties in one function, with the result that some of our theorem statements differ from that given informally. This gives an instance of Symptom 11.

An interesting issue which arose when proving one proposition surrounded the definition of another function. We defined this function in three ways and were able to show correctness for all three definitions, but termination on appropriate inputs (which was critical) only for one. While all three definitions intuitively matched the informal definition given in [3], only one led to the required conclusion. This is another instance of Symptom 11.

The use of assumptions is made clear in Isabelle by the fact that they must be referenced by *assms* whenever used. It is thus easy to tell from the proof where the assumptions are required and where they are not, showing Symptom 8. If assumptions are not used at all, they can safely be removed, giving a stronger proof. The reader may have noticed that the inductive hypothesis was not used in the inductive proof in Sect. 2 (it would have been referenced by *Suc.IH*). This suggests that induction may not be necessary there. A good improvement would be if Isabelle were able to highlight such unused assumptions in a manner similar to how Integrated Developer Environments often highlight unused variables.

The *sledgehammer* tool is also very useful from this perspective. While it may seem that some understanding is lost through the application of *sledgehammer*, in practice, it is useful mainly for locating the names of theorems which the user already knows exist. The result of sledgehammer is a *metis* command which explicitly states which assumptions, facts and theorems are being used to prove the goal, demonstrating Symptom 2.

A notable ommission in our formalisation is the explicit expression of the concept of infinity. We implicitly give this by stating various propositions to be dependent on arbitrary universal functions. Since there are infinitely many universal functions, this implies that the propositions hold for infinitely many cases. However, it could be seen that formalising this information would constitute a large project of its own. While arguably a mark against formalisation, this reinforces that concepts we informally take for granted are in fact subtly complex.

3.2   A Higher Level of Constructive Proof

As [4] notes, "a constructive proof gives more insight than a non-constructive argument".

Symptom 19. Recognise the constructive or non-constructive character of a proof.

Formalisation of computability theory can arguably lead to a more constructive proof for certain statements. For example, in proofs of universality, we actively constructed the required functions, and proved that our constructions met the requirements of the definition. Rather than claiming such functions could exist, or inferring their computability from abstract results, we built the functions from scratch and demonstrated their correctness. In some cases we were even able to construct a working Isabelle function for that given in the proofs, another symptom of understanding.

Symptom 14. Calculate a quantity used in the proof.

For one function defined informally in [3], we constructed an Isabelle function which successfully calculated values of the function. In this way, we were able to check that the function was behaving as expected (on small inputs). It was interesting to see how long the function took to calculate values, as this gave an idea of the efficiency of the algorithm.

3.3   Balancing Understanding and Tedium

An interplay was observed during formalisation between the ideas of understanding and tedium.

A type of proof that was avoided as much as practicable was that involving the manipulation of algebraic expressions, especially with a mixture of natural and real numbers, and functions defined only on naturals or only on reals. It could charitably be said that such proofs are best avoided. It is interesting to compare the process of manipulating expressions by pen and paper with the level of formalisation required to achieve the same results in Isabelle. An error that reappeared many times involved the requirement that numerals be given explicit types in some cases. Expressions involving, for example, $2\,\hat{}\,m$ sometimes need to be specified more carefully as $(2::nat)\,\hat{}\,m$. This simple inclusion of a type allows a myriad of theorems to apply to the phrase, but is easy to forget. It is interesting to note that were we completing a formalisation in a different domain such details could be the focus of our work. Rather than being a tedious means to an higher level end, they would be the very fundamental operations we would be studying. The relevant level of understanding is dependent on the field being studied. While it would be tempting to automate such proofs to a greater degree in proof assistants, consideration must be given to the field being formalised.

In other cases we found that Isabelle proofs could be very brief where a human would require more detail. For example, consider the following proofs of correctness for a recursive function (using the formalisation from [8]). The first proof is entirely obscure.

lemma *rec-exec (Cn 1 (Pr 1 (id 1 0) (id 3 1)) [z, (id 1 0)]) [x] = x − 1*
by *simp*

For the second proof, we use Isar to explain how this function works.

lemma *rec-exec (Cn 1 (Pr 1 (id 1 0) (id 3 1)) [z, (id 1 0)]) [x] = x − 1*
proof *cases*
assume *First:x = 0*
   then have *rec-exec (Cn 1 (Pr 1 (id 1 0) (id 3 1)) [z, (id 1 0)]) [x] = rec-exec (Pr 1 (id 1 0) (id 3 1)) [0, 0]*
      by *simp*
   moreover have *rec-exec (Pr 1 (id 1 0) (id 3 1)) [0, 0] = rec-exec (id 1 0) [0]* **by** *simp*
   ultimately have *rec-exec (Cn 1 (Pr 1 (id 1 0) (id 3 1)) [z, (id 1 0)]) [x] = 0* **by** *simp*
   thus *?thesis* **using** *First* **by** *simp*
next assume *Second:x ≠ 0*
   then have *rec-exec (Cn 1 (Pr 1 (id 1 0) (id 3 1)) [z, (id 1 0)]) [x] = rec-exec (Pr 1 (id 1 0) (id 3 1)) [0, x]*
      by *simp*
   moreover have *rec-exec (Pr 1 (id 1 0) (id 3 1)) [0, x] = rec-exec (id 3 1) [0, x − 1, rec-exec (Pr 1 (id 1 0) (id 3 1)) [0, x − 1]]*
      using *Second* **by** *simp*
   moreover have *rec-exec (id 3 1) [0, x − 1, rec-exec (Pr 1 (id 1 0) (id 3 1)) [0, x − 1]] = x − 1*
      by *simp*
   ultimately show *rec-exec (Cn 1 (Pr 1 (id 1 0) (id 3 1)) [z, (id 1 0)]) [x] = x − 1*
by *simp*
qed

This second proof is still not "complete" - each step is not explicitly described. However, it elucidates greatly on why the function gives that output when compared with the first proof. We have refrained from commenting within the proof to reinforce this point - at each step only one or two basic applications of the definitions for recursive functions are used.

A striking difference appears here between our intuition of what a formal proof should be, and the realisation in Isabelle. The first proof could charitably be described as "brief". However, a formal proof is meant to provide every detail, so intuitively it should be much longer than an informal proof. In the second proof, the level of detail is wholly unnecessary for the Isabelle system, yet it seems to more closely resemble what we would expect as a formal proof (or even an informal proof). Were we to try to convince a human that the lemma was true, the first proof would almost certainly not suffice. So where is the ability to test correctness? How can a reader perform, as Hilbert put it, "a mechanical procedure that will check whether the proof is correct or not, whether it obeys the rules or not" when the proof is *by simp*? The answer is by studying the code which makes up Isabelle, and deriving a proof by themselves. This seems highly unsatisfactory. While the first proof may technically constitute a formal proof in the strict sense, it does not seem in the right spirit. In practice, we can only rely upon the Isabelle system; the first proof is like saying "because I said so", without giving any compelling reason.

3.4   The Reader and the Prover

A difference may readily be discerned between the level of understanding a formal proof gives the prover versus reader. It would seem that formal proofs offer a huge window of insight to the prover, but may be quite opaque to the reader.

An example of this is in the abstraction of goals. When proving a statement, it is convenient to abstract the current goal, and prove a more general statement of a given step. In this way, proofs are kept to a manageable length, and general statements are able to be reused. A negative effect is that the reader is presented with a seemingly irrelevant proof, the justification for which is only provided later. It is up to the prover to explain a general overview of the theory, and why each proposition is proved when it is. This clearly fails the requirements of a few symptoms of understanding from [4]:

Symptom 3. Give presentations of the proof for different audiences having various degrees of expertise.
Symptom 5. Motivate the proof.

This seems a problem for formalisation. If formal proofs are to be used extensively, they need to be human understandable. At present, they often do not meet this criterion for humans not involved in the proof process. A solution to this problem may be to present theories with only the high level lemmas, with more detailed proofs available by selecting the appropriate theorem references.

In fact, the process of abstraction can hinder understanding even on the part of the prover. A difficulty which regularly appeared was that of losing sight of the goal, or proving without motivation. This situation occurs easily in Isabelle and is characterised by a series of incomplete proofs, each dependent on the last. When proving high level theorems, many abstractions present themselves easily. It is very easy to become deeply involved in such proofs, and end up trying to prove a statement which has seemingly little bearing on the original theorem. While it is interesting to see the fundamental principles a theorem relies upon, after three or four abstractions the original statement is completely forgotten. Having lost sight of the goal, the prover begins to wonder what purpose there is in proving the current statement. This confusion is often compounded when an abstracted proof fails to help prove the original goal.

In order to avoid this problem, we found the use of *sorry* statements very useful. *sorry* is a command which causes Isabelle to accept a given statement without proof. In order to avoid disappearing down a warren of abstraction, it is convenient to map out complex proofs using statements justified by *sorry*. These proof overviews often contain approximately the same amount of detail as an informal proof.

Another effective solution to the problem of forgotten goals is to complete informal proofs of the theorem on pen and paper. While this may seem like an obvious first step to proving a theorem, in many cases a formal proof seems like it should be able to proceed easily. Informally proving a statement serves both to convince the user that the proposition is true, and to give a good outline of how the formal proof should look (similar to the use of *sorry* statements). Further, the flexibility of presentation with informal pen and paper proofs means that solutions can often be found quicker than with a rigid notation mechanism.

It is interesting to consider this second solution. It says that in order to complete a formal proof it is helpful to complete an informal proof of the same statement. Does this mean that formal proofs offer no understanding to the prover? Not at all. In fact, the formal proof is the source of the statement we prove informally; if not for the process of formalisation we would never have tried to prove what is likely to be an abstract theorem, giving us a deeper understanding of the concepts at play.

3.5   Isabelle as an APE

Isabelle still has some way to go to being a good model of an APE. While the creative aspects of APEs (discovering and verifying proofs) are well served, the accessibility of formalised proofs to a general readership is not yet as envisioned. Isabelle does well as a proof assistant (as would be expected), but not yet as an intelligent interface for exploring proofs.

However even as a tool for general formalisation of the proof process, Isabelle has some way to go. While the act of proving is highly satisfying when it works, difficulties arising due to use of the system (rather than underlying problems with the mathematics) are too common and can be quite frustrating. A user interested in Isabelle as a tool for formalisation, rather than as an object of study itself, is likely to find the current learning curve unjustifiable.

An example of such a difficulty which led to great tedium was in certain proofs of termination. Specifically, if Isabelle is expecting an argument in the form $([x, y] @ [z])$ and it is instead provided with $([x, y, z])$ (both of which evaluate to the same), it will not apply relevant theorems. This can be quite frustrating, especially when the list in question has been automatically generated. A number of similar issues, while small, are nonetheless important in preventing the system feeling efficient.

However, it seems highly likely that Isabelle will mature well, and that in the future such systems will become much more widespread.

4   Conclusion

Concerns that the process of formalisation hinders understanding need not be grave. At its best, formalisation makes the prover consider and evaluate every assumption and step required to prove their goal, reinforcing just what's needed and what isn't. At its worst, formalisation can be a tedious task in determining the reasons basic algebra isn't accepted, or a far too unilluminating verification of correctness. Cases of the latter are uncommon and easily overcome. Cases of the former may increase frustration but in no way curb understanding - the inherent problem is that the prover is being made to understand more than they wish to.

An argument can be made that formalisation hinders understanding on the part of the reader. Indeed, the original four line informal proof would be much more accessible than our 40 page formalisation of it. But arguably this is a problem with informal proofs too - surely the reader of an informal proof generally understands less of the topic than the writer. Further, were a reader patient enough to make it through all 40 pages, would they not understand more than the reader of the informal proof? Such questions warrant further investigation. This being said, if systems such as Isabelle are to be used in contexts of presentation, capacity for accessibility on the part of the reader needs to be increased.

An interesting issue to consider is the impact greater automation of formalisation would have on understanding. Greater automation would lead to shorter proofs, missing more details, which might impair understanding. But perhaps in implementing the automation, that understanding would be recovered, or a deeper understanding would be found.

As a general formalisation tool, Isabelle still has some way to go. While formalisation is rewarding and enjoyable, there is still a reasonable learning curve and small annoyances affect the experience. However it seems likely that as Isabelle (and other developments) continues to improve, it will become second nature to use it in general mathematics.

Acknowledgements. Special thanks is given to Cris Calude for his generous advice, guidance and help. Thanks is also given to Robert Drummond, Mostafa Raziebrahimsaraei and Marcus Triplett for useful discussions on issues encountered during formalisation, and to the anonymous reviewers for helpful comments.

References

1. Isabelle hompage. http://isabelle.in.tum.de/
2. Ballarin, C., Belgrade 2008 - Tutorial: Introduction to the proof assistant. http://www21.in.tum.de/ballarin/belgrade08-tut/
3. Calude, C.S., Desfontaines, D.: Universality and almost decidability. Fundamenta Informaticae **21**, 1001–1006 (2014)
4. Calude, C.S., Müller, C.: Formal proof: reconciling correctness and understanding. In: Carette, J., Dixon, L., Coen, C.S., Watt, S.M. (eds.) MKM 2009, Held as Part of CICM 2009. LNCS, vol. 5625, pp. 217–232. Springer, Heidelberg (2009)

5. Gordon, M.: From LCF to HOL: a short history. In: Plotkin, G., Stirling, C.P., Tofte, M. (eds.) Proof, Language, and Interaction, pp. 169–186. MIT Press, Cambridge (2000)
6. Nipkow, T.: Programming and proving in Isabelle/HOL (2013)
7. OED Online. proof, n. http://www.oed.com/view/Entry/152578?rskey=bJkM38, October 2014
8. Xu, J., Zhang, X., Urban, C.: Mechanising turing machines and computability theory in Isabelle/HOL. In: Blazy, S., Paulin-Mohring, C., Pichardie, D. (eds.) ITP 2013. LNCS, vol. 7998, pp. 147–162. Springer, Heidelberg (2013)

Author Index

Printed in the United States
By Bookmasters